**PRESIDENTIAL
POLITICS**

PRESIDENTIAL POLITICS
Patterns and Prospects

WILLIAM W. LAMMERS

University of Southern California

Harper & Row, Publishers
New York Hagerstown San Francisco London

Sponsoring Editor: Ronald K. Taylor
Project Editor: Ralph Cato
Designer: Howard S. Leiderman
Production Supervisor: Will C. Jomarrón
Compositor: Bi-Comp, Incorporated
Printer and Binder: The Murray Printing Company

Presidential Politics: Patterns and Prospects

Library of Congress Cataloging in Publication Data

Lammers, William W
    Presidential politics.

    Bibliography: p.
    Includes index.
    1. Presidents—United States. I. Title.
JK516.L25   353.03′13   75-33948
ISBN 0-06-043829-0

For Mary, Linda, and Caroline

The Chapters . . .

Contents

Preface

The study of presidential politics today poses both fascinating dimensions and sobering questions. The rapid change in policy contexts which the United States has witnessed in the past decade constitutes one central dimension to the fascinations which now increasingly emerge. Conventional wisdom regarding the powers of the Presidency in foreign policy was largely developed out of the Cold War period, and yet today the president struggles with a variety of questions—and at points resistance within American politics—in a very different international system. We must question how these changes may affect future foreign policy roles.

Changing policy issues involving economic management and domestic policy have often seemed to rival those of a changing international system in their far-reaching implications for presidential politics. Now one finds the nation, and in turn the president, trying to cope with issues which a greater scarcity of resources and a more limited pattern of economic growth are raising in an acute way. The question of how individuals who have traditionally borne the political label of "liberal" behave in these contexts becomes particularly intriguing. Changing situations are always fascinating to the observer; presidential politics offers tremendous opportunities.

Presidential analysis today must also confront sobering questions. It has seemed all too easy for commentators to note a few of the formal reforms taken in the wake of the Watergate scandals and conclude that the constitutional crisis has been resolved. Certainly the wringing out of malfeasance with a peaceful and even orderly change in leaders was no small accomplishment as we reflect on the state of governance around the globe today. Yet we must ultimately ask: How adequate is our current thinking, and how timely and sufficient have the recent reforms actually been?

Patterns

In more concrete terms, the reader can expect three lines of analysis in this volume. First, we seek to describe and explain major patterns of behavior which can be observed in the contemporary Presidency. How do presidents tend to use staff, and why? To what extent does the personality of the occupant of the Oval Office influence both the style of his Administration and also its policy outcomes? What resources do incumbents typically bring to bear in their quest for re-election?

Second, we must seek to link presidential activities with the forces influencing actions in that institution. How did the "Imperial Presidency" of the post-World War II period develop? Is the Presidency and its internal behavior patterns really important, or is that a secondary—perhaps even trivial—consequence of power relationships within American politics? The concern for both explaining recent behavior and assessing future prospects requires that presidential politics be viewed not in isolation but in the context of the forces influencing that institution.

Prospects

Finally, the question of reform. To adequately consider the reform issue, we must utilize our expanding knowledge of the forces which do influence, and thus stand to potentially alter, presidential behavior. What can be said about different staff mechanisms, for example, or different approaches to the question of secrecy and the use of executive privilege? Would a provision for no-confidence votes and thus new elections increase accountability, or simply increase the likelihood of presidential chicanery?

Fundamentally, reform analysis must reappraise the frequent advocacy which has said: To improve American politics, one must strengthen the Presidency. If Americans now reject the fundamental assumptions of that familiar tradition, where then do we look for changes in the political system to better meet the substantial demands now confronting American politics for more effective policy as well as greater citizen confidence in government?

Presidential Politics: Patterns and Prospects can underscore key issues; the reader must appraise the answers.

WILLIAM W. LAMMERS

Acknowledgments

Any author acquires a substantial number of debts. My sense of gratitude to fellow scholars in presidential politics research is deep. The pages which follow show the substantial increase in research beginning to penetrate the Presidency on a more empirical basis. A special word is in order for the participants in the seminars on "The Contemporary Presidency" sponsored by the University of Southern California, California State University, Fullerton, and the Western Political Science Association. Conferences such as the ones held through those auspices seem indispensable in generating a more productive presidential scholarship.

A strong sense of gratitude goes also to my colleagues and students at the University of Southern California. Wise and constructive criticism are necessary, and I appreciate their willingness to listen, suggest, and tolerate various "end-runs" with interpretations. In particular, recent graduate students, Bob Erlenbusch, Michael Genovese, Ross Hopkins, and Jeff Simon have been most helpful. My University also helped in another way: Who could ask for better timing than to be on sabbatical as the Nixon Presidency fell apart! Appreciation also flows to my mentors at the University of Minnesota. In particular, Clarke Chambers, Harold Chase, William Flanigan, and Frank Sorauf have been most generous with their time and efforts.

My readers at Harper & Row, and my editor, Ron Taylor, were also most helpful. In addition, I gratefully acknowledge the assistance of my father, Claude C. Lammers, whose help has ranged from youthful library excursions to thoughtful commentary on portions of these materials.

The book is dedicated to my family with the gratitude which perhaps only fellow authors can fully comprehend. My daughters, Linda and Caroline, somehow managed to delightfully survive the preoccupations of an author-father, and my wife, Mary, gracefully managed the all too many burdens. Responsibilities are one's own; the gratitude goes to many.

**PRESIDENTIAL
POLITICS**

Issues and Concepts

American views of the Presidency have been going through a period of major convulsions. As recently as the mid-1960s, the Presidency was seen as the institution which should—and could—provide policy leadership, innovation, expertise, and a generally constructive adjustment to changing social conditions. Supporters of policy change, particularly from a liberal perspective, saw the Presidency in highly favorable terms. Institutional questions seemed largely settled. The major issue was electing the right man to office and ensuring that he was not unduly thwarted by Congress.

Assessments of presidential politics after John Kennedy's death produced a sharp alteration in views. In the wake of the Vietnam War and the Watergate scandals, a new set of concerns emerged. Presidents and the Presidency received such labels as "isolated," "above the law," "ridden with special interests," "fascist," "imperial," and—with a turn on the term Richard Nixon's press secretary used— "inoperative." Structural issues, rather than being peripheral, suddenly drew public attention. The common view that a president's problems must be the nation's problems took on a painful new meaning. Institutional questions, far from being settled, acquired a new urgency.

The state of the Presidency as it appeared in the wake of Nixon's resignation produced a widespread desire to curb the powers of that institution. Presidential staff reductions, procedures for easier presidential removal from office, and budgetary reforms were only part of a lengthy reform list. Yet difficult questions still had to be confronted. Was a reduction in presidential powers necessarily going to produce a more satisfactory national government, particularly in the face of contracting resources and the necessity of making difficult policy choices? Was an emphasis on avoiding ambitious figures in the White House inviting the stagnation in governmental operations often feared by advocates of strong presidential leadership? It seemed easier to envision ways in which the Presidency, and especially the president himself, might be reduced in power than it did to make the operations of the national government more satisfactory in the face of difficult social needs.

The post-Watergate evolution of the nation's issue agenda served to dramatically underscore the leadership question. In the aftermath of the Watergate crisis, difficult policy issues involving the most serious recession since the 1930s and the disarray in foreign-policy orientations following policy defeats in Southeast Asia combined to produce, in some, a rapid de-emphasis of concern for overzealous presidential activity. Within months after the crisis of the "imperial" Presidency, editorial writers began to wonder if President Ford was acting in a sufficiently "presidential" manner and whether he was providing adequate policy leadership.

The American Presidency is thus usefully viewed in terms of an interlocking set of dilemmas. Presidential personality, electoral expectations, staff operations, and tendencies toward stagnation in policy response are all involved. On the personality level, the dilemma involves the degree and nature of the ambition a president possesses. It has often seemed that only the ambitious individual can fulfill the leadership roles adequately. Influential political analysis, as of the mid-1960s, saw the more ambitious individuals as the more effective leaders in critical roles—with the electorate, with Congress, and with the federal bureaucracy.[1] Passive individuals might, it seemed, give a sense of continuity, but too little policy leadership. Yet the nature of the politically ambitious occupants of the White House in recent years has revealed most dramatically the potentials for manipulation, abuse of power, and vengeful disregard for seemingly established norms of presidential behavior by at least some types of ambitious politicians. This result was all too painfully apparent in Nixon's taped discussions of how to discredit "enemies," and in the vulgar disregard for legal processes which the tapes revealed.

A closely related dimension of the presidential dilemma involves electoral expectations. Presidents are frequently encouraged to build coalitions and new support for their policy proposals with electoral appeals. President Kennedy was criticized, from this perspective, for seeming at times to enjoy his high poll ratings without trying directly to build program support. Comparison of recent presidential experiences nonetheless poses a difficult issue. It was President Eisenhower, with his low-key approach to domestic matters, who was able to maintain a general electoral enthusiasm for his Presidency. President Johnson, the activist, found his support waning rather rapidly, as his drop in the Gallup Poll resembled that of President Truman in an earlier day. At worst, the activists seemed to generate a serious expectation gap when they could not produce tangible gains to meet the expectations they had aroused in the electorate. Contemporary skeptics of the capacities for presidential leadership have thus wondered whether the nation might not have to choose between leaders who are passive and those who become unpopular.

An additional aspect of the presidential dilemma involves the extent of centralization practiced in White House Staff operations. Staff expansion has often been advocated as a means of expanding the national government's capacity for achieving coordinated policies, and policies which overcome the tendency for dominance by key established interests and their friends in the agencies and in Congress. Many liberal Democrats in Congress through the 1960s were leading advocates of expanded staff, particularly in domestic policy areas. Johnson Administration aides, when testifying on President Nixon's reorganization proposals in 1971, often voiced support for reorganization seeking to ease problems of White House control.

Results have nonetheless been catastrophic in specific situations. Centralization has contributed to a lack of political accountability, fostered presidential isolation, and expanded opportunities for working out policy decisions in secret. Questions of the independence of several major federal agencies, such as the Internal Revenue Service, the Federal Bureau of Investigation, and the Central Intelligence Agency, emerged in the sordid record of the Nixon Presidency with some frequency. The staff centralization dimension of the presidential dilemma was raised as well during the term of President Johnson, as he worked out key decisions on the Vietnam War with a close set of personal advisers. One thus had to wonder: Is it possible to achieve needed policy development without inviting serious abuse of power?

Questions involving presidential personality, electoral expectations, and staff centralization produce collectively the overarching dilemma in presidential politics. The prescriptions of the strong-presidency advocate recently seemed prone to disastrous results. Yet the motivation for that advocacy continued to raise a serious question.

Would the American government, with more limited, passive, and restrained presidential roles, not be apt to suffer from an inability to achieve effective responses to difficult policy issues? Could one look with confidence at reduced presidential roles in the face of difficult tensions generated by constricting energy sources and increasingly difficult budgetary choices?

There is little need to belabor the importance of these issues to those destined to live with the results of presidential politics in the next years. As recipients of presidential policy-making activities, we can understandably hope that aspects of the presidential dilemma can be reduced. Perhaps in part, the dilemma is one of perception, rather than of concrete realities in the operation of the national government. Is it possible that advocates of strong presidential leadership have overstated the tendencies toward stagnation with a more passive president? If so, the clarified view obviously deserves strong expression. Perhaps there are also other ways in which the dilemmas of presidential politics can be reduced. If tensions and inconsistencies cannot be eliminated, might they not at least be reduced?

How best, then, to study presidential politics? The answer here is to begin with the perspectives themselves, reviewing the conflicting views of proper presidential roles which developed historically and have gained substantial expression in the period since the 1930s. One can then proceed to look at the recent evidence: How did the contemporary Presidency evolve, how do we now select presidents, and what are the central characteristics of recent occupants of the Oval Office? The focus then turns to presidential information systems, policy roles, and activities for generating support from the electorate and with Congress. After considering the difficult question of the degree of uniqueness in the Nixon Presidency, one then reassesses key issues. To what extent *are* presidential dilemmas supported by recent evidence, and how might forthcoming operations best cope with those dilemmas?

At the outset, one must consider differing perspectives, and the power relationships and socioeconomic conditions under which presidential politics must operate.

Conflicting Views of the President's Role

The proper role for the Presidency in American politics has long been in dispute. Even at the outset, the able group of men gathered at Philadelphia in the summer of 1787 were troubled by the manner in which the executive office was to be developed. They spelled out the activities and powers of Congress with some precision, but used only vague references in the stipulations for the executive—a telltale sign of uncertainty.[2] The debates themselves were marked by considerable vacillation, with basic issues often resolved fairly late in the proceedings. Even the decision providing for election by an electoral college rather than selection by Congress (which had been proposed as the Virginia Plan) came only in the final deliberations. The widespread view that George Washington would be the first executive in the new system served to reduce some of the apprehension, but not to reduce uncertainties.

In retrospect, the initial uncertainty is not surprising. The men at Philadelphia were, after all, seeking to chart unfamiliar ground in avoiding a monarchy and yet having an executive who could help to overcome problems of inadequacy in policy development which had plagued the fledgling government created by the Articles of Confederation. There were few obvious models to follow in outlining a non-monarchical executive as of 1787.

Initial uncertainty about presidential roles was followed by considerable fluctuation in both presidential behavior and major thinking about the nature of the institution. Presidential roles tended to evolve more from individual actions and specific situations than from a consistent view of the office. Andrew Jackson served to expand popular support for the Presidency through the party system, yet there was limited formal assessment of the change which was taking place. The actions of two Republicans, Abraham Lincoln and Theodore Roosevelt, were instrumental in creating precedents for active leadership roles. The Republican Party at the same time remained the frequent repository of concepts emphasizing limited presidential roles. Roosevelt's successor, portly William Howard Taft, was a frequent spokesman for a restrained interpretation of the Presidency.[3]

In recent decades, the Democratic Party has included a large number of the spokesmen for the importance of encouraging major presidential leadership roles. Woodrow Wilson contributed to this development, with his emphasis on the opinion-leading role and the importance of party leadership. The tendency for Democrats to advocate a strong set of presidential roles increased substantially as the Democratic Party developed a major coalition for controlling that office. The debate over the nature of the Presidency has intensified in recent years, along with the expansion in key roles being performed.

The major views of proper presidential roles today have their dominant moorings in the conflicts which emerged out of the changes in the Presidency spawned by Franklin Roosevelt. Although there are numerous statements by earlier participants and some students of government, the most extensive ideas emerge in the controversy over the changes and growth since the 1930s. It is thus appropriate to focus our review of conflicting perspectives on that debate.

Those taking a specific presidential perspective can be categorized into three broad groups: strong-presidency advocates, separationists, and contemporary skeptics.[4] The table below, entitled "Perspectives on the Contemporary Presidency," provides an overview of key

Perspectives on the Contemporary Presidency

General View	Major Problems Seen for the Political System	Reform Possibilities[a]
Strong presidency	Fragmentation: lack of leadership; slow policy response	Stronger parties Selection of skilled politicians Expanded staff
Separationist	President has too much power; can easily abuse it	Strengthen Congress Decentralize
Contemporary skepticism	Presidential isolation Electoral manipulation by incumbents Selection process which produces inadequate individuals	Open communication systems Greater sharing of functions

[a] See also Chapter 14.

positions. In part, the three positions involve differing views of actual institutional operations. Also, one finds major differences in how key problems with the Presidency are viewed. In turn, the nature of the reform agenda differs dramatically in the respective views.

Each of these positions has often been incorporated in a set of policy preferences, partisan orientations, and rather definite views of power relationships in American politics. The consideration of differing perspectives is thus appropriately followed by an overview of the differing interpretations of power relationships.

Strong-Presidency Views

Those emphasizing the necessity of strong presidential leadership, in the modern context, have to a striking degree been talking of the way in which Franklin Roosevelt is seen to have operated the Presidency. In particular, one finds a fondness for the manner in which Roosevelt mobilized electoral support and gained legislative victories in Congress. The strong-presidency writers have envisioned particular ways in which the president will gain his strength, and not all situations in which a president will have a major impact on the course of public policy. Now, however, given some dimensions of Nixon's Presidency, it is especially important to be specific about the manner in which the president is to be influential.

The overall picture of presidential politics which emerges from strong-presidency writers emphasizes the extent to which presidential leadership is needed if there is to be effective policy change. Congress is seen as typically too slow moving to provide major initiatives in getting new legislation promoted and accepted by the public and in Congress itself. The fear, for strong-presidency writers, has been that without a strong president, there will simply be a stalemate in American politics. Not insignificantly, this emphasis was especially pronounced during the days of domestic lethargy in the Eisenhower Presidency and the period under Kennedy, during which Congress would be characterized by some as almost literally engaging in a sit-down strike, and legislative proposals involving civil rights, aid to education, and a tax cut all languished.

The need for strong presidential leadership is thus a major theme in Richard Neustadt's classic, *Presidential Power.*[5] Writing at the end of the Eisenhower Presidency, Neustadt displayed a strong dislike for the handling of the Presidency by Eisenhower, and looked back at the Roosevelt Presidency as one in which effective use of presidential power did produce policy results. Similarly, in the early 1960s, the works of James Burns and Louis Koenig stressed the need for presidential leadership to overcome tendencies toward stalemate and lack of policy response. Koenig was most emphatic, claiming, "Our system of government tends toward paralysis except when a strong President is on hand."[6]

A strong Presidency was in turn seen as the best means of achieving policies which recognized the needs of those who were not specifically organized to plead their cases in Congress. The Presidency was seen as the place where policies for aiding middle and lower-class segments of American society gained initiation and often passage during Roosevelt's Presidency, and the institution offering the greatest chance for the "other Americans" of the 1960s to gain political recognition of their needs. Blacks, the elderly, and the rural poor were thus encouraged to seek helpful action in the orbit of presidential politics. Congress was viewed as particularly responsive to special interests, and the Presidency as more apt to speak for the entire nation. Such former key Nixon aides as H. R. Haldeman and John Ehrlichman, in arguing that only the President was speaking for all of the people, took a position which jarred many in Congress, but they were certainly expressing an idea which strong-presidency advocates had given wide circulation.

The strong president was additionally seen as providing the best opportunities for coordination and use of expertise in developing policy. This argument was more often expressed in foreign than in domestic policy areas, but could also be found in the writings which pointed to the importance of economic advice for the president. Congress again was found wanting. Its fragmented committee structure and a reluctance to develop expertise of its own constituted, for the strong-presidency advocate, a clear indication that only the Presidency could provide needed coordination and expertise. The "whiz kids" of McNamara's analytic staff in the Pentagon and the thrust toward systematic budgeting procedures under Johnson in 1965 consituted the type of development which was viewed as necessary in national politics and also more apt to occur within the Presidency rather than in Congress.

Strong-presidency writers, finally, looked to the president for the provision of necessary policy leadership in relating to the electorate. Here in particular the Roosevelt example is strong. Roosevelt's shrewd use of "fireside chats" for radio audiences and his sustained efforts at building support for such policy moves as the adoption of social security were highly praised. In *Presidential Power,* Neustadt emphasizes the opinion-leadership role with a major chapter devoted to opportunities, restraints, and techniques involved in building policy interest and support.[7] Both Eisenhower and Kennedy often received critical reviews for tending to enjoy high personal popularity but not pushing for specific policy support, especially on domestic issues. Rather than simply enjoying high popularity, the president was expected to engage in efforts at public education to gain support for policy changes.

Policy leadership with Congress, mobilization of public support, and the development of policy based upon coordination and the use of expertise have thus been key roles in the strong-presidency view. These roles have been deemed necessary because of the tendency for the political system to have too many veto points, and too often to be sluggish in its policy responses. Inertia, rather than abuses of power, has constituted the major concern.

In the wake of the Watergate scandals, one must emphasize the aspects of presidential politics which strong-presidency writers have tended *not* to fear. Possible abuse of presidential power, of great concern to the separationists, was of limited concern to the advocates of the strong presidency. In sharp contrast with the separationists and many current skeptics, before Watergate the strong-presidency advocates saw adequate alternative restraints. Interpretations of both power relationships in American politics and personal power orientations reinforced a lack of concern for possible abuses of presidential power.

Emphasis on the importance and desirability of a strong presidency was high at a time when power relationships were characterized as highly competitive. The label *pluralism* was often attached to views stressing large amounts of group competition. Such widely read works as David Truman's *The Governmental Process* described a political process with differing groups in such areas as agriculture, labor, and business competing with each other for the favor of the president.[8] Group competition in elections was seen as especially extensive, thus making elections an important check on presidential power. The pluralist view, as subsequent analysis shows, has fallen into substantial question in the face of both additional analysis and the movement toward greater concentration of economic power in American society. The belief in a pluralistic political system was nonetheless essential for the strong-presidency advocate. One could rely upon group competition rather than such formal structural arrangements as separation of power to prevent abuses by the president.

Along with group competition, the strong-presidency advocate emphasized the importance of political socialization in developing restrained and uncorrupt presidential behavior. Such leading political scientists as Robert Dahl went to great lengths to argue that the formal checks and balances of the constitutional system were overrated, and that leaders behaved with restraint in considerable part because of their learning of norms for presidential behavior.[9] A similar emphasis on the tendency for the possession of a position of power to be infrequently associated with a willingness to abuse power was developed by Lasswell and Rogow.[10] In their view, many individual factors tended to reduce the likelihood that the old maxim "Power corrupts and absolute power corrupts absolutely" would be valid. Several examples were cited of instances in which individuals behaved with greater rectitude *after* assuming the Presidency as an indication that whatever a politician's earlier involvement with petty political patronage and corruption might be, his presidential behavior would be less corrupt. A learning of norms for proper presidential behavior, coupled with a competitive political system, constituted in these writings an adequate basis for minimizing the fears some were expressing regarding dangers inherent in a strong Presidency.

Strong-presidency advocates saw various routes for the better achievement of the preferred presidential roles. Generally, a reduction in the key veto points in Congress was stressed. This typically included the seniority system, as it gave considerable power to individual committee chairmen; the use of filibusters in the Senate; and the opportunities for delay in the House stemming from the power of the House Rules Committee in deciding which measures would be debated on the floor of the House. Discussions in the early 1960s stressed problems with Congress in particular, as Kennedy faced continual frustrations with his legislative programs.

Possible strengthening of political parties emerged as an additional reform thrust. Some political scientists, looking favorably at the British party system, hoped for more cohesive political parties to provide a vehicle for presidents to gain greater support in Congress. This view did not fit well with a selection process emphasizing different constituencies for members of Congress. As analysis of the recent selection process shows, furthermore, the degree of party control seems actually to be declining. This is particularly true of the presidential selection itself. For such writers as James Burns, however, the best means of strengthening the Presidency was through modification in the party system. The attractiveness of that idea found its way, more recently, into journalist David Broder's *The Party's Over*.[11]

A different approach was voiced by Richard Neustadt, as he discounted formal changes as a feasible means for strengthening the Presidency. For Neustadt, it was crucial to elect presidents who possessed a good political sense. In his analysis, the best operation of presidential politics was to be achieved as skilled politicians guarded their choices to make sure that they maintained support in the electorate and developed high ratings among key Washington constituents. With this emphasis, such politically active presidents as Franklin Roosevelt, with their obvious enjoyment of political calculations and operations, received the high marks. Erwin Hargrove asserted a similar view in giving the personally ambitious presidents higher evaluations than their more apolitical counterparts in the major roles of leading public opinion, persuading Congress, and controlling the bureaucracy. In this view, the best means of achieving needed presidential leadership was to place skilled and ambitious politicians in the Oval Office.[12]

Supporters of the strong-presidency view, as subsequent chapters show in several contexts, came generally from the academic community, from some Democrats in Congress, and from segments of the electorate most interested in policy change. Public perceptions of the strong-presidency view have been illusive—subject to the influence of policy preferences, the popularity of particular Presidents, and even the manner in which opinion poll questions have been worded.[13] It is a fair judgment of the literature, however, to say that the popularity of the strong-presidency ideas was greater among those who thought extensively about the Presidency than within the electorate generally. In the period following World War II, a substantial segment of the electorate was more committed to the value of separation of power and a strong role for Congress than were major writers on presidential politics.

The reader may well have concluded by now that the strong-presidency ideas seem, at least at some points, to be rather dated. Credibility gaps, indictments of key presidential aides, and impeachment proceedings are surely not a part of the standard litany of the strong-presidency writers. While the views on several grounds may seem rather simplistic, it is important to stress several summary points. First, these views had a significant impact on the manner in which the Presidency was operating by the time Richard Nixon arrived at the White House. Coalition politics, with the Democratic Party often in strong support, helped carry some of these ideas into fruition. Second, however one now views these ideas, they stand as a frequent theme in many discussions of ways in which public policy can be made more effectively. Although the set of ideas involved in the strong-presidency view are most easily seen in the context of American politics in the 1950s and 1960s, the recent traumas in presidential politics have not altered the important issues in that advocacy. Thus Richard Neustadt's more recent writings, for example, caution against an over-response to Watergate abuses that could make it too difficult for other presidential personalities to function effectively.

Finally, it must be reemphasized that there are various ways in which a president can exercise a strong role in policy development. With the Roosevelt model in mind, and particularly the early years involving domestic policy, strong-presidency writers tended to talk in terms of building public support and working to gain legislative victories. That was, after all, a dominant thrust of FDR's Presidency. His constitutional fight, in contrast to the dominant early thrust of the Nixon Presidency, was with the Courts and not with Congress. President Nixon, as we will see, somewhat confounded ideas of the strong Presidency. Like Roosevelt, he sought to build a new coalition and to have an overarching impact on American politics for a substantial period. Yet because he lacked support in Congress, and distrusted the media, he was often at war with Congress, and was in the position of telling the electorate what he had done recently which was good for it, rather than building sustained support for policy decisions. To question Richard Nixon's Presidency is not necessarily to question the strong-presidency ideas altogether.

The Opposite View: Separationism

A second group of writers and political figures has long argued that the proper answer to questions of presidential power comes with a definite effort at restraining opportunity for the abuse of power. Traditionally, the most common basis for this position has been emphasis on the importance of both strengthening Congress and reducing presidential power. The label *separationist* characterizes this position. In policy terms, the separationists have not felt the same urgency expressed by most strong-presidency advocates for moving toward new or expanded policy commitments.

The separationist view has been, in the period since the 1930s, substantially a critique of the strong-presidency ideas, rather than a developed interpretation of the manner in which the American system actually operates. This is partly due to the limited interest in the separationist position within the academic community. Willmoore Kendall and Alfred deGrazia are strong exceptions to the lack of interest and academic support for the separationist position. Supporters of the Nixon Presidency during his years in office, interestingly enough, produced some discussion of decentralization but no flowering of the separationist view. Given some of Nixon's actions, this is not surprising. Nonetheless, that lack of interest constituted an important shift in traditional divisions between parties since the 1930s.

Separationists sharply disagree with the strong-presidency enthusiasts over the nature of the majorities reflected in the presidency and in Congress. For strong-presidency advocates, congressional procedures and committee structures has created, historically, a tendency for vetoes by such varying minorities as Southern whites, local elites, and business interests. The separationists argue differently. In their eyes, the Presidency emerges as the institution with a strong minority slant. The tendency for electoral college majorities in large, urban states to play a key role in presidential elections produces, for the separationist, a tendency for periodic swings toward new programs which are of primary interest to a minority within the electorate. Presidents, rather than speaking uniquely for a national interest, thus simply emerge as spokesmen for different segments of the nation. As a result, the separationist tends to view the dominant voices in Congress as having at least as much claim to full expression in the development of policy as those which tend to be most frequently heard in the orbit of presidential politics.

The amount of coordination and expertise which is applied to public policy within the executive branch is also called into question by the separationists. Alfred deGrazia considers these claims to be a gigantic myth.[14] In his view, the Presidency is like Congress—but with a tent over it. Beneath the often seeming unanimity of executive pronouncements, he sees a hidden process which, if more generally known, would make the Presidency seem more like Congress in its wrenching and groping toward policy positions.

Constitutional checks, for the separationists, are essential for avoiding abuses of power. In their eyes, formal concentration of power has long been an open invitation to abuse. It is simply not adequate to argue, for separationists, in terms of electoral checks or a prevailing competitiveness among interest groups and elites. One must maintain a formal, constitutional check in the form of separation of branches, to avoid having an executive abuse the rights of at least segments of American society. The characteristically Southern emphasis on the importance of constitutional checks which emerged in the commentary of Chairman Sam Ervin during the Senate Watergate Committee investigations in late spring of 1973 vividly reflected the separationist position.

Possible means of attainment have not been spelled out very specifically in the separationist view. Generally, there is an interest in adhering to a concept of separation of power and a tendency to equate separation with effective policy development. Proposals for making Congress more efficient occur periodically, but proposals are less often directed toward such key power questions as committee chairmanships. At the same time, the president is to be held more accountable through less general delegation of power and a reduced legislative willingness to support his proposals as a normal course of events.

Since the New Deal, the basis of support for the separationist position has come predominantly from the Republican Party and some segments of the Southern Democrats in Congress. Not a single Republican in either house of Congress, for example, voted against the Twenty-second Amendment with its limitation of presidents to two terms. The interest of white Southerners in using Congress as a base for defense against integration proposals coming from the White House was most apparent, particularly in the period prior to their fundamental defeats on civil rights matters in 1964 and 1965.

Traditional separationists can rightly note with a measure of relief—and perhaps bemusement—that several aspects of their position are now being widely expressed by academic writers and liberals in Congress. Senator McCarthy became an early skeptic as he voiced concern over abuse of presidential power (largely on foreign policy matters, and particularly Vietnam) in the 1968 presidential primaries. His shift marked a clear departure from the traditional strong-presidency ideas often expressed by Northern Democrats. One has witnessed a growing chorus of concern with presidential power coming from those who once advocated the strong-presidency position, or at least share some of the policy desires of many strong-presidency advocates. The contemporary skeptics show both several similarities and important differences as they are compared with the traditional separationists.

Contemporary Skepticism

Increasingly skeptical interpretations of the Presidency have grown dramatically since the mid-1960s. The impact of the Vietnam War and the operation of the Presidency under Richard Nixon has been instrumental in this shift. Contemporary skeptics often share with the separationists a concern for the impact of office on an individual and the likelihood that he will become arrogant in his use of power. Skeptics have also questioned the extent to which a president, often viewed as isolated from public moods and sound advice, will in fact promote policies which are in a majority interest. Fundamentally, the contemporary skeptics have come to question whether the totality of restraints on presidential operations (both constitutional and in competing power relationships among elites and interest groups) are sufficient to prevent abuse of power. Contemporary skeptics are apt to question the supposed pluralism of American politics, in sharp contrast to their strong-presidency compatriots of an earlier day. The contemporary skeptics are highly divided on the question of what should be done, however, and they tend to differ sharply with the separationists in terms of the degree of confidence expressed in separation as the necessary and sufficient step for overcoming contemporary problems.

George Reedy's *Twilight of the Presidency* stands as a major contribution to the contemporary skepticism position.[15] For Reedy, writing after serving as press secretary for Lyndon Johnson, the contemporary Presidency dangerously isolates its occupant in an atmosphere where he is treated virtually as a monarch, and has a staff which is anxious to advance personally rather than to bring needed information and viewpoints to presidential attention. Writing before the Watergate scandals, Reedy saw service in the Presidency as not necessarily producing direct corruption, but rather a situation in which the president becomes increasingly unable to make accurate political judgments. The president, in Reedy's eyes, becomes while in office an increasingly isolated bungler.

The major review of presidential personalities undertaken by James Barber has also emphasized sobering aspects of the presidential character.[16] Barber is less convinced than Reedy that the experience itself is adverse in the evolution of presidential behavior. Rather, Barber emphasizes that the type of personality we have been elevating has often been what he characterizes as an active-negative. Both Johnson and Nixon are described in this category. For the active-negative, there is a rush of activity, but a nagging sense of personal uncertainty and a perception of the political environment as essentially hostile. He must succeed by constantly striving and never letting himself be done in by opposing forces. Rather than being confident, as was

Neustadt, that an experienced politician was apt to develop skills as an effective president, Barber worries that we are now increasingly apt to get individuals in office who will make serious miscalculations because of their basic personality weaknesses. Contemporary skeptics, in short, have taken a far less optimistic view of presidential personalities than have the strong-presidency advocates.

Contemporary skepticism has seriously questioned the likelihood that presidential politics constitutes the best avenue for the achievement of policy outcomes aiding the less well organized and the less privileged in American society. For some, a dependency on presidential initiative is unrealistic simply because the president is apt to be too busy with foreign policy matters and, increasingly, questions of economic management. The president's ability to build policy support has been seriously questioned, with the suggestion that domestic policy steps are apt to reduce the popularity of a president, rather than helping in expanding support. Rather than building new support, a domestically active president is seen as often finding that he makes more enemies than new friends. The question of likely policy thrusts has been heightened mightily, as well, by the revelation of the access patterns enjoyed by business interests within the White House under Richard Nixon. The revelation of the close ties between business interests and not only the cabinet departments and regulatory commissions, but also the White House Staff under Richard Nixon simply made the concern acute.

The staunch critic of the Presidency as it has existed, especially at the hands of Richard Nixon, has added up recent tendencies as a fundamental threat to democratic politics. The picture of the Presidency which emerges in this critique is one in which an isolated White House threatens each of the checks traditionally placed on presidential action. Elections can be manipulated, at least at the hands of an incumbent. Congress can be bypassed, rather than persuaded. Interest groups held in disfavor can simply be ignored, and restraining voices in the bureaucracy dampened by a downgrading and ridiculing of the federal bureaucracy. Press criticism, in turn, can be reduced by a heavy-handed handling of access—and even threats to the freedom of reporters to operate without personal sanctions being imposed. Rather than a competitive political system, with the president bargaining and working to build public support, skeptics see little competition—and considerable manipulation and abuse of power.

Questions raised by the contemporary skeptics, and the crucial issue of what can be done, are central to the issues considered here. They become, indeed, vital questions for all Americans. For now, key summary points deserve emphasis. First, ideas about the operation of presidential politics have been closely tied to coalition positions and favored policy outcomes. This has been true historically, and is certain to be at least partially the case in the evolution away from the traumas of the Nixon Presidency. Second, it is the strong-presidency ideas which have come into particular question. They have been the most extensively developed, and are the ones which have been most directly tied to concern for the expansion of the capacity of the federal government in dealing with needed policy change. Third, positions on reform have often masked far too little knowledge of actual operations of presidential politics. The differences on factual questions found among the respective presidential perspectives underscore the importance of an expanded knowledge of actual practices and patterns. Fortunately, the emerging body of presidential scholarship is beginning to fill that void. Finally, one finds views of presidential politics closely tied to views of power relationships in American politics. It is thus appropriate to look at basic power views at the outset of one's exploration of the contemporary Presidency.

Who Influences Policy: Three Views

An intensive debate has raged in discussions of presidential politics—and of American politics generally—over the extent to which economic interests of an elite dictate the course of policy development. Some see an elite dominating, others see a tugging and pulling of interest-group activity, and some see an often noncompetitive process in which dominant interests in respective policy areas dictate the distribution of advantages in their areas of concern. Reviewing these elite, pluralist, and functional-area dominance views will provide an essential additional perspective for exploring the contemporary Presidency.

The Cohesive Elite View

Several influential analysts see the Presidency operating in close alliance with a dominant elite in American politics. The result is policies which favor that elite at the expense of interests of other Americans. Political cleavages are seen very largely in class terms, and the upper class wins. The writings of C. Wright Mills and G. William Domhoff have been major contributions to this view.[17]

The composition of the American elite is generally seen as including, first of all, "the Establishment"—those of prominent social status based upon family backgrounds; education; and economic ease, which facilitates participation in politics. One thinks here in terms of the right prep school, a degree from such an institution as Harvard or Yale, and membership in exclusive social clubs. Concretely, one thinks in terms of people like Elliot Richardson, Nelson Rockefeller, Douglas

Dillon (Kennedy's secretary of the treasury), and Dean Acheson (one of Truman's secretaries of state).

The second key component of the elite is said to be the leadership of America's corporate structure. Regardless of social origins, these are the individuals who control the major corporations which have become increasingly dominant in the American economy. Oil companies, major defense manufacturers, insurance firms, leading banking operations, auto manufacturers, and the increasingly dominant corporate agricultural operations are frequently mentioned. The internationally oriented corporations have also received greater attention in recent years. The close ties between the Nixon Administration and International Telephone and Telegraph Corporation (ITT), which erupted into one of the more persistent of the Watergate scandal issues, exemplify for the analysts of the elite the manner in which major corporate interests are closely intertwined with presidential politics.

Difficulties in deciding who should be included in the elite category have presented lingering problems. C. Wright Mills, in *The Power Elite*, gave major emphasis to the military, an emphasis which has not been entirely present in some other discussions. Observers sympathetic to Spiro Agnew's attacks on the media during his days as Vice-President have at points emphasized the communications industry as an integral part of the elite structure.[18] These views have often been associated with a conservative political orientation, and a belief that the communications industry was too internationalist and too liberal in its orientation.

The Nixon Presidency presented other issues as to the composition of the American elite as well. Nixon recruited less substantially from the Eastern-bred Establishment figures than did some previous Presidents, especially Eisenhower. Degrees from such institutions as UCLA and the University of Southern California emerged more often, and such "typical" Establishment figures as Secretary of State William Rogers had fewer peers in the Nixon Presidency than would be found in, for example, the Eisenhower cabinet. Recent social background data must be examined with care. Broadly, however, one can envision the American elite as comprising those of upper-class social status and those who dominate the major corporate operations in American society.

Several techniques for dominance by the elite over presidential politics are also emphasized. Elections are seen as largely under the control of the elite because of the necessity of raising large sums of money to run today's increasingly expensive campaigns. President Nixon's raising of well over $50 million for the 1972 campaign simply becomes the extreme case. Various writers, including those reaching elite interpretations, have pointed to both rising campaign costs (in part due to the necessity for large television budgets) and the tendency for a large portion of the necessary money to be raised from a few sources.

Issue-raising activity and the perpetuation of support for existing policies are seen, in turn, as excluding policy issues which would arise in the absence of elite financing. Such potential issues as income distribution, corporate profits, and the lack of competition in the marketplace (which in several assessments did in fact receive little attention by presidents of either party in the 1960s) are seen as falling outside the range of extensive political controversy, because of the implied threat which the elite holds over political leaders, who often depend upon them for campaign support. The perpetuation of large expenditures in such areas as defense spending, and of agricultural benefits increasingly directed toward agribusinesses is seen as a clear indication of the elite's ability to sustain its position. Political leaders, it is argued, sense that certain topics are simply not good ones for the person who wants to advance.

Control involves, in addition, the placing of individuals in positions of leadership who either were raised in a context of elite values, or have moved into elite life-styles through upward mobility. Upward mobility must be emphasized for presidents, since, as we shall see, they have tended not to be of elite origin. For cabinet positions, the emphasis is on elite backgrounds from birth, particularly in the important older cabinet positions such as those of the secretaries of treasury, defense, state, and justice.

The measure of conflict which does occur in presidential politics is seen by elite writers as involving peripheral issues in which the elite has little interest and by which it does not feel threatened. Such issues as federal aid to education and the management of welfare payments could be placed in the category which such elite writers as Mills have regarded as "middle level."[19] The pluralists, who have generally emphasized open competitiveness, are seen as ignoring the central forces which determine the nature of the issues being debated. Policy outcomes, according to elite writers, will continue to be highly beneficial to the elite until their bases of control are reduced.

Competitive Interest Groups

A major thrust in writings on American politics in the period between about 1950 and 1965 emphasized the openness of group competition. David Truman and Robert Dahl are the best known exponents. In Truman's view, American politics is characterized by the formation of new interest groups when there is a disruption of smooth-flowing relationships in social or economic arrangements.

Those who are disadvantaged (or become so) will unite, Truman argues, to press their case for governmental redress of grievances.[20] The emphasis is on open access to decision makers, including an important bargaining role for the president. Elections become, far more than in the elite view, an important ingredient for policy development, as groups organize, form coalitions, and aid in the selection of a president who will move in their preferred policy direction. Interests which lack such political resources as money and elite position are seen, in Dahl's view, as often being able to compensate by more extensive use of other resources, such as extensive organization and the impact of their numbers at the ballot box.

Questioning of pluralistic views has become increasingly common in recent years. The range of organizational activity has for many observers tended to be weighted in two directions. Tangible, specific interests often seem easier to organize than more general ones. One thus sees economic interests emerging more readily than interests in more general values, such as clean air, low noise levels, or safe and inexpensive foods.[21] Similarly, studies of electoral participation have repeatedly shown very limited amounts of activity on the part of lower-class and, at points, middle-class individuals.[22] There have also been some important exceptions to these tendencies, with interesting consequences for presidential policy roles, as such interests as consumers, environmentalists, and minorities have sought entrance to the group process. For now, it is sufficient to emphasize that criticisms of the pluralistic view have led to an important alternative view.

Autonomous and Uncompetitive Interests

A third view of power relationships in American politics has generated enough interest in recent years to warrant separate attention. Theodore Lowi is the most widely read of the writers emphasizing the tendency for major interests to dominant in their primary area of policy concern.[23] Lowi is highly critical of the tendency for power in national politics to be parceled out to the dominant interest or interests in respective function areas of governmental operation. For Lowi, key interests dominate, for example, in such areas as agriculture, regulatory commission operations, and federal government efforts in such fields as transportation and urban renewal.

Lowi differs from the elite writers in tending *not* to see the elite exercising interconnected and coordinated control over the federal government's operations. He also gives more attention to ways in which the structure of the federal government allows and promotes current practices. The key problem for Lowi is not dominance by a cohesive elite, but rather the inability of the federal government to achieve any sense of direction or purpose. The present governmental structures, for Lowi, can neither plan nor achieve justice. The president is seen as generally at the mercy of the dominant interests in respective functional areas, thus eliminating the potential leadership role others have envisioned.

The net result, for Lowi, is a political system which gives preferential treatment to the organized voices in politics—and those voices are very often of elite status. There is room in this view for both elite interests and other organized groups to win in their respective areas of concern through the essential use of friendly bureaucrats, interested congressmen, and supporting clienteles. The resulting policy-making interactions, with their frequent drives for autonomy from outside control by any political actors (including the president), become an important ingredient in analyzing presidential politics.

The President: Puppet or Policy-maker?

Differences in views of presidential politics resulting from the respective power interpretations are enormous. For the believer in the power of the elite, the major question is how the president interacts with the elite. Questions such as presidential isolation or legislative-executive relations take on only peripheral importance. One simply looks to the policy preferences of the elite for clues as to the evolution of public policy. For those emphasizing functional-area autonomy, presidential politics also becomes quite secondary. Presidential activities themselves take on minor importance, except insofar as a president's symbolic activities can be viewed as a consequence of his inability to achieve tangible policy changes when confronting the key interest or interests in respective functional areas. The pluralist is considerably more interested in presidential politics, as he looks for coalition building, bargaining, and access being provided to a wide range of interests.

Both explanations of contemporary presidential politics and assessments of reform opportunities must consider the accuracy of different power interpretations. Presidential policy roles are explored in subsequent chapters with an eye toward major issues in the power debate. Although definitive answers can be elusive, power questions are essential as one reviews the contemporary Presidency.

The Contemporary Context

Presidential politics is fundamentally influenced by the changing social and economic context in which it operates. Observers of the Presidency have often, it seems, tended to give particular individuals both too much credit and too much blame for the events taking place during their tenure. The American political scene, historically, has often allowed Presidents and the Presidency to be associated with a general sense of social progress. In recent years, the situation has to some extent reversed; the opportunities for gaining high evaluations have dropped sharply. Only in part can Presidents be blamed for those changing conditions. The contemporary context must be kept in mind both in evaluating recent Presidents and in considering the nature of the Presidency which is likely to emerge. Central in this perspective are the growing conditions of scarcity and the degree of uniqueness in the American political experiment.

The Increasing Scarcity of Resources and Revenue

The nature of the policy demands unfolding by the 1970s presented severe challenges for national policymakers. Questions which had dominated the course of presidential politics in the 1960s remained only partially resolved. Policies involving changing life-styles, life in the central cities, and economic management were in many respects inadequate, even if in some instances less openly controversial. The nation had struggled through a difficult period in the late 1960s with its institutions more intact than some had thought possible at the height of the urban upheavals. Yet major aspects of the policy problems remained.

The 1970s added a fundamental new dimension to the forces buffeting presidential politics. American policy making has characteristically involved a substantial amount of the something-for-everyone approach.[24] Even the poverty programs of the 1960s were to be financed not out of a redistribution of tax impacts or a curtailment of services to some Americans, but from additional money which a growing economy would provide. The Johnson Administration thus launched a War on Poverty and a substantially across-the-board tax *cut* at the same time. Overall budgetary expansion throughout the 1960s, and mounting federal deficits, were a testament to the tendency for policy making to avoid hard choices on allocation alternatives among key competing interests.

In the 1970s, the necessity for choice became far more apparent. The abundance of the American economy made the expansion of the public sector a possibility, if support was developed for that option. An aging population, with its service and income-maintenance needs, nonetheless narrowed the possibilities for modifying domestic policies without facing hard choices. Even if one made the politically questionable assumption of a major cut in defense spending, there was still not expected to be enough revenue to satisfy the costs of many of the popularly advocated programs. Annual budget reviews by the Brookings Institution sounded an increasingly somber tone.

By 1973, authors of those reviews placed greater emphasis on the development of improved capacities for making effective choices.[25] Inflation and recession served, as of the mid-1970s, to intensify the scarcity issue. Some room for maneuver could be found, but only through a harder look at alternatives than political leaders had generally wanted to take.

Greater scarcity of resources throughout the world emerged as a further complicating factor for presidential politics. Few would have thought, even a few years earlier, that presidential roles would verge upon the difficult task of establishing rationing policies for major necessities of life. Yet even if immediate resource problems were overcome, the longer-range picture remained one in which shortages and related problems of inflation were apt to be more serious than in the past. The demands on policymakers, in short, were certain to be difficult and complex. A nation which had enjoyed substantial advantages in the past faced major challenges to its rather unique political experiment.

The Uniqueness of the American Experiment

Americans have created a unique context for their continuing political experiment. Both the scope of the system and the nature of political attitudes contribute to that uniqueness. There *are* important similarities between current American experiences and those of other nations. One must be careful not to reemphasize the American tendency to view their political experiments as somehow removing them from difficulties experienced in other advanced industrial societies. Nonetheless, in some respects there remains a uniqueness to the American political experiment.

The sheer size of the American political system constitutes one unique feature. Executive politics in other countries with somewhat similar political values are not taking place in nations which approach America in size, either geographically or in total population. Of the industrialized nations loosely categorized as democratic, Japan has about half the population of the United States, but is compactly located as an island nation. Even the largest Western European nations are about one-fourth as large in population and far more compact geographically. Great Britain, for example, could be fitted into an area about the size of Oregon. Size has recently been recognized as having more than peripheral importance in the operation of political systems.[26] Interestingly enough, several of the experiments with executive-centered planning which some Americans have admired are taking place in such nations as Sweden, the Netherlands, and Israel—countries with populations reaching at best the size of a moderately large American state.

American attitudes also serve to magnify the uniqueness of the contemporary experiment. With some exceptions, and with significant variation in definition, Americans have generally desired a presidential politics which is basically democratic. Secret deals, lack of access, and manipulation of elections run counter to desires for a democratic political process.[27] As a result, practices undertaken in the name of efficiency in some countries are apt to produce sharp criticism from at least segments of the American electorate. The ultimately strong response to the abuses of the Nixon Presidency was in part a reflection of widespread American desires for a democratic presidential politics.

Americans simultaneously expect a politics which produces reasonably satisfactory solutions to major policy questions. Rather than viewing problems as inevitable, Americans have historically tended to view themselves as being unique among nations in their ability to pursue progress across a wide variety of policy fronts.[28] Presidents themselves have often seemed to be at the center of this belief pattern. Presidential rhetoric gradually shifted from a frequent celebration of the wonders of American accomplishment to a combined emphasis on both earlier American accomplishments and forthcoming progress. State of the Union addresses in recent decades, for example, have been replete with references to a wide variety of problems which the federal government has been about to solve.[29] It has been largely out of character for either presidents or the electorate to emphasize the sometimes intractable nature of social problems.

American values, finally, have traditionally involved a confident view of the American political system. The authors of *The Civic Culture* found a substantially higher level of confidence in America than was present in several other nations, including Great Britain, as they analyzed data which tapped electoral perceptions as of the late 1950s.[30] Americans were uniquely apt to believe that their government was responsive if one had a grievance, and that it was a system worth taking pride in.

The period between Vietnam and Watergate produced a massive plunge in American confidence. A general feeling that government was unresponsive to public needs grew very substantially. In the wake of a tumultuous decade capped by the Watergate scandals, a majority of Americans expressed alienation and a feeling of powerlessness. As pollster Louis Harris tapped that attitude in a survey done for a Senate committee, he found alienation in broad segments of American society, including Southerners, skilled laborers, and residents of rural communities. Major changes were found since that question had first been asked in 1966—and American confidence had already begun to decline by that year.[31]

Significantly, Americans appeared not to have abandoned their underlying faith in the ability of the system to perform. Some 89 percent in the same Harris survey still felt that the system could work well. The gap between hostility toward recent events and the underlying view that the system could work thus created a major problem for the president, as the most visible figure in the political system. By the mid-1970s, American politics not only faced low levels of evaluation but a sense that things had somehow gone wrong.

Some began to wonder, by the 1970s, whether the answer to tensions in political attitudes might not rest with a burying of the American myth. That myth, it seemed, tended to convey unrealistic assumptions as to what could be accomplished with public policies and in the achievement of a democratic political system. This issue is vital, particularly as one subsequently assesses electoral expectations and presidential rhetoric. One might nonetheless ask at the outset: Where is it appropriate and necessary to alter those views? Does one simply become a cynic and conclude that all progress is impossible and all politicians necessarily corrupt, or that a substantial measure of democracy is unattainable in an advanced industrial society such as the contemporary United States? American confidence and optimism may have contributed to unrealistic expectations, yet wholesale abandonment of those attitudes could not easily be viewed with enthusiasm.

The contemporary context thus intensifies problems with presidential politics. The shift to scarcity has made the solution of political questions by a something-for-everybody approach less feasible. Power relationships, as seen by some, make the attainment of democratic politics difficult and unlikely—at least with anything close to the present political system. Citizen confidence in presidential politics has simultaneously been badly shaken, with uncertain implications. At the same time, the most common ideas for strengthening the capacities of the national government by strengthening presidential leadership roles have come under massive attack. Rather than a settled political system with easy answers derived from the past, Americans face a continuing political experiment. To begin our consideration of that experiment, it is essential to examine the forces contributing to the growth and evolution of the institution which has recently come under such heavy fire.

NOTES

[1] See Erwin C. Hargrove, *Presidential Leadership: Personality and Political Style*, New York, Macmillan, 1966.

[2] A useful general account of these struggles is contained in Charles

C. Thach, *The Creation of the Presidency, 1775–1789,* Baltimore, Johns Hopkins Press, 1922.

[3] Presidential statements and early scholarly views are presented in Robert S. Hirschfield, ed., *The Power of the Presidency,* Chicago, Aldine, 1968.

[4] For another classification scheme, see David Paletz, "Perspectives on the Presidency," *Law and Contemporary Problems,* Summer 1970, chap. 1.

[5] Richard E. Neustadt, *Presidential Power: The Politics of Leadership,* New York, Wiley, 1960. For his more recent view, see "The Constraining of the President: The Presidency after Watergate," *British Journal of Politics* 4 (October 1974), 383–397.

[6] Louis Koenig, *The Chief Executive,* New York, Harcourt, Brace, and World, 1968, pp. 186.

[7] Neustadt, op. cit., chap. 5.

[8] David B. Truman, *The Governmental Process,* New York, Knopf, 1951.

[9] Robert A. Dahl, *A Preface to Democratic Theory,* Chicago, University of Chicago Press, 1956.

[10] See Arnold Rogow and Harold Lasswell, *Power, Corruption, and Rectitude,* Englewood Cliffs, N.J., Prentice-Hall, 1963.

[11] David Broder, *The Party's Over,* New York, Harper & Row, 1972.

[12] Hargrove, op. cit. For his more recent views, see Erwin C. Hargrove, *The Power of the Modern Presidency,* New York, Knopf, 1974.

[13] Changing public perceptions are traced in Donald Devine, *The Political Cultures of the United States,* Boston, Little, Brown, 1972, pp. 151–161.

[14] See Alfred deGrazia, "The Myth of the President," in *The Presidency,* ed. by Aaron Wildavsky, Boston, Little, Brown, 1969, pp. 49–73.

[15] George Reedy, *The Twilight of the Presidency,* New York, Mentor, 1970.

[16] James David Barber, *The Presidential Character: Predicting Performance in the White House,* Englewood Cliffs, N.J., Prentice-Hall, 1972.

[17] See the classic work by C. Wright Mills, *The Power Elite,* New York, Oxford University Press, 1956. G. William Domhoff's writings include *Who Rules America?* Englewood Cliffs, N.J., Prentice-Hall, 1967, and *The Higher Circles,* New York, Vintage, 1970.

[18] See Domhoff, *The Higher Circles,* chap. 8, for one review of this position.

[19] The classic discussion is in Mills, op. cit., chap. 11.

[20] See Truman, op. cit., especially, pp. 101–102.

[21] The difficulties involved in organizing more general interests and values are disscussed in Mancor Olson, Jr., *The Logic of Collective Action: Public Goods and the Theory of Groups,* Cambridge, Harvard University Press, 1965.

[22] Major new data have emerged in Sidney Verba and Norman H. Nie, *Participation in America: Political Democracy and Social Equality,* New York, Harper & Row, 1972.

[23] The major work is Theodore J. Lowi, Jr., *The End of Liberalism:*

Ideology, Policy, and the Crisis of Public Authority, New York, Norton, 1969. Also useful as a theoretical perspective is Robert Presthus, *Elite Accommodation in Canadian Politics,* Cambridge, England, The University Press, 1973. See especially chap. 13.

[24] The importance of abundance in American political development is effectively discussed in David Potter, *People of Plenty,* Chicago, University of Chicago Press, 1954; see especially chap. 5.

[25] Charles L. Schultze et al., *Setting National Priorities: The 1974 Budget,* Washington, Brookings, 1973. See especially chaps. 1, 13.

[26] See Robert A. Dahl and Edward R. Tufte, *Size and Democracy,* Stanford, Stanford University Press, 1973.

[27] The question of just how deep the American commitment to democratic politics actually is, and the confusions over definitions, poses sobering questions. For a provocative review of recent data, see Thomas R. Dye and Harmon Zeigler, *The Irony of Democracy,* Belmont, Calif. Wadsworth, 1970.

[28] The optimism in American thought has been usefully traced by David Noble, in *The Paradox of Progressive Thought,* Minneapolis, University of Minnesota Press, 1958.

[29] A useful review of those messages is contained in Seymour H. Fersh, *View from the White House,* Washington, Public Affairs Press, 1961.

[30] See Gabriel A. Almond and Sidney Verba, *The Civic Culture: Political Attitudes and Democracy in Five Nations,* Princeton, N.J., Princeton University Press, 1963.

[31] See "Confidence and Concern: Citizens View American Government: A Survey of Public Attitudes," by the Subcommittee on Intergovernmental Relations of the Committee on Government Operations, U.S. Senate, pt. 1, 93rd Cong. 1st sess., December 1973.

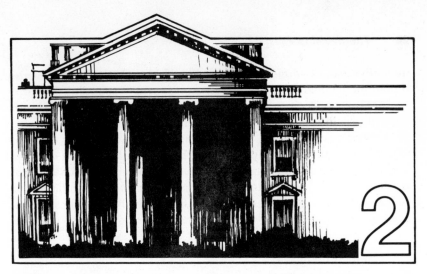

The Evolving Presidency

The contemporary Presidency is a vastly different institution from the one which existed during most of America's political history. The Presidency of Calvin Coolidge's day more closely resembles a minor department today than it does present presidential operations. A reincarnated President from the nineteenth century might recognize some of the responsibilities, but would certainly be astonished at both the range of responsibilities his presentday counterparts face and the immense structure with which modern occupants of the Oval Office are involved.

Four key developments have taken place since the early 1930s. In structural terms, the Presidency has expanded in size and in the development of an elaborate and substantially institutionalized set of roles around the president. Second, the Presidency has expanded its scope of policy concerns in the areas of foreign policy, economic management, and general domestic policy questions. Third, vis-à-vis other institutions, and most importantly Congress, the Presidency has acquired a substantial advantage in policy development, often through means which do not directly require congressional consent. The fourth key development follows from the above changes: The contemporary Presidency has significantly increased problems for ·the president as an individual in terms of the likelihood that he will be seriously uninformed on important aspects of his own responsibilities.

Many developments have taken place with little notice and often surprisingly little controversy. Evolution of informal practices rather than specific authorization was often critical to the changing character of the contemporary Presidency. Yet the tumultuous events of recent years have dramatically intensified the basic question: What factors produced the immense office, with its potentials for abuse? Both functional and structural development must be sketched before confronting key developmental influences directly.

Major Functions

Modern Presidents (defined as those beginning with Franklin Roosevelt) have engaged in a variety of activities which have tremendous consequences for every aspect of the political system. Furthermore, there is widespread agreement that at least a large number of those activities are essential for effective functioning of the political system. Even a president who wishes to define his role in fairly passive terms finds himself doing considerably more than his more active predecessors in earlier days. Many doubt the possibility—aside from questionable desirability—of a Presidency which is again as passive in many areas as was Eisenhower's. It has been common in discussions of presidential functions to develop rather lengthy lists of the various "hats" which are worn by the president. Rather than creating a lengthy list, it is more useful to review major overall presidential functions. These include his functioning as chief of state, foreign policy leader, economic manager, domestic policy developer, and partisan leader.[1]

Chief of State

All American chief executives are involved in activities as ceremonial heads of government. Mayors cut ribbons; governors speak when there is a major event in their state, or when a major disaster occurs. Presidents similarly find themselves welcoming foreign visitors, issuing awards of various kinds, welcoming astronauts, and making statements when major events occur. A passive president may rather enjoy these roles; for the active occupant of the White House, the time spent may be considered more of a waste. All presidents nevertheless find these events having a significant impact on their calendar. The East Room always seems to be full of visitors, and one is forever wondering what to give foreign guests, as gifts are exchanged in state visists.

Presidential functioning as chief of state, despite the seemingly trivial aspects, has considerable significance for the totality of presidential politics. The British, by maintaining the monarchy for cere-mony and using the prime minister position for policy matters, achieve a highly useful distinction which has never been a part of the Ameri-can system. In American politics, the Presidency, embodied by its occupant at a given point in time, constitutes an extremely important symbol of nationhood. Children tend to learn an early veneration of the Presidency. (This pattern, it must be emphasized, may change as a result of recent events.)[2] Americans also react in very strong emotional terms to such events as the death or assassination of a president, again showing his place as considerably more than simply a director of policy change. Even Harding's death, coming as his popularity was sagging—although before the scandals of Teapot Dome—produced a major outpouring of public grief.[3]

The strong response to John Kennedy's assassination has been the best-studied indication of the ties between the occupant of the White House and a sense of nationhood. There is no precise manner in which Kennedy's personal popularity can be isolated from the sense of an attack on the nation when he was gunned down in Dallas. His popularity in the Gallup Poll ratings had fallen to a record low of 59 percent in the last survey before his death. In any event, the public responded in very strong terms. Religious expressions were common. Many indicated personal symptons of physical distress. Chil-dren were widely reported to be upset by the level of distress reflected in their parents. Interestingly enough, the nature of the dominant response was *not* primarily one of concern for personal impacts of change in policy. American confidence in its political system, as of 1963, was nicely born out by the absence of that concern.

Professor Sidney Verba, in looking at the totality of the electoral response, expressed surprise at its depth. For Verba, the response suggested a quasi-religious nature in American orientations toward the Presidency. He wrote specifically:

> The reactions to the assassination—the intense emotion, the reli-gious observances, and the politico-religious symbolism—are evidence (although hardly proof) that such commitment exists. And the Presi-dent is the appropriate focus of this commitment, for like the medieval king he is the concrete human individual whom one can see, on whom one can focus attention, and with whom one can share common human emotions, and yet he is something transcending his concrete human aspects, for he is also the symbol of the nation.[4]

The identification of the president with the symbols of the nation was also evident in the responses to impeachment discussion as the Nixon Presidency began to collapse in 1973. The act of impeachment seemed similar for many Americans to that of killing a king. The Nixon Administration remained in office long after its lack of support would have caused a fall in most other systems only in part because of the lack of a politically established mechanism for removal. By December 1973, a large majority felt that the President was guilty of serious distortions which probably covered illegal activities, yet the number of voters favoring impeachment remained in the 40 percent range. The merged identification of a president as both partisan leader and symbol of the nation, given past impact, must certainly have contributed to the reluctance with which Americans moved toward an acceptance of impeachment as a feasible course of action.

Chief-of-state activities, while they appear peripheral at times, constitute an extremely important component of presidential functions. No president is going to be able to get away from the state dinners, welcoming speeches, and holiday celebrations. Furthermore, an astute president would not wish to do so. This is one of several instances in which presidential functions become blurred, and it may well be advantageous for a president to emphasize the ceremonial aspects of his position when he is in trouble with the more specific policy-making activities. Richard Nixon's emphasis in 1972 on a campaign to "reelect the President" was a classic example of the manner in which functions can be blurred. The thrust of the appeal was to ask voters to reaffirm faith in the President and not choose between two partisan candidates for a given office, and it had considerable success. A clarification and modification of electoral orientations, given past tendencies to merge partisan, policy-making, and chief-of-state functions, is one important dimension of possible reform.

Foreign Policy Leader

In the period since World War II, presidents have performed a dominant role in the evolution of foreign policy decisions. Presidential dominance has been especially clear when a crisis and the possible or actual use of force is involved. A president, be he John Kennedy deciding on the American response to the Soviet placement of missiles in Cuba in 1962 or Nixon considering American responses in the Middle East in October, 1973, tends to dominate. A few congressmen are often called after the decision has been made and told what has happened, or what is about to happen. Often this occurs minutes before the president addresses the nation to explain his decision. James Robinson, in looking at some 22 cases in the period between 1933 and the early 1960s, found a repeated and dramatic indication of the tendency for presidential dominance where possible use of force was involved.[5]

Time commitments vary, but all recent Presidents have engaged in a substantial amount of foreign policy activity. William Manchester estimated that John Kennedy spent approximately 80 percent of his time during his first year involved in foreign policy matters.[6] Thomas Cronin placed the foreign policy time commitments for the contemporary president at 60 percent.[7] To a cabinet officer interested in domestic problems, the President might well have seemed to be "a prisoner of Berlin" when the issue of the Berlin Wall emerged in 1961. A reading of the memoirs of Lyndon Johnson is similarly revealing. Although deeply interested in his domestic program, he found his administration and his own time increasingly involved with Vietnam questions. Even the chapter breakdowns in Johnson's book show the substantial involvement with the foreign policy dimensions of his Presidency.[8] Richard Nixon was also frequently regarded as primarily interested in foreign policy matters, and his own statements as to his responsibilities emphasized the importance of the foreign policy area.

There may be some modification in the congressional role in foreign policy matters in the future, but this is not apt to fundamentally alter the substantial amount of time and energy expended by future presidents. There is also some degree of choice open to a president, as on occasion foreign policy roles are sought simply because they seem to offer more of a chance for results than many of the perennial domestic issues. What cannot be avoided is the likelihood that foreign policy activities will continue to be a major component of the Presidency in the foreseeable future.

Economic Manager

A basic expansion took place during the 1960s in the president's economic management function. Presidents had been involved with economic questions for several decades, and with tendencies toward increased concern. The 1946 establishment of the Council of Economic Advisers was a major step in expanding the expectation of an economic management role for the president. There was substantial disagreement as to the necessity for these activities in key segments of the population such as the business community, however, especially in the 1950s. Eisenhower was able to maintain his popularity while defining his economic role in very limited, budget-balancing terms. John Kennedy contributed substantially to the acceptance of a more active presidential role, with his own acceptance of the necessity for a more active economic planning role and his willingness to pursue support for that philosophy in such formerly unlikely quarters as the business community. Yet despite those efforts at building support, Kennedy was unsuccessful in selling Congress on a tax cut to stimulate economic growth. A mere eight years later, Richard Nixon launched his major step toward wage and price controls after receiving criticism from his own party for not acting sooner. An unprecedented 71 percent of the electorate indicated support in the next Gallup Poll. By fall 1974, President Ford also found a strong expectation that his administration develop a comprehensive economic policy.

Several writers have emphasized the importance of the president's expanded involvement with economic management questions. Lawrence C. Pierce, in *The Politics of Fiscal Policymaking*, saw greater presidential involvement as a major development in governmental policy making on economic matters generally.[9] Thomas Cronin, in looking at presidential functions, argued that the greater economic activity had developed a distinctiveness from other domestic activities.[10] The electorate of the 1970s expected that there would be presidential action and often judged the president's performance in economic terms. Presidents themselves sensed this concern. Thus even the presence of several economic advisers who resisted an emphasis on direct economic planning did not deter Richard Nixon from taking the giant step of extensive wage and price controls in August 1971.

The expectation of presidential involvement in managing the economy is now widespread. Presidents in turn spend more time with this activity. The question is increasingly not whether the president will act in seeking to manage overall economic forces, but rather what the proper choices are.

Domestic Policy Developer

Presidential activities relating to domestic policy development show considerable variation. Expectations are less uniform than in the economic management area. The strong-presidency advocates expect the president to be very actively involved. In terms of actual behavior, one can expect a president to deliver such major addresses as the State of the Union address, and present a budget message and set of proposals to Congress. A substantial number of legislative proposals will generally be forthcoming, with widely differing levels of subsequent effort toward gaining support. Supervision of the federal bureaucracy also occurs in varying degrees, although the amount of actual time spent may be limited. The size of the domestic bureaucracy and the scope of its actions makes domestic management at least potentially a very extensive activity.

Presidents also respond to domestic crises, such as oil spills, racial outbreaks, labor strikes, and energy shortages. A president in some instances may well be stalling rather than trying to lead policy development, but at least some action is usually forthcoming.

During times of crisis in another area of presidential responsibility, domestic activities may virtually cease. A foreign policy crisis is the most apt to intervene, such as Kennedy's October 1962 involvement in the 13 days of decisions leading to the blockade response to the Soviet missiles in Cuba. For Richard Nixon, the threat to his very political survival reduced other involvement by 1973. Some domestic activity virtually always occurs, but with major variation as to the exact roles being performed. Consideration of reform in domestic policy making must be sensitive to the forces which influence and restrict presidential involvement.

Partisan Officeholder

Americans have long had a measure of ambivalence about partisan politics.[11] Even one presidential candidate—Dwight Eisenhower—seemed confused by the intricacies and implications of partisan politics. A belief that somehow partisan matters were getting in the way of what was good for America subsequently permeated several of the positions taken in the early days of the Eisenhower Presidency. Many observers believe that the president must somehow be above nasty things like partisan politics.

There can be no denying, however, that partisan matters are significant to the occupant of the White House. Most first-term presidents will be thinking of reelection, which requires party nomination. Second-term presidents have often had considerable interest in shaping both the choice of and the possibilities for success of their successors. Furthermore, to get his policies through Congress a president finds that the political party mechanism is often crucial. Despite a decline in or elimination of patronage involving such areas as postmasterships and minor offices, many appointment questions are of partisan concern. Patronage is important to presidents in terms of political control in key states and may relate to their ability to control major votes in Congress. The motivation for Kennedy's fateful trip to Dallas a year before the 1964 election sadly illustrates the importance of partisan activities; Kennedy sought to improve his position with the faction-ridden Texas Democrats on that trip. Partisan involvement has at some points increased in recent years, as presidents have been involved in a larger number of primary contests for selection of congressmen in their own parties.

Partisan activities are essential. If party mechanisms were to be strengthened, as the strong-presidency position has at points suggested, one would necessarily have an increase in the extent to which the Presidency is identified and operates in partisan terms. As long as the selection process involves nomination by party and Congress organizes on a party basis, one can expect a substantial amount of partisan presidential activity.

Summary

Presidential functions have expanded enormously since the 1930s. Foreign policy and economic management activities have involved a broad range of decisions of immense importance. Structural dimensions, as will be seen, have grown along with the expanding functions. It is useful to conclude the discussion of functions by considering the distinctiveness and the interrelatedness of the respective functional areas of the modern Presidency.

Aaron Wildavsky has persuasively argued that the foreign policy functions of the Presidency differ in important respects from other policy areas.[12] The foreign policy roles, in this analysis, give more flexibility and more chance for success than occurs in other policy areas. Flexibility is increased by greater congressional willingness to support presidential initiatives, a lack of interest groups, and less tendency for critical electoral evaluation. It is the domestic and economic functions which produce the extensive conflicts, deadlocks, and lack of presidential influence on final outcomes. This view was developed prior to the protest over the Vietnam War, and will require careful attention. It is nevertheless important to determine functional-area differences in order to avoid overly hasty generalizations regarding key aspects of presidential behavior.

Functional areas are also extensively interrelated. The president's ceremonial activities as chief of state may be blurred with basic partisan and policy issues and activities. Partisan concerns may have a very direct impact on economic policy making as elections approach. International steps may relate to the strengths or weaknesses of the president in other areas. Conversely, a catastrophe in the foreign policy area, such as Johnson's loss of support over the Vietnam War, will drastically alter activities in economic and general domestic areas. From the vantagepoint of the Oval Office, as Richard Neustadt has argued, there are not respective functional areas to be taken care of, but rather a constant set of activities which must interrelate to produce (for a successful president) the support of key groups and electoral confidence.[13] Because catastrophe in one area can be devastating for other areas, it is proper for the president to see his job in its totality. A functional breakdown nonetheless reveals major patterns of activity in the modern Presidency.

Structures Surrounding the President

Growth in presidential functions has been accompanied by a sharp increase in the structures operating within the context of the Executive Office and in turn of the federal bureaucracy. There has unfortunately been a retarded development of a clear understanding of these structures. A desire for anonymity, public acceptance of secrecy, and the very complexity of presidential operations have contributed to a situation in which presidential structures have often remained a mystery even to reasonably well-informed followers of

American politics. One of the constructive developments of the extensive Watergate hearings is the greater recognition, even though rather sordid in too many respects, of the structures around the president.

The level of institutionalization in presidential structures must be considered at the outset. In terms of the roles which are filled in successive Presidencies, there has been more continuity than has sometimes been recognized. It is thus possible in sketching the key components to present a picture which involves substantial continuity. There is widespread expectation that key responsibilities will be carried out and that a structure will be employed in each Presidency to implement those responsibilities. At numerous points there is a recognition among staffers of comparable roles filled by individuals in previous administrations. Some of the structures, particularly in the economic and foreign policy areas, are also defined with a measure of precision by statute. From these facts, one may argue that we have an institutionalized Presidency.[14]

Despite a substantial degree of institutionalization, there can be a significant amount of modification from one incumbent to the next. Revelations of Nixon's numerous changes made the room for flexibility most apparent. Observers had commonly assumed, for example, that the formal press conference was an institutionalized aspect of the communications activities. Yet President Nixon went over a year without such a gathering; and Lyndon Johnson used a variety of ad hoc procedures, even including gatherings on the hay bales at his Texas ranch. The specific manner in which the top aide or aides are used also differs drastically. Richard Nixon's reliance upon H. R. Haldeman, prior to the Watergate debacle, constituted a rigid hierarchical pattern (even including Haldeman's routine presence at key presidential conferences with other individuals in the Oval Office) which differed substantially from the manner in which, for example, John Kennedy employed Theodore Sorenson and Kenneth O'Donnell.

Of the three major institutions, Congress and the Supreme Court seem to reveal greater regularity in procedures. In part, the Supreme Court is simply so much smaller. For Congress, there is greater public awareness of procedures, and open controversy surrounding most changes. A committee chairman or a majority leader in Congress has a built-in opposition, which tends to complain if procedural changes are attempted which others see as detrimental.

Fluidity in presidential structures has been allowed in part because of the view that each new president must be able to devise the procedures which he finds most compatible with his own personality and work style. The stipulations of the Reorganization Act of 1939 give the president a virtual free hand in organizing the White House Staff and, to a considerable extent, the Executive Office of the President. Secrecy has also contributed to the ease with which procedures can be modified, as revelations of activities in the Nixon years have made painfully apparent. With a recognition of both fluidity and a measure of continuity, we can review key structures.

Two major organizational entities overlap within the formal organization of the modern Presidency.[15] The White House Staff, as the more immediate organization, is comprised of various special counsels and advisers, including both some key advisers and those with personal support roles. Besides assistance with the management of the president's own time, staff aides have been extensively involved with issues of presidential communication and the generation of political support for their boss and his programs. The Executive Office of the President encompasses both the White House Staff and also a series of advisory and planning units possessing varying degrees of influence. For example, such major policy-making units as the Office of Management and Budget, and the Council of Economic Advisers are part of the Executive Office of the President. In practice, individuals may combine both White House Staff roles and positions in the more formal advisory units such as the National Security Council or an energy or international economic planning group. As is so often the case, organizational charts are not a clear indication of the importance or actual functions of respective positions. Although individuals may also shift on occasion between either the White House Staff or the Executive Office of the President and one of the regular departments or agencies (e.g., the Departments of State and Defense, the Atomic Energy Commission), it is imperative to recognize the different organizational bases of the federal bureaucracy and the Executive Office. The president is expected to exercise some supervision over the federal bureaucracy, but the establishment of the Executive Office of the President was specifically for the purpose of aiding the president in the discharge of his various responsibilities.

As of 1974, the components of the Executive Office of the President were:[16]

> White House Staff
> National Security Council
> Council of Economic Advisers
> Council on Economic Policy
> Office of Management and Budget
> Domestic Council
> Energy Policy Office
> Office of Economic Opportunity
> Council on Environmental Quality
> Council on International Economic Policy
> Office of Special Representative for Trade Negotiations

Federal Property Council
Special Action Office for Drug Abuse Prevention
Office of Telecommunication Policy

In looking at the structures of the modern Presidency, one must first consider the White House Staff, with its combination of immediate advisers, communications specialists, political support promoters, and general logistical support groups. In turn, examination of the Executive Office of the President involves both major policy advisers and the various specialized units which often assume limited importance.

Immediate Advisers

All presidents have individuals around them with whom they interact on a frequent basis. The controversy around H. R. Haldeman's role as top staff coordinator in the Nixon Presidency should not obscure this basic point. There are vital differences in the manner in which key advisers are used, but the existence of such individuals cannot be avoided. Roosevelt used Harry Hopkins in such a proximate manner in the war years that he actually had him move into the White House. Truman relied critically upon such advisers as John Steelman and Clark Clifford. Eisenhower had Sherman Adams as his coordinator of staff operations and as a key adviser on domestic matters. Kennedy relied upon his brother Robert, Theodore Sorenson, and Kenneth O'Donnell in immediate, generalist roles. Johnson tended to wear advisers out, using Jack Valenti, William Moyers, and several others in immediate advising roles at various points.[17]

The key question is not whether such people will exist, but how they are used. The feature which distinguished the Eisenhower and Nixon operations was the extent to which a given aide was clearly superior in a hierarchy from others, and was responsible for the flow of information and the direction of staff activities. There will always be key figures around the Oval Office in the West Wing of the White House. The crucial question is how they relate to the president, and to others.

Communications Specialists

The extensive activity involving presidential communication is increasingly striking as one surveys the operations of the White House Staff. All recent Presidents have employed a substantial number of individuals to help in dispensing information. The central positions have been those of speech writer and press secretary. Regardless of how good a president may be at writing speeches, the dictates of time frequently prevent his proceeding without assistance. Speech writers help in addition with the wide variety of verbiage, from toasts for foreign visitors to presidential proclamations, which must come from the White House. Because they interact frequently with the president, the speech writers may also become important lobbyists for particular positions in their own right.

The position of the press secretary is also of great importance. Under President Nixon, titles were altered somewhat. Nixon wanted to extend his jurisdiction beyond the news coming out of the White House, and therefore made his communications director (Herbert Klein) responsible for coordinating the release of information not only from the White House but from the cabinet departments. The more specific task of meeting at least once daily with the White House press corps was given to his then assistant, Ron Zeigler. President Ford faced early difficulty with the press secretary role, as his first press secretary (Gerald terHorst) resigned in the face of the sudden decision by President Ford to pardon former President Nixon. There is simply no way for a modern president to avoid including on his staff persons with a major role involving relationships with the press.

The Nixon Presidency also produced an expanded example of the importance of a more general communications role, including the use of television and various public relations techniques. Although no specific comparative data are available, it was frequently noted that the Nixon Presidency used a surprisingly large number of people in staff roles who came from advertising backgrounds. H. R. Haldeman's earlier position as manager of a Los Angeles advertising agency was frequently noted, and he had recruited a number of individuals from his contacts in the advertising industry. President Nixon also used people such as Richard Moore for the specific purpose of aiding in public relations approaches. These activities, as we will see, corresponded to both a greater use of television than had previously been the case and a substantial amount of innovation in that use. Presidential staffs seem inextricably involved with the communications process.

Promoters of Political Support

A substantial number of White House Staff positions are also involved with efforts at generating political support for the incumbent and his programs. The head of legislative lobbying activities, at least for Nixon, was prominently located in close proximity to the Oval Office. The period since World War II has seen the Office of Legislative Liaison become an accepted feature of the White House Staff, with easily better than a dozen individuals involved in lobbying for presidential programs on Capital Hill. Lawrence O'Brien's energetic efforts for President Kennedy in this role have been among the more noticeable in recent years.

Some aides will be primarily responsible for liaison with key political groups. This often involves a measure of symbolic representation. Presidents generally seek some expression of representation for such groups as women, blacks, Southerners, ethnics, union members, academics, and youth. Staff aides for Lyndon Johnson were particularly sensitive to these roles and used to joke about the various representational roles, including attention to even fairly specific groups such as Greek Americans. It is helpful to have individuals available to meet with specific groups, from the academic gatherings in the White House to the youthful protesters demonstrating in the wake of unpopular foreign policy decisions.

The interest in generating political support may also take on far more tangible forms. For Nixon, Peter Flanigan performed an important role in relating to the business community, and Harry Dent served as a liaison with spokesmen for the South. More generally, one finds interest in the reelection effort centered within the presidential staff. This was not new to the Nixon Presidency. Kenneth O'Donnell was a major political strategist as Kennedy began thinking about reelection in 1963. In 1948, Clark Clifford played an important role in developing Truman's uniquely successful reelection plan. The peripheral position of the national party organizations has been noted for some time. One author even entitled a major study *Politics Without Power*.[18] The extent to which the Nixon staff expanded upon and altered the tendency for reelection to be a staff function becomes an important question in the collapse of his Presidency. What cannot be ignored is the general tendency for major segments of the staff operations to take on a highly political orientation.

Lesser Staff Roles

Other staff roles at points do take on some importance. The office of legal counsel is often a fairly uneventful position. Presidents need help with such matters as drafting executive orders, working out the language of executive agreements, and dealing with the states in meeting requirements for filing reelection papers. This was the position held by John Dean, the subsequent key witness in the case against President Nixon as it unfolded before the Ervin Committee in June 1973. The string of lawyers subsequently working on Nixon's defense gave the staff legal roles a most unprecedented importance in the 1973–1974 period.

Some of the individuals on the White House Staff occupy positions of limited influence even though they may have such titles as counselor to the president. These positions on occasion are a safety valve in presidential operations, as individuals are given peripheral functions in the counselor role after they have been eased out of other positions. Symbolic activities may also be involved, rather than important policy functions.

Other individuals working at the White House are involved with various types of logistical support. Mail must be answered, and letters must be typed. The Christmas cards must be prepared and mailed. In addition, a president will have his own ushers, gardeners, chefs, and maids. With some exceptions, the importance of these individuals is not in their policy impacts. Rather, they serve to remove the president from the daily concerns of life which affect all but the most wealthy Americans. One would literally have to be a millionaire many times over to have a comparable set of luxuries, including a rent-free estate, vacation retreats, a personal airplane, and a treasured collection of American art and antiques.

Even excluding the logistical-support personnel, the White House Staff may easily number well over 500 persons for a modern president. The actual set of supporting structures is nonetheless only partially described as one considers those positions. Intertwined with the operations of the White House Staff are the activities of persons with major roles in other areas of the Executive Office of the President. These individuals are more apt to be housed away from the White House itself, with its center of activities around the Oval Office in the West Wing. Location in either the Old or the New Executive Office Building is in part simply a function of size for the other units, however, and their heads often have prominent locations in the West Wing. Both vital policy roles and a number of relatively unimportant advisory mechanisms are found in the Executive Office of the President.

Policymatter Experts

Foreign, economic, and to some extent, domestic policy functions, have produced an expanded structuring of advisers within the Executive Office. The National Security Council and its staff, along with the crucial position of the national security adviser, have been recognized by both statute and general practice. The national security adviser (who is also a member of the White House Staff) has had at his disposal in recent years an extensive staff organized to support the National Security Council. That staff can easily number more than 100 individuals, and they are always located at the center of the flow of information in national security matters. Presidents have made varying use of the National Security Council in recent years, but they invariably confront a major staff apparatus.[19]

The largest of the national security intelligence operations, the

Central Intelligence Agency (CIA), is also included in some discussions as a part of the Executive Office of the President. In terms of operating relationships, this is most appropriate. Although confirmed by Congress, the head of the CIA reports to the president and sits with the National Security Council. If the nearly one billion-dollar budget of the CIA was included as part of that of the Executive Office, both the size and the cost of the Executive Office would appear much larger than is presently the case.

Economic advisers have also grown in stature in recent years, as presidential responsibility for the economy has expanded. The staff of the Council of Economic Advisers had grown past 80 at recent count. The top three positions, including the chairmanship, were defined by the Employment Act of 1946.[20] In the Nixon Administration there was also considerable experimentation with the economic apparatus. In June 1973, an Economic Policy Council was formed to include the chairman of the Council of Economic Advisers and also a number of cabinet officials. In addition, wage and price controls produced a Cost of Living Council, including both a Pay Board and a Price Commission. The Cost of Living Council was not technically a part of the Executive Office of the President, but in fact had close relationships. The Federal Reserve Board, possessing the important role of determining interest rates, also remains outside the Executive Office, but with substantial interaction, and often conflicts, with the president.

Along with the growing importance of economic advice has come an expanded role for the Office of Management and Budget (OMB, formerly the Bureau of the Budget), with its key role in developing the annual budget proposals. With a staff of easily over 500, the OMB has assumed great importance not only in budgeting, but in the development and coordination of presidential programs. A hostile review from OMB can be a serious blow to new proposals. Unfavorable assessments of management capabilities in an agency can produce considerable outside review. The growing importance of OMB is even reflected in its physical dimensions: A new office building had to be constructed as its staff became increasingly overcrowded in the Old Executive Office Building.

President Nixon also undertook a substantial effort during his first Administration to formalize the advising process on a broad range of domestic issues. This is the area where individuals may hold positions which blur into more political roles. Law degrees and political experience are more apt to appear as credentials for these positions than Ph.D.'s, when compared with foreign-policy- and economic-advising roles. That these positions entailed close relationship to political activities was borne out by the tendency for the frightened witnesses before the Ervin Committee to come from this area (and the directly political-assignment positions) rather than from foreign and economic policy positions.

The specific step taken by President Nixon was to establish a Domestic Council. He first experimented with an Urban Council (giving Daniel Moynihan a substantial role) and then established the Domestic Council in 1970. At one point, the Council numbered 70 individuals. The Council was headed by John Ehrlichman, constituting an increase in his power in the Nixon hierarchy. This domestic step was rather comparable to the use of greater social science advising support which had often been advocated by such liberals in Congress as Senator Humphrey. Ironically, this was also the step which seemed for some in Congress to make the President more removed, rather than to increase his use of expertise.

Special Access Positions

Presidents continue to experiment with the organization of the Executive Office, and the shifting structures reflect changing degrees of importance attached to various policy questions at particular points in time. Some of the assignments in the Executive Office also reflect successful lobbying by particular interests as they seek placement in the Executive Office, in hopes of achieving greater access to key decision points. They may be physically scattered throughout Washington, but desperately fight to gain and hold their legal position in the Executive Office. The more fluid positions may attract considerable presidential attention on occasion, but often they are relegated to reporting through members of the White House Staff.

Several once-prominent advisory groups have faded or been eliminated. As Johnson rushed to establish his War on Poverty in 1964, he also established the Office of Economic Opportunity (OEO) as part of the Executive Office. The poverty programs were not to be trusted to such regular organizations as the Departments of Labor, or Health, Education, and Welfare. As a result, both the top planners and the federal staff of better than 2,000 individuals were actually employed as part of the Executive Office. President Nixon sought to dismantle this structure in 1973, on the basis of his authority to reorganize the Executive Office. Congressional supporters were successful in delaying the step, arguing that a program which Congress had established by law could not be eliminated by presidential reorganization activities. Another once-prominent agency, the Office of Science and Technology, was eliminated by Nixon in 1973. The sense of crisis in the nation's handling of science matters at the time of the Kennedy Presidency gave way to the view by 1973 that the president was better off without a separate science-advising unit.

New units have also emerged. The Environmental Quality Council was created, with the help of Congress, to deal with the new standards for environmental control being established in 1969. The Nixon Administration continued its experimentation with the establishment of an Energy Policy Board, in an effort to coordinate the nation's energy policies. Other recent units have dealt with such specific concerns as drug abuse, international trade, the handling of federal procurement, and telecommunications policy. The rise and fall of advising mechanisms in the Executive Office indeed represents a most interesting indication of the changing focus on political issues within the country.

Interests seeking access are also on occasion reflected in the special task forces and commissions which are periodically created. Use of this device substantially increased during the 1960s, with the thrust of Kennedy and the continuation of Johnson. Nixon was less enthusiastic. These groups are typically formed for a fairly short duration and asked to submit recommendations to the president on a myriad of topics, from obscenity to possible improvement in racial policies. Lack of a sustained position to lobby one's cause in presidential politics is often a problem for commission members seeking a real policy impact. Furthermore, a commission may have been set up in the first place as a stalling device, rather than a problem-solving or idea-generating mechanism. The commissions do nonetheless periodically take on some importance, and they do comprise yet another dimension of the Executive Office operations.[21]

The Vice-President

Located somewhat in limbo, both figuratively and literally, across the street from the White House, in the ancient Old Executive Office Building, stands the office of the vice-president. New administrations typically open with statements of a new high to be attained in constructive relations between the president and his second-in-command, only to be followed some months later by reports that the vice-president feels slighted and is unhappy in his work. The role for Nelson Rockefeller with President Ford opened with the typical statements of the importance of the Vice-President's activities. It remained to be seen how that role would evolve, with an unusually experienced number-two man and a President who initially displayed limited aggressiveness on some major policy matters. The past record was in any event sobering. Accounts stressing difficulties have appeared in recent years involving Spiro Agnew, Hubert Humphrey, and Lyndon Jonson.[22] By his own say, Richard Nixon regarded Eisenhower's ambivalence toward his renomination in 1956 as one of his early crises.[23] Eisenhower also contributed more to an understanding of the common vice-presidential role than to a lowering of Nixon's anxieties when he answered a reporter's question by suggesting that he might be able to think of an important contribution by Nixon if given a week's time.

A vice-president will generally sit in on major meetings, yet he often sees the president alone very infrequently. Lyndon Johnson was even reported to take unnecessary trips across to the West Wing of the White House to make it appear that he was more actively involved. A vice-president may get involved with some policy matters. On occasion there may be a domestic role, as exemplified in particular by Nelson Rockefeller's position with President Ford. The vice-president, beginning with Lyndon Johnson, took an active role in space policy. Presiding over the Senate can take some time, as can some legislative lobbying activities on occasion. Vice-presidents are also expected to be spokesmen for the administration and on occasion have done some of the harsher campaigning. This role for Nixon in 1954 was part of the basis of the anger his name subsequently produced in Democratic circles.

The vice-president does not generally function at the center of presidential activities. In the eyes of the president he is a potential rival, and he may well have been selected with an eye toward balancing the ticket rather than toward a close working relationship. The overall state of the office within presidential operations was nicely illustrated by the widespread belief, prior to the unearthing of his own miserable trail of corruption, that Spiro Agnew knew little of the Watergate activities, for the simple reason that those in his position have tended not to know the key secrets of presidential operations.[24]

Summary

The modern presidency has expanded tremendously in structure as well as function. Presidents typically speak of a desire for curtailment, yet continue to find the office expanding. It is difficult to get precise figures because of the tendency for a mingling of assignments at points between the Executive Office and various departments and agencies. The general trend is nonetheless clear. Howard McCurdy has calculated recent White House Staff sizes as follows:[25]

FDR in 1938:   45
FDR in 1944:   48
Truman in 1952:   252
Eisenhower in 1960:   275
Kennedy in 1963:   263
Johnson in 1968:   202
Nixon in 1973:   510

The Nixon expansion is also revealed in budgetary terms. The budget for the White House Staff increased from $8.5 million at the outset to $16.5 million by 1974.[26]

The size of the Executive Office is even more impressive. The inclusion of the Office of Economic Opportunity, with a staff of approximately 2,000, provided a unique expansion in the Johnson and early Nixon years. Yet even without OEO, one is easily talking of a total Executive Office of over 2,000 individuals. If one included even the top levels of the CIA, the figure would also expand tremendously.

It is not surprising that President Ford would announce an interest in reducing staff size as one of his first objectives. The inability of recent successors to accomplish that objective nonetheless had to inspire a measure of skepticism. The modern president seems inevitably to find himself surrounded with a staff operation of massive proportions.

Sources of Change in the Presidency

A combination of forces has contributed to the growth of the modern Presidency. Because there is little chance for precise comparison, it is difficult to give specific weights to respective factors. One can nonetheless gain a general understanding of factors altering the nature of presidential politics. The developments one seeks to explain thus involve an expanded set of functions, an enlarged structure, greater power vis-à-vis other institutions, and—as an all-too-common result—greater problems of isolation for the president. Some of these factors have been changing in the wake of the collapse of the Nixon Presidency. A look at factors influencing recent developments is a sobering reminder: Alteration in the nature of the Presidency is not an easy task.

The Expanding Scope of Government

Students of political systems on a comparative basis have often found the more industrial and urban societies tending to have a larger range of activity within the public sector. Expenditure analysis within the United States has also pointed toward a tendency for several factors related to industrialization and urbanization to be correlated with higher levels of public spending.[27] Massachusetts and California spend more, per capita, than Mississippi and North Dakota, and Los Angeles spends more than Sioux Falls. Regulatory activity has also tended to grow with urbanization and industrialization. This overall trend is basic, but it does not help to explain why the Presidency should grow at the expense of other aspects of the political structure.

The Complexity of Policy Questions

There is no question but that the nature of the policy questions confronting the national government has shifted and is continuing to change. Allocation questions, which could often be handled on a pork barrel basis and with Congress playing a major role, have become less important. Rather than having the location of custom houses, agricultural experiment stations, and tariff impacts as major decisions, the contemporary political process has involved definitions of policy questions which involve complex, interrelated social and economic phenomena. One is now attempting to deal with individual motivation and behavior in seeking to control inflationary impulses, direct individuals back into the job market, and improve the educational performances of ghetto children. Even the shift in the nature of policy questions being considered between the 1950s and the 1960s was substantial, as the emphasis on physical issues such as highways and atomic energy plants declined while issues involving social behavior increased. All three areas of presidential involvement—foreign, economic, and general domestic—have seen a shift toward a consideration of more complex questions.

At crucial points, congressmen have recognized the difficulties created by complexity with a graceful yielding to larger presidential roles. In one unusually extensive study, the authors of *American Business and Public Policy* found a surprising readiness, rather than reluctance, in congressional approval of the shift to executive dominance in the working out of tariff policies.[28] The last tariff bill to go through Congress in detail contained over 1,200 amendments, and congressmen seemed reluctant to continue dealing with such bills. It was striking in 1973 to find Congress, despite the emerging collapse of the Nixon Presidency, still willing to authorize major presidential discretion in trade negotiations. The action in other areas has been comparable. The major delegation of wage and price control authority to President Nixon by a Democratically controlled Congress was passed with a large majority favoring virtual carte blanche authorization for the President to work out the specifics of regulation. Some expected that Nixon would not use the authority, thus giving them a campaign issue against him in 1972, but they were still willing to go along with widespread delegation.

It is fair to ask why the Presidency, rather than Congress, has often moved to develop expanded capacity for handling complex policy questions. Some of the executive advantages have been seen in a variety of industrial societies. The legislature seems unable to respond with the speed and flexibility which may be needed. Louis Fisher, in discussing the growth of the American tendency toward widespread legislative delegation to the Presidency, has emphasized this factor.[29]

A different set of past legislative leaders, more attentive to the uses of expertise, might have made a more substantial effort. Key committees were until recently often run by individuals (frequently from the South) who sought to hold on to their bases of power with traditional methods, rather than implementing specialists, computers, and a more expanded knowledge base. Belatedly, the period since about 1968 has seen some response in this direction.

The willingness on the part of Congress to go along with executive growth is also significantly related to the coalition pattern in American politics since the 1930s.

The Democratic Party Preference for Presidential Power

Major segments of the Democratic Party in Congress persisted in a staunch desire to expand executive power. An expanded Presidency was often seen as the best means of accomplishing their policy objectives, given the distribution of coalition strength in the two branches. Chapter 3 underscores that Democratic advantage in terms of tendencies to control the Presidency. All members of Congress would, to be sure, express some interest in separation of power. Roger Davidson and his colleagues, in studying the House of Representatives in the mid-1960s, found substantial willingness, in principle, to have Congress play a large role.[30] Yet on crucial issues of either gradual expansion of presidential power or of specific presidential staff additions, the Democrats were generally in strong support. Foreign policy expansion often had substantial bipartisan support, as in the 1947–1948 period. Major domestic moves deserve specific consideration.

The establishment of the Executive Office of the President, with the important inclusion of the Bureau of the Budget, transferred from the Treasury, was proposed by Roosevelt and finally passed in 1939, despite opposition from some Republicans and some major interest groups. The conservative coalition had been able to thwart Roosevelt's initial proposals in 1937. Only a handful of Democratic legislators dissented in the major 1939 votes.[31]

The major thrust toward the defining of economic roles after World War II, culminating in the establishment of the Council of Economic Advisers, found Democratic sentiment again behind a strong role for the president, rather than a more independent, or legislatively oriented economic mechanism.[32] Access to the White House for specific interests, such as scientists, with the establishment of the advising mechanisms following Sputnik, and the poor, with the establishment of the Office of Economic Opportunity in 1964, was also achieved with substantial Democratic support.

Some tinkering with the Presidency, such as the enactment of the new procedures for handling disability with the Twenty-fifth

Amendment, came with a highly generalized support.[33] Such matters have often depended on gaining enough interest, rather than winning in partisan or coalition divisions. At the cutting edge of changes, where policy and power matters were closer to the surface, the Democratic Party was a mainstay in both structural and functional expansion of the Presidency. The strong-presidency concept being expressed in academic circles was at several points supported in specific steps involving Democratic votes.

The President's Awe-Inspiring Foreign Policy Role

The key role of foreign policy matters in institutional evolution since World War II is difficult to overestimate.[34] A large share of presidential time after the war was devoted to foreign policy matters. The critical and often irreversible nature of the decisions which were periodically made led in turn to extensive support and a general awe of the president. Both structures and general attitudes were involved. Structurally, the practices of secrecy in presidential politics quickly surfaced. Background briefings, with their inevitable references to "high administration sources" were a product of World War II. Extensive use of security classification came along at about the same time. The 1947–1948 decisions on reorganization, with the formation of the National Security Council and the CIA, produced a major expansion in total presidential machinery.

Orientations of both advisers and the electorate also seem to have been affected by the importance of the president's foreign policy role. It is increasingly common for critics to note that advisers do not as regularly as in earlier days tell the president that his ideas are stupid or that he has made a blunder on a given decision. The president today lacks, as George Reedy argues, individuals with whom he interacts as peers. Presidential communication with advisers reflects an awareness that the president must be concerned with foreign policy issues potentially involving the literal destruction of millions of people.

The impact of the president's foreign policy role has also produced unique results on the electorate. When a president makes what seems to have been a major mistake, such as Kennedy's authorization of the Bay of Pigs invasion in 1961, he may suddenly enjoy a sharp *rise* in his popularity. It has seemed difficult, in short, during the Cold War period for either advisers or the electorate to greet a president in conventional terms.

Foreign policy concerns have also expanded the growth of the tendency to cloak the president in an extensive apparatus to protect his personal security. Truman was the last President to venture out very much on his own, and even his morning walks produced concern in the Secret Service. It has seemed increasingly impossible for a

President to do common, everyday things. Prior to his marriage, Canada's Trudeau dated women while in office. Chile's Frei occasionally walked home to his residence where he continued to dwell, while his wife continued teaching school. The American president has been denied the common experiences. The emergency phone equipment never leaves a president's side, and it is rare that he has even a brief amount of time away from the prying eyes of the press and the Secret Service.

The Nixon Presidency seemed to reveal one other key impact. At several points, the methods and orientations for domestic and partisan functions were rather like those employed in foreign policy matters. A few highlights illustrate the point for now. Secrecy was rampant. The use of spies was condoned. The opposing party was at points not seen as a loyal opposition, but an "enemy." Announcement of policy steps, rather than sustained policy-support building, often seemed to dominate. If Congress could not be won over, then the appropriate tactic was simply to take the policy step anyway, using some aspect of the vague powers which had become associated with the Presidency in previous years. Although one must be wary of pushing the analogy too far, it almost seemed at times as though President Nixon sought to operate all aspects of the Presidency in the manner in which he (and other recent presidents, in several respects) had often conducted the foreign policy roles. In short, the operation of the Presidency as an institution with primary and often overwhelming concern for foreign policy matters also influenced other aspects of presidential behavior.

Glorification of the President by the Electorate

Several factors have contributed to a tendency for the electorate to glorify the Presidency. Traditional political socialization, with its emphasis on reverence, has been involved, along with the tendency not to disassociate the ceremonial from the partisan, policy-making dimensions of the office. High expectations held by those espousing the strong-persidency view were also contributing factors. The president's involvement with foreign policy issues, as considered here, has given the electorate an additional shove toward a larger-than-life view of the occupant of the Oval Office.

Television has also contributed to his glorification by the electorate. Presidents have far better access to the electorate through the use of television than any other politicians. When George Washington announced his retirement, his words, in print, without any image, took 4 days to reach New York and 10 days to reach outlying regions. When Lyndon Johnson made the same announcement in 1968, he faced an audience of 75 million people.[35] Furthermore, the Nixon

Presidency saw a marked increase in emphasis on presidential use of television. The importance of television was demonstrated in October 1973, as Nixon spokesmen lashed out not at the opposing party but at the media as being responsible for the "firestorm" of opposition to the firing of Special Prosecutor Cox and the resignation of Attorney General Elliot Richardson. Presidents have become used not only to extensive television coverage, but to often flattering coverage.

Presidential glorification, intensified by television, has contributed to the perception of the Presidency as being above the normal political process. In this context, it has been comparatively easy for recent Presidents to operate in a manner which increasingly removed them from at least some of the normal political restraints.

The Impact of Individual Presidents

The developing Presidency has repeatedly seen the impact of individuals and their ideas of the office. Despite widespread agreement on some procedures, the president has an opportunity to influence both presidential structure and political practices which goes to no other individual in the American system. The impact of individual strengths and weaknesses are readily apparent. George Reedy's argument that the Presidency magnifies a president's personality—both good and bad—is an indication that there is enough flexibility for individuals to have a major impact.[36] Each President in the modern period has left an impact on the institution.

Roosevelt's contribution was both functional and structural. He expanded domestic roles, but perhaps more important were the precedents he set involving mobilizing roles and relationships with the electorate. Roosevelt also contributed to the growth of the White House Staff and the federal bureaucracy, although it is worth recalling that the budget was still under $10 billion for the entire federal government when World War II began.

Truman and Eisenhower were the first presidents to operate in the context of the expanded formal institutions which evolved after World War II. Truman took the first cautious steps in bringing organizations such as the Council of Economic Advisers into the orbit of presidential decision-making. Eisenhower perpetuated (to the surprise of some) the economic advising activities, and made a concerted effort at strengthening the cabinet. The use of formal agencies such as the National Security Council and the establishment of a formal hierarchy for advising were major Eisenhower impacts.

President Kennedy liked to look back to the Roosevelt Presidency rather than to those of immediate predecessors. He sought to mobilize particular groups with advisory commissions more extensively than had been done in the past. In addition, he made a major impact on the expansion of systematic analysis and the role of econo-mists in governmental planning. Functionally, Kennedy also began expansion in economic planning, as he sought support for more active fiscal policy.

Lyndon Johnson's design for the Presidency was to mobilize and to establish a Great Society with new domestic programs. He also carried forward vigorously the use of outside commissions and task forces. The thrust of his successful legislative efforts has been substantial; it was Johnson who showed how the legislative process could be activated by an aggressive president supported by unusual majorities. Johnson's other, unwitting impact on the Presidency was to cause a sharp increase in questioning of leader isolation and in criticism by the media and the public.

Richard Nixon intended a major impact on the Presidency. Rather than operating a status quo Presidency, Nixon sought funda-mental change. His actions, prior to public knowledge of the Water-gate scandals, led former Supreme Court Justice (and Johnson confi-dant) Abe Fortas to categorize him as a radical.[37] The White House was to be decreased in size (although it had expanded again in his first term) and the cabinet departments were to be reorganized. Reve-nue sharing was to reduce the direct necessity for federal policy mak-ing in several domestic areas. One irony of the Nixon Presidency is that a President who had a definite design for personal impact so unwittingly contributed to a vastly different impact—an impact which is sure to be felt for years in American politics.

The Ambitiousness of Presidential Staffs

Presidents are not the only individuals whose personal desires have helped shape the institution. Some expansion, particularly in terms of staff size, but also, at points, in overall functions, has been a result of the rivalries for status, prestige, and influence on the part of presidential staffs. Richard Whalen has emphasized this point in his highly critical account of the Nixon staff.[38] George Reedy has expressed a similar concern in his assessments. As our review of staff backgrounds will show, there has been an increasing tendency in recent years for presidents to recruit highly ambitious individuals in large numbers. They may have some of the anonymity so often attributed to presidential aides. Key aides, just like officials within departments and agencies, have nonetheless had a tendency to view the size and scope of their operations imperialistically. As a result, increases in one staff are apt to produce pressures for increases in other staff units to maintain comparable ratios of personnel. Some pressure for expansion must ultimately be attributed to individual ambition, rather than more general forces such as increased complexity of contemporary policy issues.

The Conflicting Pressures for Change

For a variety of reasons, Americans have witnessed the evolution of a Presidency with both multiple functions and a large, complex structure. The complexity of policy questions, Democratic preferences, the impact of the president's foreign policy involvement, his glorification by the electorate, ideas and actions of incumbents, and the ambitions of staff aides have all been involved.

The response to the actions of Johnson and Nixon did most clearly begin to produce changes in some of the support for the Presidency, which had begun to receive such names as "isolated," "imperial," and "swollen." Democratic Party support eroded precipitously, as disillusioned former supporters of the Presidency led efforts to curtail recent practices. Electoral disaffection began to produce some decline in aspects of the more worshipful views of the institution. The shift away from the Cold War international system also reduced some of the more automatic justifications of strong presidential roles.

Key supporting factors nonetheless remained. The discussions of reform often did not address themselves to the possible reduction in the scope of governmental operations. Many former supporters of the strong-presidency view talked primarily in terms of strengthening Congress, rather than confronting the possible inevitableness of massive presidential power if the scope of federal activities was not reduced or at least altered in form. Problems of complexity also remained, and an advocacy of price and wage controls emerged early in the Ford Presidency, at the very time that concern for reducing presidential power was also rampant. The underlying problem of complexity in governmental operations which had often fostered expansion of presidential power in the past remained at least as important as in earlier decades. Questions of possible directions which the cross-cutting forces of change might and should take must await a more direct look at recent operations.

NOTES

[1] There is fair consistency in functional breakdowns. See, for example, Clinton Rossiter, *The American Presidency*, New York, Mentor, 1956, chap. 1.

[2] The major findings came from the Kennedy period, and some questions are emerging as to the validity of generalizing those findings. See Fred Greenstein, *Children and Politics*, New Haven, Conn., Yale University Press, 1965.

[3] For a discussion of the highly emotional responses to Harding's death,

see Francis Russell, *The Shadow of Blooming Grove,* New York, McGraw-Hill, 1968.

[4] Sidney Verba, "The Kennedy Assassination and the Nature of Political Commitment," in *The Kennedy Assassination and the American Public,* ed. by Bradley S. Greenberg and Edwin B. Parker, Stanford, Calif., Stanford University Press, 1965, p. 348.

[5] James A. Robinson, *Congress and Foreign Policymaking,* Homewood, Ill., Dorsey, 1967.

[6] William Manchester, *Portrait of a President,* Boston, Little, Brown, 1963, p. 32.

[7] Thomas Cronin and Rexford Tugwell, eds., *The Presidency Reappraised,* New York, Praeger, 1974.

[8] See Lyndon B. Johnson, *The Vantagepoint,* New York, Holt, Rinehart & Winston, 1971.

[9] Lawrence C. Pierce, *The Politics of Fiscal Policy Formation,* Pacific Palisades, Calif., Goodyear, 1971.

[10] The distinctiveness of presidential economic activities was developed by Thomas Cronin as an extension of remarks on the swelling of the presidency at a meeting of the Conference on the Contemporary Presidency, University of Southern California, January 13, 1973.

[11] The tendency for Americans to worship their political system but to view party politics and politicians skeptically has been documented in many sources. See, for example, William Mitchell, "The Ambivalent Status of the American Politician," *Western Political Quarterly* 12 (1959), 683–699.

[12] Aaron Wildavsky, "The Two Presidencies," in Aaron Wildavsky, ed., *The Presidency,* Boston, Little, Brown, 1969, pp. 230–243.

[13] The interrelationships of functions is a major theme in Richard Neustadt's *Presidential Power: The Politics of Leadership,* New York, Wiley, 1960.

[14] The development of institutionalized procedures for the Presidency is discussed in Richard Neustadt, "Presidency and Legislation: Planning the President's Program," *American Political Science Review 49* (1955), 980–1021.

[15] A useful description of the respective components is found in Howard E. McCurdy, "The Physical Manifestations of an Expanding Presidency: A Tour of the White House and Executive Offices." Prepared for delivery at the 1974 Annual Meeting of the American Political Science Association, Chicago, Ill., September 1, 1974.

[16] *U.S. Government Organizational Manual,* Washington, D.C., GPO, 1974.

[17] An informative account of these relationships is found in Patrick Anderson, *The Presidents' Men,* Garden City, N.Y., Doubleday, 1968. Useful historical reviews are provided in Louis Koenig, *The Invisible Presidency,* New York, Rinehart, 1960.

[18] Bernard C. Hennessy and Cornelius P. Cotter, *Politics Without Power,* New York, Atherton, 1964.

[19] For general review of this role, see Roger Hilsman, *The Politics*

of Policy Making in Defense and Foreign Affairs, New York, Harper & Row, 1971. See also Chapter 9 of this book.

[20] The growth in the economic advising role is traced in Edward S. Flash, Jr., *Economic Advice and Presidential Leadership: The Council of Economic Advisers,* New York, Columbia University Press, 1965.

[21] On the commission role, see Thomas E. Cronin and Sanford D. Greenberg, *The Presidential Advisory System,* New York, Harper & Row, 1969, pp. 89–149.

[22] On Johnson's role, see Leonard Baker, *The Eclipse of Lyndon Johnson,* New York, Macmillan, 1966. On Humphrey's role and frustrations, see Allan B. Ryskind, *Hubert,* New York, Arlington, 1968. The difficulties of Spiro Agnew prior to his acknowledged role in personal abuses is traced in Theodore Lippman, *Spiro Agnew's America,* New York, Norton, 1972.

[23] Richard M. Nixon, *My Six Crises,* Pyramid Books, New York, 1968.

[24] On Agnew's roles, see Richard W. Cohen and Jules Witcover, *A Heartbeat Away,* New York, Viking, 1974. On the general ineffectiveness of the Vice-Presidency, see Arthur M. Schlesinger, Jr., "Is the Vice-Presidency Necessary?" *Atlantic,* May 1974, pp. 37–44.

[25] McCurdy, op. cit.

[26] *National Journal,* April 6, 1974, p. 495.

[27] This line of analysis is explored in Thomas R. Dye, *Politics, Economics, and the Public,* New York, Rand McNally, 1966.

[28] Raymond Bauer et al., *American Business and Public Policy,* New York, Atherton, 1963.

[29] Louis Fisher, *President and Congress,* New York, Free Press, 1972, chap. 3.

[30] Roger Davidson, et al., *Congress in Crisis,* Belmont, Calif., Wadsworth, 1966, chap. 3.

[31] The passage of the Reorganization Act of 1939 is extensively reviewed in Richard Polenberg, *Reorganizing Roosevelt's Government,* Cambridge, Harvard University Press, 1966. Only five Democrats and seven Republicans deviated from a straight party vote in the House.

[32] These events are effectively traced in Stephen K. Bailey, *Congress Makes a Law,* New York, Columbia University Press, 1950. See especially chap. 6.

[33] Birch Bayh, *One Heartbeat Away: Presidential Disability and Succession,* Indianapolis, Ind., Bobbs-Merrill, 1968.

[34] The impact of foreign policy functions is stressed in Arthur M. Schlesinger, Jr., *The Imperial Presidency,* Boston, Houghton Mifflin, 1973. See also Emmet John Hughes, *The Living Presidency,* New York, Coward-McCann & Geoghegan, 1972.

[35] Newton Minow et al., *Presidential Television,* New York, Basic Books, 1973, p. 7.

[36] George Reedy, *The Twilight of the Presidency,* New York, Mentor, 1970, chap. 1.

[37] Emmet John Hughes, op. cit., p. 333.

[38] Richard Whalen, *Catch the Falling Flag,* Boston, Houghton Mifflin, 1972.

The Selection Process

Recent presidential performances have dramatically shown the importance of presidential selection. One must wonder how public policy and the state of the Presidency would be different today if Nelson Rockefeller had emerged as the Republican Party candidate in 1968, or if Hubert Humphrey had finished narrowing Richard Nixon's lead that year. Or if John Kennedy had served two full terms instead of his 1000 days.

The question of individual impacts ultimately becomes a vital one in overall evaluations of the contemporary Presidency. What kinds of individuals are tending to emerge, and why? This is a most difficult question. One part of the answer must reside in the selection process itself.

Major changes have been taking place in the presidential selection process, and with consequences which are only partly felt and understood. The standard coalition division, with the Democrats apt to control the Presidency and the conservative coalition of Republicans and Southern Democrats apt to control Congress, has been shattered. Furthermore, changes in party-identification voting habits make it unlikely that a new solidification of coalition and party comparable to that of the 1936–1964 period will emerge. At the same time, party control of the nominating process has declined and the process has become more individualized and more demanding for prospective candidates. One of the key results is the power of incumbency. It seems increasingly difficult to vote incumbents out. The changes in coalition patterns, which are affecting presidential politics in so many ways, deserve careful attention.

Changing Coalitions

Despite the Republic interlude of the Eisenhower years, the dominant coalition pattern in American politics between 1936 and 1968 was one in which the Democratic Party had a substantially better chance than the Republicans of capturing the Presidency. At the same time, supporters of expanded federal domestic programs had a better chance in presidential politics than in Congress. Beginning in 1968, this pattern partially reversed. President Nixon moved, despite overall domestic program expenditure increases, in directions seeking to reduce the scope of federal domestic programs. His budget as proposed in 1973 not only emphasized an unusual amount of change, but sought to reduce or end major aspects of Johnson's domestic program. Conversely, Congress tended to be the center for "new priority politics," with a pattern of decreasing defense appropriations from the levels requested by the President and increasing domestic allocations. The resulting conflict was a basic underpinning for many of the tensions between Nixon and Congress.

The New Deal Democratic Coalition

The reelection of Roosevelt in 1936, which crystallized developments which had been moving in the Democratic direction for several years, produced a coalescence of the Democratic presidential coalition. This coalition victory represented in many respects the classic case, perhaps even *the* case, of a strong president building policy support while in office and gaining reaffirmation with electoral support. In retrospect, that election produced not just a victory of landslide proportions but a shift in party identification for a group of voters sizeable enough to dominate the course of presidential politics for a generation.

The generally familiar basic elements of the Democratic coalition can be reviewed quickly, along with key dimensions of policy change involved:[1]

Southern Democrats. A maintenance of traditional voting habits was involved here, with few tensions, because the New Deal did not select blacks for specific policy attention.

Labor. The New Deal gave basic recognition to the trade unions in terms of bargaining rights with the Wagner Act in 1935, and gained a major and often well-organized union vote for the Democratic Party.

Farmers. Efforts toward stabilizing agriculture were frequent in the first term and caused substantial swings toward the Democrats, particularly in areas of the Midwest which had often voted Republican in the past.

Ethnic and urban voters. Roosevelt and the Democrats made a major effort to aid urban Americans with various relief programs. There was also a conscious effort to attract various ethnic groups (and particularly Jews) with appointments and symbolic reinforcement. Interest in ethnic voters was not directed toward the blacks, however. They were effectively prevented from voting in the South during the 1930s and were not an important electoral force.

Middle-class Americans. Such New Deal programs as the establishment of banking and home mortgage reform were of substantial benefit to middle-class citizens, and contributed to the new support among voters (particularly in the Midwest) who had previously identified with the Republican Party.

Westerners. Irrigation and public works projects spawned by the New Deal were popular in the West, and brought support from some formerly Republican strongholds.

In sum, the election of 1936 brought to fruition a coalition which replaced the Republican coalition which had largely dominated national politics (and particularly the Presidency) in the entire period since the Civil War.

Conservative Coalition Strength in Congress

Congressional resistance to the Democratic presidential coalition was often effective, despite the fact that the Democrats were able after 1930 to hold majorities in Congress in all elections except 1946 and 1952. Although Roosevelt could write his legislative program largely without serious resistance in his first term, the conservative coalition crystallized in 1937 and became a major roadblock to further presidential initiatives in domestic policy areas. Struggles over the Supreme-Court-packing issue in 1937 (as Roosevelt sought to end conservative control with expanded Court membership), and reorganization and agricultural issues, produced a recognition by conservatives in Congress of their ability to block new programs.[2] During the entire period between 1937 and 1964, the conservative coalition was very often able to thwart domestic proposals by Presidents which were supported by liberal Democrats. President Truman faced an often rancorous stalemate, Eisenhower often attempted little change, and Kennedy faced an unusually hostile and unproductive Congress.

Several factors contributed to the limited success of the liberal

Democrats in Congress. Legislative majorities are often hard to organize, and some felt that the liberals were often not the most astute members of Congress in handling rules and procedures. Legislative elections also produced, in off-year elections, a somewhat different segment of the electorate than the one voting in presidential elections. At points, the more likely supporters of expanded federal programs were among the nonvoters in congressional races, thus reducing chances for a strong activist majority.[3]

Key congressional structures were also central to Democratic activist frustrations with Congress. Seniority selection requirements for committee chairmanships, especially the position of the Rules Committee in the House of Representatives, served to slow several presidentially endorsed measures.[4] As the Rules Committee politics and House procedures operated in the late 1950s and early 1960s in particular, liberals could easily lose simply because they could not get bills reported out of the Rules Committee. The Senate filibuster also allowed the Southern segment of the Democratic coalition a critical veto, particularly when civil rights measures were involved. The net result was clear: Those seeking a more active federal domestic role generally found more potential in presidential, rather than congressional, political action.

The Democratic Presidential Coalition, 1948–1968

Greater Democratic than Republican opportunity for capturing the Presidency obviously did not produce an unblemished pattern of support in elections. Eisenhower's personal popularity, particularly in 1956, coupled with electoral disinterest in domestic matters in the 1950s, produced two decisive Republican victories. The Democratic victories of 1948 and 1960 were also very close. The entire period was nonetheless characterized by a persistence in electoral tendencies to identify with the Democratic Party. The postwar elections deserve specific note.

In 1948, President Truman barely won reelection, after being counted out by virtually everyone, in the face of not one, but two, minor party splits. Strom Thurmond led the bolt from the Democratic Party of the Southerners over the emerging racial issues, ultimately carrying the states with the heaviest black populations—Alabama, Louisiana, South Carolina, and Mississippi. Henry Wallace simultaneously led a protest by the political left over foreign policy matters, as the Cold War solidified and the more radical views on domestic policies sought expression in presidential politics. Truman was able to eke out a narrow and surprising victory by emphasizing the domestic programs of the New Deal coalition and, as a result, substantially reducing the initially projected disaffection to Wallace. A close election can be explained in many ways. It is important simply to emphasize that Truman campaigned very heavily on the domestic policy appeals of the New Deal and did bring supporters in such categories as labor and agriculture to a substantial reassertion of their Democratic allegiance.[5]

The Eisenhower elections produced victory for a man, far more than for a party. Eisenhower was helped in 1952 by issues as well as personal appeal, as questions involving the Korean War and government corruption made a significant impact. In 1956, Ike was helped even more by the comparison of his personality with Adlai Stevenson's, and somewhat less by issue differences. Yet in both elections the key victory ingredient was not a realignment of individuals calling themselves Republicans but rather a defection by voters still regarding themselves as at least weak Democrats.[6] Ike won both elections with the percentage of voters identifying as Republicans remaining under 40 percent. (The Democrats had strong and weak identifiers numbering close to 50 percent. The others classified themselves as independents and apoliticals.) Eisenhower's personal popularity through his eight years in office was simply not translated into voter increases in Republican identification.

John Kennedy's scant victory over Richard Nixon in 1960 (by a mere 118,574 votes) again showed frailties with the Democratic coalition. Counting defections of both Protestant Democrats and Catholic Republicans on the question of Kennedy's Catholicism, Kennedy suffered a net loss. In part because of the defections of Democratic Protestants (and also because of the racial issue), Kennedy lost Virginia, Tennessee, and Florida, while carrying Texas by only a few votes.[7] Yet Kennedy was able to keep enough other segments of the basic New Deal coalition together to win over the initially more widely recognized candidate.

In 1964, Johnson showed what having a weak Republican opponent plus an emphasis on the New Deal coalition could still accomplish. With the exception of white Southern defection on the racial issue in the Deep South, Johnson was able to hold every segment of the coalition intact, gaining over 61 percent on the total vote cast.[8] The subsequent enactment of key domestic programs, including aid to education, Medicare, and civil rights legislation, marked the culmination of basic aspects of the policy agenda which had been a part of the Democratic coalition ever since the New Deal (or the 1950s, for civil rights). The Democrats have since then often had to defend existing programs rather than advocating new ones, and simultaneously face the underlying racial issue in many policy questions.

The Recent Decline of Traditional Coalitions

Both continuing volatility in electoral activity and the difficulty of analyzing political trends make it hazardous to view single events as clear shifts in voting patterns. The combined impacts of 1968 and 1972, coupled with the changing use of party identification cues, nevertheless give clear indications that the Democratic coalition has lost its dominant hold on the Presidency. Despite the narrowness of Nixon's 1968 election victory and the remarkable job which Senator Humphrey performed in building a near-victory after the turmoil of the Chicago convention, the 1968 election nonetheless found 57 percent of the electorate supporting either Nixon or Wallace.[9]

The 1972 election saw Nixon able to combine some former Wallace support with his own 1968 vote. The Democrats also showed innumerable confusions in their coalition. A convention which substantially excluded and certainly alienated such traditional supporters as labor leaders, city leaders, and Southerners, dramatized Democratic uncertainties. It was indeed strange to traditional viewers of Democratic conventions to see both Mayor Daley and many labor leaders on the sidelines. Some would even refer to McGovern's subsequent 37.5 percent of the total vote as the largest vote for a third party in history![10]

The Democrats did seem to work awfully hard in putting on as poor a presidential race as finally occurred. The ensnarement of George McGovern in the Eagleton episode not only revealed difficulties with the time-honored selection process for vice-presidents, but left the McGovern campaign disheartened from the start. McGovern also raised such issues as income support for the poor in ways destined to confuse and alienate the increasingly middle-class segments of the traditional Democratic coalition. Roosevelt, it is worth noting, was very vague about his policy steps until after assuming office. By the summer of 1973, it was also evident that acts of sabotage, perhaps in particular of the Muskie candidacy in the primaries, had worked to the disadvantage of the final Democratic showing in 1972. The Republicans also profited, as we shall see shortly, from the many advantages of incumbency.

After due apologies are made for 1972, it is apparent that the Democratic coalition lost in ways making it difficult to reestablish the New Deal coalition hegemony in presidential politics. Several factors stand out:

The South is increasingly lost to the Democratic coalition on the presidential level. There may be opportunities in the more industrial and urban states, particularly Florida and Texas. There may also be possibilities of combining blacks and poor whites on economic issues. The expectation of easy Democratic victory in the South is nonetheless increasingly nonexistent. The Deep South has, in fact, voted against the Democratic nominee for three straight elections.

Ethnic Americans and workers generally show considerable restiveness with the Democrats, in part because of the Democratic support for advancement of the black population in situations where competition for jobs, houses, and schools produces conflict. This was expressed in the Wallace vote in 1968 and in his continuing political appeal in the 1970s.

Labor leaders have difficulty uniting a vote behind the old appeals of the New Deal coalition as they deal with an increasingly young membership—one for which the 1930s is ancient history. Some labor leaders, in fact, had drifted into Republican support as of the 1972 election.

Farmers have always been somewhat unstable in their Democratic support. Their declining number in the face of the agribusinesses of today's agricultural economy in turn further reduces the opportunities for a strong farm bloc behind the Democrats.

In terms of size, the Democratic rural areas and the inner city Democratic areas have been losing population to the vast suburbanization of metropolitan areas. Democrats have had some impressive victories in the suburbs, but the older organizations and issues have faded.

The decline in the Democratic coalition for controlling presidential politics is substantial as one reviews recent defections. The likelihood of future Democratic presidents easily returning to the old coalition is remote. Yet coalitions can regroup, and that remained a possibility in the wake of the Nixon debacle. Before considering future coalition possibilities, recent changes in coalition strength within Congress must also be recognized.

A major shift has occurred in the position of Congress. It is informative to compare the record as seen by Willmoore Kendall in 1960 with the situation a decade later. Looking at relations between the president and Congress in the decades prior to 1960, Kendall saw several key differences.[11] His list is summarized in the table on page 62.

The situation changed markedly by the early 1970s. On foreign policy, it was in Congress where resistance to the Vietnam War focused, under both Johnson and Nixon. On defense and welfare expenditure conflicts, the Nixon Presidency found a sharp tendency for the President to propose welfare cuts and for Congress to propose increases. At the same time, Congress sought to cut the defense budget by as much as $5 billion in a single year. On civil rights, the Nixon Presidency found the chief executive actively seeking ways of modifying initial commitments. Unlike Eisenhower, Nixon sought to alter policy commitments across a broad range of policy concerns.[12] In the process, the traditional divisions between president and Congress underwent basic revision.

The picture which emerges can be stated simply. A Democratic coalition which had enjoyed its best access in the Presidency, and

Presidential Versus Congressional Policy Emphases Prior to 1960

Public Policy Area	Congressional Emphasis	Presidential Emphasis
Internal security	Strong legislation supplemented by permanent congressional investigating staff	Active only when pushed by Congress
Public works	Unabashedly for the "pork barrel"	Appeals to national interest rather than local constituencies
Foreign trade	Protectionist	Free trade
Foreign aid	Drags its feet	Deeply committed
Integration	Tends to withhold authority for governmental action	Ready to act, even without a public mandate
Economic policy	Watches the national debt; emphasizes sound finance	Accepts Keynesian position on debt and governmental spending
Defense, welfare	Increases size of air force; defense spending comes first	Tends to cut military requests and to resist Congress
Foreign policy	Nationalistic; no quarrels with right-wing dictatorships	Internationally minded; committed to democratic forms of government

at least periodically had enjoyed considerable influence in domestic policy areas, found itself in disarray by 1972, while at the same time enjoying somewhat greater influence in Congress. A bad-luck factor was partly involved in the McGovern debacle, but the traditional coalition alignments had clearly been broken.

Possible Future Coalitions

The nature of possible future coalitions will have vast implications for presidential politics. If a new coalition emerges which is anti-black, anti-poor, and (perhaps most importantly) opposed to a strong governmental role in promoting social change, massive impacts on presidential politics could occur.[13] This is basically the coalition seen by such writers as Richard Scammon and Benjamin Wattenberg in the late 1960s. On the other hand, if there is a resurgence of economic protest in the Democratic Party in the context of a new populist commitment against corporate and upper-class interests, policy consequences of great magnitude may also follow.

An additional key question is involved in looking at coalition possibilities. How permanent will future alignments be? The period between the 1930s and the 1960s produced several fairly stable features of presidential politics. The Democratic Party was in the majority in terms of party identification. The Republicans might capture the White House with a popular military leader, but they could not alter basic party alignments. Issues dividing the parties, especially on the domestic agenda, were also fairly fixed. The Democratic Party could not always win in Congress, given the conservative coalition strength in that body. Yet the tendency for the Democratic legislators, with the exception of *some* Southern defectors, to support an expanded federal domestic role, with an eye toward attempting to help the have-not social groups, was also persistent.

One interpretation of the recent evolutions taking place in presidential politics has emphasized an emerging Republican majority. Republican enthusiast Kevin Phillips received a warm welcome in Nixon circles as he proclaimed the emergence (in 1968) of a new Republican majority.[14] That new majority was said to include the South, business groups (particularly in areas outside the Northeast), substantial segments of the newer metropolitan areas of the Southwest and the West—the "sunshine belt"—and substantial segments of the Midwest. Phillips saw the Democrats as a minority party including only New England, blacks, and some remaining Democratic identifiers in other geographic areas and social groupings. With obvious indignation directed toward the liberal Democrats of the Northeast, Phillips saw the Democratic Party going the way of the Federalists in an earlier day.

There are some historical patterns on Phillips' side of the argument. Great historical upheavals such as the Civil War and the Depression have been the source of past realignments. It is not difficult to see the convulsions of the 1960s over issues of race and the Vietnam War constituting a comparable set of social tensions. There is also some basis for the argument that the party realignments have taken place about every 40 years, making the 1970s the logical time for another realignment.[15] Problems nonetheless arise in analyses pointing to a new Republican majority.

It is not easy to prejudge the impact of the Watergate scandals on the presidential fortunes of the Republican Party. The collapse of the Nixon Presidency was simply unprecedented. Significantly, past electoral responses to issues of corruption in government do not show a revulsion permanently harming the affected party. The scandals of the Grant Administration were followed by a series of Republican victories, including the 1876 election with its very questionable granting of disputed electoral college votes from two southern states to achieve victory for President Hayes. Voter support for Republicans in the post-Grant period was not shaken by the Republican association with corruption in government.

The Teapot Dome scandals of the Harding Administration were well known by 1924, yet Coolidge was able to win handsomely as the factional frustrations of the Democrats became even more pronounced.[16] A generation later, Eisenhower campaigned hard on the issue of corruption in government and did have some impact, although the Korean War and personality factors were also central to his victory.[17] Yet conversely, the substantial instances of corruption in the Eisenhower Presidency (as discussed in Chapter 12) never became a serious campaign issue.[18]

The congressional landslide for the Democrats in 1974, with gains of 43 seats in the House and 3 in the Senate, could be the beginning of a different response. Widespread frustration with the economy as of 1974 may nonetheless prove, in the wake of careful analysis and future experiences, to be a dominant factor in that result. Although past experiences do not speak to an issue with the magnitude of the Watergate scandals, they do serve as a hope-dampening set of precedents for those who expect corruption to prevent party realignment. The electorate's tendencies to remember and act on issues of corruption in government have been remarkably short-lived.

There were other, more serious difficulties with the theory of the emerging Republican majority even prior to the Watergate scandals. The elections of 1968 and 1972 found voters caught in a situation in which racial issues, though partially blurred by references to such issues as crime, often predominated over economic matters. Nixon was actually running behind Senator Muskie in the 1971 polls, as Nixon's economic performance drew extensive criticism. A combination of the somewhat improved economic situation and the voter uncertainty over Senator McGovern's economic policies aided Nixon mightily in 1972. There is no assurance, however, particularly in the wake of the disastrous economic results during the 1968–1976 period, that future Republican candidates will be able to avoid having Democrats unite around pocketbook issues.

The continuing Democratic identification of middle-class segments of the electorate is also given insufficient attention in the Phillips analysis.[19] Party identification has proven to be a fairly lasting phenomena, and not one easily shaken by an occasional defection on the basis of candidates or issues. In the wake of the Watergate scandals, it is furthermore clear that the Republican identification is giving way to greater degrees of independent orientations. By 1974, the Republicans were technically a *third* party, with independent identifiers the second category behind the Democrats. Republicans could take some consolation in the fact that the independents were increasing rather than the Democrats, despite all Richard Nixon and the country had been through. Continuing Democratic and independent identification nonetheless certainly does not speak well for a prognosis looking to a *permanent* new Republican majority.

Historical analogies must also be questioned. One possibility is that the Democratic Party will regroup in the context of a realigning process.[20] There is in fact a historical parallel for that phenomena, as the Republicans went through a realignment process in the 1896 election. To assert itself as a new majority party, it is necessary for the former minority party to capture a position on issues which makes it popular with a majority. The conditions necessary for this to occur seem fairly restrictive. There may be too many issues, or the opposing party may quickly capture the same position. Furthermore, to go through a realignment, the newly emerging majority party cannot maintain a commitment to past issue positions which have lost their attraction. The problem of party ideologues can thus be serious, and there have been indications of this problem in the resistance to change within the Republican Party.

The best guess is that neither party will enjoy the dominance in presidential politics which went to the Democrats with the New Deal and the Republicans for the entire period between Lincoln and Franklin Roosevelt. More than realigning, the parties appear to be disintegrating. Ticket splitting, independent identification, and decline in party organizational strength are all involved.

Voters have vastly increased their tendency to split votes between parties. The commitment of voters to being party regulars in earlier days has yielded to a common tendency to cross party lines. The trend line for ticket splitting between votes for Congress and for the president has gone up like a steeply pitched staircase, from less than 5 percent in 1920 to over 40 percent in 1972.[21] The 1972 election was even more astonishing to those with concepts of party regularity. A whopping 44 percent of the Democratic identifiers voted against Senator McGovern. Futhermore, that simply represented a trend and not an exception. Whereas straight ticket voting represented in the neighborhood of 80 percent of the vote prior to World War II, it fell to 63 percent in 1952, and only 43 percent in 1968.[22]

The shift in identification away from any of the parties and toward an independent posture also manifests a growing disenchantment with all political parties. The independent group, which had comprised approximately one-fifth of the population as of 1952, had grown to almost a third by 1974. Furthermore, the disaffection among those under 30 was especially strong. In that group, the independent identifiers comprised a larger category than not only Republicans, but Democrats as well.

Voters have also been increasingly inclined to show their disregard for parties and the political process by not voting at all. After a general advance in participation between 1920 and 1960, voter participation levels began to decline. In 1920 some 43.4 percent of the electorate went to the polls, and the figure for 1960 had advanced to 63.1 percent. Yet by 1972, there was the second lowest turnout since 1932, with only 55.6 percent of the electorate contributing to Richard Nixon's victory.[23] Even if 1968 levels had been maintained, over seven million additional people would have voted. The 1974 congressional elections again showed the general inclination to avoid participation even through the voting act, with less of the electorate bothering to vote in the first post-Watergate election than at any time since the 1940s in many states. A lack of involvement not only with the political parties but with the electoral process itself was clearly growing.

Disintegration of the political parties can also be seen in organizational terms.[24] There never was a time when the American parties were truly mass-based organizations. Furthermore, insofar as they did build substantial bases of organizational strength, these tended to be oriented toward a patronage and personal payoff politics which both widespread public preference and substantial legal restriction has made increasingly rare. The parties today vie with an increasing range of organizations in carrying out their modest involvement with the electoral process. Special political organizations, interest groups, and various elite groupings are all substantially involved. The impact of the Watergate scandals on the Republican Party gave indications of being yet another blow to any sense of widespread party organization. Many Republican stalwarts felt abused and betrayed, with a resulting drop in party activity within a group which had traditionally maintained some willingness to help perpetuate viable party organizations.

There remains some possibility of renewed party vitality. The decade between Vietnam and Watergate was a hard one for all institutions, and there were some expressing a strong interest in reviving the parties. A revitalizing of the parties to a level at least resembling their position in presidential politics of several decades ago is not inconceivable. Given the recent decline, however, efforts at strengthening the parties will have to be undertaken to reach even the earlier levels.[25]

Consequences of possible greater fluidity in presidential voting and party coalitions will be enormous. There will be more opportunity for incumbents to build support while in office. More votes are apt to be persuadable prior to each election. There may correspondingly be a greater problem for incumbents in working toward reelection if they can depend with less certainty on a solid base of partisan supporters. The possibility of incumbents resorting more extensively to symbolic appeals in the face of difficulties in uniting partisans on the basis of party identification is also very real. Although several of these implications must be explored in various contexts in the forthcoming chapters, some of the likely results deserve immediate exploration.

Emerging Issues

Fluctuating electoral orientations and declining party dominance of presidential selection constitute the basis for several emerging issues in the selection process. That process itself is becoming increasingly arduous for prospective candidates. Declining party control also increases the chances of factional victories, making voter choice and control difficult. The power of incumbents is simultaneously increasing in ways which challenge notions of electoral control. One must wonder, finally, whether the present process is likely to produce effective presidential personalities.

The Arduousness of Getting Nominated

The evolving selection process is making increased demands on those seeking office. The withdrawal of Senator Walter Mondale from pursuit of the Democratic nomination in late 1974, after sensing both the magnitude of the task and its personal costs, was a forceful demonstration of the sacrifices which must be made by a prospective nominee. It is difficult to envision an individual in the next years gaining the Presidency with as little early effort as was expended by Dwight Eisenhower. Others (notably leaders in the Eastern wing of the Republican Party) worked extensively for Ike, but their efforts pale by comparison with the more recent nominating activities. Itemizing the necessary activities underscores the magnitude of the task.[26] To be selected as a major party nominee, one must:

Make the necessary speeches and cultivate the press enough to gain attention and categorization as one of the hopefuls. (This is easier if one has a logical institutional position, but may also create real problems if it conflicts with one's role as governor or senator.)
Build an organization which is sufficiently widespread to begin pursuing delegate support in each of the 50 states. Of necessity, this must go right down to the congressional-district and county level, since a majority of the delegates are selected at that level. Senators Gold-

water and McGovern both showed at once the opportunities and the magnitude of this responsibility.

Build an organization to enable one to contest in as many as 6 to 10 state primaries. This usually includes California, which constitutes in and of itself one-tenth of the population of the nation.

Raise funds to finance the early activities, without formal party support. This must at a minimum involve several million dollars. (Federal financial support will help as of 1976, but more substantially after one's campaign is established.)

Learn enough about local situations to avoid stumbling amidst all of the confusions of favorite-son candidates and local issues. In addition, one must deal in the fledgling organizations with acts of sabotage by opponents at least within one's own party and—at least for Democrats in 1972—on the part of the opposing party as well.

Organize a convention communication system and decision process which, with little prior use, can handle a sudden rush of opposition efforts to find weaknesses, promote rival coalitions, and thwart a nomination.

There is no question but that the present nominating process serves some useful purposes.[27] Candidates learn more about the country and its people. Local campaigning also has the advantage of giving the electorate the opportunity to have some direct contact with potential officeholders. The rise of television campaigning is, however, reducing that phenomenon. There is additionally some advantage in requiring that candidates have political experience, and the necessities of the present selection process have generally achieved that objective.

Other consequences of the process are not so reassuring. The organizational and financial requirements are such that only a few individuals can realistically consider the Presidency. Individuals emerge who have better access to money, organizational capacities, and media attention. The difficulties involved in gaining the nomination, and in turn election, are such that one must not only be ambitious, but also have an ability and a willingness to avoid any actions which the zealous examination of one's personal weaknesses by opponents might uncover. A skepticism about others, rather than trust, and even an overly acute sense of possible danger in relating to others can be useful. In the next chapter, a look at the personalities which have emerged will indicate some sobering tendencies.

The Structuring of Voting Alternatives

Political parties have often been criticized for not providing clear choices at the polls. Tendencies for selection and nominating processes to produce candidates of the tweedledee-tweedledum variety have produced criticism from both academic observers and voters feeling that their side (whether left or right) would be victorious if only policy positions were clearly presented. For the issue-oriented segment of the electorate, it was preposterous for issue differences to emerge, as in 1960, only as questions of how the islands of Quemoy and Matsu, near Formosa, would be defended, or whether the expansion of federal aid to education should include funds for science labs and dorms but not libraries.

Forces at work in the party system are *decreasing* the likelihood that centrist campaigns will occur as frequently as in the past. There is always the possibility that the Wallace phenomenon of 1968 (with 13 percent of the vote to a third party) will mark the beginning of a complete shattering of the two-party system. Multiparty races might increase the selectivity voters could exercise at the ballot box, but also leave unresolved the question of the policy and leader orientations preferred by a majority of the public.

Structural developments in both major parties may also work against centrist campaigns. One of the consequences of opening the nominating process to greater participation by those with intense political concerns is that the often rather moderate segments of the electorate find their views less clearly reflected. For all the abuse so frequently heaped upon practical politicians, their tendency to place a very high priority on winning has often had the consequence of presenting the electorate with center candidates. Today, nominating processes of both parties are subject to forces which decrease the likelihood of centrist campaigns.

The thrust of these forces in the Democratic Party in 1972 was obvious. The quota system for representing minorities, which the traditional Democratic politicians had acquiesced to in the turmoil of Chicago in 1968, was instrumental in helping George McGovern capture the 1972 nomination. In December 1974, the Democrats held a special party convention to deal with this issue. The resulting compromise eliminated specific quotas but maintained language urging representative delegations. The issue seems destined to be a recurring one.

In the Republican Party, rules for allocating delegates to each state, coupled with the enthusiastic work of conservative segments in the party, give a major advantage to conservative nominees. The willingness of Goldwater supporters in the 1962–1964 period to engage in the tedious business of gaining control of local party machinery was instrumental in Goldwater's nomination, and some of that kind of willingness continued among conservatives into the 1970s. At the same time, the distribution of convention delegate votes between the larger industrial states (which are less apt to support conservative candidates) and the more rural states was set up at the 1972 convention in a manner likely to aid prospective conservative nominees. A Ronald Reagan, more than a Charles Percy, stood to profit from that distribution.

A faction which wins a nominating victory and which redefines the political center in American politics according to its own beliefs may, obviously, reflect periodic shifts in the location of the political center. To note with a measure of concern that the parties are not always nominating at what the professional politicians judge to be the exact center does not suggest that the nominating process ought to stay forever on its present center ground. Judgments of factional wings, especially of the out-parties, are nonetheless apt to produce distorted conclusions as to where the center resides.

The danger presented by present nominating processes is evident. Where a nominee, especially from the out-party, represents a faction, the vote is apt to produce a huge majority for his opponent, who is often an incumbent. Because of the decline in regional bastions of strength for both parties, the electoral college majorities are apt to magnify the appearance of victory margins greatly. Large majorities can lead to miscalculations on the part of incumbents, as they tend to view large majorities as a reflection of a clear voter policy choice. The track record of second-term incumbents, as we will see, has been strikingly mediocre, despite frequent large reelection majorities. The question of incumbency itself is thus involved.

The Advantages of Incumbency

Incumbency is an extremely important resource in presidential elections. Incumbents tend not only to be reelected, but to receive a larger vote the second time they face the electorate. Specifically, in this century the results have been as follows.

President	Election Year	Percentage of Vote	Special Circumstances
William Howard Taft	1908	54.5%	
William Howard Taft	1912	25.1%	(3-party race)
Woodrow Wilson	1912	41.9%	(3-party race)
Woodrow Wilson	1916	49.3%	
Herbert Hoover	1928	58.1%	
Herbert Hoover	1932	39.1%	
Franklin Roosevelt	1932	57.4%	
Franklin Roosevelt	1936	60.8%	
Franklin Roosevelt	1940	55.0%	
Franklin Roosevelt	1944	53.8%	
Dwight Eisenhower	1952	55.1%	
Dwight Eisenhower	1956	57.4%	
Richard Nixon	1968	43.4%	(Wallace, 13%)
Richard Nixon	1972	60.7%	

The remarkable success of incumbents is most apparent. Only three incumbents have lost in bids for reelection since the Civil War. Grover Cleveland received more popular votes than his opponent, but lost in the electoral college, and William Howard Taft lost as Theodore Roosevelt forced a three-way split in 1912. Thus, Herbert Hoover, running in the midst of a depression, with a fourth of the work force unemployed, was the only clearly rejected incumbent in recent decades. Johnson, it should be noted, was in serious difficulty after five years in office and declined to run despite his eligibility for a second complete term. The tendency for incumbents to do so well in their second attempts may be partly related to a tendency for the most attractive potential out-party candidate not to challenge an incumbent. The large margins registered by Johnson against Goldwater, and Nixon against McGovern were in part a consequence of weak opposition. Yet it is striking that incumbents have done so well, especially in the face of frequent interpretations suggesting that they have difficulty in maintaining support for their specific policy choices.

The frequency of incumbent victories can be traced to an impressive set of resources. President Nixon displayed a good use of one resource in emphasizing the majesty of his office during the 1972 campaign. Voters were asked to support the Presidency, not to choose between two partisan candidates. Television coverage of one's role makes an emphasis on office very easy. Incumbents can choose to emphasize foreign policy activities, such as a trip to China or Russia, in order to far outdistance the coverage and dramatic attention given their opponents.

A president may on occasion also avoid domestic issues. Lyndon Johnson did not take this step, but instead rushed about the country proclaiming his new domestic programs. Conversely, Richard Nixon chose an "above-politics" orientation, emphasizing his attention to other presidential business. Cabinet officials and perhaps a vice-president can stand in for the president, with a tendency to talk to specialized groups. The president can easily avoid a direct debate with his opponent in such situations.

Incumbents also have a built-in resource of organizational support. They can simply transfer members of the White House staff to campaign activities, and at points use the services of individuals who are still on the payroll of the White House Staff. Nixon was not the first incumbent to operate a shuffle of personnel between staff duties and campaign involvement. Both staffers and postmaster generals in an earlier day have had major campaign and patronage involvement. Despite the restrictions on political activity rooted in the Hatch Act, governmental employees in some agencies may also be used for partisan purposes. This was the basis for Democratic accusations in 1972 against pro-Nixon activities by employees of ACTION (the merged unit including the Peace Corps and Vista). The Nixon operations in 1972 constituted a major modification in the use of the existing bureaucracy at key points, as is clear in our examination of the collapse of the Nixon Presidency. Nonetheless, there have long been major advantages for incumbents in having staff and federal bureaucracy resources at their disposal.

A final resource for incumbents has emerged in recent years. Historically, the incumbent was largely at the mercy of events dictating the conditions under which he would seek reelection. If the business cycle created difficult economic conditions, he simply had to suffer the likely political consequences. The growth of economic management roles has partially altered the incumbent's position in recent elections. A president can now give a boost to the economy during an election year in order to increase his reelection chances. Richard Nixon, interestingly enough, was reported to have been resentful that Eisenhower did not let federal funds for such activities as highway construction go into circulation faster as a means of reducing unemployment prior to the 1960 election. Neither Lyndon Johnson nor many Democratic supporters of the tax cut in March 1964 were unmindful of either the general popularity of a tax cut in an election year nor the advantages of standing for reelection in a more rapidly expanding economy. In August 1971, Richard Nixon moved to freeze wages and prices and also stimulate the economy in a dramatic attempt to improve economic conditions for 1972.[28] Furthermore, the attractions were sufficiently strong so that this step was taken despite the presence in the Nixon advisory system of several strong supporters of a more limited role.

Economic forces can make it impossible for a president to create good economic situations for an election year. Lyndon Johnson finally felt it necessary to confront his would-be Democratic successor, Hubert Humphrey, with the necessity of running in the face of a tax increase in 1968. President Ford also faced difficult choices by 1975. A deteriorating international economic system is certainly not easily altered by presidential decision, no matter how strong the desire to improve conditions may be. What a president does often possess, however, is the power to run for reelection under at least improving economic conditions. Given voter tendencies to respond often to rather immediate economic events, the president's ability to influence economic upswings can be an important resource.

The ability of the incumbent to enjoy public exposure, the benefits of his title and the ceremony surrounding it, opportunities for avoiding issues, and opportunities for building an organization constitute major electoral resources, as we have seen. The growth of his economic management activities is thus an important addition to an already impressive list of incumbent advantages. The message is clear: Despite what appears at times to be limited ability to build support for specific policy steps, incumbents can often gain reelection. An extraordinary aspect of the 1972 campaign is also very clear. Even without spies and illegal collection of funds, Richard Nixon possessed impressive natural advantages as an incumbent. Yet neither he nor his pack of overzealous advisers considered these to be adequate.

Summary

The process of presidential selection is undergoing substantial change. Presidential election results are becoming more fluid and uncertain. It is unlikely that the Democratic Party can look forward to control of the Presidency comparable to the hegemony seen between 1932 and 1968. We could conceivably still be moving toward a realignment with a new Republican majority. We may also see a resurgence of the Democratic Party around economic issues and some agitation over the corrupt record of the Nixon Administration. Uncertainty in future elections is the more likely pattern. The nominating process is a more intricate affair than many, who take a ho-hum view of internal party and nominating activities, have suspected. The power of incumbency simultaneously raises difficult questions as to the ease with which effective political competition can be maintained. An additional sounding of the operation of the current nominating process can be taken by looking at the actual results. What kinds of people emerge?

NOTES

[1] For an extensive discussion of the policy measures leading to the 1936 coalition victory, see Arthur Schlesinger, Jr., *The Politics of Upheaval,* Boston, Houghton Mifflin, 1960, pt. 4; and William E. Leuchtenberg, *The New Deal,* Columbia, S.C., University of South Carolina Press, 1968.

[2] The formation of the conservative coalition as a conscious voting bloc is well documented in James T. Patterson, *Conservative Coalition and the New Deal,* Lexington, Ky., University of Kentucky Press, 1967.

[3] On the impact of mid-term elections, see Barbara Hinckley, *Stability and Change in Congress,* New York, Harper & Row, 1971, chap. 2.

[4] The impact of the House Rules Committee is analyzed in James Robinson, *The House Rules Committee,* Indianapolis, Ind., Bobbs-Merrill, 1963.

[5] For a highly readable account of the 1948 election, see Irwin Ross, *The Loneliest Campaign,* New York, New American Library, 1968.

[6] The Eisenhower elections were the first to be systematically studied

by the use of academic-sponsored polls. See Angus Campbell et al., *The American Voter,* New York, Wiley, 1960.

[7] On the Kennedy victory, see Philip Converse, "Religion and Politics: The 1960 Election," in *Elections and the Political Order,* ed. by Angus Campbell et al., New York, Wiley, 1967, chap. 6.

[8] For an account emphasizing the Republican problems in combating the New Deal coalition, see John Kessel, *The Goldwater Coalition,* Indianapolis, Ind., Bobbs-Merrill, 1968.

[9] For an account emphasizing the cumulative nature of those respective votes, see Philip E. Converse et al., "Continuity and Change in American Politics: Parties and Issues in the 1968 Election," *American Political Science Review* 63 (December 1969), 1062–1082.

[10] Problems with the 1972 election as experienced by the McGovern camp are discussed extensively by key staffer Gary Hart. See his *Right from the Start,* New York, Quadrangle, 1973.

[11] Willmoore Kendall, "The Two Majorities," *Midwest Journal of Political Science,* November 1960, pp. 317–345.

[12] For one statement of differences with Congress, see William T. Murphy, Jr. and Edward Schneider, *Vote Power,* New York, Anchor Books, 1974, chap. 1. These issues are additionally explored in Chapter 10 of this book.

[13] A popular emphasis on the emergence of a majority resistant to social change is found in Richard M. Scammon and Ben J. Wattenberg, *The Real Majority,* New York, Coward-McCann & Geoghegan, 1970.

[14] Kevin Phillips, *The Emerging Republican Majority,* New York, Arlington, 1969.

[15] The emphasis on cyclical aspects of voting behavior is found in Walter Dean Burnham, *Critical Elections and the Mainsprings of American Politics,* New York, Norton, 1970.

[16] On Teapot Dome scandals and their impact, see Francis Russell, *The Shadow of Blooming Grove,* New York, McGraw-Hill, 1968; and Burl Noggle, *Teapot Dome,* New York, Norton, 1962.

[17] Campbell, op. cit., p. 50.

[18] On the Eisenhower pattern of corruption, see David Frier, *Conflict of Interest in the Eisenhower Administration,* New York, Penguin Books, 1970.

[19] The importance of the middle-class identifiers is stressed in Everett Ladd, Jr., *American Political Parties,* New York, Norton, 1970.

[20] An excellent analysis of this possibility is found in James L. Sundquist, *Dynamics of the Party System,* Washington, Brookings, 1973. See especially chap. 13.

[21] For the rise of independent voter identification and tendencies to split tickets, see Walter deVries and V. Lance Tarrance, Jr., *The Ticket Splitter,* Grand Rapids, Mich., Eerdmans, 1972.

[22] Richard W. Boyd, "Electoral Trends in Postwar Politics," in *Choosing the President,* ed. by James David Barber, Englewood Cliffs, N.J., Prentice-Hall, 1974, p. 185.

[23] Ibid., pp. 182–183.

[24] The underlying factors involved in the decline of American parties are effectively discussed in Frank J. Sorauf, *Party Politics in America,* Boston, Little, Brown, 1972. See especially chaps. 16, 17. For a forceful statement of the strong party position in the wake of Watergate, see Charles M. Hardin, *Presidential Power and Accountability: Toward A New Constitution,* Chicago, University of Chicago Press, 1974.

[25] See on this point, Sundquist, op. cit., chap. 13.

[26] The volumes by Theodore White beginning in 1966 provide highly readable discussions of problems with the contemporary nominating process. See, for example, *The Making of the President, 1972,* New York, Atheneum, 1973.

[27] The Brookings Institution has sponsored a series of useful discussions on problems with contemporary nominating practices. See in particular, Judith Parris, *The Convention Problem,* Washington, Brookings, 1972.

[28] The impact of political calculation has been stressed in several discussions of the August 1971 decisions. See Leonard Silk, *Nixonomics,* New York, Praeger, 1972; and Rowland Evans, Jr. and Robert D. Novak, *Nixon in the White House,* New York, Vintage, 1971, chap. 7.

The Cast of Characters

White House personalities have recently been viewed very negatively. Presidents often seem arrogant, self-aggrandizing, and prone to cunning political maneuvers, which ultimately cost them dearly in loss of electoral confidence. Staff members appear to be young men on the make, willing to tell the president whatever he wants to hear in exchange for an enhanced career, perhaps with a major corporation or a Washington law firm. At the outer limits stand the political appointees, often viewed as inexperienced, ineffectual, and little more than tools of the interests that promoted their initial nomination.

Recent occupants of the Oval Office must be examined from several perspectives. Examination of their general social backgrounds provides useful insights into the question of elite dominance of the Presidency. Knowledge of the varying impacts of the political experience of recent presidents is also important in understanding their behavior in office. Just what have the often-praised political experiences actually been contributing? More fundamentally, an understanding of recent presidential personalities is important. This becomes especially important in light of the problems had by Johnson and Nixon, active, politically experienced individuals who got into major difficulties while in office. Initially, then, we must seek perspective on the question of the impact recent personalities have had on the operations and policy responses occurring during their tenure.

Theories of Presidential Personality

A growing number of studies seek to interpret both individual Presidents and the role of personality in presidential behavior. Valuable insights are beginning to emerge, and there have been important advances in the concepts employed in interpretation. It is possible to decipher the impact of individuals on their administrations somewhat more clearly. Greater difficulties occur as efforts are made to explain the origins of differing types of presidential personalities. It is easier, for example, to see the impact of Nixon's crisis-oriented personality on his Watergate decisions than to explain the origins of that personality. The primary concern in this work is with the impact of personality on the totality of given presidential activities, and not the origins of behavior for particular individuals. The contributions of Richard Neustadt, Erwin Hargrove, and James Barber to studies of presidential personalities must be considered before reviewing characteristics of recent incumbents.

In *Presidential Power*, Neustadt does not develop a specific set of categories for looking at presidential behavior.[1] The focus is instead on the nature of necessary presidential roles and the ways in which they are best filled. To be effective, presidents, in his analysis, must be able to see their own power stakes in given situations, and to think of their appearances in the eyes of both Washington's president-watchers and the general electorate. In effect, he distinguishes those with a keen political sense from those who lack that skill. Neustadt generally expects successful presidents to come from political backgrounds, since these are the individuals most apt to possess the needed political skills. Neustadt also suggests that the politically skilled president must possess a suitable temperament, but this is not defined in specific terms. From the use of examples, Neustadt shows a clear preference for Franklin Roosevelt as an example of a President with the successful combination of traits and gives Eisenhower a critical evaluation. Thus, according to Neustadt, in studying presidential personality one should look primarily at the degree of political skills different individuals possess.

Erwin Hargrove is somewhat more specific in his categorizing.[2] Presidents emerge as either active or passive. For the actives, there are personality needs which drive them toward political activities in a quest for dominance over others. The personality needs of the actives thus presumably fit well in major presidential roles. The two Roosevelts and Woodrow Wilson are studied as examples of this category. The passives do not possess a comparable need for mastery over others. Taft, Hoover, and Eisenhower are presented in the passive category. Writing as of the mid-1960s, Hargrove argued that the passives were less apt to perform adequately in key relationships with Congress, the bureaucracy, and the electorate. It is essential to emphasize that Hargrove was not describing the passives as marginal men. They were viewed as highly competent in their original fields of endeavor: Taft, the competent judge; Hoover, the highly successful engineer; Eisenhower, the effective coordinator as a military leader. Problems with their administrations could thus not be traced to a lack of competence. Rather, Hargrove saw these individuals lacking personal needs for political action which would motivate them toward effective leadership.

The high marks for leadership went to the actives, and particularly to Franklin Roosevelt. Hargroye's analysis came early in the Johnson Administration, and he was already sensing some difficulties with the Johnson behavior pattern. Hargrove has since modified his position, now stressing the degree of risk involved with insecure but active personalities. His earlier work nonetheless stands as a major example of recent categorization, suggesting examination of Presidents in terms of the degree of motivation they possessed for political roles.

James Barber's analysis is more elaborate. *The Presidential Character,* published in 1972, quickly became a widely read volume on presidential behavior.[3] Presidential personalities are paired in a table, producing four categories: active-positive, active-negative, passive-positive, and passive-negative. The activity dimension involves the amount of energy which is generated in the routines of a president, ranging from the rush of activity in Johnson's Presidency, with his double-shift routines, to the quiet pace of individuals like Harding and Coolidge. The positive-negative dimension involves the degree of security, confidence, and enjoyment with which the president performs his tasks.

The Barber analysis thus produced four categories:

Active-Positive. Substantial activity and an enthusiastic confidence in the results.

Active-Negative. A rush of activity, sometimes rather frenzied, but with a brooding sense that one is fighting against difficult odds and a hostile environment.

Passive-Positive. Limited energy displayed, but with an enjoyment of the routines of office.

Passive-Negative. Limited activity, and a sense of frustration with the activities of the office.

There are major problems involved in seeking to categorize presidential personalities into one of four types. Professor Barber has defended his work by arguing that one can identify central tendencies even though there may be aspects of a given individual's behavior which do not fit perfectly into one or another of the categories.[4] Problems are also apparent as one notes (along with Barber) that few Presidents of recent years fall into either of the passive categories. Insofar as this does occur, the actual choice of categories is reduced still further.

Barber's analysis does very effectively show problems with some types of active, ambitious politicians, such as Richard Nixon or Lyndon Johnson, who display considerable anxiety about themselves and their performances. Barber correctly senses that these types of individuals may take uncompromising positions on key issues by perceiving them as threats to their ability to stand firm. Thus, not only Johnson and Nixon, but also Woodrow Wilson (regarding the League of Nations) and Herbert Hoover (in the face of a worsening depression) are seen to have placed too much emphasis in their decisions on the necessity of standing firm in the face of criticism. This resistance is traced to behavior characteristics of the active-negative personality. Thus, Barber's analysis does have the major usefulness of identifying a category of behavior for the active and often politically experienced personality which had not received specific attention in earlier formulations.

It is often difficult to develop highly accurate interpretations of individual presidential personalities. For that matter, individuals in a host of lesser positions in American society are interpreted in substantially different ways. In analyzing a president, there is not only the problem of access to the president, but the necessity of dealing with the various images of him which tend to be fabricated. Presidents may do some of this themselves, in trying to establish characterizations of themselves which will be popular with the electorate. The first accounts of a new president will also frequently have a partisan overtone. For this reason, accounts by participants in a Presidency are often very useful as they relate to presidential routines, but of limited value in determining the character of the individual in the Oval Office. For our purposes, it is therefore often appropriate to identify areas of disagreement about the personalities of specific presidents rather than to seek a resolution of all debates.

The Recent Presidents

With due apologies to the earlier Presidents, the sketch of presidential backgrounds begins with Franklin Roosevelt. The Presidency certainly did not begin (as some of the more admiring statements virtually seem to suggest) with Franklin Roosevelt crossing the

Potomac. Most of the actions and events of concern in subsequent chapters are nonetheless encompassed in the line of presidents beginning with Franklin Roosevelt.

Roosevelt

All the advantages of upper-class birth went to Franklin Roosevelt. His credentials for membership in upper-class New York society were impeccable.[5] The Roosevelts' prominent status could be traced back to pre-Revolutionary days in New York. As a result, Roosevelt's schooling took place at the proper private schools, culminating with degrees from Harvard and Columbia Law School. His entry into politics was also facilitated not only by the family contacts which come easily to one in his position, but also by the distinction of having an uncle serve as President during his adolescence.

Roosevelt's political experiences prior to 1933 involved several different roles. Early experiences included service in the New York state legislature, a tour as assistant secretary of the Navy, and a frustrating national campaign in 1920 as the Democratic nominee for vice-president. After the quiet years in which he only partially recovered from his polio attack of 1921, Roosevelt was elected in 1928 to serve four eventful years as governor of New York. Those years in Albany exposed Roosevelt to substantially the same range of domestic issues which confronted him in 1933, and both a substantial number of ideas and key individuals came with Roosevelt from Albany to the White House. Although it would certainly not have been guessed at the time, this also marked the last instance in better than 40 years that the then-familiar pattern of sending a governor to the White House would occur.

There is very widespread agreement on Roosevelt's basic enjoyment of his White House roles. Barber sees him as a clear example of an active-positive. Relating to a large number of individuals was comparatively easy for him, and political maneuvers were often downright enjoyable. The reader who is suspicious of the Roosevelt interpretations might well examine the now completely published press conferences as a remarkable example of the generally enthusiastic and good-humored manner in which at least one aspect of his presidential roles developed. His obvious enjoyment of press conferences in that more informal period of relationships with the press stands in incredible contrast to the acrimonious Johnson and Nixon years.[6]

Neither the Roosevelt staff system nor the Roosevelt personality in office were without failings. Increasingly critical evaluations are made of both during the war years, and Roosevelt was increasingly capable during his second term of serious political miscalculations. Roosevelt's staff problems will be apparent in our direct look at staff systems. The policy steps themselves were often inadequate and at points downright confused; they certainly did not end the depression, as economic conditions in fact worsened again in 1937. It is nonetheless not surprising to find the Roosevelt personality and staff system causing substantial favorable comment. His personality fit the difficult depression period well, and did produce an effective handling of several key roles.

Truman

Harry Truman had precious few of Roosevelt's initial advantages.[7] His Missouri family was industrious but modestly middle-class. His schooling was limited. Despite some night-school work, Truman was the only modern president without a college degree. His early business experiences were also frustrating and at one point ended with a substantial debt. When he entered local politics in Independence, Missouri in an essentially administrative position as a county judge, Truman, who was in his late thirties, had few obvious, tangible accomplishments to his credit. His persistence in a moderate life-style was also pronounced. Even as a senator, he lived frugally in Washington. In economic terms, he was the poorest of the modern occupants of the Oval Office.

Truman's political career began in 1922 with his election to a county judgeship. This office, in Missouri local government of his day,. was actually an administrative position. He was then defeated in 1924 in a campaign marked by intense Ku Klux Klan opposition to his re-election. He returned to local office in 1926, with the endorsement of the dominant state leader (Boss Pendergast), who was looking for a solid local candidate. His concerns were those of local public administration until his 1934 race for the Senate. Following his Senate victory that year, ten years in the Senate offered Truman few really significant experiences. He did surprise many by winning a difficult primary fight in 1940, as the Pendergast machine was by then in disarray. His most noteworthy activity was heading the Senate committee examining conflict of interest in wartime contract operations. When Truman was thrust into the Presidency by Roosevelt's death only weeks after the inaugural (April 12, 1945), he had had two decades in a political career, but very limited experience in critical political roles and only a couple months as vice-president.

Truman's character has produced both an interesting public response and a growing debate. After receiving an extraordinarily high initial popularity rating, Truman's popularity fell to extreme lows by his second term. Yet by the 1960s he was being given high ratings and seemed to be remembered for an ability to make major policy decisions rather than the fiesty attitude which caused part of the unfavorable view while he was in office. By the early 1970s, a major group of writers had emerged with a far more critical view, stressing Truman's role as a simplistic anti-Communist in the evolution of the Cold War.

Truman's personality in the White House tends to be praised on three grounds. The first involves his ability to learn, both in general and on the job. Though lacking the advantages of a formal education, Truman did have an appreciation for books which led him to a wide range of reading. He frequently enjoyed drawing analogies to the actions of earlier presidents or other political leaders. His ability to learn is also stressed in the context of his gradual assumption of command as he stepped into a difficult wartime transition. Secondly, it has been argued to the point of cliché that Truman had a capacity for making large decisions correctly even though he may have been somewhat impulsive on some minor matters. Finally, Truman is remembered today as a President who was more able than most to avoid the fanfare of the White House and, in the process, to avoid some of the tendencies toward egotistical identification with the office.

The directness of Truman's views on numerous matters is vividly presented in Merle Miller's *Plain Speaking*. Truman directed himself specifically to the question of power in that oral biography, suggesting that "if a man can accept a situation in a place of power with the thought that it's only temporary, he comes out all right. But when he thinks that he is the *cause* of the power, that can be his ruination."[8] More recent presidents, for all their formal schooling, might well have profited from that perspective emanating from a self-educated man.

One thrust of Truman criticism has been directed toward his pettiness and his tendency to surround himself with a staff of old friends of limited ability.[9] Where matters involved his family, Truman could respond in very strong terms, as with his famous defense of his daughter's singing ability. Truman also had a staff of very mixed ability, with both high points and some lows, which he seemed willing to tolerate. The amount of corruption in his Administration was somewhat overrated, but he did have a tendency to stick with old friends. It is not certain just how much these criticisms tell us, however, about the general impact of Truman's personality while in office.

Critics have also argued that Truman suffered from an unfortunately narrow world view. This has led a group of revisionist historians to argue that Truman had a major responsibility for the development of the Cold War.[10] It has been fairly easy to show that Truman took a simple view of foreign policy matters at some points. The possibility of showing the effects of the atomic bomb before dropping it on Japanese cities was never given serious consideration by Truman. In some respects, critics are really arguing that the culture he reflected was a narrow one, and not that his personality per se was poorly developed for the Presidency. This is one of the points at which personality-oriented writing has been imprecise.[11]

The initial laudatory comments about Truman's foreign policy roles did come without sufficient analysis of specific cases, making a more careful analysis essential. The alternative picture of Truman as an aggressive "cold warrior" now emerging in some quarters may ultimately contribute to a more definitive understanding. This is one of the instances where an earlier release of key presidential papers would have been useful. As that documented picture does unfold, one is apt to find a clearer view of a genuinely simple man whose critics and admirers have both overstated his contributions.

Eisenhower

That Dwight Eisenhower went to West Point to gain an education is a reflection of the extremely modest situation of his west Kansas family.[12] The Eisenhowers lived on the "wrong side of the tracks" in Abilene, Kansas, and money for college education was not readily available. Subsequent military positions and the royalties from his writings (particularly *Crusade in Europe*) gradually added to his economic worth. Eisenhower also expanded his economic position with the acquisition of the Gettysberg farm and additional royalties, so that he left a substantial estate at the time of his death. Eisenhower represents one of several cases in which individuals of modest background have risen in their social and economic positions very substantially prior to entering the White House.

Eisenhower's absence of experience in elected politics makes him a marked exception to the general recruitment practice. He had obviously engaged in substantial decision making and management activity in his military positions, and he did serve a brief stint as president of Columbia University. Eisenhower was rather defensive about his nonpolitical background at points and spoke harshly in his memoirs of the authors of books on management at the White House who had neither served as president nor managed large organizations.[13]

Eisenhower's personality and military experience clearly had a dramatic impact on his staff organization. Eisenhower thought consistently in terms of the military staff system, with definite delegation and with a chief of staff serving the top official. Sherman Adams was thus the counterpart of a chief of staff in a military command, at least on many domestic matters. As Eisenhower writes, "At the top of the staff was, of course, Governor Sherman Adams."[14] Seldom had the impact of presidential personality on staff operations been as pronounced.

The Eisenhower personality was easily misunderstood. His very real tendencies toward restraint could easily be characterized and exaggerated. Eisenhower's enjoyment of Western movies and golfing could easily be amplified by critics to give a picture of a President who did extremely little. Press conferences generally did little to reinforce a favorable view of Eisenhower as an effective presidential personality.[15] It also seems reasonably clear that "Ike" tended not to think of issues in terms of political feasibility and political maneuver, unlike most other recent Presidents.

Several writers have more recently been suggesting more in the Eisenhower presidential character than was immediately apparent to many observers. Arthur Larson, another former Eisenhower speech writer, produced a substantially more praiseworthy account than most others which are available.[16] Peter Lyon, in *Eisenhower: Portrait of the Hero,* seems reluctant to come to firm conclusions but generally does not share the criticisms of the more unflattering biographers.[17] Writers who would be expected to take different views than those which they author are always interesting, and liberal columnist Murray Kempton has penned an interesting account arguing that Eisenhower's ability to grasp the significance of foreign policy situations was inadequately appreciated during his years in office. Kempton specifically writes:

> The Eisenhower who emerges here intermittently free from his habitual veils is the President most superbly equipped for truly consequential decisions we may ever have had, a mind neither rash nor hesitant, free of the slightest concern for how things might look, indifferent to any sentiment, as calm when he was demonstrating the wisdom of leaving a bad situation alone as when was moving to meet it on those occasions when he absolutely had to.[18]

The praise of Eisenhower's decision process which Kempton expresses will receive some support in our subsequent look at staff systems.

It would be all too easy to create a nostalgia for Eisenhower's style in the wake of problems with more recent Presidents. The tendency for decisions often to be avoided and for domestic political information to be filtered out of Eisenhower's staff system must remain as part of the assessment of Eisenhower's personality in office. Eisenhower's performance is destined to remain a reminder of the difficulties involved in selecting a president who is effective in all of the multiple roles now required.

Kennedy

Ike's successor seems destined to occupy a long-disputed position in American politics. The Kennedy legacy has been strongly influenced by his position not only as a martyred President, but as one who held office during the last period in which American optimism was firmly wedded to the Presidency. Widely differing views of the Kennedy family have simultaneously produced both contempt for "an overly ambitious bunch of upstarts" and a longing for a perpetuation of the Kennedy tradition.

Even the Kennedy social standing creates a measure of confusion.[19] He was obviously born to wealth and never had to worry about money. While President, he donated his salary to charity and even persisted (to the periodic irritation of his associates) in avoiding the bother of even carrying money. Yet there was a vast difference in Massachusetts social circles between having a father who made a fortune in the Scotch market and went to Mass, and having an ancestor who made a fortune (perhaps in rum running) while attending the Anglican church. The Kennedys had the money of upper-class Americans, but not the same social status, in at least some eyes. A Kennedy could attend Harvard, but not always travel in the same social circles as a member of Boston's Wasp Establishment.

Political experiences were nonetheless forthcoming. A grandfather who had served as mayor of Boston and a father who served as chairman of the Securities Exchange Commission (SEC) and ambassador to England indicated the beginning of a most highly politicized family. The experience in London would produce a book as well—*While England Slept*. After returning from the war, Kennedy won election to Congress in 1946 along with many other veterans, including young Richard Nixon out in California's San Gabriel Valley. Election to the Senate in 1952 gave his career a more prestigious turn, but did not bring him great prominence or responsibility. Kennedy remained a lesser figure in a Senate dominated by senior committee chairmen and such Democratic party figures as Lyndon Johnson, even as he began flirting with national office in 1956, with his brief bid for the vice-presidential nomination. Kennedy thus came to the Presidency comparatively young (43), with 14 years in Washington and a highly politicized family background, if not a particularly large amount of prior political responsibility.

The Kennedy character as it unfolded in the White House has produced another intense debate. Barber emphasizes the late maturation of Kennedy because of the growing sense of purpose he displayed while in office, and categorizes him as an active-positive. Barber has a fairly favorable view of the amenability of the Kennedy personality to the necessities of office. The Kennedy wit is also duly noted by Barber, in the context of Kennedy's seeming ability to work diligently but not without a measure of perspective. Few writers are more laudatory than his key aide, Theodore Sorenson. In Sorenson's *Kennedy,* one is given an account of a personality both able to learn and grow while in office and able to handle various responsibilities with a high level of effectiveness.[20]

Others emphatically disagree. Nancy Clinch has recently produced a lengthy account from an attempted psychohistorical perspective, *The Kennedy Neurosis*.[21] In her work, Clinch traces the long-standing ambition for office in the Kennedy family and the constant drive for spectacular successes while in office. Specific decisions, from the approval of the Bay of Pigs invasion to the space program to the assault on the steel industry to rescind price increases, are discussed in an attempt to portray Kennedy as a dangerously ambitious person. Henry Fairlie's *The Kennedy Promise* develops a somewhat similar theme, stressing the Kennedy contribution to Cold War tensions and the tendency to operate the Presidency in crisis terms.[22] For these writers, the real Kennedy is seen in vast contrast to the Camelot image he at points successfully conveyed to the electorate. Though aspects of these accounts are somewhat slanted, the Kennedy record does raise more questions about the impact of ambition on presidential operations than is sometimes recognized. It is nonetheless in the actions of the two following presidents that one sees the clear, obvious, and ultimately tragic problem of presidential ambition and personality needs leading to grave difficulties.

Johnson

Lyndon Johnson was yet another example of a President who rose from modest family circumstances. He was not quite the poor boy he sometimes liked to suggest, but life in west Texas in the days of his youth was generally not very prosperous.[23] Johnson was educated at Southwest Texas State Teachers College rather than the University of Texas, where sons and daughters of elite families in Texas often gravitated. Johnson also began his career, as he liked to mention in promoting federal aid to education, in the role of a local schoolteacher.

There is no disputing Johnson's ultimate economic rise along with his lengthy political career. He loved gadgets and the things money could buy. The actual sources of Johnson's fortune have been in some dispute. Lady Bird was an effective businesswoman and contributed some property through inheritance. Mainstays in Johnson's economic growth were land, starting with his ranch; ownership of the television station in Austin, Texas; and investment in bank stock in Texas. Texas grew rapidly in the period after World War II, and so did the Johnson estate. *Life* magazine, in August 1964, listed his fortune at $14 million. Johnson was disturbed by this release, and had an audit prepared which placed his fortune at $3.5 million. (In part, the lower figure was achieved by listing his properties at their purchase price rather than their actual value.)[24]

Johnson reigned as the most experienced Washington figure to enter the White House in modern times until the arrival of Gerald Ford. Beginning with service for a conservative Texas congressman, Richard Kleberg, in 1932, Johnson lived in Washington until 1968, with only a brief time out for service in the National Youth Administration in Texas prior to his 1937 election to Congress. He not only served in the Senate from 1948 to 1963, but he held a uniquely influential position as Democratic majority leader. Johnson's constant attention to every legislative detail made him one of the most influential Senate party leaders of this century, if not in fact the most influential. Johnson was a master in the process of legislative bargaining and constantly sought ways to piece together majority coalitions in the often fragmented Senate political process. The claim that he talked to every member of the Senate every day exaggerates his personalized leadership role, but highlights the nature of his energetic performance.[25]

The White House nonetheless revealed most forcefully Johnson's limitations as a political leader. He did have an ability to understand the legislative process, and no one ever accused Johnson of lacking an ability to sense the political dimensions of various issues. Few questioned his basic intelligence, either. Eric Goldman, an aide whose dismissal could easily have embittered him, nonetheless considered Johnson to have been one of the most intelligent men he had met, even during his years as a historian at Princeton.[26] Some liberals also felt more comfortable with Johnson's seemingly fundamental and instinctive desire to accomplish his domestic objectives than with Kennedy's sometimes less directly sensed commitment.

The difficulties with Johnson in the White House basically had to do with his underlying insecurity and resulting tendency to respond badly to criticism and suggestions that he should proceed differently. Being an aide to Johnson was consequently no easy task. When he was in a bad mood, his outbursts at critics could be quite extreme. For all the frequently noted feisty side of Harry Truman, it was Johnson who would turn on a reporter and ask why he had raised such a "chickenshit" question with a President.

The Vietnam conflict brought out the worst in Johnson. First, there was his effort to hide the magnitude of the war. As the situation worsened, those with critical information had serious difficulties in trying to communicate with the President. It was not fundamentally a failure of the foreign policy apparatus to supply sobering information which led Johnson to search continuously for military victory, but rather an unwillingness on Johnson's part to confront the adverse information and its implications. Professor Barber correctly sees the continuation of Johnson's commitment to his Vietnam policies as a tragic consequence of his personal inability to confront the failures of that policy. The reader need not accept all of Barber's framework for analyzing presidential personality to see Johnson as a prime example of the sad way in which ego defensiveness can affect presidential decision processes.[27]

Nixon

It remained for Richard Nixon to show the extremes to which personal insecurities could go in influencing presidential operations. Like his predecessor, Nixon had been born in modest circumstances. His father was perennially changing from menial jobs to shaky business ventures, and the family knew considerable economic misfortune. The deaths of two young brothers further contributed to a childhood with frequent unpleasantness.[28] Nixon did manage nonetheless to attend nearby Whittier College and do well enough to gain admission to Duke Law School. After graduation (third in his class) Nixon returned to Whittier and engaged in a modest law practice, and then completed his naval service prior to entering the congressional race in 1946.

Although he served 14 years in Washington prior to his election in 1968, Nixon's political career was somewhat unique. Only six years were spent in Congress, including two in the Senate. Nixon learned in those years an ability to gain press attention through committee activities. His dramatic efforts in helping to corroborate Whittaker Chambers' testimony against Alger Hiss brought him sudden public attention. In other respects, Nixon was not involved in the legislative process in a central way (as is virtually always the case with young legislators), and he went on to spend eight years as Vice-President.

The Vice-Presidency placed Nixon close to ultimate power and yet very far away. He was repeatedly anxious in his relationships with Eisenhower, never quite sure where he stood. He attended formal meetings, but he was simply not integrally involved with making decisions. His Vice-Presidency was followed by two losing elections, including the race for governor of California, after which Nixon seemingly ended his political career for keeps with his emotional suggestion that the press would no longer have Richard Nixon to "kick around." Thus, although Nixon had spent the same number of years in Washington as John Kennedy, he had had only a brief legislative experience, and he was unique among recent Presidents (with of course the exception of Eisenhower) in having been absent not only from Washington but also from public office for eight years immediately prior to his ascendence to the Presidency.

The intervening years as a New York lawyer did give Nixon

some new social contacts, and they allowed him to expand somewhat his personal estate. In 1969 he recruited one of his law partners, John Mitchell, taking him away from the technicalities of municipal bonds and into the attorney general's office. Financially, Nixon was able to claim an estate of $307,141 by 1968. The *tripling* of that estate in his first four years in the Presidency became a substantial topic in and of itself, and one of the factors, as we will see, in the collapse of his Presidency.

There has been substantial agreement on the central characteristics of Richard Nixon's personality. A few writers, such as Theodore White in 1972, have tended to be impressed with Nixon's factual knowledge and ability to organize himself on foreign policy matters. At the other extreme, Nixon has been seen by some as suffering from serious emotional problems. Although one may not necessarily accept the more scathing interpretations of the Nixon personality, there is fairly substantial agreement among "Nixonologists" regarding key personality limitations.[29]

Nixon is often described as a loner. Even members of his family have referred to his basic shyness. His public speaking tended to be forced, rather than natural and confident. Critically, Nixon in his shyness disliked interpersonal conflict. He preferred written communication to the give and take of direct contact. The creation of a separate office in the Executive Office Building for his use to escape the pressures of the Oval Office was but one indication of his reluctance to engage in extensive interpersonal communication. While in the Presidency, Nixon also preferred, despite the periodic toughness of his rhetoric, to avoid difficult situations with individuals. His early secretary of the interior, Walter Hickel, was in fact the only person who was directly dismissed in his entire Presidency. Furthermore, Nixon preferred to have that step communicated to Hickel by John Ehrlichman, even though Nixon had met with Hickel during the same day. To some extent, the staff system which H. R. Haldeman and John Ehrlichman devised was one which met basic characteristics of Nixon's personality.

Nixon also displayed a high degree of suspicion toward others in general. This quality was extremely apparent in the transcripts of the Watergate conversations. Few aides could emerge from listening to Nixon's own references to them without feeling saddened at his lack of trust and confidence in their ability. It was very much in character for Nixon to sanction the development of an enemies list and to orient his actions more substantially toward punishing enemies rather than toward rewarding friends. Nixon was always seeing enemies, be they the communists of the Alger Hiss days or the columnists of the 1970s.

A high degree of ambition was also apparent in Nixon's makeup.

He tried to prove himself, from an early age, with a rush of activities, including his persistent football efforts at Whittier and his involvement first with debate and then with dramatics. After doggedly pursuing the Presidency, he was simply not willing to replicate Eisenhower's example of slow change in policy and use of a steady administrative hand. Nixon wanted to be another Roosevelt, in terms of substantially reordering American politics and the partisan alignments. Given his minority position with Congress and the lack of majority party identification in the country, Nixon was easily motivated to find more questionable means of accomplishing his objectives.

The Nixon personality operated, finally, in terms of a periodic effort to prove himself, by showing that difficult situations could be overcome.[30] If Nixon could not be sure of his identity and self-esteem in other ways, he could at least take satisfaction in being able to overcome crisis situations. Thus, in an extraordinary sequence of events, a person who had penned a lengthy book about the ways in which he had learned to handle crisis situations, a decade later precipitated a supreme crisis for himself. A basically shy but nevertheless ambitious and often ruthless President hid within the comfortable orbit of a few key advisers to conduct a bizarre and dangerous sequence of events ultimately leading to his own downfall.

Ford

The change in presidential personalities was dramatic when the deposed Richard Nixon boarded the airplane for San Clemente and Gerald Ford entered the White House. In several respects, Ford represented common presidential characteristics. A Wasp background was again most evident, including membership in the Episcopal church. Ford also came from a small-town business background: His stepfather (with whom he lived from childhood) operated a paint business in Grand Rapids. While the 1920s were prosperous, the depression restricted the family's finances. Ford's athletic ability thus helped him through school, including both the University of Michigan and Yale Law School.

Like Nixon and Kennedy, Ford began in the House of Representatives shortly after military service, after his successful campaign in 1948. Ford rose gradually in the House, ultimately serving as Republican Party leader. He was the only recent President to come directly from the House, and he had a longevity record in Washington rivaled only by Lyndon Johnson. Unlike Johnson's, however, his business dealings were modest. His net worth as he assumed the Presidency was placed at approximately $250,000, consisting primarily of real estate holdings for direct family use.

An understanding of the Ford personality was slow to emerge.

Some doubted that he was always quite as much the nice guy he initially appeared to be in press accounts and the first works of friendly biographers.[31] It was very evident that he was highly partisan in his orientations. The long years on the Hill had reinforced a sense of partisanship which differed fundamentally from Eisenhower's orientation to the Republican Party, in particular. Ford's commitment to a generally conservative political philosophy also seemed more consistent than that of Nixon.

The most striking aspect of the Ford personality, coming as it did after Nixon's resignation, was his casual and friendly interpersonal relations.[32] He proclaimed an enjoyment of the Presidency shortly after arriving in office, and did seem to enjoy many of the activities. He also sought to refrain from the "Mr. President" ethos of earlier operations by insisting that he be called Jerry in a variety of contexts. Ironically, some columnists soon began to wonder whether his bearing was in fact "presidential" enough. The extent to which Ford would either change the White House, or be changed by it, remained an intriguing question early in his tenure.

Recent Presidents have, in sum, been only partially representative of the American population. Wasp backgrounds still predominate, with the sole exception of John Kennedy. Some Jews, blacks, women, Chicanos, Italians, and Eastern Europeans might be found in Congress, but not in the White House. Curiously, the large cities have not contributed any presidents, either (with the exception of John Kennedy). The long-standing tendency to recruit presidents from the Northeast has been decisively broken, however, with Presidents' boyhood homes suddenly including such places as Independence, Missouri; Abilene, Kansas; Johnson City, Texas; and Whittier, California. Even Ford, despite all his Michigan years, was born in Nebraska. Beyond questions of geography, the recent presidential backgrounds and personalities pose several basic issues.

Underlying Issues

Questions involving presidential backgrounds and personalities revolve about social class issues, the impact of political experience, and the difficulties recently experienced with some of the more active political figures. One must also seek some perspective on the influence an individual presidential personality has on the activities of his administration.

Social origins of recent Presidents do not show a pattern of elite-born and -raised individuals dominating the Oval Office. In this century, the two Roosevelts were clearly from upper-class families, and Kennedy was born to fortune but had ambiguous Irish Catholic social status. The common pattern finds middle or lower-middle-class individuals moving upward socially and economically prior to arriving at the White House. Educational experiences have often been part of the upward mobility. With the exception of Truman, who had no college degree, and Johnson, with his diploma from Southwest Texas State Teachers College, recent Presidents have had degrees from Harvard, West Point, Duke Law School, and Yale Law School. Economically, those born in modest positions had generally acquired some means prior to ascending to the White House. Johnson was uniquely successful, while Truman continued to live modestly.

Ultimately, social background data does not give great insight into presidential behavior. The self-made man has at points been more friendly to elite interests than the individual born to wealth and position. Thus, Franklin Roosevelt was regarded in some circles as a traitor to his class, while several Presidents born in very modest economic circumstances were apt to be especially friendly to elite interests.[33] It is nonetheless important to recognize that several recent Presidents, though certainly not raised in log cabins, grew up in modest homes—perhaps aging white frame houses—in small-town America.

Prior political experience has had very differing impacts on recent incumbents. Overall, it is striking how little experience may help in preparing prospective presidents. Knowledge of both foreign policy and certain economic management questions may be developed only to a very limited extent. Presidents who were legislators may well have specialized in another area. The legislative experience is also of virtually no use in aiding in the development of managerial skills. After running an office with at best a couple dozen people, a legislator is confronted with a White House Staff of more than 500 and an Executive Office of over 2,000 to say nothing of his responsibilities for administrative oversight of the entire federal government. He may have some knowledge of various governmental agencies, but not of the managerial responsibilities themselves. Congressmen may also have learned very little in dealing with the press, and they may actually have developed bad habits. Some felt that Lyndon Johnson had been spoiled in his legislative years by the ease with which he could handle the local Texas reporters. Occasional interviews and appearances on one of the Sunday television interview shows are certainly limited training for the problems of daily interaction (at least through one's press secretary) with a press numbering hundreds of individuals.

Ironically, a legislative background may not even be particularly helpful to the president in learning to lead Congress, although Lyndon

Johnson was clearly aided by his prior experience in his early dealings with Congress while President, and President Ford was at least sensitive to the legislative desire to be consulted on major issues (although not that of the pardon of Nixon himself). President Kennedy was never in a leadership position in Congress, and seemed at points to be somewhat in awe of the legislative leaders he had formerly worked with in a subordinate position. Richard Nixon never was extensively involved with legislative process, and he had a uniquely difficult time dealing with Congress.

In the final analysis, there is no experience in American politics which truly prepares one for the range of responsibilities now focused in the Presidency. Although he lacks involvement with foreign policy matters, the role relationships which are learned by the governor of a major state are probably more useful than those which the legislative background produces. Presidents do need a sense of coalitions, a sense of timing on issues, and an ability to sense when people are trying to con them or simply salve their egos. These skills can often be acquired in a political career, but there is no assurance that this will be the case.

There is a danger as one focuses on presidential personalities of attributing too much of the total response during their terms to their individual characteristics. Structural factors and the impact of social and economic conditions can be all too easily overlooked. Individual Presidents do have a major impact on the manner and style in which their Presidencies operate. The latitude characteristically given incumbents thus allows for an Eisenhower, a Kennedy, and a Johnson to make their own impacts on staff relationships within a brief four-year period. The Nixon-Ford transition also began to show important staff differences. Presidential personality may actually influence the way in which things are done more than the final outcomes themselves. The grinding of social and economic forces during a given tenure often makes the general contours of an administration inevitable. Richard Neustadt nicely argues this view in claiming that Harry Truman influenced the specific nature and timing of the American response to the economic collapse of Western Europe in the 1947–1948 period, but that the American government would inevitably have come to some policy response.[34]

Presidential personalities also make a comparatively greater difference in the more unstructured and more secret situations. Fred Greenstein has usefully reviewed a range of situations in which presidential personality is apt to have a significant influence.[35] An absence of sanctions (which can come with secrecy) and a fluid, unstructured situation are among the key factors listed. There is some evidence for this position in the tendency of those emphasizing personality failures to find them in the foreign policy operations of the President. Two of three major cases of failures discussed by James Barber involve foreign policy (Wilson in regard to the League of Nations, and Johnson over Vietnam), with Hoover's persistence in going slow on antidepression measures the only major domestic example. The foreign policy roles will emerge in our analysis as comparatively more secretive and unstructured. It is thus plausible to argue that the personality factor may be greatest in aspects of presidential foreign policy activities.

Presidential personalities do ultimately contribute to the dilemmas of presidential politics. The problems with active but insecure personalities are now far more evident than in the Eisenhower days. The qualities which Barber identified with his active-negatives can produce serious difficulties, as a president may identify his own ego strength with an ability to withstand criticism. The nature of the staff systems presidents create as a manifestation of their own personalities may also contribute to serious limitations in both the information they receive and the final decisions reached.

Simply hoping for presidents who define their responsibilities in limited ways is inadequate. The government does continue to function with a passive chief executive, be his passivity due to political incapacitation (as with Nixon in the throes of an impeachment struggle), a physical ailment, or to a limited presidential view of his own responsibilities (as occurred in some respects with Eisenhower). Yet the impact of a president functioning effectively in key roles has periodically been critical in the development of policy response and represents a resource for system response which cannot easily be abandoned.

Recent Presidents are an impressive testament to the difficulties in getting the right mix of qualities in a chief executive. Presidents have tended to be good in some responsibilities and not in others. An Eisenhower could deliberate on aspects of foreign policy strategy at points with a useful sense of restraint and detachment, yet he never seemed to sense some of the potentials for domestic policy leadership. Conversely, Lyndon Johnson could lead Congress masterfully in his early days, but suffered dreadfully in his ability to manage foreign policy decision making. The very range of roles and responsibilities makes it extremely difficult to select presidents who are effective across a whole range of relationships.

Impacts of individual presidential personalities emerge in numerous cases and relationships as one explores aspects of the Presidency more specifically. With the backgrounds and salient personality characteristics of recent Presidents in mind, we can turn to the second grouping in our cast of characters, the presidential aides and advisers.

Aides and Advisers

Presidents do not do their work alone. Both the aides on the White House Staff and the larger group of advisers within the Executive Office occupy positions of growing importance. The Watergate hearings brought to light for millions of Americans a picture not only of staff importance, but of some of the types of personalities involved. Any presidential staff will reflect the styles and preferences of a given president. A president has considerable latitude both in selecting aides and in staffing the Executive Office, since these positions often do not require legislative confirmation. Furthermore, there are fewer traditions of interest group and party influence than in cabinet member selection. A president can fairly easily fill positions with friends. Given this type of recruitment and the lack of clearly defined procedures, Lester Seligman has used a most apt analogy in suggesting that in organizational terms the recent staffs have most closely resembled—of all things—a sect.[36]

Presidential advisers in recent years have been surprisingly young. Both Theodore Sorenson, a key aide to Kennedy, and William Moyers, a major Johnson aide, came to power at about the time of their thirtieth birthdays. H. R. Haldeman and John Ehrlichman were both in their early forties when they assumed major responsibilities with Richard Nixon. A full third of the staffers in recent Presidencies have, in fact, been in their thirties.[37] With the partial exception of the Eisenhower Presidency, White House assignments have been stepping-stones for younger men, far more than sinecures for elderly party figures.

Presidential aides have generally not come up through the ranks of elected political positions. Almost two-thirds in recent staffs have come from immediate prior service outside the government.[38] Some aides will have been involved in either the election efforts or prior advising roles if the president-elect comes from the Senate. Yet they tend not to have run for elective office themselves. Their backgrounds tend to be those of press secretary, legislative assistant, and advance man; they are not former candidates or officeholders. Melvin Laird's stay on Nixon's staff after prior service as both secretary of defense and as a congressman was most unusual, as was John Connally's brief stay on the staff after having served as governor of Texas. President Ford initially turned a little more often to Congress, with key aides John Marsh and Donald Rumsfeld both having formerly held office in the House of Representatives.

Presidential aides tend to acquire their positions through a combination of good fortune plus a display of ability which is deemed useful by the president. There is a pattern among aides of reasonable success at law school and in a prior advising role, more than a process of direct elite recruitment. In recent staffs, about a fifth of the members were educated in elite Eastern schools at the B.A. level.[39] There are some exceptions, but staff members have tended not to come overwhelmingly from the ranks of upper-class America. The number of upper-class backgrounds *is* disproportionate to the total numbers of the upper class in the electorate, but a substantial number of staff members are from upper-middle and middle-class backgrounds.

Perhaps more important than staff backgrounds is the question of where the staffers go after service in the White House. Kennedy and Johnson aides showed, more at least than the Eisenhower aides, a tendency to acquire prominent positions *after* their service in the White House.[40] Eisenhower's staff aides tended more often to return to their former activities. Nixon staffers show a unique pattern: from White House to jail cell! The early success of several aides in landing business jobs may portend a most interesting relationship—upward mobility from the White House Staff despite Watergate.

The Kennedy and Johnson Presidencies and the subsequent fortunes of their staff aides revealed both the growing importance of governmental access for business and also the expansion and increasingly lucrative operations of the Washington lawyers. Patrick Anderson describes some of the subsequent employment offered recent aides. Major advances in both incomes and positions of responsibility were made by such former aides as McGeorge Bundy, Joseph Califino, Myer Fellman, William Moyers, Theodore Sorenson, and Jack Valenti.[41] Younger ex-aides could also look forward in several instances to the prospect of a return to influence, if not direct appointment, with future Democratic victories. The example of Clark Clifford seemed likely to continue. Clifford had moved from a position on Truman's staff to great prominence both as a lawyer and as a periodic adviser to Democratic political figures, including Presidents Kennedy and Johnson. Strikingly, academics on occasion had more difficulty, as involvement in either the staff or the cabinet could—in the wake of academic opposition to the Vietnam War—place the individual who had been gone from academic life more than two years and had resigned from his home institution in considerable jeopardy, if he ultimately chose to reenter academic life.

Staff members have also tended to reflect the regional backgrounds of the Presidents they served. All recent Presidents did recruit heavily from the mid-Atlantic area (which includes Washington). They also drew heavily from their home states. Kennedy recruited disproportionately from his native Massachusetts, and in particular from Boston's academic circles. Johnson drew heavily from Texas; 6 of the top 10 aides were at one point from his home state. Nixon aides again revealed the tendency for home-state backgrounds to appear in substantial numbers. California and New York were disproportionately represented. New York contributed John Mitchell (as confidant as well as cabinet member), Leonard Garment, and Daniel Moynihan. The list of Californians seemed almost endless (in top cabinet spots as well as in aide and adviser roles). One thinks of H. R. Haldeman, Roy Ash, Robert Finch, Herbert Klein, Jeb Magruder, Ronald Zeigler, and a host of lesser-known individuals (Washingtonian John Ehrlichman had his degree from UCLA).[42] Nixon's recruitment of Californians was in keeping with the tradition for staff members to be recruited on the basis of personal contact, without undue pressure for regional balance.

Those individuals operating within the ever-growing advisory units of the Executive Office of the President are somewhat more apt to be selected on the basis of educational qualifications, and less on the basis of specific acquaintance with the president. Education has been a route for advancement particularly in the economic and foreign policy advisory staffs. Ph.D.'s are fairly common in those areas, whereas law degrees are more common in the domestic policy areas. Better than half of the recent domestic staffs have, in fact, held law degrees.

Some of the advisory personnel in the Executive Office must be approved in their positions by Congress. In a move hotly disputed between Nixon and Congress, the positions of director and deputy director of the Office of Management and Budget went into the Senate confirmation category. (Nixon's veto of this was one of the few Nixon vetoes which the Senate successfully overturned.) In addition, the members of the Council of Economic Advisers, the director of the CIA, and several lesser advisory unit heads are now also confirmed. Confirmation tends to be automatic, but the necessity of gaining confirmation can produce some prior consultation. Perhaps most importantly, confirmation also provides the basis for some subsequent interaction between advisers and Congress. As a result, a chairman of the Council of Economic Advisers may on occasion relate to Congress, whereas those within the White House Staff have more consistently avoided that role. In the eyes of these aides, such a role would take away from more valuable time, and confront them with the same problems facing members of the cabinet.

It is difficult to generalize about the ability level of presidential staffs. In terms of educational backgrounds, there has been a steady rise beginning with the Kennedy staff. Taking all staffers beginning with Truman, some 13 percent have had Ph.D.'s. The absence of a college degree has become increasingly rare. The opportunity for upward advancement following staff assignment has, in the eyes of some observers, made staff positions increasingly attractive to able, ambitious individuals. We can better assess the question of staff competence by looking at specific aides and advisers and their actions as we begin shortly to unravel the specifics of presidential information systems.

To sum up for now, aides and advisers in the contemporary Presidency are often young men with high ambitions who have gotten their positions through a combination of hard work, educational success, and knowing the right individuals. The economic and foreign policy positions, and many lesser positions in the Executive Office, are more apt to reflect success with academic activities. Patrick Anderson describes aides effectively as "young, highly intelligent, and unashamedly on the make."[43]

Staffing the Bureaucracy

Presidents often have considerable difficulty in staffing positions in departments and key agencies. Despite efforts at systematizing this task, appointment activities are replete with confusion, irritation, and—too often—private disappointment with some of the results. Melvin Laird may not have been, as was widely rumored, precisely the fifth Nixon choice for secretary of defense in 1969, but the persistence of the rumor reflected the widespread recognition that presidents often have extreme difficulty in filling positions. Nixon used a mass mailing to thousands of prominent people looking for possible recommendations in 1969, partly as a public relations adventure; yet the problems of filling major positions remained substantial.

Problems with the Selection Process

At the core of the presidential difficulty in selecting personnel for the executive branch is one central fact: Political appointments are often not attractive to the individuals a president would like to have working for him. At the same time, the president is constrained by a set of party and interest-group norms (as well as direct pressures) for selection which are enough to discount many possibilities, but which do not provide a pool of effective talent which a president can easily tap.

One difficulty surrounds the position of American legislators. In the cabinet system employed by the British, the chief executive has a built-in set of legislators ready to fill administrative positions. This may restrict recruitment of talent somewhat, since outsiders are excluded, but it also provides a ready source of leadership. In contrast, American legislators are reluctant to give up their positions. Reasons are obvious. An established legislator can look forward to a lengthy career in Congress, barring unusual developments. He can also look forward to a gradually increasing position of influence in his area of specialization. In some policy systems, he may indeed conclude that he would rather run things from the Hill than bother with administrative detail in departmental operations.

The disruption of a legislative career tends to be substantial. Very few legislators who give up their positions ever return. Senators Anderson and Ribicoff in recent administrations have been exceptions. There also tend to be few individuals who go from cabinet positions to Congress. Robert Kennedy, in going from the Justice Department to the Senate, was a major exception—and certainly a unique case. There is, in sum, little traffic between legislative and cabinet positions. An occasional individual such as Melvin Laird, who left the House to be secretary of defense, constitutes an unusual exception.

Insofar as individuals with elective office experience are recruited, they tend to come from the state governor's offices. A given administration may well have several former governors. Nixon, for example, used Walter Hickel from Alaska as his first secretary of the interior, George Romney from Michigan as his first secretary of housing and urban development, and John Volpe from Massachusetts as his first secretary of transportation. Significantly, as Nixon sought in the wake of the 1972 election victory to strengthen control in the White House, his cabinet came to include no individuals with previous positions in major elective office. Graduate degrees, more than political backgrounds, became the common background.

Presidents will generally recruit some businessmen. The extreme case may well continue to be Eisenhower's cabinet—not too affectionately known by some as "nine millionaires and a plumber." There are also difficulties with the recruitment of businessmen. Conflicts of interest may make it difficult for an individual to accept a measure of legislative scrutiny and the required disinvolvement with his firm. There may also be substantial financial sacrifice involved if an individual contemplates leaving a high-level managerial position for a position paying (at recent levels) some $42,500 a year.

Job satisfaction problems are also involved. This presents something of a vicious circle. As presidents have difficulty filling cabinet posts, they often tend to rely upon staff appointees for the more interesting policy development tasks. Yet as the departmental positions thus become more routine, their attractiveness to potential appointees tends to be reduced. Thus in the extreme case, President Nixon found himself in 1973 in the position of asking individuals to fill cabinet posts which he had publicly stated ought to be abolished.

Cabinet officials often find themselves isolated from the president, and spending considerable time trying to deal with Congress and seeking to manage cumbersome governmental bureaucracies. Spending extensive time testifying before Congress is, with few exceptions, a rather dreaded task in Washington. Bureaucratic management, in turn, can seem unrewarding, as direct accomplishments are often difficult to achieve. It is not surprising that the turnover rate is high, or that there are substantial numbers of rejections of presidential offers.

Limitations are also present in the fairly extensive set of norms for particular offices. Franklin Roosevelt reportedly desired to appoint Henry Morganthau as secretary of agriculture. Morganthau was in fact keenly interested in agricultural problems and was involved with his estate in New York. Yet to appoint a nonfarmer, a New Yorker, and a Jew was far more than those involved with Agricultural Department politics were anxious to contemplate. Tradition said that the secretary should be a farmer and a Midwesterner, aside from the question of ethnic background. More recently, lawyer Orville Freeman emphasized the time he had spent on the family farm as he was being considered for the secretary of agriculture position.

Richard Fenno undertook an extensive study of cabinet appointment politics, and found definite norms for several departments.[44] He also found clear patterns in terms of the types of people who were selected for posts. There have been some changes since Fenno's study, as a secretary of the interior came from the East (Morton from Maryland under Nixon) and an immigrant Jewish professor— Henry Kissinger—was appointed secretary of state. Drawing substantially from Fenno's work, the following patterns can be sketched.

The older and most prestigous departments are:

Attorney General. Historically, an attorney who has had political experience. Frequently, this post has gone to the president's campaign manager.
Defense. Generally a person with business background, often in one of the large industries such as auto manufacturing.
State. Often an Easterner, and often a member of the American upper class.
Treasury. Generally a businessman with at least some direct involvement with the banking industry.

The older clientele departments are:

Agriculture. Generally a person with a farming background, and often from the Midwest.
Commerce. Usually a businessman, at points selected to balance regional distribution in a cabinet.
Interior. Generally a Westerner, given the importance of irrigation issues in Interior Department activities.

Labor. Periodically a labor official; more frequently an academic person with involvement in labor policies, when the Republicans are in power.

The new departments are:

Health, Education, and Welfare (HEW); Housing and Urban Development (HUD); Department of Transportation (DOT). The three new departments have less well developed patterns of recruitment. Either political backgrounds such as governorships or else managerial skills in business or related academic fields tend to emerge.

Interest-group pressure can at points be intense. If there is little controversy in a given policy area, and the appointments follow established norms, there may be few difficulties. Where the opposite situation occurs, interest-group pressure can be both intense and successful. This was dramatically evident with Nixon's selection of the nation's top health official in 1969.[45] Robert Finch, the HEW secretary, first wanted to appoint Dr. John Knowles as Assistant Secretary for Health. The American Medical Association (AMA), smarting from its defeat in the establishment of Medicare in 1965, violently objected to the proposed appointment of a person who testified sympathetically toward a comprehensive prepaid health plan. AMA friends in Congress were contacted, as their lobbyists sought to utilize some of the leverage the rather generous recent political contributions ($680,000 in 1968) had attempted to provide. Nixon assured Finch that he would support the nominee of his choice, but that the decision was up to Finch to make. Finch vacillated in the face of strong opposition, made one more effort to clarify support at the White House, and then capitulated. Ironically, the subsequent rapid appointment of Roger Egeberg brought to the position an individual whose attitudes on some issues caused no rejoicing in AMA circles. The Knowles case is one of many examples of the difficulties cabinet officials had in dealing with Nixon's White House; for present purposes it also stands as an excellent example of the veto interest groups can exercise in the appointment process.

There are some shifts occurring in terms of the pressures which operate on a president. Cabinet appointments in the Eisenhower years and before seemed to be perceived more in terms of representing factional divisions within the parties. The Nixon changes in particular were undertaken with limited party pressures for ideological balance; the issue was more predominantly one of technological and managerial competence. A president's appointments, particularly as he forms his first cabinet, seem nonetheless destined to be influenced by interest both in balancing policy orientations and meeting the prevailing norms of several of the specific offices.

Presidential concern for staffing the bureaucracy also extends beyond the cabinet itself. Several top positions in departments such as State and Defense receive considerable attention. There are also the positions in the regulatory commissions and independent agencies, such as the Federal Power Commission (FPC) and the National Aeronautics and Space Administration (NASA), which must be considered. Beyond the first several dozen appointments, a president increasingly finds himself involved with the ratification of choices made by others.

White House Staff and Cabinet Compared

Differences in staff and cabinet backgrounds take on particular importance in the light of the tendency for recent Presidents to emphasize White House Staff at the expense of cabinet members. Key staff positions are apt to be attained on the basis of personal contact with the president in his years prior to election. This is particularly true of his immediate advisers and his political aides. Staff positions will also go, somewhat more than the cabinet positions, to individuals who have advanced their social status through educational activities.

Cabinet positions show a substantial amount of elite recruitment. This is particularly evident in the old-line departments—which are also, with minor exceptions, the most important cabinet positions.[46] Domestic positions in both the older clientele departments and the new domestic units are filled somewhat more broadly.

An emphasis on decision making by the White House Staff rather than by the cabinet can have key impacts. Presidents may try to overcome the influence of dominant interests in specific policy areas by adding to the decision-making responsibilities of the White House. From the standpoint of those who criticize the inability of the American system to produce more general policies, and to overcome the dominance of key interests, one can sympathize with at least aspects of this tendency. Interestingly enough, some of Johnson's aides testified in favor of Nixon's reorganizing efforts in 1971, which were directed both toward a reduction of some of the veto points in the bureaucracy and establishing a more centralized basis for presidential control.

Yet the centralizing thrust also has highly questionable impacts. The shift to White House rather than cabinet-level decision making can reduce access of all groups but those which have established a privileged base of operation among presidential advisers. The departmental access which is criticized by those with a desire for more centralized policy making is also the access which others have seen as giving the political system at least a measure of openness to interest groups.

Decision making by staffers rather than cabinet officials also raises questions of political control. Staffers, as we have seen, are more apt to gain their position on the basis of personal ties with the president, and they are apt to have little independent base of political strength. They can easily contribute to a high leader-follower dependency in policy making operations. Presidential staffers also reduce the control of Congress, in that they are often not confirmed, and they may more easily use the claim of executive privilege as a basis for refusing to testify in congressional hearings.

Summary

Reviewing characteristics of major participants in contemporary presidential politics provides insights into the dilemmas of presidential politics on two levels. For presidents themselves, difficult questions have surrounded the nature and impact of their ambitions. Presidents Kennedy, Johnson, and Nixon were all highly ambitious individuals, although Kennedy was not as obviously the striving politician in the eyes of major segments of the electorate—and in the interpretations of many of his admirers. Each was an experienced politician. Two of the three represented the American dream of individuals being born in common circumstances and then being elevated to the Presidency. Yet the actions of each, in ascending order, raised serious questions as to the type of personality which is effective in the Oval Office. Clearly, an effective mix of qualities in an individual president was proving most difficult to achieve. Is it still possible to select presidents who are both ambitious enough to avoid a lethargic Presidency but balanced enough in their drives not to overtax the ability of the system to respond?

Presidents now surround themselves with aides and advisers, reflecting a growing use of expertise, but also a more pronounced emphasis on using young men interested in advancing their careers. Presidents have often also sought to use these individuals to gain greater control over the operations of the federal bureaucracy. Yet as they have done so, they have increased the problems of accountability in policy development. Issues involving impacts of ambition and of centralization abound as one looks more directly at presidential information-gathering and policy-making activity.

NOTES

¹ Richard E. Neustadt, *Presidential Power: The Politics of Leadership*, New York, Wiley, 1960.

² A more recent effort by Erwin C. Hargrove to deal with a limited

set of propositions rather than categories is found in his "Presidential Personality and the Revisiónist Views of the Presidency," *American Journal of
Political Science* 17 (November, 1973), 819–835.

[3] James David Barber, *Presidential Character: Predicting Performance
in the White House*, Englewood Cliffs, N.J., Prentice-Hall, 1972.

[4] James David Barber, "Strategies for Understanding Politicians," paper
delivered at the American Political Science Association meeting, Chicago,
Ill., September 1, 1974.

[5] The totally upper-class background in which Franklin Roosevelt was
raised can be sensed from many volumes. See, for example, Frank Freidel,
Franklin D. Roosevelt: The Apprenticeship, Boston, Little, Brown, 1952;
and James MacGregor Burns, *Roosevelt: The Lion and the Fox*, New
York, Harcourt Brace Jovanovich, 1956.

[6] A summary of press conference activities is contained in Elmer Cornwell, *Presidential Leadership of Public Opinion*, Bloomington, Ind., Indiana
University Press, 1965.

[7] For Truman's background, see Alfred Steinberg, *The Man From Missouri*, New York, Putnam, 1962; and Bertram Cochran, *Crisis and the
Truman Presidency*, New York, Funk & Wagnalls, 1973.

[8] Merle Miller, *Plain Speaking: An Oral Biography of Harry S. Truman*,
New York, Berkeley, 1973, p. 384.

[9] Cochran, op. cit., chap. 7.

[10] Ibid., chap. 20.

[11] On this problem, see Erwin C. Hargrove, *The Power of the Modern
Presidency*, New York, Knopf, 1974, chap. 2.

[12] For Eisenhower's background, see Peter Lyon, *Portrait of the Hero*,
Boston, Little, Brown, 1974.

[13] Dwight D. Eisenhower, *Mandate for Change: The White House
Years*, New York, Signet, 1963, p. 154.

[14] Ibid., p. 158.

[15] Many of the critical views are found in Marquis Childs, *Eisenhower:
Captive Hero*, New York, Harcourt Brace Jovanovich, 1958.

[16] Arthur Larson, *The Eisenhower Nobody Knew*, New York, Scribner,
1968.

[17] Lyon, op. cit.

[18] Larson, op. cit., p. 200.

[19] G. William Domhoff argues that he was clearly a member of the
upper class. For a view emphasizing the ambiguity of the Kennedy social
position, see Richard J. Whalen, *The Founding Father: The Story of Joseph
P. Kennedy*, New York, Signet, 1964.

[20] Theodore C. Sorenson, *Kennedy*, New York, Harper & Row, 1965.

[21] Nancy Clinch, *The Kennedy Neurosis*, New York, Grosset & Dunlap,
1973.

[22] Henry Fairlie, *The Kennedy Promise: The Politics of Expectation*,
New York, Dell, 1974.

[23] On Johnson's background, see Booth Mooney, *The Lyndon Johnson
Story*, New York, Avon, 1964; and Eric Goldman, *The Tragedy of LBJ*, New
York, Dell, 1968.

[24] Johnson's finances are discussed in Rowland Evans, Jr., and Robert Novak, *LBJ: The Exercise of Power,* New York, New American Library, 1966, pp. 31–32.

[25] On Johnson's legislative role, see ibid., chap. 8.

[26] Goldman, op. cit., chap. 18.

[27] See Barber, op. cit., chap. 2.

[28] On Nixon's youth, see Bruce Mazlich, *In Search of Nixon,* New York, Basic Books, 1972.

[29] A particularly strong statement emphasizing Nixon's psychological problems is Eli S. Chesen, *President Nixon's Psychiatric Profile: A Psychodynamic-genetic Interpretation,* New York, Wyden, 1973.

[30] Nixon's orientation toward crisis is discussed in Barber, op. cit., pp. 388–394.

[31] An early account of the Ford background was Bud Vestal, *Jerry Ford Up Close,* New York, Coward-McCann & Geoghegan, 1974.

[32] On Ford, see also James David Barber, "Ford, Will He Be Tough Enough?" *U.S. News and World Report,* September 2, 1974, pp. 22–25.

[33] For a view arguing the limited challenge Roosevelt presented to elite interests, see G. William Domhoff, *Who Rules America?,* Englewood Cliffs, N.J., Prentice-Hall, 1967, pp. 152–154.

[34] Neustadt, *Presidential Power,* chap. 3.

[35] Fred I. Greenstein, *Personality and Politics: Problems of Evidence, Inference, and Conceptualization,* Chicago, Markham, 1969, pp. 48–57.

[36] Lester G. Seligman, comments on paper presentation, American Political Science Association meeting, Chicago, Ill., September 1, 1974.

[37] Patricia S. Florestano, "The White House Staff: Bibliographical Study," unpublished manuscript, University of Maryland. This study examined all members of the presidential staffs listed in the U.S. Government Organizational Manual from Truman through early Nixon.

[38] Ibid., p. 20.

[39] Ibid., p. 12.

[40] See Patrick Anderson, *The Presidents' Men,* Garden City, N.Y., Doubleday, 1969, chap. 7.

[41] Ibid.

[42] For backgrounds of the Nixon staff, see Dan Rather and Gary P. Gates, *The Palace Guard,* New York, Harper & Row, 1974.

[43] Anderson, op. cit., p. 469.

[44] Richard F. Fenno, Jr., *The President's Cabinet,* New York, Vintage, 1959.

[45] This case is effectively presented in Rowland Evans, Jr., and Robert D. Novak, *Nixon in the White House: The Frustration of Power,* New York, Vintage, 1971, pp. 59–66.

[46] There is some confusion in these data, since some individuals will be given social standing, such as listing in the Social Register, because of their political accomplishments. For one review, see Domhoff, op. cit., pp. 97–102.

The President's Quest
for Information

The Oval Office stands at the center of a massive information system, Presidents generally receive extensive data and staff summaries on everything from unemployment levels to troop casualties. The public information system is monitored through newspapers, television, and the commentary flowing in various specialized groups of the population—labor, intellectuals, businessmen, and others.

The president frequently meets with various advisory bodies, including the National Security Council; policy matter experts, such as the head of the Council of Economic Advisers; and, in varying degrees, the cabinet and legislative leaders. Numerous interest-group leaders, members of the press, individual legislators, and presidential friends find their way to the Oval Office, or to one of the president's alternative business and vacation settings—perhaps Key West, San Clemente, or a Colorado ski lodge. In addition, key presidential aides both meet with the president frequently and engage in their own intelligence-gathering activities. A president has literally thousands of individuals engaged directly in the task of helping reach informed decisions. Furthermore, presidents generally have had a lifetime in politics to develop knowledge of America and the policy questions confronting the nation. Yet issues of presidential isolation seemed particularly acute in recent years.

Presidential information systems must be explored from several perspectives. A critical first question involves the factors contributing to presidential awareness and involvement with some questions and not others. Secondly, one must explore the various sources, from the routine printed word to the advising process, which bring information and analysis to the president. Finally, it is essential to provide an initial consideration of the vexing issue of presidential isolation.

The Contest for Presidential Attention

What does tend to gain the attention of the president, and why? That basic question is fundamental to the nature of presidential information systems. Presidents are clearly only peripherally involved with many matters which seem at least potentially to be of major interest. Budgets are signed with but a cursory knowledge of the workings of particular agencies, individuals are hired (or fired) with little direct presidential knowledge, and positions taken in presidential speeches may be developed with little direct presidential involvement. Yet presidential interest and involvement is on occasion very substantial. Some agency operations are known in detail, personnel issues are directly reviewed, and policy positions result periodically from clear knowledge and involvement.

From the perspective of foreign policy operations, Morton Halperin has provided one thoughtful overview.[1] He sees presidential attention being molded by (1) dramatic changes in the actions of other nations which may trigger interest, along with (2) new technology, and (3) changes in the shared images of society or bureaucracy. (4) Routine events may also require attention. Speeches, or visits, become the vessel through which a new policy proposal may emerge. In these instances, the formal event triggers the interest, rather than the initial interest leading to a proposal for a speech. (5) Changes in personnel may also precipitate the raising of issues, including ones not immediately related to the initial departure. (6) Finally, there are some self-generated efforts. The central thrust of Halperin's most useful account of presidents and the foreign policy bureaucracy clearly suggests a limited range of concerns which are self-generated by presidents.

Theodore Sorenson, a key Kennedy aide, reviewed the decision process more generally.[2] In his view, there is a great deal of choosing which goes on both of the information which is received and the issues which are carried through to decision. Time is viewed as an extremely limited resource, with an inevitable set of forced choices as to what the president is able to examine. The general thrust of Sorenson's work is decidedly toward the restraints operating on the presidential agenda.

A review of the records of recent incumbents, and of several interesting specific studies, gives a general indication of factors determining recent presidential agendas. These include fixed responsibilities, crisis situations, electoral support factors, the threat of acknowledged failure, personal interest, and the impact of effective lobbying. The weights attached to respective factors vary from one president to another, but not the underlying impact of key forces.

Fixed Presidential Responsibilities

Some presidential information and activity flows, from the required activities in any given year. Budgets must be submitted to Congress, and a State of the Union address must be prepared. Top-level turnovers in personnel, even if not precipitated by presidential action, must be followed by some recommendation to Congress. Professor Halperin correctly notes the tendency for these fixed events to periodically precipitate presidential involvement. Preparing a speech or a budget may force a president to look more closely at what is being done in a given area. Speech writers have on occasion been very clever in this role. It is nonetheless never certain that formal involvement will produce more than a cursory presidential exploration of a given issue. Frequently, other, more specific factors are involved.

Crisis Situations

Even the most casual observer of presidential politics has doubtlessly witnessed presidential involvement with "crisis" policy issues. Troop commitments and responses to foreign military actions are perhaps the clearest examples. The involvement may easily be so substantial, in fact, that other information processing virtually stops. Recall, for example, Kennedy's extensive involvement with formulating the American response to the knowledge (through American intelligence efforts) of the presence of Soviet missiles in Cuba in October 1962. Similar observations have been made about Johnson's preoccupation with the Santo Domingo crisis in April 1965. Conferences and phone calls predominate, be the president at Camp David or in the White House; other information is pushed into the background.

Crisis-oriented domestic matters also predominate on occasion. Labor disputes have a long history of presidential involvement, although at points these are handled at the staff level. Racial upheavals, with the periodic threat of violence, similarly may focus presidential attention. Even a president who is reluctant to become involved, as was Eisenhower in 1957, may find himself confronted with the necessity for involvement as tensions mount. In 1957, Eisenhower found himself trying to negotiate with several Southern governors and ultimately sending federal troops to Arkansas to enforce the federal desegregation order at Little Rock's Central High School.[3]

It is unfortunately easier to point to crisis situations in which presidents have become highly informed and involved than it is to specify the conditions which force a particular set of events to be identified as a crisis. American politics has witnessed a substantial increase since about 1960 in the tendency to talk in crisis terms. In one brief decade, crisis-oriented discussions filled the air regarding the crisis of the cities, the racial crisis, the environmental crisis, and the energy crisis. Other groups have sought to express their concerns in crisis terms, but with less success.

Presidential involvement is often related to the cyclical behavior which is apparent in the national focus on policy issues. Policy questions frequently go through a fairly definite cycle, including, as Anthony Downs has described: (1) the preproblem stage, (2) alarmed discovery and euphoric enthusiasm, (3) realization of costs of significant progress, (4) gradual decline of intense public interest, and (5) the postproblem state.[4] Unless there is a threat of violence, a president will often try to avoid getting involved with the initial cries of alarm. He may respond more in terms of trying to slow the fears, perhaps with task forces and promises of future action. The tendency for a president not to respond quickly, along with other problems of political access, may in fact be one of the factors promoting an escalation in crisis rhetoric. Proponents of new policies try to outshout each other in order to somehow gain presidential attention. Presidents do tend to be involved if a crisis issue has been on the national issue agenda for some time, often in the context of the third stage in the Downs analysis, which involves developing a specific proposal and thus confronting the costs of significant change.

One major incentive for the president not to become involved with domestic policy issues on a crisis basis deserves emphasis. Presidents are much more likely to get a rally-round-the-flag response on foreign than on domestic policy issues. Unless the country confronts a crisis which takes on the appearance of a natural disaster, there are generally enough partisan and ideological overtones in a problem situation to win more enemies than friends for the person who tries at solution. It seems doubtful, for example, that President Ford could easily have gained much electoral popularity if he had sought more extensive involvement with the busing furor which developed in South Boston during the first weeks of his tenure. Domestic crisis situations do nonetheless periodically bring presidential involvement, especially where the possibility of substantial violence is involved.

Reelection Concerns

Presidential elections often look more uncertain to the incumbent trying to plan for reelection than to the analyst who looks at the record of previous elections and has a hard time identifying "issues." Nowhere is this more evident than in reflecting on the difficult position of the Nixon Presidency by mid-1971. Nixon and his aides faced the 1972 elections with a sagging economy and a definite possibility that George Wallace might run once again. Nixon trailed Democratic frontrunner Senator Edward Muskie, and there was always the possibility that Senator Edward Kennedy would emerge from his murky noncandidate status. His ultimate landslide victory in 1972 bears little resemblance to the preceding uncertainties.

Presidential interest in particular policy questions is often highly motivated by a sense of what will be important in the coming election. In Nixon's case, questions of Southern support took on importance both for the President and his staff, and were reflected in the Supreme Court appointments repeatedly offered to the South and the efforts at stringing out the enforcement of school desegregation.[5] Other Presidents have also had their attention focused by election concerns. Concern for possible electoral sanction, as we will see, was a factor in focusing Johnson's attention on Vietnam.

The view that reelection concerns tend to influence presidential agendas gains some support in an interesting study undertaken by John Kessel. He examined State of the Union addresses since Truman in an effort to determine presidential agendas with the aid of content analysis.[6] All recent incumbents displayed a tendency to let domestic policy references decline in comparison to foreign policy references during the four years between elections. A predominance of foreign policy issues was especially pronounced in the second terms. Yet in the fourth year for an incumbent facing reelection, there was a turn away from foreign policy references toward various domestic matters. State of the Union addresses are obviously not a perfect measure of presidential concern; they may in part involve symbolic references. Yet the turn to "bread-and-butter" issues in reelection years is an interesting indication of the general presidential concern with reelection.

A president is also influenced by electoral factors in traditional party coalitions. He certainly does not sit down frequently to review what the party platform committee suggested he, as its nominee, would accomplish if elected. Platforms may well reflect a small concession made by a factional victor to other interests in his party. Platforms do nonetheless periodically reflect various coalition interests, and serve to focus issues. This was clearly the case in the Kennedy and Johnson Presidencies, as commitments to such programs as aid to education, medical care for the aged, and aid for the unemployed were firmly supported programs for key groups in the Democratic coalition. James Sundquist has effectively shown a strong tie between parties and policy ideas in that period.[7] Party positions, coupled with continued lobbying, can motivate presidents to an interest in specific programs.

Presidents also become directly involved as they adjudicate specific allocation decisions and patronage issues with an eye toward electoral and legislative support. Patronage issues may reach the Oval Office, at least for the President to "sign off," even if not actively review. Where it becomes difficult for a president to generate support for general policy steps, specific, tangible rewards may be sought with particular interest as a basis for developing support. Government contracts constitute one important example. The granting of large contracts for a major weapons system really has the effect of a major program of regional economic aid. More money may be involved in a single defense contract than one finds in an entire program designated for regional aid. The largest military contracts have involved amounts in the $10 billion or better range, while the Area Redevelopment Administration was never funded at more than a fraction of that figure. A president may believe that an upswing in the economic fortunes of a large, pivotal state is of major importance to his own reelection chances, and thus decide to become involved on contract issues. The debate over presidential involvement tends thus to center not on whether presidents take an interest, but rather on the extent to which political factors override other concerns.[8]

The scandals of the Nixon Administration further pointed to the presidential willingness to become involved with specific political support matters. The debate over such issues as the merger between ITT and Hartford Insurance, and the price structure for the dairy industry, as discussed in Chapter 12, was not whether or not the President was aware of contributions. The debate involved instead the interpretation of the impact that knowledge had on the President, and on his orders to subordinates. For now, one need simply emphasize that the presidential agenda does periodically include the trading of favors and the pursuit of support for reelection.

Reelection has also motivated the pursuit of political intelligence from various sources. This information generally relates to the strengths, weaknesses, and possible strategies of various political actors with whom the president is concerned. Party channels have traditionally buzzed with this type of information, and such figures as party chairmen and key presidential aides have tended to provide a conduit for this type of information. Such names as Louis Howe and James Farley for Franklin Roosevelt and Kenneth O'Donnell for Kennedy come readily to mind.

The Nixon Presidency revealed most dramatically how far a Presidency would go in efforts to gain political information. Chapter 12 considers some of the specifics of those practices and the nature of Nixon's involvement. The Watergate eavesdropping and burglary were the most dramatic and captured much of the public attention. Equally indicative of the extent of Nixon's desire for political information was the interest in gaining information from governmental agencies, particularly the FBI and the Internal Revenue Service. Both election strategies and the gathering of specific information deemed necessary for building support are a recurring part of the presidential agenda.

Avoiding Publicly Recognized Failure

Presidents frequently show an interest in issues which may confront them with embarrassing failures. The briefings they receive for press conferences are one manifestation of this concern, as several hours may be spent by the president going over likely troublespots reporters are apt to raise. One of the results of the retreat from press conferences in recent years may well, in fact, be the loss of this prod for presidents to inform themselves.

President Kennedy's strong response on the proposed steel price increase in April 1962 is a good example of the importance of a president's sense that he may be facing a publicly acknowledged failure.[9] Kennedy felt that the steel price increases not only went against his guidelines, but that they made him look bad in the eyes of the labor leaders who had been given reassurances that steel industry management was going to exercise greater restraint in their price demands that year. Kennedy mobilized an impressive array of resources in his response, including his indignation at a press conference, Defense Department promises to buy only from those who refused to go along with a general industry-wide increase, and renewed antitrust discussion. After an intense week, Inland Steel agreed to hold the line, and ultimately U.S. Steel backed down. The critical importance of the fear of publicly recognized failure was born out most dramatically by events a year later. Steel prices were increased more than had been proposed the year before, and yet there was no presidential response.

The threat of failure in the legislative arena also often produces presidential interest and involvement. One reason that a president may be reluctant to get behind legislation more directly than does occur involves the desire of avoiding publicly acknowledged failures. Presidential involvement may also be triggered at points by the president's veto power. President Nixon, for example, would often have messages prepared both for signing and for vetoing a bill; the bill was then in a context to force his involvement. The legislative impact may focus on specific incidents more than general policy issues, but at least there is some pressure for presidential involvement.

Presidents' Personal Interests

Presidents periodically take a personal interest in questions which cannot easily be explained in other terms. President Roosevelt retained an interest in naval issues which could be traced back to his early days as an assistant navy secretary and to his longtime interest in sailing and boating activities. President Kennedy, also a former navy man, got personally involved in the naming of new ships. Kennedy also made aid to Appalachia one of his pets, in part because of his long interest in regional economic issues as a legislator from somewhat economically depressed New England. His interest also increased after the West Virginia primary election. President Johnson's interest in educational issues could be traced in part to his early teaching days and to his continuing faith in the importance of the educational process. President Nixon's genuine concern for the work ethic fostered rather direct involvement with the family assistance approach to welfare reform as a way to reduce welfare dependency. In a policy system with few resources for lobbying a president, the fond hope of lobbyists is that he will develop a personal interest in their cause which surpasses concern which could be generated with normal political pressures.

The Lobbying Process

Issues frequently gain presidential attention as the result of successful lobbying by key proponents. Competition for presidential interest and attention is often intense. Given the size of today's presidential bureaucracy, to lobby successfully it is very often necessary to have proponents within the staff process rather than outsiders operating through commissions, or engaging in general issue-promoting activity. White House access is frequently essential for success in bringing an issue to the president's attention, let alone obtaining a favorable response.

Summary

Basic points emerge from an examination of the forces influencing presidential attention. The forces which do motivate the president to personal knowledge of particular relationships and perhaps to some specific involvement are highly sporadic. Many potential concerns must inevitably be left out. There are always more issues and areas of exploration occupying the attention of the staff, the federal government, and the country than a president can absorb. As a result, there is in any Presidency, regardless of how it is organized, a necessity for choice as to both information and resulting issue involvement. There are nonetheless major differences in the degree of success presidents achieve in using their available information sources and staffs.

Sources of Information

Advisers must inevitably be the cornerstone of a presidential information system. Presidents spend a substantial amount of time with their advisers. President Nixon, in a typical day, would schedule Henry Kissinger perhaps three times, and H. R. Haldeman as many as seven times.[10] Presidents do have other sources of information, however, which are used in varying degrees, and these deserve specific note before the critical role of the advisers is discussed. These include newspapers, television, polls, the mail bag, comments from friends and family, and meetings with such outsiders as legislators and interest-group leaders.

Presidents make varying use of newspapers. President Kennedy was an avid newspaper reader. In part, he retained a former journalist's interest in newspaper activities. According to his key aide, Theodore Sorenson, Kennedy read

> all of the Washington newspapers (*Post, Star, News*), most of the New York papers (*Times, News, Wall Street Journal,* at one time the *Herald Tribune,* and frequently most of the others), the *Baltimore Sun,* the *Boston Globe,* the *Philadelphia Inquirer,* the *Miami Herald,* the *Chicago Sun-Times,* the *Chicago Tribune,* and the *St. Louis Post Dispatch.*[11]

Kennedy staffers loved to point to instances in which specific stores were recollected by President Kennedy. President Johnson read in varying degrees the *Washington Post, New York Times, Baltimore Sun, Wall Street Journal,* and *Christian Science Monitor.*[12] President Nixon preferred a daily news summary, generally prepared by Patrick Buchanan on his speech-writing staff. (It did not go unnoticed among Nixon-watchers that Buchanan was also noted for his conservative political leanings.)[13] Various magazines also make their way into presidential reading; staffers often function on an ad hoc basis as conduits for articles which they feel may be of particular interest to their boss.

President Johnson, among recent Presidents, was the most intrigued with television. Johnson had a panel installed so that he could monitor three stations simultaneously in his quest for awareness of the manner in which his moves were being presented to the electorate. Presidents Kennedy and Nixon were somewhat less avid watchers of television news. Nixon even went to the trouble of having Johnson's television sets removed. Johnson was also the most avid follower of the ticker tapes which the Associated Press machine made available.

Presidents receive a voluminous amount of mail. President Kennedy averaged over 30,000 letters a week. A major appeal for support may bring 100,000 or more. Various sampling procedures are used by the staff in handling the mail. Kennedy tried to read every fiftieth letter, plus summaries of others. Presidents have often concluded that much of the mail is inspired by interest groups and is not very representative. In this judgment they are in fact supported by a variety of academic studies.[14] They nonetheless have a substantial flow, which receives at least the attention of their staffs.

Public opinion polls, both as reported in the media and as commissioned by the president, often get considerable attention. Presidents tend to be conscious of their Gallup Poll ratings; Johnson is reported to have even periodically carried them about on his person. The presidential commissioning of private polls has become common, as leads are sought which may help with strategies, rather than simple reports of general public perceptions.

Written reports and analyses also abound in presidential operations. The *Congressional Record* was extensively summarized for Johnson. His legislative leadership days had made him an eager follower of the implications of materials in the *Congressional Record*. Economic indicators and staff studies of various kinds are also used extensively. The obvious problem for the president is that he cannot read much of the available material. As a result, various practices are developed for providing summaries of pro and con interpretations, along with indications of suggested action.

Information can also come from meetings outside the context of staff operations. Cabinet meetings vary widely in frequency. They may be more frequently held in the early stages of an administration. Meetings with legislative leaders are often held at breakfast meetings and are frequently held several times a month when Congress is in session. There are also wide variations in the frequency with which presidents meet with individual legislators. Johnson liked to meet and also liked to use the telephone. Nixon was the most reluctant of recent occupants of the Oval Office. He did not meet, for example, with even Barry Goldwater (the acknowledged party leader after Nixon) for months following the beginnings of the Watergate investigations.

Presidents also meet interest-group leaders with some frequency. President Johnson made one of the largest displays of this activity early in his administration, as representatives of business, labor, civil rights groups, and spokesmen for such policy areas as medicine and education all found their way to the White House.[15] If a call comes that a key figure such as Roger Blough (head of U.S. Steel) wants to see the President—as when the steel price increase was about to be announced in April 1962—a meeting is quickly arranged.

Presidents may cultivate a group of individuals with whom they can interact on a fairly informal basis. These relationships range from privileged access to genuine personal friendships. Several members of the press corps, such as Charles Bartlett, enjoyed this status with John Kennedy. President Johnson maintained a close relationship with Abe Fortas, in the days when Fortas was a Washington lawyer. (This pattern of access was so persistent that Johnson had difficulty redefining the Fortas role after Fortas was appointed to the Supreme Court.) President Nixon enjoyed close friendships with two Eastern businessmen he had known in his New York days, Robert Abplanalp and Beebe Rebozo.

In varying degrees, personal friends have an opportunity for providing outside advice and for influencing presidential thinking in relaxed atmospheres. Often, however, the outsider is enjoyed primarily because his company helps the president enjoy nonpolitical activities. It is doubtful, in the age of highly information-oriented policy making, that one will again find an outsider playing a role such as that of Colonel House with Woodrow Wilson. House actually had a major impact on foreign policy for several years, even though he remained a private citizen.[16]

Presidential families and especially their wives also occasionally constitute a sounding board for presidential ideas. Raising young adults (a responsibility Johnson, Nixon, and Ford all faced while in the White House) can on occasion produce exposure to ideas and problems of the young. These may not be very representative, but they can provide stimulus from a noninstitutionalized source.

First ladies engage in differing roles. In some instances, their husbands welcome a chance to discuss subjects unrelated to politics and simply enjoy the comforts of family. Cultural topics sometimes provided diversion for John Kennedy. Eleanor Roosevelt may well long remain the most unique example of a first lady who in fact occupied a significant role as part of the presidential staff.[17] More recently, Lady Byrd Johnson was the most politicized of the first ladies. Some even gave her significant credit for helping restrain some of her husband's more compulsive instincts.[18]

There are tremendous differences in presidential uses of information sources. Personality factors are extremely important not only in determining how many individuals see the president, but the effectiveness of that interaction. President Roosevelt's willingness while in office to allow as many as 100 different individuals to see him, without requiring that their visit or topic be "cleared," may well continue to be the exceptional case. President Nixon may well remain the extreme case in terms of reluctance for personal contact. Nixon was so formal in interpersonal relations that he actually at points had aides prepare not only suggested agendas but suggested small talk to use when he received visitors. A president who sticks doggedly to an agenda may well not gain extra bits of information which can be most useful.[19] Other differences in recent practices, and their strengths and weaknesses, emerge as one looks at the advisory role and the question of competition more directly.

Advisers, Groups—and Groupthink

Policy advisers at points have very important influences in the development of presidential policy ideas and commitments. The periodic major changes in policy positions which do come from the Presidency are most assuredly not conceived in a vacuum. The tugging and pulling among advisers for influential positions and victory for their policy ideas is often intense.

Advisers do also frequently circulate papers among themselves and attend meetings to "coordinate" various matters with precious little real impact. The decline in status and the ultimate elimination of the Office of Science and Technology in the Nixon Administration is a good example of staff impotence. The science advisers were suspect because of the number of holdovers from the Johnson Administration, and Nixon gradually found it more convenient to simply bypass that office. Ultimately, the office was actually abolished, in the reorganization which began following the 1972 election.

Several factors can facilitate the success of major advisers. It is often necessary to win a battle for presidential attention. This is less true in some of the foreign policy situations than in those involving choices among domestic issues. The staffer must also convince the president that he has ideas which are of genuine usefulness. In this respect, economic advisers may have an advantage over advisers in other domestic areas; it does not take much imagination for a president to realize that he needs help when the economy is in trouble. An adviser also needs to convince the president that he is loyal and that he shares key values which the president deems important. Where the area of expertise is itself difficult for the president, the sense of shared values can be particularly crucial. Especially for a president who dislikes interpersonal conflict, an aide's stature may also be enhanced if a president senses that the aide can fend off various opponents to a policy, thus sparing the president personal involvement.

The roles of Walter Heller, Daniel Moynihan, and Clark Clifford illustrate ways in which advisers can have a decided impact on presidential decisions. As Kennedy's chairman of the Council of Economic Advisers, Walter Heller played an important role both in educating Kennedy to economic policy issues in general and promoting Kennedy's interest in tax cuts as a means of stimulating the economy. Given the stagnant economy which Kennedy inherited and his fairly ambitious goals, the situation was ripe for an economic adviser to gain access. Heller had had previous experience in translating economic issues for the layman, having advised Orville Freeman in his days as governor of Minnesota. Accounts of the Heller-Kennedy relationship have thus frequently talked of the importance of the economist's role in altering Kennedy's economic orientations.[20]

Daniel Moynihan's role was perhaps more unusual.[21] As an experienced Washington policy adviser from Democratic administrations, Moynihan was able to gain Nixon's attention with both telling arguments and a sense of the factors which would be influential with Nixon. Institutionally, he initially functioned in 1969 as head of Nixon's Urban Council. The Nixon commitment to the family assistance plan in 1969, with features comparable in some respects to a guaranteed income, was in the eyes of many a most surprising step for the Nixon Presidency. A major influence can be attributed to an adviser who gained access to the President and explained family assistance in terms of a method of avoiding welfare dependency—thus enabling Nixon to see family assistance as in keeping with his own commitment to the work ethic.

Turning to foreign policy, Clark Clifford's role with Lyndon Johnson in the spring of 1968 was a striking example of adviser influence. (Clifford at that point served as secretary of defense.)[22] Clifford was not the first adviser to develop a questioning stand on the issue of how extensively military requests should be granted in pursuing the Vietnam War. George Ball, Robert McNamara, and several others had taken a questioning view. Johnson's firm commitment to the view that he must persevere on Vietnam had simply made earlier efforts hopeless.

Clifford was brought to the Defense Department in the wake of McNamara's Johnson-induced departure to the World Bank, with Johnson anticipating that a long-trusted friend could be counted on to aid in holding a firm line against internal staff dissidents on the Vietnam issue. Clifford's actual role proved to be very different. In the wake of the Tet offensive in early 1968 and its shattering impact on Administration views held through 1967 that the war was being won, Clifford engaged in a substantial review of the Vietnam War. Clifford himself became increasingly skeptical of the wisdom of continuing with periodic increases in troops. By mid-March, he was emphatically against the request from General Westmoreland for 200,000 additional troops. This position obviously did not endear Clifford to Johnson; by summer his access was in fact restricted. Townsend Hoopes (himself an important civilian working in the Defense Department against the honoring of that request) nonetheless gives Clifford a key role in influencing Johnson to resist the military. Some combination of the dissent which was focused around Clifford and the startling showing of Senator McCarthy in the New Hampshire primary did, ultimately, produce a decision on Johnson's part by the end of the month both to resist the military and renew the bombing halt. (In the dramatic speech announcing that decision, Johnson also declared his decision not to run for another term in 1968.)

All three advisers were well informed on their respective policy issues. They had also had considerable skill in advising roles. Heller was aided by Kennedy's sense that economic issues offered his Administration new potential, Moynihan was aided by his ability to sense the appeals needed to reach Nixon, and Clifford was aided by the crush of events which was forcing a reappraisal by Johnson of his crumbling Vietnam position. These roles are nonetheless delicate, as was perhaps most apparent in Clifford's case. The role of bringing bad news to a committed president is never an easy one. An influential adviser may not find his position comfortable and lasting, but he can have an important impact on presidential thinking.

A substantial amount of presidential information-gathering and, at points, decision-making takes place in group situations. As a result, the limitations as well as the strengths of group meetings emerge. Cabinet meetings and their limitations have been most frequently discussed, but the problems of group meetings are apparent in other contexts as well.

The overwhelming conclusion of presidential observers is that cabinet meetings are neither a particularly effective communication device nor very often an actual decision-making body. Abe Fortas expressed a doubt that any really important decisions had been reached in cabinet meetings in many years.[23] John Kennedy even left the cabinet meetings on occasion for what he considered to be more important matters. Extensive efforts to utilize the cabinet may occur, as with Eisenhower, but the results are generally disappointing.

Problems with cabinet meetings are numerous.[24] A president may not trust the individuals who are in attendance. Press leaks are frequent, and a president will often feel more secure in dealing with his hand-picked key staff aides. Members of the cabinet are often reluctant to discuss matters which are difficult for them. They are after all in competition for funds with the other men around the table and are reticent to discuss their own difficulties. As a result, tangents or highly generalized formulations often receive primary attention. The sheer size of the cabinet meetings, which, with several persons besides department heads being given cabinet status, often numbers over 20, tends to make close dialogue difficult. Cabinet meetings of this size, just like those of student councils, academic faculty, and any other group, can easily become unwieldy.

Cabinet meetings also raise difficult issues involving specialization of knowledge. Henry Fairlie makes the valuable observation that a president may become overly involved with decision making by specialized groups and thereby miss the useful skepticism which can come from those who lack tremendous expertise but have good insight into problems.[25] He sees aspects of this in Kennedy's tendency to rely upon functional groups rather than the cabinet. It nonetheless remains true that cabinet meetings can involve rather lengthy dialogues by individuals who want to apply rather strained analogies to a variety of situations. Kennedy cabinet members wondered at points, for example, how applicable some of the analogies drawn by Anthony Celebreeze from his experiences as mayor of Cleveland were when used for a wide variety of policy interpretations.

Cabinet meetings, as well as other group meetings, are also subject all too frequently to the devastating impact of what Irving Janis has labeled "groupthink." Looking at presidential information systems from the standpoint of a group psychologist, Janis argued that there are many situations in which important information is not pursued because of the tendency for group meetings to emphasize the importance of group loyalties. Janis writes, "The more amiability and esprit de corps among the members of a policy-making in-group, the greater is the danger that independent critical thinking will be replaced by groupthink, which is likely to result in irrational and dehumanizing actions directed against out-groups."[26]

Janis developed his concern for groupthink as he began examining presidential decisions such as the Bay of Pigs invasion of Cuba, approved by President Kennedy in early 1961. The key question was how individuals of substantial intelligence (Ph.D.'s, Harvard deans, etc.) could approve a decision which allowed major questionable assumptions to go unexplored. As Arthur Schlesinger, Jr. has subsequently written, even a close look at a map of the route which escaping troops would have to follow raises serious questions regarding the assumption that a defeat would not be disastrous. The belated recognition by President Kennedy that his Administration had approved American support of the Cuban invasion, in the wake of its disastrous defeat, revealed a serious early debacle in his Presidency.

The view which Janis develops does not emphasize a "yes man" staff orientation such as one finds depicted in Reedy's *Twilight of the Presidency*. Rather, one finds a sense of loyalty to the team which discourages the raising of seemingly hostile or skeptical questions. This sense of loyalty is seen as being reinforced by the sense of a common enemy which the group must oppose. As a result, individuals who have skepticism about aspects of an emerging plan will not express those views in group discussion.

It is tempting to view aspects of the Nixon Presidency in a similar context. Consider, for example, the March 30, 1972 meeting at Key Biscayne (with Mitchell, Magruder, and La Rue present) where the final commitment of $250,000 for Liddy's political espionage was apparently made.[27] The sense on the part of innumerable figures in the Watergate scandals of a common enemy has been most apparent. One could hardly be more specific about a sense of being opposed by enemies than actually making a list of those considered to be hostile! In terms of the Magruder testimony, one sees a decision of momentous import made at the end of a busy day and not taken very seriously. Furthermore, the picture one gets is that reservations were felt, but no members of the group took a strong stand in demanding that possible negative implications be explored.

It is easy for individuals to magnify the degree of skepticism they felt about a decision at the time it was made when the decision subsequently turns out to be a bad one. This is a difficulty with the Janis analysis, as he uses postdecision statements by participants for his interpretation. Even when legal sanctions are not a possible result of their statements, presidential aides have a tendency to justify their own positions by magnifying aspects of their roles. The Janis concept is nevertheless a useful one in helping explain sources of miscalculation.

Groupthink, as seen by Janis, is not inevitable. He devotes an entire chapter to ways in which the tendencies of groupthink to inhibit completeness of discussion can be reduced. President Kennedy demonstrated one important lesson. After having been served badly by the decision process leading to the Bay of Pigs invasion, Kennedy was very conscious during the deliberations leading to the American responses in the Cuban missle crisis of 1962 to avoid similar pitfalls.[28] One of his strategies during the fateful 13 days of deliberation was to absent himself periodically from the discussion in order to reduce chances of a premature focusing on what would seem to be the preferred position in Kennedy's mind. Encouragement of dissent among advisers by a president can be helpful. Some have argued that Kennedy himself was rather aggressive in his decisions in that process, particularly in not considering the trade for outmoded American bases in Turkey. The final results of Kennedy's decision process need not be defended, however, to argue that he was quite successful in avoiding miscalculation as a result of the groupthink phenomenon.

The question of how one obtains thoroughness in group deliberations is a recurring issue in any administration. A frequently advocated solution to the information problem in both groups and individual advising situations is for the president to employ a competitive staff process. That approach deserves specific consideration.

Should the President Encourage Staff Competition?

Will Sparks, a Johnson speechwriter, has vividly illustrated the concern for competition in staff relationships.[29] A president, argues Sparks, should watch his aides and the flow of traffic around his office carefully. If a given individual seems to be fading from view, and a little checking indicates that he is doing inconsequential background studies, the president should then praise him to a White House reporter with a seemingly offhand reference to the staffer's fine contribution. With this reference duly reported as a recent scoop, the aide will push his position, and others will listen to him more. Then, to cut the aide back down to manageable size, the president should privately criticize him for talking so much to the press. The net result: The president avoids the creation of a firm pecking order and overconfidence on the part of the staff.

The most widely expressed statement of the importance of staff competition is in Richard Neustadt's *Presidential Power*.[30] For Neustadt, the key to a president's avoiding mistakes based upon lack of information is to maintain a staff process which allows a flow of key information upward to the ears of the president himself. To maintain a competitive process, Neustadt believes the president should avoid assigning fixed jurisdictions. By having more than one person report individually on a topic, the president can create an incentive for individuals to report first and extensively; they are never entirely sure what slant someone else may have given.

There has been wide variation in the degree of competition maintained in presidential advising operations. Norman Thomas, writing before the Watergate-generated picture of the Nixon Presidency, categorized the recent administrations in terms of the degree of formality in staff arrangements. Presidents were ranked from the most to the least formal as follows: Eisenhower, Nixon, Truman, Johnson, Kennedy, Roosevelt.[31] It was easier to identify the extremes, with the ranking of Truman and Johnson in the middle presenting some difficulties.

The highly useful recent study by Richard Johnson, *Managing the White House,* also categorizes recent administrations.[32] Johnson develops three basic patterns: formalistic, competitive, and collegial. The formalistic style is seen predominating for Eisenhower and Nixon. In that process, there is an emphasis on delegation and use of a key aide as, in effect, chief of staff. Frequent references by White House staffers in the Nixon years to the effect that H. R. Haldeman "ran the place" were a likely indication that he fulfilled that role. Along with a formal hierarchy and extensive delegation, the formalistic approach tends to emphasize careful staff work and staff reports in designated areas of responsibility. The competitive process is in turn best illustrated by the Roosevelt staff. Few jurisdictions were fixed, and a large number of individuals reported to the President on various topics. The collegial approach is seen as exemplified only by the Kennedy Presidency. Its essentially compromise features will be discussed shortly. Following the Johnson analysis substantially, staff operations can be considered in terms of their costs and benefits.

Qualifications of the view that staff relationships should overwhelmingly stress competition have been growing. Several authors have noted that a loosely structured, competitive process is less well suited for foreign policy matters.[33] In this regard, it must be emphasized that Roosevelt's success with the competitive process was achieved primarily during the period prior to World War II, during which the major issues were domestic.[34] Roosevelt's staff system has received a less favorable review in its adaptation to foreign policy matters.

The sheer size of the federal government today also raises questions about the applicability of the competitive model. Rather than a staff of about 50 as in Roosevelt's day, the president now deals with a staff of over 500, plus an extensive Executive Office of several thousand. In turn, the federal government is now responsible for a budget of over $300 billion, whereas the budgets of the 1930s were well under $10 billion. The problem of scale is enormous. A president who seems to distrust everyone and is continually double-checking, as Neustadt seems to be suggesting he should do, is very quickly going to run out of time for meeting his various responsibilities.

The competitive approach also can create strains on the staff. Staffs presumably exist to best serve the president, but a chief executive must be sensitive to the impact of undue insecurity on staff morale and rates of turnover. The pressures which President Johnson's personal involvement in so many issues created are the best recent example of staff strain: Johnson was plagued with staff turnover.

The information process may also be incomplete if there is a constant tendency to emphasize political feasibility at the expense of searching through a complete set of policy alternatives. The emphasis in a competitive staff is on coalitions and power relationships. As a result, there is less incentive for the more careful reviews. Both a president and his staff can be so busy counting votes in Congress, and for the next election, that they simply do not take the time to probe the larger picture of policy alternatives in which they operate. This problem contrasts with one of the key benefits in the alternative formalistic approach.

There are some benefits surrounding the formalistic approach. Staffs and the president may tend to focus on a broader range of alterantives than if the competitive approach were stressed, and the president himself tends to have more time for considering those alternatives. The focus is often on trying to find the "correct" answer among alternatives, and not immediately raising questions of political feasibility. Nixon's staff apparatus is most illustrative on this point. He was able to develop a number of impressive new foreign policy moves. It will take time to digest the wisdom of some of those steps, yet whatever the final judgment, they must be related to his staff system. The formalistic approach did allow for a consideration of a number of major new foreign policy moves.

The costs of the formalistic approach are also most apparent. The traditional argument has been that the president is apt not to gain bits of political information which are useful, and that he may get involved with issues too late because of the delegated nature of his operations and the lack of staff members informing on each other, in effect. The Eisenhower cases, such as his finding out about serious conflict-of-interest issues in his Bureau of the Budget regarding the Dixon-Yates contract only when the information was revealed by the opposing party in Congress, have been overshadowed by more recent events.[35]

President Nixon showed very painfully the problems with a formalistic staff. Information about some of the political activities going on in his staff was screened from him. This point obviously must be made carefully. Nixon sought for months to hide behind the excuse of total ignorance, when in fact he was orchestrating the cover-up activities with considerable knowledge of what had been going on. Yet the record which unfolded in the transcripts also showed both presidential surprise and outrage when he initially became aware of the close tie between his White House and the break-in at the Democratic National Headquarters.[36] Nixon's staff operation, in short, was such that one would expect the President to be uninformed on a variety of specific bits of political information.

More generally, one would also expect the formalistic operation to lead to decisions being made without adequate understanding of likely public responses. This was very uniquely the Nixon pattern. The magnitude of public sentiment was seriously misjudged on such issues as the invasion of Cambodia in May, 1970, his choices of Supreme Court nominees, and then his whole series of attempts at containing the "Watergate matter."

The Nixon case is obviously extreme in many matters. Part of the problem with his decision processes resulted from his own personality and could not easily be corrected with any staff system. Although extreme, the nature of his staff limitations are nonetheless characteristic of the formal approach. A president is apt to interact with too few people having a good "political sense." He also may interact with too few people in general, thus increasing the likelihood that a few aides will predominate in shaping his perception of likely public responses.

Advantages of an effective use of the competitive approach are again evident from the problems confronting Nixon and Eisenhower, with their formal approach. Yet the restraints of time make the competitive model difficult to sustain fully, and there may be too little quest for new alternatives and solutions. Compromises are necessary, and Richard Johnson feels that the collegial approach as manifested in the Kennedy Presidency is one possible alternative.

In the collegial approach, there is not a single "chief of staff," and individuals are rotated in some of their assignments. The president seeks to manage differing groups of advisers for work on specific problems. Conflict is promoted in the group activities, with an effort toward encouraging a wide range of alternatives for consideration. The handling of the Cuban missile crisis illustrates this thrust. Rather than simply relying upon those in fixed positions in the national security apparatus, as he had in the Bay of Pigs fiasco, Kennedy put together an executive committee to specifically confront the problem of responding to the Russian missiles in Cuba.

The aim of the collegial approach is both to achieve workable solutions and also to maintain the review of a variety of alternatives. With an astute president in charge, this can be an effective system. The demands on him are nonetheless awesome. Not only is this more time consuming than dealing with a fixed hierarchy and a pattern of routine delegation, but it also requires a high level of presidential skill in managing the personalities on his staff. Because staffs are substantially influenced by both the skills and limitations of the president, it is clearly not a compromise which all occupants of the Oval Office can employ.

The question of what staff system to promote in a given Presidency thus remains somewhat illusive. Staffs inevitably reflect presidential personality. The importance of the personality factor was forcefully revealed in the frequent interpretation that Richard Nixon sought, even in the wake of the Watergate scandals and the loss in April 1973 of his key aides, to reestablish his formalistic approach with a new cast of characters. Richard Johnson's conclusion is a sensible one: Whatever the tendencies in staff patterns, there should be a sensitivity on the part of the president to the likely negative results, and he should make period efforts toward compensating action. A highly competitive staff can profit from an effort at overall policy review, and a highly formalistic operation can profit from at least some presidential actions which are outside the prevailing pattern. The possibility of more basic surgery must also arise and is considered here in the context of the emerging reform agenda. Given recent staff operations, the seriousness of the isolation issue demands analysis.

Dimensions of Presidential Isolation

Any political system is vulnerable to a lack of leader awareness of mass preferences and their intensities. Furthermore, any set of leaders within the American system is vulnerable to this difficulty. Basic tensions surround both the manner in which messages are submitted to leaders and the way in which they are received. Those who participate politically in various ways are not representative of a cross section of the electorate. Letter writers, interest-group members, and even White House pickets generally come from concentrations within the electorate which have higher social status, greater degrees of education, and a higher sense of political efficacy than the general public.[37] Even presidential voting itself leaves out a substantial segment of the electorate, as 40 percent or more of the eligible voters may not find their way to the voting booth in presidential elections. A president and his staff who systematically sift through the various messages which individuals write get a distorted view if these are taken as representative of the entire population. Public opinion polls, despite their key limitation of not tapping opinion in the context of discussion and debate, do provide somewhat more representative information.

The task of maintaining adequate knowledge of public opinion is further complicated by the manner in which messages are filtered through staff operations and are received in the Oval Office. Presidents are not alone in their tendency to perceive events and opinions through a filter which involves their own values and preferences. Analysis of members of Congress has shown a comparable tendency for different individuals to see the same set of events and opinions differently.[38] This point deserves emphasis, given the tendency in some discussions to assume that presidential vulnerability to inadequate information somehow necessarily signifies greater capacities for accurate perception in the legislative branch. In reducing the myth of an omnipotent president, it is essential to avoid romanticizing Congress. What can be said specifically, then, about the common charge among contemporary skeptics that the modern president has become increasingly isolated?

The president does indeed have at his disposal a tremendous amount of factual data. These sources have been reviewed, including polls, statistical analyses of various kinds, and the outpourings of analytic staffs in major policy areas. In a lifetime in politics, each of the recent Presidents has acquired a substantial reservoir of knowledge about the nation. Kennedy was an avid reader, in addition having traveled extensively. Johnson was highly intelligent and liked to gobble up information. Nixon impressed such observers as Theodore White with his extensive knowledge of aspects of American life. Presidents have traveled the country; they have talked with people from all regions; they will generally have developed a substantial base of factual information.

There are nonetheless several respects in which isolation does occur. Presidents lack the common experiences of most Americans. They read of price increases, but do not usually have to worry about food bills. They read of problems with mortgages, but do not have to confront these problems directly (unless they continue to invest in real estate!) They jet around the country without having to experience the abandonment of vacation plans because of increased air rates. In terms of factors which produce changes in views, presidents are confronted with data, far more than emotionally wrenching experiences.

It is not surprising that the issue of presidential isolation has been raised at a time when American values have become more uncertain. Presidents Johnson and Nixon were in their sixties when in the White House, and their early political socialization occurred during vastly different times. Woodrow Wilson and the problems of World War I were salient in their boyhoods, and a simple and optimistic view of America and the world prevailed far more than in recent times. Age does not preclude changes in attitudes. There have been, among political executives around the globe, remarkable instances of elderly leaders seizing essentially new or "young" ideas and providing strong leadership. Major European leaders including both Charles de Gaulle and Konrad Adenauer served at ages making Johnson and Nixon seem mere youngsters. Yet a rapid change in values does intensify the problem of elderly leaders who are out of touch with the emerging concerns of the nation.

The question of presidential isolation becomes clearer as one specifies the type of information which may be missing. Four basic categories are involved. First, a president may lack knowledge of policy consequences or alternatives, including the consequences of no action. Kennedy's information system as it operated in the approval of the Bay of Pigs landing was clearly an example of this failure. The full implications of the perilous position the invaders would likely be in was simply never made clear.

Two types of missing information relate to political relationships. There may be an inadequate assessment of the degree of political support for a particular alternative. Decisions which produce a firestorm of public response or, less dramatically, simply rejection, are indicative of communication failures surrounding the support question. Politically necessary information may also be lacking about specific individuals and situations which subsequently prove embarrassing for a president. Conflict of interest questions often arise in this category.

Finally, presidents may simply be unaware of the specifics, or the importance, of actions being taken by their staffs. The frequent pattern is that information is simply not brought to the attention of the president. Staffers seem all too often to make commitments, or to imply that a given step is preferred by the president, when he is not even aware of their actions. The restricted nature of his own agenda makes this to some degree an inevitable phenomena.

It is useful to review the factors which can contribute to each of the information gaps. These relate to presidential personalities and to the nature of the staff system. Absence of a consideration of alternatives and consequences may be the product of a groupthink orientation among advisers, as described by Janis. A highly informal process with an emphasis on politically feasible solutions may also reduce the likelihood that alternatives and possible consequences will be adequately explored.

Poor judgments as to levels of political support can be fostered by both staff operations and the general environment of the White House. It is in these calculations that the overly comfortable atmosphere of the White House can be detrimental. A major argument of Reedy's *Twilight of the Presidency* is that the problem of inadequate political sense grows while a president is in office.[39] Selectively drawn cases do indicate a tendency for longevity in office to be associated with a growing tendency to miscalculate. Even a President such as Roosevelt, who sought to maintain a staff system which would give him good political information, badly miscalculated with his effort at expanding the Supreme Court in 1937. This relationship requires additional analysis. In part, there is the tendency for incumbents to be reelected by large margins, margins which artifically magnify any real electoral commitment to the president's next policy moves, simply because of the great advantages going to the incumbent in an election. Staff turnover may also contribute, since the president will be surrounded increasingly by individuals who did not know him when he was just a Harry, Dick, or Jerry, but who instead rose in the maze of staff politics.[40]

Both poor judgments and the lack of politically sensitive information are also, as we have seen, related to personalities and staff systems. A president who does not like informal conversation and an adversary staff process can easily fall victim to an inadequate exposure to the specific information about people and situations which might prevent his looking bad later. Periodic and embarrassing revelations in the press, Congress, and the opposing party testify to the impact of staff and personality.

Ultimately, any president is also isolated in the sense that he is not aware of some activities in his own Presidency. This can involve both potential policy issues and specific actions of individuals. Given the scope of national policy matters today, there is simply no way for either the best of presidential personalities or an "ideal" compromise on staff procedures to avoid aspects of this problem. In some degree, any president is, in that sense, isolated.

Summary

It is easy to overstate the problem of presidential isolation when the decisions which are being reached by the president are counter to those the observer prefers. In some situations, the president may simply be reaching conclusions one opposes after operating an extensive information process. The issue is then not directly one of isolation, but of either the basic values the incumbent possesses or his correct assessment of political support for various alternatives. Similarly, the crush of events in specific situations may mean that no information system and no president can arrive at very satisfying answers. Recent economic issues have revealed aspects of this problem. The Ford Presidency promised an interesting experiment, in that there were initially some attempts at operating in a less isolated manner, and yet the economic developments of his first months in office were surely anything but reassuring.

At points, the issue of presidential isolation is significantly one of electoral confidence as well as policy effectiveness. Even if major new policy moves are not forthcoming, it can be reassuring to have the president get out from behind the gates on occasion. Lyndon Johnson by 1968 and Richard Nixon by 1974 substantially confined their ventures from the White House to either military bases or other carefully selected, friendly audiences. Such a closed presidential environment can hardly be reassuring to major segments of the electorate.

It is not surprising to find the issue of presidential isolation frequently raised in foreign policy contexts. In the foreign policy roles, the president has had the greater opportunity for both molding his own information system and for reaching final decisions. The question of presidential isolation is closely related to the nature of the policy roles being performed. It is essential now to explore those roles directly.

NOTES

[1] Morton Halperin, *The Foreign Policy Bureaucracy*, Washington, Brookings, 1974, pp. 101–104.

[2] Theodore C. Sorenson, *Decision-Making in the White House*, New York, Columbia University Press, 1963.

[3] Richard E. Neustadt, *Presidential Power: The Politics of Leadership*, New York, Wiley, 1960, p. 28.

[4] Anthony Downs, "The Issue-Attention Cycle and Improving Our Environment," Chicago, February 1971. Mimeographed.

[5] Nixon's Southern strategy has been discussed in numerous sources. On educational matters, see Leon Panetta and Peter Gall, *Bring Us Together*, Philadelphia, Lippincott, 1971. For a more general discussion, see Reg Murphy and Hal Gulliver, *The Southern Strategy*, New York, Scribner, 1971.

[6] John H. Kessel, "The Parameters of Presidential Politics," paper delivered at the 1972 annual meeting of the American Political Science Association, Washington, D.C., September 5–9, 1972, p. 9.

[7] James L. Sundquist, *Politics and Policy: The Eisenhower, Kennedy, and Johnson Years*, Washington, D.C., Brookings, 1968, chap. 9.

[8] For an account emphasizing political concerns, see Jack Raymond, *Power at the Pentagon*, New York, Harper & Row, 1964. For an account minimizing the number of political concerns, see Morton J. Peck and Frederic M. Scherer, *The Weapons Acquisition Process: An Economic Analysis*, Boston, Harvard Business School, 1962.

[9] See Grant McConnell, *Steel and the Presidency, 1962*, New York, Norton, 1963.

[10] Howard E. McCurdy, "The Physical Manifestations of an Expanding Presidency: A Tour of the White House and Executive Offices," paper delivered at the 1974 annual meeting of the American Political Science Association, Chicago, Ill., August 29–September 2, 1974, p. 14.

[11] Theodore C. Sorenson, *Kennedy*, New York, Harper & Row, 1965, p. 316.

[12] A useful account of Johnson's information channels is contained in George Christian, *The President Steps Down*, New York, Macmillan, 1970, chap. 1.

[13] A minor furor was created by the publication of Nixon's daily digest. See the *National Journal*, January 26, 1974, pp. 131–134, for a sample of the daily digest.

[14] One major study of those who participate actively in politics is Lester Milbrath, *Political Paticipation*, Chicago, Rand McNally, 1965. On letter writing, see Leila Sussman, "Mass Political Letter Writing in America: The Growth of an Institution," *Public Opinion Quarterly*, Summer 1959, pp. 203–212.

[15] President Johnson discusses the interest-group meetings in *The Vantagepoint*, New York, Holt, Rinehart & Winston, 1971, p. 29.

[16] On the uniqueness of the role played by Colonel House, see Alexander L. and Juliette L. George, *Woodrow Wilson and Colonel House*, New York, Day, 1956.

[17] The sections dealing with the White House years are most informative in Joseph Lash, *Eleanor and Franklin*, New York, New American Library, 1973.

[18] See Louis Heren, *No Hail, No Farewell*, New York, Harper & Row, 1970, pp. 204–205.

[19] The formality of Nixon's interpersonal relations is discussed in Richard Whalen, *Catch the Falling Flag*, Boston, Houghton Mifflin, 1972, p. 255.

[20] On the Heller-Kennedy relationship, see Edward S. Flash, Jr., *Economic Advice and Presidential Leadership: The Council of Economic Advisers*, New York, Columbia University Press, 1965, chaps. 6–8.

[21] On Moynihan's role, see Daniel P. Moynihan, *The Politics of a Guaranteed Income*, New York, Vintage, 1973.

[22] The Clifford role is discussed in Townsend Hoopes, *The Limits of Intervention*, New York, McKay, 1965; and David Halberstam, *The Best and the Brightest*, New York, Random House, 1969.

[23] Remarks by Abe Fortas in Emmet John Hughes, *The Living Presidency*, New York, Coward-McCann & Geoghegan, 1972, p. 335.

[24] The tendency for cabinet members to be replaced by staff advisers is discussed by Bill Moyers and Hugh Sidey, "The White House Staff vs. the Cabinet," *Washington Monthly*, February 1969, pp. 3–17. On cabinet meetings generally, see Richard R. Fenno, *The President's Cabinet*, New York, Vintage, 1959, chaps. 3, 4.

[25] Henry Fairlie, *The Kennedy Promise: The Politics of Expectation*, Garden City, N.Y., Doubleday, 1973.

[26] Irving L. Janis, *Victims of Groupthink*, Boston, Houghton Mifflin, 1973, p. 13.

[27] See the testimony by Jeb Stuart Magruder before the Ervin Committee, as reported in *The Watergate Hearings: Break-in and Cover-up*, New York, Bantam, 1973, pp. 157–159.

[28] The most extensive account of the decision process leading to the blockade is Graham Allison, *Essence of Decision*, Boston, Little, Brown, 1971.

[29] Will Sparks, *Who Talked to the President Last?* New York, Norton, 1971, p. 120.

[30] Richard E. Neustadt, *Presidential Power: The Politics of Leadership,* New York, Wiley, 1960, especially chap. 7.

[31] Norman S. Thomas, "Presidential Advice and Information: Policy and Program Formation," *Law and Contemporary Problems,* Summer 1970, p. 554.

[32] Richard T. Johnson, *Managing the White House,* New York, Harper & Row, 1974.

[33] Louis Koenig, *The Chief Executive,* New York, Harcourt Brace Jovanovich, 1964, chap. 9.

[34] The comparison between the evaluation of Roosevelt by James MacGregor Burns in *Roosevelt: The Lion and the Fox,* New York, Harcourt Brace Jovanovich, 1956, and in *Roosevelt: Soldier of Freedom,* New York, Harcourt Brace Jovanovich, 1970, is striking. The domestic staff operations receive decidedly higher evaluations.

[35] In the Eisenhower case a serious conflict of interest in the awarding of the Dixon-Yates contract was first revealed by the Democrats.

[36] For President Nixon's response, see Carl Bernstein and Bob Woodward, *All the President's Men,* New York, Warner Paperback Library, 1975, pp. 138–139.

[37] On the selective nature of constituent messages, see Leila A. Sussman, "FDR and the White House Mail," *Public Opinion Quarterly,* Spring 1956, pp. 14–16.

[38] See Louis Dexter, "The Representative and His District," in *New Perspectives on the House of Representatives,* ed. by Robert Peabody and Nelson Polsby, Chicago, Rand McNally, 1969, chap. 1.

[39] George E. Reedy, *The Twilight of the Presidency,* New York, Mentor, 1970, chap. 7.

[40] Staff turnover is rapid. Eisenhower's staff was the most durable. Johnson had a high turnover. Overall, about half of a staff will serve from 13 to 36 months. Patricia S. Florestano, "The White House Staff: Bibliographical Study," unpublished manuscript, University of Maryland, pp. 32–33.

Presidential Policy Roles

Presidents and their staffs have widely differing impacts on the actions of the federal government. A president may sign papers over which he has had no real influence in the morning and go on television in the evening to announce a new surprise policy step which his administration has taken. Often, the amount of personal influence the President exercises seems far more extensive than is actually the case. Presidents ratify many decisions made elsewhere, not only by their own staffs, but at points by Congress, the bureaucracy, and interested participants. It is thus necessary to consider the nature of presidential policy roles and how they can be interpreted, prior to examining policy responsibilities directly.

Differing Policy Roles

Both presidents as individuals and the institution of the Presidency perform a variety of policy roles. It is useful to view these roles on a continuum from minimum to maximum influence on a given policy. The major roles are ratifying the decisions of others, altering bargaining outcomes, mobilizing, and taking fait accompli action.[1] At important points, there are major differences between the influence of the president as an individual and the impact of the institution of the Presidency. Both these differences and the characteristics of each role become apparent in reviewing major cases and examples.

Ratifying the Decisions of Others

Presidents very often engage in the ratification of decisions made by others. This is an inevitable consequence of the range of issues with which incumbents have some involvement. Bills are signed with scant knowledge of their content, let alone any involvement in their development. Budgets are approved with only the most limited knowledge of the actual operations of an agency. Appointments may be made without the president's having known, or even met, the newly named individual. Because these actions often come flowing out in news briefings, it is fairly easy to get an impression of a larger amount of presidential activity than actually takes place.

Ratification is often of decisions made by one's own staff. Staffers often speak of the tendency to bring the president the "hard cases." This has sometimes been done as an effort at minimizing public awareness of the staff role. Yet the staff decision as to what constitutes a "hard case" screens out many matters of some significance.

Ratification may also come in response to agreements or solutions worked out in the bureaucracy, in Congress, and among various interests and elites. Where the ratification comes in response to a decision in Congress, the president signs the bill and often tends to take credit even if he really had little or nothing to do with its passage.

Presidential acceptance of practices in which policies are worked out by others is nicely illustrated by the cigarette advertising controversy. Support for a health warning on cigarette packages emerged in 1965 within Congress as part of the growing consumer movement. Interest in having the Food and Drug Administration take a stronger stand gained some support. The Tobacco Institute in turn mobilized its lobbying muscle, led by ex-Senator Clements. President Johnson had ample opportunity to enter the conflict, but chose not to. As A. Lee Fritschler states in his fine case study, "The disparity of views and even the bickering between agencies was allowed to exist up to and through congressional hearings in 1965. President Johnson made no attempt to coordinate agency programs although he had the administrative mechanism to do so."[2] A bill was ultimately passed in Congress which in effect insured that a tougher posture would not be taken by the Food and Drug Administration. President Johnson then quietly signed the bill despite some last-minute efforts at promoting a veto on the part of consumer-minded legislators. The President had most emphatically ratified a policy step resulting from the actions of others.

The ratification role is thus one of minimal influence for the president but not necessarily of minimal role for his staff. Staffs will generally engage in extensive efforts at supervising and implementing various policies which have significant consequences, even though such implementation has not been debated in the context of inherent policy change. The frequent tendency to avoid policy questions in American politics by simply leaving issues to administrative discretion can easily magnify the importance of the actions taken in the name of supervising various policies.

Altering Bargaining Outcomes

Presidents do at points interject themselves into a bargaining process by influencing choices between policy options which are festering in their Presidency, or by working to move otherwise stalemated bargaining processes. This thrust can come in the president's own staff, or in policy-making activities including the bureaucracy, key interests, and Congress.

President Johnson provided a good example of this role (and some aspects of the mobilizing role) in the posture he took regarding federal aid to education in 1965.[3] Various forms of aid to education had been proposed for a long time. The concept had in fact been mentioned by President Hayes, and it was a permanent issue at least since the early Truman days. A combination of racial and Protestant-Catholic cleavages had nonetheless repeatedly stymied a general aid-to-education measure. The South profited handsomely from the aid to impacted areas (school districts near military bases, primarily) and resisted a program which could be tied to an expanded effort at federal desegregation policy. The church-state issue further confused matters, with no single proposal easily winning support of both Protestant and Catholic groups. The result was a frequent stalemate in Congress, as various amendments were used to insure that no majority could be formed. The veto of the House Rules Committee further thwarted Kennedy's efforts toward achieving a major education bill.

Johnson seized the issue in 1965, with his encouragement of a compromise to be worked out in the Office of Education which would be agreeable to the widest possible number of interests. His Commissioner of Education, Francis Keppel, was instrumental in responding to Johnson's plea that a bill be worked out to avoid a church-state fight. As that measure did develop, Johnson closely monitored committee and floor activities to ensure that there would not be the familiar kiss of death amendments which had deadlocked earlier proposals. Johnson was successful, as Congress passed the basic aid to education measure in 1965.

Final budgeting decisions involving key policy alternatives may also thrust the president into a bargaining role. Cutting a budget in keeping with a need for overall reduction can involve the president directly. President Johnson in 1963–1964 exercised this role quite aggressively, for example. Often, presidents are in the ratifying role as they deal with budgetary matters, as we shall see.

Attempts to alter bargaining outcomes are often made by the more active presidents, but can often by unsuccessful. The president may have to act first to convince members of his own staff of the merits of a given solution. More generally, the limitations of a direct bargaining role come back to the problem of autonomous policy-making activity which finds some groups able to resist a president. Thus, in a role analysis similar to the one being used here, John Ries concludes, "Folklore about the decisive man of action, the man at the top who gets things done, and the strong and dynamic leader are preposterous misrepresentations of both the realities and possibilities for executive leadership."[4]

Mobilizing Policy Support

The mobilizing role differs from that of altering bargains in the extent to which the president is involved with promoting interest in an issue and working to gain support for the preferred policy in the electorate and in other decision groups such as Congress. The distinction between mobilizing and altering bargains is not always clear in specific cases. There are nonetheless differences in central tendencies. In altering bargains, a president is often working on perennial issues, often in an inside role either with the bureaucracy or with Congress. In mobilizing, the president takes a larger role in generating initial interest in a particular issue and a larger role in working for both electoral support and approval by other decision makers. Cases are again helpful.

Poverty efforts by both Johnson and Nixon illustrate the mobilizing role. Johnson wanted a program which he could call his own and seized upon the concept of a War on Poverty which had been getting attention in the bureaucracy during the Kennedy Presidency. Rather than accepting the advice of some staffers in favor of a more gradual approach, Johnson decided during his first weeks in office to make a major effort toward alleviating poverty in the country. Johnson clearly did not invent interest in the poverty issue. Various writers, such as Michael Harrington in *The Other America* and Harry Caudill in *Night Comes to the Cumberlands,* had begun to popularize the issue. Task force operations, led by Sargent Shriver, were also in operation as a basis for developing specific plans. The Budget

Bureau and the Council of Economic Advisers also had engaged in some planning. The Johnson thrust was to give the issue top priority, and to engage in an extensive electoral sales appeal for the War on Poverty. As James Sundquist writes, the poverty concern was now central even in State of the Union rhetoric.[5] The War on Poverty legislation became one of the first major pieces of domestic legislation under President Johnson.

The gestation of the Family Assistance Plan in the Nixon Presidency in 1969 was a rather curious, and ultimately unsuccessful, attempt at a mobilizing role.[6] Nixon, just like Johnson, was interested in a major new program which could be identified with his Presidency. There had been no extensive national debate over a guaranteed income approach as he came to office, and the nation was certainly not expecting this step from a Republican President. Nixon could have chosen the more limited role of ratifying a modest change from the status quo. Instead, Nixon encouraged the development of the proposal which ultimately became known as the Family Assistance Plan. The basic innovative feature of that plan was its provision of a modest minimum income figure for all families while also providing increases in compensation as individuals engaged in some employment activity. Rather than being penalized for working, the poor would have an incentive to augment their incomes up to a figure substantially above the minimum guaranteed income.

Nixon took what was for him a very rare step on family assistance; he devoted a televised broadcast to the advocacy of a new domestic plan. The mobilizing attempts were nonetheless ultimately unsuccessful. Supporters were victorious in the House, but the plan got bogged down in the Senate Finance Committee. Nixon strategists were unable to prevent a rash of amendments or to reduce the mounting confusion as to just what would be provided in respective plans. Though unsuccessful, the Nixon effort illustrates the basic characteristics of the mobilizing role. A new solution had been seized and promoted by the President.

President Kennedy also practiced the mobilizing role on occasion. Perhaps the most dramatic instance was his role in the development of the American commitment to landing a man on the moon within the decade of the 1960s. President Kennedy took that step in April 1961, to the surprise of many. There had been a declining interest in space research among some opinion groups prior to the announcement of the Apollo mission and the request for congressional funding approval. Electoral interest, according to a poll taken at that very time, was exceedingly modest. Space research was one of the programs, in fact, which was most frequently mentioned as an area of possible reduction by the electorate.[7]

Congress reacted very quickly to Kennedy's televised address calling for a major new commitment. It was not until 1963–1964 that serious congressional debate about space-program spending began to emerge. Before the decade was over, the American space program had evolved with a high priority attached to reaching the moon with a manned landing, and the nation found itself spending $4 billion to $5 billion annually on the total space program. The ease with which Congress accepted the additional budgeting for NASA made the case partially resemble, in fact, an instance of the fait accompli presidential role.

Taking Fait Accompli Action

There have been a substantial number of fait accompli actions by presidents in recent years. In these cases, there is little prior discussion anywhere in the political system, and once a decision is reached, it is final. President Ford's pardon of Nixon is a classic example. There was not only little discussion of the issue prior to actual announcement, but even a disclaimer of the immediacy of the issue by President Ford. By refusing to let even his press secretary know of the pending decision, President Ford ended up losing Gerald terHorst, who resigned as a result. More fundamentally, the startled nation was faced with a fait accompli action, in that there were no recourses to Ford's action through the normal political process. The sudden dismissal of Special Prosecutor Archibald Cox in October 1973 by President Nixon was another classic case. Not only was there no advance warning, but the President was doing the very thing he had promised the nation he would not do. The "firestorm" of response, as Nixon's own chief of staff (Alexander Haig) categorized the instant rash of telegrams and calls for impeachment, was also characteristic of the fait accompli response. Where there are few other possible courses of action, a surprised citizenry may turn to more unconventional approaches, be they impeachment resolutions or sit-in demonstrations.

Foreign policy actions are often of the fait accompli variety.[8] A classic example is the commitment of troops, as with the invasion of Cambodia announced in May 1970. There was little advanced indication that this was to come, and once the step was taken there was no ready course of appeal. Ultimately, the disruptions on the campuses and the anger in Congress produced a resolution against future actions, but the troops were not removed until the end of June.

Economic policy may also come as a fait accompli step. Again, Nixon provides a major example. There had been some discussion of the possibility of wage and price controls, and Congress in 1970 had passed legislation authorizing the President to take that step if he chose to do so. Yet Nixon had specifically stated that controls were not being considered, right down to his dramatic announcement of wage and price controls in August 1971. Furthermore, with the exception of tax measures which had to be approved by Congress, there was again no recourse. The public could only hope that the President had decided wisely.

There is an important reason why a president may not want advance announcement. Labor unions, businessmen, consumers and foreign speculators will all alter their behavior if they suspect that a major step such as controls or dollar devaluation is forthcoming. This can have adverse short-run consequences. Nonetheless, the result for the electorate is evident: announcement of a major decision with little public knowledge of its imminence, and little recourse regarding the results.

The most extreme form of the fait accompli role occurs where actions are taken and an effort is made to hide them even after they have occurred. This was characteristic of the 1969 bombing of Cambodia by the Nixon Administration, for example. The policy of spying on the opposing political party and then engaging in an elaborate secret cover-up is also a dramatic manifestation of the fait accompli role.

Presidents do not often make the fait accompli decisions alone. Nixon's economic decision in August 1971, for example, was preceded by an extensive weekend of deliberations at Camp David with a diverse group of economic and political advisers.[9] Staffs again may have an important influence. The dependence on staff is nonetheless one of the characteristics which has led to so much recent criticism of the fait accompli pattern of presidential decision making. The process is highly dependent upon the quality of the staff apparatus, along with the president's own personality. Groupthink tendencies or a staff of deferential yes-men can be all too common.

Steps taken in a fait accompli manner do ultimately require some defense. A president cannot go on forever with an unpopular war, or with a ravaging inflation, and not face the necessity of seeking electoral support for his policies. There may well be an after-the-fact effort at justifying and maintaining support for the fait accompli actions. The fait accompli actions nonetheless differ from other approaches in the extent to which the President simply asks the electorate and Congress to support him in what he has done rather than to express support for a policy which is in the process of being developed.

The fait accompli role potentially offers the president his maximum influence. However, he will not often literally sit alone and decide to "do the right thing" and then announce his decision, although at points this seems close to the truth. It is therefore possible for fait accompli decisions to come out of the Presidency which have actually involved a limited presidential role. It is precisely for this reason that fait accompli decisions raise important questions as to the effectiveness of the advising process and the nature of access to that process, as well as questions of presidential personalities themselves.

Summary

The significance of different presidential policy roles can be usefully summarized in reviewing the relationship of policy roles to differing views of presidential politics. Writers who see a high degree of autonomy among interest groups tend to visualize the president often ratifying decisions fostered by a key interest. The strong-presidency advocate at least hopes that the president can engage in a substantial amount of bargaining and mobilizing activity. Contemporary skeptics often emphasize the tendency for fait accompli roles to result from inadequate presidential personalities or staff operations oriented toward a groupthink process. Elite-oriented writers tend to see the president (and also the Presidency) taking a ratifying role, with decisions made by the elite itself.

Factors Shaping Presidential Policy Roles

It is necessary to ask why there are such wide variations in presidential policy roles. Why do some presidents often go on television to promote a policy step, or rush to the telephone to deal with an uncertain congressman, while others more often choose to accept the outcome of policymaking activities dominated by others? Several factors should be considered prior to our consideration of respective presidential policy responsibilities in Chapters 7, 8, and 9.

Individual presidential personalities constitute one major factor. As we have seen in the work of James Barber, there are tendencies for individuals to reflect their own personalities in the choices of roles. One would expect the passive personality to engage in the ratifying role more often than would the active one under similar circumstances. Among the actives, bargaining and mobilizing roles may be well chosen by a variety of specific presidential personalities. The insecure individual, however, may be more prone to engage in the fait accompli route, in that the prospect of facing conflict and possible defeat by being more open with the public can be distasteful. Aspects of the Johnson Presidency regarding Vietnam and the Nixon Presidency in relation to Watergate will clearly show this tendency.

The distribution, intensity, and general expectations involved in public orientations toward respective policy questions are also important. Presidents often seem to have their greatest difficulties in mobilizing support and bargaining effectively when public opinion is both intensely held and fairly evenly divided. In particular, mobilizing roles can be difficult on issues in which public opinion has become substantially settled, as seemed to be the case on such issues as school busing by the mid 1970s. There may be more room for maneuver on foreign policy issues where polarization is not intense, or on domestic issues which have not received enough attention to produce clear divisions in the electorate. Some presidents will still be more willing than others to seek a mobilizing role, but they do tend to be influenced by their perceptions of public opinion. Furthermore, initial attempts at a major policy role on some specific issue may produce a negative result; this initial failure may discourage future activities other than simple ratification of a decision made by underlings.

Power relationships are also of major importance. If a president cannot bring to bear some pressure on key benefactors of a given policy, then he may have to ratify whether he wants to or not. Conversely, where there are opportunities for new coalitions and for building different groups of supporters, a president may be able to bargain effectively.

More generally, roles are influenced by the policy environment confronting the president. In part, the policy environment is reflected in electoral orientations and in key power relationships. The concept of policy environments is broader, however, in that it emphasizes the kinds of restraints and opportunities provided for presidents by such forces as a decline in economic resources in regard to domestic policy or a shift from Cold War patterns regarding foreign policy. The impact of these policy-environment changes is an important factor in looking at recent presidential politics.

Structural relationships also have some impacts. In an age dominated by concern for reform, it is easy to overstate the extent to which structural arrangements determine presidential roles and presidential behavior in general. Our look at the reform agenda must be sensitive to this issue. Basically, structural relationships can be important where they provide, for example, limited presidential opportunity for reviewing aspects of budgetary allocations, or where they allow a president to undertake some foreign policy decision in secret, without prior public deliberation. Relationships with Congress are also of critical importance since several of the limits on presidential ability to influence Congress are firmly imbeded in basic structural relationships. In the wake of the Watergate scandals, Congress repeatedly sought to alter presidential roles and general presidential behavior by modifying such structural factors as the conditions under which troops could be committed, the manner in which discretion could be exercised on budgetary operations, and the conditions under which information could be legally withheld from Congress and from the public.

Key elements for understanding the presidential handling of policy responsibilities are thus apparent. Presidential personality, electoral expectations, power relationships, the general policy context, and structural relationships are all involved. With these factors in mind, it is time to begin looking at recent policy activities and their outcomes.

NOTES

[1] This analysis draws from the useful work of John C. Ries, *Executives in the American Political System*, Belmont, Calif., Dickenson, 1969. See especially pp. 117–125.

[2] A. Lee Fritschler, *Smoking and Politics: Policymaking and the Federal Bureaucracy*, New York, Meredith, 1969, p. 33.

[3] The Johnson case is skillfully described in Eugene Eidenberg and Roy B. Morey, *An Act of Congress*, New York, Norton, 1969. See especially chap. 4.

[4] Ries, op. cit., p. 125.

[5] James L. Sundquist, *Politics and Policy: The Eisenhower, Kennedy, and Johnson Years*, Washington, D.C., Brookings, 1968. See especially chap. 6.

[6] An unusually extensive case by a key Nixon adviser is in Daniel P. Moynihan, *The Politics of a Guaranteed Income*, New York, Vintage, 1973.

[7] Eva Mueller, "Public Attitudes Toward Fiscal Programs" *Quarterly Journal of Economics* 77 (May 1963), 210–235.

[8] An important early discussion emphasizing the closed nature of foreign policy decisions is in Samuel P. Huntington, *The Common Defense*, New York, Columbia University Press, 1961.

[9] Several discussions have emphasized the intense nature of those deliberations. See for example, Roger Miller and Raburn Williams, *The New Economics of Richard Nixon*, New York, Harper & Row, 1972.

Domestic Policy

Presidents sit at the center of an impressive domestic policy apparatus. In recent years, better than $200 billion has been spent annually to fund its components. Well over half of the easily better than 400 bills sent to Congress by the Presidency involve domestic policy questions. The Office of Management and Budget houses more than 500 employees in its new quarters, equipped with substantial analytic capacities for measuring agency and policy performance.

Yet domestic responsibilities for the president often seem frustrating and ineffectual. Some have suspected that presidential interest shifts to foreign policy on occasion simply to get away from nagging domestic questions, or in an effort at generating some favorable publicity. To begin unraveling this issue, as with each major policy responsibility, one must first consider the nature of the policy context and policy process in which the president operates. In turn, the managerial problems emerging from the federal bureaucracy, and the degree of presidential discretion in budgeting operations deserve attention.

The Constraining Domestic Policy Context

The domestic policy context in which the president operates has become increasingly difficult in recent years. Key factors reducing opportunities for strong presidential roles include the increased complexity of many issues, a decline in consensus on possible solutions, and the impact of scarcity. These are not necessarily permanent, although they may be more so than the optimist likes to admit.

Domestic policy issues within presidential politics have become increasingly complex. In part, the greater complexity is a consequence of some expansion of knowledge of what does (and especially what does not) work. Earlier programs, such as the interstate freeway program of the 1950s, could have been examined in terms of a whole range of possible impacts, from the decline of small towns to the displacement of inner-city residents—and especially blacks. It was simpler to debate the costs of freeways or dams in Eisenhower's day than to confront a large number of social consequences. The tendency to proceed less simply today is in some respects commendable, yet it does have the consequence of making the development of programs more difficult, since a president and his advisers must discuss an extended set of ramifications stemming from a new policy venture.

Today's issues are more apt to involve questions of human behavior. How does one motivate individuals to seek new employment opportunities and training? What approaches might best help the ghetto child overcome reading difficulties? Is it possible to alter incentives within the medical care delivery system to avoid increases in medical fees when more money is added into that system, as happened too often with Medicare? How does one overcome decades of unequal treatment of blacks without producing a backlash of intense resentment on the part of whites who feel threatened? As the federal government began to do more domestically in the 1960s, policy questions did become more complex and difficult.

The domestic policy context is also complicated by low levels of public consensus on many issues. Lyndon Johnson showed as recently as 1964–1965 that a skilled president may have fair success in getting legislation through the frequent veto points in Congress when a fairly high level of consensus prevails. Support for several of his early domestic measures was better than 60 percent.[1] It is far more difficult to develop a consensus when the electorate is either sharply divided or confused in a vague way. In the wake of the urban upheavals of the 1960s, public consensus on a number of key issues has become more elusive. The confusions in the Democratic Party coalition are one dimension of that shift. Both whites and blacks were divided on such racial questions as school desegregation through busing to a greater extent than in the 1960s.

There remained the possibility as of the mid-1970s that a fairly high consensus might be formed around different issues. There has been a cyclical nature in the development of support for major policy thrusts in the past. Economic issues clearly offered the greatest likelihood for a consensus on some new policies. Yet in the wake of the national malaise following Watergate, it remained to be seen how much consensus might emerge on key domestic issues.[2] The decline in consensus after the policy breakthroughs of the mid-1960s under Johnson had to be recognized, in any event, as an important ingredient affecting presidential politics in the ensuing decade.

Domestic presidential roles were also becoming more difficult as a result of the shift in the age of the population and the slowing of economic growth. The 1960s stood, in retrospect, as a period of unique growth in the economy and as a period in which a high level of young people in the population had helped stimulate not only a need for such services as schools, but a substantial amount of economic activity in general. Population projections and economic developments and forecasts by the mid-1970s were describing a very different situation. The recession of 1974 actually reduced the gross national product, to introduce the reverse of the typical "growth dividend" of the sixties, in which an expanding economy meant that the same tax structure brought in additional revenue. Longer-run projections were also sobering, as some economists saw an increase in the gross national product of under 3 percent being common by the end of the decade, as compared with the 6 percent and better which had at points been achieved in the 1960s.[3]

Population projections also showed a sharp aging of the population in the foreseeable future as a result of declining birth rates. As a result, projections of expenditures for income maintenance programs for the elderly were becoming increasingly somber. Not only social security, but the increasingly costly pensions for government employees were involved. Thus, the Ford Presidency found itself in late 1974 considering another increase in the social security tax in the face of increased concern with the actual soundness of the social security system. A slow population growth and a modest level of economic growth are developments which can be readily applauded by those who take a long-range perspective on American and global resources. Yet the consequences for presidential roles were already showing up as definite problems in the Nixon Presidency.

The domestic policy context, in sum, was not an easy one as it evolved in the 1970s. Issues were more complex than they were thought to be in the 1950s, consensus was often lacking, and the amount of money available for new programs through economic growth was in sharp decline. Changes in the distribution of wealth in the country could alter the amounts of revenue available, but not without difficulties for a president who undertook that approach.

The Policy-Making Process

Both power relationships and major structural arrangements often reinforce the limitations on domestic policy leadership. Presidents often confront centers of policy-making and, in particular, resistance to change in which there is a mutual exchange of benefits among key supporters of given legislation and prevailing administrative practices. These relationships have been variously categorized as "whirlpools of activity," "policy subsystems," and—with reference to both the tendency for three specific components to be involved and a wry comment on many of the results achieved—"the unholy trinity."[4] At times, both domestic interest in policies like urban renewal and educational assistance, and concern for economic programs involving such issues as consumer protection tend to confront these patterns of mutual benefit-exchange.

Organizations within the federal bureaucracy comprise one key component. Officials within many federal agencies tend to be selected under strong pressure from the concerned clientele, and will in turn tend to reinforce support for their own operations by building and working to expand the organization of key clientele groups. Thus doctors and the health operations of the Department of Health, Education and Welfare (HEW) have a close relationship, as do educational groups with HEW and labor unions with the Department of Labor. Individuals will often, in fact, move rather easily from governmental positions back to private employment with the recipient of public policy with which they have been involved as a government employee. Natural resource operations have produced some of the more intense questions about this seeming conflict of interest as individuals pivot from regulatory agency and White House Staff positions back to employment with, for example, the oil industry.

Clientele groups pursue close relationships with governmental officials for obvious reasons. There are opportunities for influencing the overall direction of policy, and for adjudicating specific benefits within existing programs. Clientele groups also seek the aid of key congressmen for the same reasons.

The ties congressmen have to specific agencies and programs can be developed in various ways. Some will actually have a personal involvement, and are in fact confronted with conflict-of-interest issues. A Senator Russell Long, for example, may sit as chairman of the Senate Finance Committee which must consider the tax laws for the oil industry, even if he also has a personal and family income from oil which has exceeded $2 million in a recent 6-year period. Often, the tie for a congressman stems from aid which can be forthcoming for his district or state. The committee process in Congress has facilitated the importance of these relationships. Such committee operations as interior, agriculture, and public works have shown a large number of influential congressmen with a constituency interest in particular programs they are presumably helping to "objectively" oversee and evaluate.

Presidents are at points restricted from entering influentially into these centers of mutual benefit exchange because of formal restrictions. These restrictions are basically the result of successful attempts by those who have gained a strong position in claiming public benefits to insure also that it will be difficult for those with more general policy concerns to intervene. Avoidance of action by either presidents or legislative majorities is eagerly sought. Thus the highway lobby has fought to obtain—and to keep—the trust-fund policy for the federal highway program, a policy that makes presidential review difficult. Similarly, industries being monitored by various regulatory commissions have often opposed reforms which would make it less likely that regulators would possess favorable dispositions toward their operations.

The questions which presidents face in seeking to develop and to coordinate domestic policies thus often amount to controlling the federal bureaucracy. Presidents have taken various approaches in recent years, and with varying degrees of success. It is thus essential, in looking at presidential policy-making activities, to consider the problem of presidential control over the federal bureaucracy.

Controlling the Bureaucracy

In his domestic role, a president is faced with major problems of bureaucratic management. It is useful to review major components briefly and then look at the management problem in specific terms. A review of the totality of the federal bureaucracy serves to emphasize, particularly in terms of the fragmented set of commissions and agencies, the scope of the domestic responsibilities. A brief sketch of employees and budgets gives some indication of the volume of activity taking place (see table on page 148).

The grouping of cabinet departments reflects an easy means of categorizing. The first four—Treasury, Defense, State, and Justice—are all old departments and are involved with key general functions. State has been somewhat eclipsed by Defense and the national security adviser, but still has some significant activities. Treasury considerations are increasingly important, as the very management of the government's debt (which explains the large cost of operating the Treasury Department) becomes a major policy question. Such key divisions as the Civil Rights and Anti-Trust divisions make the

Cabinet Departments

Department	1972 Expenditures (actual; in millions)	1972 Personnel Level
Treasury	22,198,000	95,728
State	553,000	22,669
Defense	75,084,000	1,009,562
(Civilian purposes)	(1,625,000)	(30,585)
Justice	1,571,000	45,446
Interior	1,652,000	56,892
Labor	9,354,000	12,339
Commerce	1,459,000	28,412
Agriculture	12,825,000	85,511
Transportation	8,658,000	67,232
Housing and Urban Development	4,081,000	15,200
Health, Education and Welfare	75,708,000	105,764

SOURCE: *The Budget of the United States: FY 1974* (Washington: Government Printing Office, 1973), pp. 328, 338.

Justice Department's involvement with policy questions a major one. Defense impacts scarcely need to be emphasized, as the department has not only operated the military establishment but has taken on important foreign policy development roles.

The second group of departments—Interior, Agriculture, Commerce, and Labor—comprise the older clientele-focused organizations. These are the cabinet departments which are the subject of repeated reorganization proposals. The final three departments are new, domestic organizations. Particularly in the case of HEW, the organization is really a loosely organized conglomerate. The Post Office lost cabinet status with its reorganization in 1971.

The Regulatory Commissions

Americans made a unique choice, beginning with the establishment of the Interstate Commerce Commission (ICC) in 1887, to carry out economic matters through regulation by the mechanism of commissions which were presumably to be free of the influence of both Congress and the president. Commissioners' terms are staggered and lengthy. The commissions, despite initially proclaimed intentions, are often free from neither presidential involvement nor congressional pressure. The acceptance of campaign funds by Nixon aide Maurice Stans from Robert Vesco when Vesco was in trouble with the Securities and Exchange Commission (SEC) constituted one of the first damaging incidents in the Nixon Administration. Regulatory commission operations have been the subject of repeated indications of dissatisfaction and reorganization proposals. In an age of greater concern for environmental matters and policy, a review of the major commissions is a good reminder of the policy significance of the regulatory agency jurisdictions.[5]

Major Regulatory Commissions

Civil Aeronautics Board (1938). Authorized to encourage and develop civil aviation (The safety regulations are the responsibility of the Federal Aviation Administration.)

Federal Communication Commission (1934). Authorized to regulate interstate and foreign communications by wire and radio. (Television licensing and the interpretation of equal time for political candidates have been particularly controversial aspects of FCC operations.)

Federal Power Commission (originally formed in 1920). Authorized to regulate the interstate aspects of electric power and natural gas production and distribution.

Federal Trade Commission (1915). Authorized to examine such issues as price fixing and deceptive advertising in an effort to keep economic competition both free and fair.

Interstate Commerce Commission (1887). Authorized to regulate surface transportation, including railroads, trucking companies, bus lines, freight forwarders, water carriers, and express agencies.

National Labor Relations Board (1935). Authorized to oversee collective bargaining practices and procedures.

Securities and Exchange Commission (1934). Authorized to protect the interests and rights of the public and of investors against malpractices in the securities and financial markets.

Major Agencies

Periodically, new activities have been given an agency format rather than being assigned to departments. These may have regulatory powers, but are not often headed by commissions. There has been a continuing search for independence on the part of advocates of certain federal activities, and an interest in experimenting with organizational formats. As a result, several of the activities which the federal government has estabished, particularly since the 1930s, have been given separate agency status. In addition, the Civil Service Commission was left outside the Executive Office of the President because of the hope that patronage politics would thereby be reduced. As the following list indicates, agencies oversee such major activities as promotion of atomic energy, space exploration, and the development of the Tennessee Valley.

Major Agencies

Atomic Energy Commission (1946). Authorized to promote the development and use of atomic energy, including private participation, and to control for safe use. (Modified in 1974.)

Environmental Protection Agency (1970). Authorized to promote coordination and effective governmental action to assure the protection of the environment by abating and controlling pollution on a systematic basis.

National Space and Aeronautics Administration (1958). Authorized to promote research and exploration into problems of flight within and outside the earth's atmosphere, and to operate programs for such purposes.

National Science Foundation (1950). Authorized to promote the strengthening of science research and education.

Selective Service Commission (1948). Established to operate the military draft system.

Small Business Administration (1953). Authorized to promote, aid, counsel, and assist in the maintenance and development of small businesses.

Tennessee Valley Authority (1933). Established to promote unified programs of resource conservation and economic development in the Tennessee Valley region.

United States Civil Service Commission (1883). Authorized to develop and operate a merit civil service system for federal personnel.

Veterans Administration (1930). Authorized to administer laws covering benefits for former members of the armed forces, their dependents and dependent children, and seriously disabled veterans.

The size and scope of the domestic bureaucracy present a managerial task of considerable magnitude. President Kennedy once graphically expressed his frustration in dealing with the bureaucracy by suggesting that trying to gain a response was like trying to have a fist fight with a pillow; wherever one punched, there was a shift somewhere else. The desire to increase control by the president has involved both organizational issues and the critical question of budgetary control.

The experience of the Nixon Administration was probably destined to involve difficulties with the bureaucracy, and its destiny was more than fulfilled. In part, the Nixon Presidency faced the problem of any new administration which brings a change in party.[6] There is apt to be a residue of employees in the higher levels of the civil service who are sympathetic to the values of the previous administration. For two reasons, this problem is apt to be worse for Republicans. Overall, the top levels of the civil service have been more attracted in recent decades to the domestic policy orientations of the Democratic Party. At the same time, a Republican generally does not have the opportunity sometimes afforded a Democratic president of developing control of the bureaucracy through rapid expansion. In 1933–1934, for example, Franklin Roosevelt adopted a strategy of establishing new agencies, which had as one of its consequences a lessening of the problem of controlling previous appointees. Conversely, in 1953 Eisenhower finally felt it necessary to eliminate approximately 500 positions from the civil service as a means establishing presidential control. Eisenhower could not be easily accused of being overly partisan or imperialistic; rather, he reflected the typical problem of control confronting new Republican presidents.

Nixon's problems with the bureaucracy were not simply those which came to light in the wake of the Watergate investigations, although those scandals vividly displayed, as we shall see, a White House desire to use aspects of the operations at the Internal Revenue Service, the Federal Bureau of Investigation, and the Central Intelligence Agency for political purposes. Issues of control were also apparent in the rest of the domestic bureaucracy. One reason for the unprecedented cabinet shuffle following the 1972 election was Nixon's desire to gain better control of several cabinet operations. He produced a more rapid turnover following that election than any other recently reelected incumbent, generally replacing some of the politically experienced (and in his eyes, sometimes too independent) top people with those recruited primarily for managerial skills.[7] In such departments as Health, Education, and Welfare, the President had been repeatedly confronted with managerial problems.

Frustrations at the White House with problems of bureaucratic management also produced, in the first term, a sweeping set of reorganization proposals for the entire executive branch.

An extensive study chaired by Roy Ash (later Nixon's head of budgeting operations) provided the basis for proposed reorganization which would have realigned the cabinet positions by retaining key departments (State, Defense, Justice, and Treasury) and adding four major new departments organized around natural resources, human resources, community development, and economic affairs. Several changes in agencies and regulatory commissions were also involved. The Nixon proposals, interestingly enough, drew a substantial amount of favorable comment and testimony from Johnson Administration officials who had grown weary in their day of dealing with the existing department structure. Joseph Califano, a major coordinator of domestic programs for Johnson, spoke in very approving terms.

Congressmen and lobbies enjoying access in the existing structure were far less impressed. Employees with stakes in existing personnel systems also constituted a decidedly hostile faction, and in the end only the minor step of merging Vista and the Peace Corps was achieved, despite the substantial set of proposals.[8] Nixon was in the midst of seeking to achieve some of the intended coordination with a new supercabinet structure when the woes of Watergate disrupted the flow of reorganization business.

The managerial issues often raised once again the problem of presidential relationships to specific centers of specialized interaction, whose clienteles (including, very importantly, organizational employees themselves) and various friends in Congress were able to successfully resist presidential direction. Presidential disfavor might be a bit disconcerting, but often by no means devastating. There remains nonetheless the question of the budget as a potential vehicle for presidential control. To what extent do budgetary operations give the president an opportunity for control not only of the bureaucracy, but of policy-making activity in general?

The Budgetary Process

Presidents now submit budgets to Congress which are well beyond $300 billion, and include domestic components beyond the $200 billion range. Presumably, budgetary control should be both a major tool for controlling the bureaucracy and for exercising a strong role in domestic policy development. Yet despite repeated reform efforts, this is often not the case. The Office of Management and Budget has more influence than the president on many specifics, and even the entire presidential impact is sometimes surprisingly small.

Presidents cannot be accused of failing to seek more comprehensive budgetary control.[9] There has been a general growth since World War II in efforts seeking to use budgeting as a management tool and not simply as an accounting mechanism. President Kennedy sought major changes in the Department of Defense in 1961, with the recruitment of Rand specialists in defense budgeting and proponents of systems analysis. As comptroller in the Pentagon, Charles Hitch played a major role in modifying budgetary analysis within the Department of Defense. The appointment of Robert McNamara as defense secretary was also motivated by the desire for more systematic analysis.

President Johnson sought, as of August 1965, to extend the more systematic budgetary process to the domestic operations of the federal government. His instructions promised a "revolution" in budgeting practices for the federal government. Presumably, the ideas being borrowed from the experiences of the Department of Defense would produce more coherent planning and, in the process, an opportunity for a president to exercise greater control. Yet in 1971 President Nixon officially indicated an end to the so-called "planning-programming-budgeting system" (PPB), and there was little remorse throughout the Washington bureaucracy. Some doubted in retrospect whether the PPB system had been as successful within the military budgeting channel as it had been proclaimed. It was in any event apparent that the more systematic system caused difficulties in its domestic applications. The five major features of the PPB system are reviewed below, along with the problems they presented.

Program identification. The new system attempted to define budgeting activities in the context of objectives rather than specific objects of expenditure. Rather than indicating costs of salaries, equipment, and new construction as they differed from the previous year, PPB encouraged the statement of programs and their goals. This rather quickly produced difficulties. In part, a clear statement of purposes for some domestic operations was not politically expedient. A further decline in small farms might be the objective of some Department of Agriculture activities, but it was politically most inopportune to advertise that fact. In retrospect, it also became apparent that some of the program definition within the PPB system at the Pentagon had circumvented the difficult task of identifying programs by using rather ambiguous concepts, such as strategic reserves.

Benefit-cost analysis. Efforts at calculating benefits and costs from various federal programs were not really new. The Army Corps of Engineers had been doing this for some time with irrigation and flood control projects, for example. Benefit-cost analysis did also provide some useful comparisons between weapons systems in military budgeting. Comparisons between bombers and missiles, for example, could produce fairly specific results. (They led, in fact, to an intense struggle between the generals and the "whiz kids" over the usefulness of an expanded bomber capacity during the Kennedy years.) Yet at best, such analysis seemed highly influenced by the assumptions one had to make, such as the fairly simple issue of how interest costs were assessed for longer-range expenditures.

The efforts at benefit-cost analysis of domestic programs proved even more vexing. There was an incentive to try to use it on domestic programs, since there seemed to be advantages in the first couple years under Johnson in being able to show that domestic programs such as urban renewal did have favorable benefit-cost ratios. It seemed necessary to develop these projections in order the compete effectively for funds. The efforts nonetheless quickly became rather tenuous. How does an analyst realistically ascribe costs to the individual who must be moved because of an urban renewal effort? Dollar values of intangibles are difficult to develop without being extremely arbitrary.

Multiple-year forecasting. One of the most useful aspects of the PPB effort was in generating an expanded concern for budgets covering a several-year period. There had been a strong tendency to view budgets in a single-year frame, with longer-run comparative costs rather easily ignored. By looking ahead, it was possible to produce total expenditure comparisons in a three to five-year period which were more useful than the annual reviews. Fortunately, this thrust was not lost either on more recent budgeting officials or on outsiders looking at budgeting alternatives. Some of the former Johnson Administration officials who gravitated to the Brookings Institution in Washington helped produce useful multiple-year forecasts.

Zero-based budgeting and detailed descriptions. The most arduous aspect of the budgeting reform was the call for zero-based budgets. The basic concept here is fairly simple. The budgeting official is asked not simply to justify his changes from the budget of the previous year, but to justify all of the expenditures in his budget. Ignoring past history and precedents, the budget official was to proceed as though he were starting from scratch and then compare and justify respective programs. In that process, detailed descriptions were also requested. Only a few agencies were ever successful in even undertaking the zero-based budgets. Perhaps in part because of the problem of recruiting experienced personnel, this was an extremely difficult task.

Problems with the PPB system were also evident in a more general context. Questions of political feasibility must be confronted by a president, yet this system was highly geared away from those considerations. Getting an irrigation budget approved in Congress might be easier if it provided for several smaller dams in order to please a variety of congressmen, even if the systematic analysis indicated that there were higher benefit-cost yields with fewer but larger projects. Or approval for Amtrack funds might (as actually happened) be more readily approved if plans deviated from the original program enough to run one route to West Virginia—which happened to be the home region of a key committee supporter. As a practical matter, it also became apparent that budgeting reform could not easily be accomplished by efforts of the Presidency alone. Where Congress persisted with the older categories and the old committee jurisdictions, the revisions could quickly produce confusion.

By the second Nixon administration, a more flexible approach to budgeting was undertaken. Systematic analysis was not forsaken, but the rigors of PPB were not systematically required. With the reorganization of the budgeting operations into the Office of Management and Budget (OMB), there was also a greater emphasis on the collection of data on agency performances by OMB. A substantial number of individuals with training in management disciplines were hired; the approach employed had the rubric "management by objective." This involved analysis of policy consequences at points, and some effort at relating those accomplishments to budgeting costs.

Neither the PPB system nor the more flexible use of policy analysis since PPB's abandonment has made the task of the president who wants to be intelligently involved with budgetary issues an easy one. Budgets as he sees them very often involve fairly small changes from the previous year for many agencies. Budget requests for the Patent Office, the Coast Guard, or the Bureau of Land Management, for example, may well show little variation from one year to the next. Such changes as do occur are worked out at the OMB level to an overwhelming degree simply because the president lacks the time and the incentive to become involved. Agency heads often feel reluctant to protest OMB decisions, since they sense that they must deal with the budgeting officials on a continuing basis. Protests from major departments do come at points, but there is a tendency for issues to be resolved at the staff level for many departments. It is at this point that budgeting expands the power of presidential budgeting officials rather than the president himself.

On occasion, presidents do become directly involved with budgetary matters. Basic presidential agenda factors may be present, such as personal interest, electoral concerns, or successful lobbying. Presidents may also develop an interest indirectly as they worry about ways in which the budget can be cut. President Kennedy found, for example, that agricultural costs were running a seemingly high third among his costly programs, and was motivated toward an interest in change on that basis. President Johnson took the budget materials with him to his ranch in December 1963, and amazed reporters as he produced a budget substantially under the expected $100 billion. He had partly created those expectations, but also took a rather direct hand in reducing the budget to under $98 billion. Budget cutting is nonetheless often an across-the-board process, thus giving the President and/or his budgeting officials an overall role, but not a specific influence on the development of priorities.

The ease with which presidents can influence budgets and, through them, priorities is further restricted in three important ways. Presidents may find themselves limited at given points in time by the number of budgeting commitments which cannot be altered in that year's proposal. Restrictions involve trust funds, programs funded

by statutory formulas, and multiple-year commitments. It is technically possible for a president to propose changes in statutory formulas
or trust funds. Such steps nonetheless require separate action and
cannot be planned for in a given budget proposal. The incentives
created by budgetary operations are thus away from comparing funds
in such fixed areas as social security, agricultural subsidies, and highway funds with other annual budget items. The proportion of the
budget which can be altered in a single year's proposals is clearly
under half of the total governmental expenditures, and in some esti-
mates has been as low as a fourth of the total expenditures.[10]

There have been some interesting exceptions to the view that
budgetary rigidity makes it impossible for a president and/or his
budgeting officials to significantly alter established programs. The
budget Richard Nixon proposed in 1973 (for fiscal year 1974) was
in several respects a startling document. Nixon proposed a savings
of $17 billion over originally projected expenditures for 1974, with
over $15 billion of the suggested cuts in categories which required
no action other than legislative approval of the revised budget figure.
The places where Nixon was proposing savings were also striking.
In his budget review, major cuts were to be made in supposedly
sacred policy areas. The Department of Agriculture was to be reduced
from original projections by 21 percent, the Army Corps of Engineers
by 26 percent, and the Veterans Administration by 14 percent. These
changes represented a presidential willingness to make significant alterations in budgets which have frequently been viewed as substantially immune from outside attack.[11] A Presidency eager to cut rather
than engage in a tax increase or major defense reductions could propose cuts in the regular budget which significantly affected supposedly
strong agencies and departments. It nonetheless remains true that
this level of presidentially proposed alterations in seemingly established agency operations is infrequent.

Presidential ability to control through the budgetary process
is also limited by the budgeting practice which separates indirect
subsidy questions from direct expenditure proposals. Subsidies are
built into the tax structure in basic—and increasingly controversial—
ways. Tax exemptions allowing various deductions may be viewed
as either tax loopholes, or as a method of promoting activity without
expanding the federal bureaucracy. Such diverse activities as home
ownership, art museum development, and lower costs on state and
local bonds are all encouraged by existing tax deductions. Development of hobby farms by millionaires, speculative real estate adven-
tures, and purposely poor management of housing projects are also
encouraged by advantageous tax deductions. The subsidies are usually
designated as "tax expenditures." This label underscores a basic

point: Without the various deductions, the federal government would be collecting substantially greater amounts of revenue. The sums, furthermore, can be large. In fiscal year 1970, approximately $20 billion went to health and welfare deductions, and about $10 billion to commerce and transportation deductions.[12] Various defenses are made for some of the "tax expenditures"; they may become, for example, indirect means of aiding local government finance (through lower costs for borrowing money through tax-exempt bonds) or of encouraging private charities. Intense supporters often cluster around these specific provisions, as any tax reform effort will show. Depending upon whose tax advantages are involved, there can be intense lobbying from such diverse groups as the oil industry, state and local finance officials, home owners associations, and real estate promoters.

The relative merit of specific provisions need not be debated here. Rather, it is essential to emphasize that the budgeting process does not present opportunities for choosing between the indirect subsidies and direct expenditures. A president is not in the position of trying to determine how valuable the two alternatives are; he deals only with the existing set of direct budgetary expenditures.

One other type of information has also been generally lacking. Despite the emphasis on expanded policy information in the PPB thrust, there has often been a reluctance to discuss the social class income distribution and benefit distributions. Only belatedly have policy analysts even begun to ask questions as to how expenditures on such activities as education or transportation facilities will affect income distribution issues. As a result, even if a president wanted to make a series of redistributive decisions, he would often lack the appropriate informaton.[13]

Despite limitations, presidents do have some opportunities for influence through the budgetary process. Program supporters have a right to worry at Christmastime as the next year's budget sits on the president's desk. Yet given the restraints on him, it is not easy for a president to significantly alter many of the allocations in the budget he proposes for any given year. Moreover, presidential limitations become significantly greater with a slowly growing (or declining) economy and the restrictions on presidential ability to develop priorities through the commitments of new money to new programs. The budgeting process for the president, in short, is often one of either ratifying or engaging in minor bargaining processes.

Domestic Frustrations

Opportunities for the president to confront major domestic problems often suffer from serious constraints. Perhaps the liberals who have abandoned the pursuit of the Presidency, such as Senators Kennedy and Mondale, had other than personal reasons for concluding that the office was not worth struggling to obtain. There are also indications as to why Aaron Wildavsky argues the likelihood that presidents retreat voluntarily from domestic responsibilities in exchange for international diplomacy and travel.

Limitations of presidential domestic roles seen thus far can be summarized as follows: Social consensus on many issues is often lacking and is often difficult to build. Opportunities for playing something-for-everyone politics are restricted by the emerging impact on American society of a proportionately older population and scarcity of resources. The managerial tasks called for by the rise of the domestic bureaucracy are substantial, and they are not easily influenced by such developments as a reformed budgetary process. Finally, even if a president genuinely desires a strong domestic role, the demands of foreign policy and economic management responsibilities often required attention elsewhere.

The resulting picture is not a happy one for those hoping for strong domestic presidential roles. Simply hoping that a president can somehow wave a magic wand and transform difficult policy issues is wishful thinking. There are somewhat more hopeful developments which can be explored in terms of alternative approaches to policy change, and they must be central to the thinking about reform and reduction of the dilemmas of presidential politics. Interest group activities which emerge without presidential leadership, and changing resources of some of the participants in the policy process *can* alter what policies come from the Presidency and from the political system generally. From the presidential standpoint, it is nonetheless not difficult to sense the reasons for a president's frequent sense of limitation in dealing with domestic policy issues.

NOTES

[1] James L. Sundquist, *Politics and Policy: The Eisenhower, Kennedy, and Johnson Years,* Washington, D.C., Brookings, 1968, chap. 10.

[2] Data suggesting possible areas for policy agreement is reported by John G. Stewart in *One Last Chance: The Democratic Party, 1974–76,* New York, Praeger, 1974, pp. 109–110. Majorities could be found supporting such steps as increasing social security payments and providing additional funds for improving educational opportunities for children from low-income families. Although this material is suggestive of possible areas of support, it does not confront respondents with the forced choices between tax increases and new programs, which often complicate decisions for both presidents and Congress.

[3] *Los Angeles Times,* August 3, 1974, p. 1.

[4] A major discussion emphasizing the policy subsystem concept is contained in Emmette S. Redford, *Democracy in the Administrative State,* New York, Oxford University Press, 1969, chaps. 3–5. Redford's model is highly influenced by the strong-presidency tradition, as he sees most policy subsystems as highly stable unless altered by presidential leadership.

[5] Descriptions for agencies and commissions are adapted from governmental descriptions. See for example, *U.S. Government Organizational Manual 1971–72;* Washington, D.C., GPO, 1971.

[6] Historical dimensions of this problem are traced in Henry L. Laurin, *Presidential Transitions,* Washington, D.C., Brookings, 1960.

[7] William W. Lammers, "Interpreting the Contemporary Presidency," paper delivered at the Western Political Science Association Meeting, San Diego, Calif., March 30, 1973, p. 20.

[8] The hearings on Nixon's reorganization proposals make very illustrative reading about veto processes facing a president. See "Reorganization of Executive Departments: Part I—Overview," Hearings before a Subcommittee of the Committee on Governmental Operations, U.S. House of Representatives, 92nd Cong., 1st sess., June 1971. For Joseph Califino's comments, see pp. 389–408.

[9] There is now an extensive literature on the budgeting question. A good recent critical review and source of references is in Leonard Merewitz and Stephen H. Sosnick, *The Budget's New Clothes,* Chicago, Markham, 1971.

[10] On budgeting restraints, see Murray Weidenbaum, *The Modern Public Sector: New Ways of Doing the Government's Business,* New York, Basic Books, 1969, pp. 174–177.

[11] Lammers, op. cit., p. 22.

[12] These figures are drawn from Robert Eyestone, *Political Economy,* Chicago, Markham, 1972, p. 76.

[13] A few examples of the income distribution impacts have begun to emerge. See in particular Robert H. Haveman and Julius Margolis, eds., *Public Expenditures and Policy Analysis,* Chicago, Markham, 1970, especially chap. 9.

Economic Management

The tumultuous economic events of recent years have thrust presidents increasingly into an economic management responsibility. Questions of overall growth, unemployment levels, and rates of inflation have occupied considerable attention of both the president and the electorate. The increase in unemployment concerns as the ranks of the unemployed increased to over 8 million in 1975 simply intensified a growing tendency for economic concerns to assume major importance in presidential politics.

The public has clearly come to expect economic leadership from the Oval Office. Public support for strong economic leadership has even tended on occasion to precede presidential willingness to take the most far-reaching step, the establishment of wage and price controls. Concern for economic matters seemed by 1974 to impinge on presidential abilities to do other things, as President Ford discovered as he received considerable editorial critcism of his foreign policy activities and partisan campaign activities at a time when the economy was in an increasingly disastrous condition. A president simply cannot escape public awareness of major economic indicators and their direct, personal impact experienced at the grocery checkout stand and the unemployment office. Indeed, the rapidly deteriorating economic condition of the United States by the mid-1970s raised more seriously than in many years the question of whether the electorate would be willing to follow a prospective leader on a white horse who promised to right the economy even at the cost of substantial changes in both the economic *and* the political organization of the nation.

Presidents do have a substantial range of policy tools for use in the economic management role. Neither general students of the Presidency nor, for that matter, presidents, on at least some occasions, are quickly able to sort out the economic theories behind respective policy tools. Without seeking to resolve the policy issues directly, it is essential that we examine the political implications and ramifications of the respective policy tools. At the outset, the nature of the recently deteriorating policy context must be highlighted. Several things have happened to reemphasize reasons why the findings of economists have at points produced references to a "dismal science."

The Worsening Economic Context

Presidential economic management shifted in the short space of 10 years from a golden age of the "new economics" to the aggravating realities of "stagflation." In the early 1960s, the major issue was how to use policy tools for improving growth and levels of employment. President Kennedy inherited in 1961 an economy which had been performing poorly in terms of both unemployment and sluggish growth. An expansionist policy was fairly quickly settled upon in this context, with a particular emphasis on a tax cut as a means of stimulating the economy. The passage of the tax cut measure in 1964, after earlier failures during the Kennedy years, represented a major victory for those desirous of a strong economic management role for the federal government.

The wisdom of economic policies pursued in the Kennedy and Johnson years has been debated, particularly by those who felt that there was too much emphasis on tax policy.[1] What is undisputable is the performance of the economy during the 1960–1968 period. Economic growth was substantial, as it surpassed the sluggish performances of the Eisenhower period. Unemployment also declined overall between 1960 and 1968, with levels often under 4 percent. Yet the rate of inflation was also low, with increases in the consumer price index over 3 percent occurring only once prior to Nixon's inauguration; the then seemingly high figure of 4.2 percent was reached in 1967–1968.

The economic events under Nixon were a disaster.[2] The nation experienced recessions in both 1970 and 1974, with various debates over the labels which should be applied. Unemployment was also much higher, as it often hovered around the 6 percent figure. Yet simultaneously, the inflation rates produced the infamous "double digit inflation," as figures soared over the 10 percent figure by the end of Nixon's Presidency. Were the human impacts not so devastating for millions of Americans, one might smile at the humor produced, such as the references to "Nixonomics" as a situation in which those indicators which should rise, fall, and those which should fall, rise. The economic disarray of the Nixon Presidency reached its climax as the President went on national television to announce yet another set of proposals and make confident statements in the midst of the televised hearings of the impeachment proceedings.

It is not easy to sort out the degree of responsibility which should be given to Nixon and his economic advisers. In the eyes of many, they acted very slowly in 1970 and 1971. Somewhat more obvious is the highly expansionary thrust of monetary and fiscal policy as part of the wage and price freeze of 1971. An expansionary economic policy was then followed by a rapid and confused turning on and off of wage and price controls. Some even wondered if the real intent in the use of those controls was to show the country how ineffective controls actually were. It seems likely that Nixon and his managers will seldom receive very high ratings in economics.

Underlying pressures nonetheless were involved, pressures which proved difficult for President Ford and which seem destined to make the economic management roles more difficult in the coming years than during the 1960s. The last pressure on Nixon's economic managers was perhaps the most devastating. Arab oil prices were raised between October 1973 and January 1974, from slightly over $3 per barrel to well over $11. The resulting inflationary pressures on the American economy were substantial. At the same time, balance of payment issues intensified as industrial nations including the United States found oil payments to be a serious drain on their economic position, and Americans found themselves locked into an international monetary system which was both ill-equipped to deal with the sudden shifts and also difficult to readily transform.

Other factors were involved earlier in the Nixon Presidency. The inability of the national government to adequately finance the Vietnam War in 1967 produced an unusually large debt and had a destabilizing impact on a variety of economic relationships. The political economy which Richard Nixon inherited was facing the problem of running deficits when they were not appropriate.

Declining world food resources and shrinking American surpluses also complicated economic policy making by the early 1970s. In their search for scarce food resources, the industrialized nations at points tended to promote inflation in each other's economies through increased demand in the international markets. The American situation was exacerbated by the clumsy sale of American wheat to the Russians, but the basic situation was only part of a worldwide shift.

The economic policymakers faced, finally, the grim impact of dilemmas which economic theorists have isolated. Under many conditions, it is impossible to develop policies which both combat inflation and reduce unemployment. The problem may not be figuring out how to correctly maximize all values, but rather having to make difficult forced choices.

By the mid-1970s, the nation seemed ready to explore more substantially a variety of techniques for dealing with the economy. Those tools, in their political context, can now be reviewed.

Policy Tools

Presidents do not want for a variety of potential tools and techniques in their economic management role. These include fiscal policy, monetary policy, structural approaches, enforcement of competition, use of guidelines, and wage and price controls. Each of these steps has important ramifications for presidential politics.

Fiscal Policy

Fiscal policy involves the impacts of government taxing and spending on overall forces in the economy.[3] In economic terms, there has been a widespread recognition that the budgetary deficit or surplus of the federal government has important consequences for the entire economy. A deficit can stimulate the economy by increasing demand, as both government spending and the untaxed individual and business incomes compete for goods and services. A budgetary surplus, conversely, can play an important role in reducing overall demand in the economy. The notion that the federal budget should be viewed in terms of its overall impact and not simply in terms of analogies to individual household budgets gained substantial acceptance in the 1960s. Yet that acceptance was followed shortly by conditions which made the politically more easily accepted concept less helpful economically.

Fiscal policy presents definite political problems for a president. Fiscal decision making is most attractive when the appropriate step is a tax decrease, and for increases in spending. Even this step was resisted in Congress in the early 1960s, while the tendency to view the federal budget as analogous to a household budget persisted. That view was held by a declining minority by the 1970s.

The difficulties confronting fiscal policy come as the necessary step moves counter to the political instincts and political preferences of the president and/or Congress. There clearly should have been an adjustment of the financing of the Vietnam War in 1966–1967, but there was instead a massive shift to deficit spending. The exact nature of the responsibility has been disputed, with Johnson pointing to his attempt at interesting congressional leaders in a tax increase, and others feeling that Johnson did not push hard enough due to his basic desire to minimize public awareness of the magnitude and costs of the Vietnam War.[4] The hope that both guns and butter could be pursued as policy objectives persisted, rather than acceptance of the less popular steps which wise fiscal policy dictated. Persistently, implications of fiscal policy are more readily accepted if they suggest courses of action which accord with other aspects of a person's political philosophy. Democrats in particular tend to be enthusiastic when the appropriate step is to increase federal programs; Republicans at points like to use the suggested directions of fiscal policy as a rationale for cutting their most hated federal programs. A president may be guided into economically unwise positions because of his own tendency to accept fiscal policy solutions with varying degrees of enthusiasm. He will also most certainly run into resistance in Congress from those whose policy desires make a given fiscal policy step uninviting. As a result, it may be hard to get fiscal policy steps accepted at the time they could be of maximum effectiveness.[5]

Monetary Policy

Changes in the available money supply also constitute an important tool in economic management. Questions involving the money supply are labeled monetary to distinguish them from the taxing and spending, or fiscal policy, issues. The basic policy concept is fairly simple. By acting to increase interest rates, policy seeks to lower demand in the economy, as fewer individuals and firms will borrow for new purchases and capital improvements. Conversely, a low interest rate is seen as likely to stimulate the economy as more demand is generated through the borrowing process.

A major debate in recent years has surrounded the extent to which monetary policy should be employed in lieu of an active fiscal policy. Generally, those aligned with the Republican Party have been somewhat more apt to promote a monetary policy rather than an active fiscal policy. In the Nixon Presidency, his second chairman of the Council of Economic Advisers, Herbert Stein, was a major proponent of the monetary policy approach. Stein was a former student of Milton Friedman, the University of Chicago economist, who has developed considerable prominence in emphasizing the importance of monetary rates to economic performance.

The question of how the federal government is to proceed with monetary policy is intensified by the formal separation of the Federal Reserve Board from the operations of the Presidency. The "Feds" are comprised of a group of 12 individuals appointed for no less than 14-year terms. Their responsibilities in regulating the nation's banks include the critical role of influencing interest rates. Chairman Martin was often at odds with President Kennedy on the interest-rate issue. President Nixon sought to achieve a smoother relationship by the appointment of his former aide, Arthur Burns, as head of the Federal Reserve Board. Informal interaction among key policymakers is also often fairly substantial, despite formal separation. The head of the Federal Reserve Board, the secretary of the treasury, and the chairman of the Council of Economic Advisers, along with, at points, the head of the Office of Management and Budget, often meet frequently. At points, such labels as "the quadrad" are applied to this foursome by observers who sense the importance of these meetings. Informal consultation can nonetheless be rather cumbersome for a president interested in aggressively pursuing monetary policy objectives.

Structural Approaches

Economic management has included, especially since the Kennedy period, efforts at achieving economic objectives by directly aiding segments of the economy such as depressed regions and undertrained workers. Kennedy made a major push on both aid to depressed regions and also manpower retraining. The Area Redevelopment Administration was to aid areas such as Appalachia, which Kennedy had mentioned extensively in his campaigns, and numerous new programs were to help workers gain the skills for better jobs.

In economic terms, structural approaches make little sense where the issue is lack of overall demand in the economy. Kennedy faced this problem, as workers were sometimes trained for jobs which did not exist and attempts at aiding depressed areas found marginal firms shuffling around the country in pursuit of one government incentive after another, rather than sustaining real economic growth. Having a textile plant leave already depressed New England to take advantage of low interest loans and low tax rates in South Carolina might make a few people in South Carolina happy for a time, but would do little to reduce overall unemployment rates.

Direct aid approaches have differing political impacts.[6] They do have the advantage of giving a president something tangible to talk about in terms of what his administration is doing. They also tend to generate specific rewards which a president can distribute with an eye toward gaining support for various legislative thrusts. (In time, however, the resentment of those who are excluded can also be substantial.) A president may also find over time, as did Kennedy and Johnson, that the lack of clearly documented accomplishment makes the structural approaches ready targets for critics of federal programs. There may well be good reasons why the costs in educating a ghetto youth at a Job Corps camp surpass those of sending a youngster to Harvard. Many indirect benefits and supports which the college student receives tend not to be measured. Yet such comparisons can be devastating politically. Such popular magazines as the *Reader's Digest* and *Human Events* can fairly easily find aspects of such programs to criticize.

Specific favors to industry are also structural steps with mixed political impacts. Campaign contributions have been one practical political consequence, as firms contribute with an eye toward possible—or at points rather immediate—benefits. Other impacts can raise problems. Thus, the Nixon effort to help sustain the economy of southern California by providing special government loans to the beleaguered Lockheed Corporation became a ready target for criticism in 1971.[7] Such loans often become, as critics of the Lockheed arrangement argued, unwarranted subsidies to firms which would be better served by major adjustments in their operations. Yet such assistance can also be a more effective means of maintaining jobs than trying to get new industries to move into depressed areas. A president worried about unemployment is often impressed with this argument. Structural approaches thus present key political liabilities as well as assets for a president.

Enforcing Competition

Enforcement of competition was a rather lightly used policy tool in the period from Kennedy through Nixon. Kennedy became impatient with the zealousness of his first key antitrust enforcer, Lee Lovenger. Johnson was more interested in approaching policy issues by stressing growth, plus programs directly aimed at the poor. The lack of commitment to antitrust policy was abundantly clear in the Nixon Presidency. In such specific situations as that involving the proposed merger between ITT and Hartford Insurance, Nixon was very specific in denouncing a stern antitrust approach. Some felt that political ties accounted for this attitude, and others felt that the philosophy of the Nixon Administration was primarily involved. In any event, the Administration's lack of interest in enforcement was evident.

Americans have long had, in fact, a measure of ambivalence regarding antitrust approaches. Several writers have been impressed with the extent to which *both* the electorate and corporate leaders have tended to enjoy and at points revere big business. Thurman Arnold's *Folklore of Capitalism* describes his skepticism about the

American commitment to controlling big business on the basis in part of his own experiences trying to enforce antitrust measures in the 1930s.[8] John K. Galbraith's *New Industrial State* traces both the growth of economic concentration and also the tendency for corporate leaders to prefer managed markets.[9] Theodore Lowi's *End of Liberalism* reviews what he sees as a shift away from capitalism as the dominant ideology in the 1930s.[10]

The results of American regulatory policies, or lack thereof, have been immense. Concentration in the economy has continued to grow. By 1969, the 200 largest manufacturing corporations controlled about two-thirds of all assets held by corporations engaged primarily in manufacturing. The trend was also clear. The largest 100 corporations had a greater share of all manufacturing assets than the largest 200 did in 1950.

The immensity of economic concentration could be seen in another way also. As of 1968–69, the United States government was at the top of the 10 organizations with the largest total revenues; the next 9 included *only 2 states* (California and New York). Revenues of such corporations as General Motors, American Telephone and Telegraph, Standard Oil (New Jersey), Ford Motors, Sears and Roebuck, General Electric, and IBM *all dwarfed any other state.*[11]

By 1975, the issue of competition as an economic management tool seemed apt to receive renewed interest. With a strong emphasis from the Joint Economic Committee of Congress, the question of lack of competition was reexamined as a possible cause of inflation. Concern over lack of competition came as no surprise to those who were impressed, as was Theodore Lowi, with the tendency for various functional areas of the economy to have little competition either in their markets or in the nature of their relationships to the government. The absence of competition was seen not just as a question of legally defined antitrust issues, but one involving as well a variety of governmental practices. Allowing physicians to prescribe generic labels rather than brand labels for drugs, for example, can substantially increase competition in drug pricing. The actions of the regulatory commissions and the strong position granted to some unions were skeptically reviewed in terms of their impact on economic performance.

There is tremendous pressure on a president not to confront the antitrust area more directly. The specific advantages various firms and industries enjoy through limitations on competition produce intense lobbying pressures if they are threatened. Charles Schultze, a former head of Johnson's budgeting operations, recognized these pressures as he suggested that there might be some opportunities for an assault on the issue if one combined a variety of measures into a package with several simultaneous changes.[12] By 1975, the very impact of the Watergate scandals seemed to be giving new life to the interest in antitrust enforcement, both within governmental circles and in some segments of the electorate. Such major firms as American Telephone and Telegraph, Xerox, Goodyear, and Firestone, found themselves subject to new legal challenges as part of renewed antitrust efforts.

Guidelines

The odd term *jawboning* crept into economic discussions in the Kennedy Presidency. Both Presidents Kennedy and Johnson sought to influence economic development by exercising "moral suasion" on key segments of business and labor. In addition, consumers were at points encouraged to orient their buying habits in keeping with a need for shifts in overall demand in the economy. In 1974, the Nixon Administration, despite its reluctance to use guidelines prior to launching wage and price controls, reverted to aspects of a guideline approach.

Guidelines obviously suffer from the absence of specific sanctions. One should recall, however, that it was Kennedy's sense that the steel industry had not kept its gentleman's agreement on prices in relationship to labor restraint which prompted the major flexing of political muscle in April 1962. Kennedy had been seeking to "jawbone," in the sense of putting pressure on both business and labor to avoid excessive price and wage increases. In response to the initially announced steel price increase, Kennedy took several steps. An unusually angry press conference was held, the threat of antitrust investigation emerged, and there was the assurance that any companies not following U.S. Steel's lead in the price increase would be in a highly advantageous position in relation to government contracting through the Department of Defense. For an intense week, Kennedy was showing (and successfully, as U.S. Steel rescinded the price increase) that there were indeed resources in the Presidency which could back up the guideline approach.[13]

Guidelines do tend to promote a measure of discussion and, at points, bargaining without the necessity of establishing a major regulatory unit to police all transactions. A popular president, and one skilled in bargaining processes, can have some impact. Problems can nonetheless occur, as his credibility may be marred by frequent noncompliance. Furthermore, economic pressures can fairly easily destroy the measure of restraint which guideline tactics introduce.

Wage and Price Controls

The most far-reaching step a president can take is to establish wage and price controls. These have been primarily a wartime phenomena in the United States. Even during the Korean War, the

Truman Administration embarked only very reluctantly on a partial course of wage and price controls. The frustrations with the World War II regulatory activities, which were substantial by 1945–1946, contributed to Truman's reluctance.[14] The Nixon attempt at wage and price controls between August 1971 and April 1974 (when they ended entirely), some six years after the costs of the Vietnam War had begun to mount, was from an historical perspective a most unusual step. In economic terms, there is no question but that wage and price controls constitute a policy tool with tremendous consequences. Anyone who experienced the cancellation of 1971–1972 raises can well testify to the direct impact! The central economic problem, in turn, is that controls may delay adjustments in economic activity which are needed.

Wage and price controls cause an interesting set of political responses. Controls are often greeted with initial enthusiasm. This was particularly the case in 1971, as the Nixon Administration had increasingly been badgered for doing too little to combat inflation and recession. Truman was also under substantial pressure to move to meet inflationary pressures in the wake of the outbreak of the Korean War in June 1950. Over time, controls nonetheless encounter considerable resistance. Initial enthusiasm that difficult conditions will be corrected often gives way to irritations with specific decisions and frustration with the inevitable delays and confusions which the bureaucratic mechanisms create. A president may also find that the political responses to economic adjustments as controls are removed is particularly adverse. Truman in 1946 and in 1952, and Nixon in 1974, both felt the adverse responses to the longer-run impact of wage and price controls.

A president moving to establish wage and price controls is also confronted with major internal problems. New capacities for administration must be quickly developed. In both 1950–1951 and in 1971, there was intense concern with the inadequacies of the policing machinery. Previously existing units tend to be understaffed if not downright incompetent, and there is a rush to create more adequate mechanisms. As these mechanisms evolve, opportunities for creating new patterns of access for bargaining become important to both the president and key interests. Individual interest-group leaders and corporate spokesmen vie for access. This may create some new opportunities for a president. Over time, it can also generate substantial conflict, as manifested for example in the hostility of organized labor toward Nixon's operation of the Cost of Living Council.

President Nixon's implementation of wage and price controls did not serve to enhance public confidence in that policy technique. A detailed economic review is necessary to sort out the extent to which specific decisions made within the period of full and partial controls contributed to the sad results. It certainly does not help to sell off a fourth of the American wheat crop to the Soviet Union and then turn around and realize that the country faces inflationary pressures because of an inadequate supply for internal consumption. Given the short-run political gains which are apt to be associated with wage and price controls, a future president may well again look toward those political advantages. Yet the longer-run consequences both economically and politically, for either the incumbent or his successor, dictate a careful look before this most substantial policy step is implemented. Wage and price controls, just like each of the other major tools, have tremendous political consequences for presidential politics.

It is necessary to point out a certain datedness in the available policy techniques. Policy tools developed in the 1960s were substantially oriented toward problems of growth and unemployment. They were also substantially directed toward the internal dynamics of the American economy. Inflation, recession and sharp alterations in the international economy had not been confronted to a comparable degree for several decades. Uncertainty was felt by the mid-1970s about the adequacy of existing policy tools in confronting changes in the international markets and changes in consumer attitudes.

The Policy Process

Major political consequences stem from the president's growing economic management role. Where speed seems necessary, the role of Congress tends to be very peripheral. Congressmen often criticize policy, but are reluctant to face the difficult choices themselves. Presidential power thus often increases. Presidents also may face serious problems of credibility with the electorate. The frequent tendency has been for a president to appear on television and announce that economic conditions are soon going to improve, and the electorate need only have confidence. There are certain conditions of inadequate demand in which efforts at promoting consumer confidence are justified. Yet such efforts can easily reflect an unrealistic presidential hope and serve as a convenient reason for not pursuing other policies. As conditions worsen, the president is then confronted with an economic credibility gap with the electorate.

Power issues are also important in the president's growing economic management role. From the vantagepoint of the president and his advisers, the economic role can be seen taking place in a highly competitive process. The negotiating which tends to take place on economic policy issues clearly produces a competitive environment.

Thus C. Jackson Grayson's description of the pressures confronting the Price Commission he headed for Nixon is a continuing account of conflicting pressures from industry.[15] A substantial amount of economic management activity involves economic decision makers with either individual firm impacts or concerns for their industry.[16] Individual firms and at points unions and other participants lobby for a specific favorable decision, thus producing competition. Industry-wide activities also produce substantial conflict. Those affected by monetary operations are desirous of policies reducing the difficulties in their operations. Those involved with the airlines have been desirous of policies which would reduce the hardship to their industry. Automobile manufacturers have sought relief from the antipollution constraints which have limited their ability to produce cars as cheaply as they would like. Bargaining roles thus often emerge in the president's efforts at dealing with the major actors involved with these constellations of interests.

There has, at the same time, certainly not been uniform access for various interests. Labor union leaders have often spoken with a very definite and overriding interest in the problems of a particular industry. In interacting with dominant voices within areas of the economy, the president and his economic managers have also often been interacting with individuals identified in elite interpretations of presidential politics.[17] The tendency in these discussions has often been to seek quick decisions and speedy results, thus also tending to emphasize such strategies as changes in investment taxes or quick changes in the available supply of energy. Economic discussions in these conditions have generally avoided the longer-run implications of such general issues as income distribution in American society, and the operation of markets in ways destined to give those with dominant positions an ability to influence prices (and their own profits) as well as the quality of goods available to the average citizen. The ability of corporate interests, collectively, to maintain a relatively stable position in the American economy was not influenced by the shift since the early 1960s to a more active presidential responsibility for economic management.

From a presidential perspective, the question of economic management has nonetheless tended to be one of seeking to devise effective policy in the face of both conflicting advice and various economic forces nationally and internationally which can make the develop of effective policy very difficult. An easy reliance upon either past wisdom or existing structures seems, in many perspectives, to be inadequate. From the presidential vantagepoint, economic management responsibilities loom as both increasingly important and increasingly difficult.

NOTES

[1] Considerable useful material is contained in the debate between Walter Heller and Milton Friedman, *Monetary vs. Fiscal Policy*, New York, Norton, 1969.

[2] Two useful books on Nixon's economic policy from a general perspective are Roger Miller and Raburn Williams, *The New Economics of Richard Nixon*, New York, Harper & Row, 1972, and Leonard Silk, *Nixonomics*, New York, Praeger, 1972.

[3] A highly readable discussion of the importance of fiscal policy is found in Robert L. Heilbroner and Peter L. Bernstein, *A Primer on Government Spending*, New York, Vintage, 1963.

[4] On this point, see Robert Eyestone, *Political Economy: Politics and Policy Analysis*, Chicago, Markham, 1972, pp. 60–61.

[5] Problems in presidential development of fiscal policy are usefully discussed in Lawrence C. Pierce, *The Politics of Policy Formation*, Pacific Palisades, Calif., Goodyear, 1971.

[6] Some of Kennedy's difficulties are discussed in James L. Sundquist, *Politics and Policy: The Eisenhower, Kennedy, and Johnson Years*, Washington, D.C., Brookings, 1968, chap. 3.

[7] For a critical legislator's view, see William Proxmire, *Uncle Sam: The Last of the Bigtime Spenders*, New York, Simon & Schuster, 1972, p. 231.

[8] Thurmon Arnold, *The Folklore of Capitalism*, New Haven, Conn., Yale University Press, 1937.

[9] John K. Galbraith, *The New Industrial State*, Boston, Houghton Mifflin, 1967.

[10] Theodore J. Lowi, *The End of Liberalism*, New York, Norton, 1970, chaps. 2, 3.

[11] "The Biggest Corporations by Revenues," *Forbes* 105 (May 1970), 75–76.

[12] *Los Angeles Times*, August 4, 1974, p. 18.

[13] An interesting case account of this use of presidential power is found in Grant McConnell, *Steel and the Presidency*, New York, Norton, 1963.

[14] Truman's use of wage and price controls is discussed in Edward S. Flash, Jr., *Economic Advice and Presidential Leadership: The Council of Economic Advisers*, New York, Columbia University Press, 1965, chap. 3.

[15] For an informative discussion of issues confronting the Price Commission, see C. Jackson Grayson, Jr., *Confessions of a Price Controller*, Homewood, Illinois, Dow Jones-Irwin, 1974, esp. chap. 7.

[16] The extensive individual firm pressures and pressures from major functional areas of the economy are graphically portrayed in Proxmire, op. cit., pp. 130–162.

[17] The presence of individuals from the corporate structure in the making of economic policy decisions is emphasized in G. William Domhoff, *The Higher Circles*, New York, Vintage, 1970, chap. 6. See also Michael Parenti, *Democracy for the Few*, New York, St. Martin, 1973, chap. 3.

The Foreign Policy Presidency

Foreign policy actions are of immense importance to the contemporary Presidency. Presidents are involved with foreign policy concerns to a degree often overshadowing other presidential functions. The question of unrestrained presidential power has also been most forcefully raised in the foreign policy roles.

Presidential foreign policy roles nonetheless vary widely. An important development has been the shift in the nature of the international system. In looking at the foreign policy roles, it is thus appropriate to begin with that shifting international system, moving in turn to the characteristics of the foreign policy bureaucracy, the Vietnam case, and the congressional role. Finally, a review of major differences between foreign and domestic roles is important. How do they differ and to what extent?

The Changing Policy Context

The international political system of the 1970s differs fundamentally from that of the 1950s and early 1960s.[1] The new international system is described as "multipolar" to distinguish it from that which existed during the period of continuing confrontation between the

United States and the Soviet Union. In this new international system, changing degrees of friendship and differing interactions take place among at least five major international actors. President Nixon, in describing this system during his first term, looked to the development of a five-part cast of major international actors, including the United States, the Soviet Union, China, Japan, and Western Europe. In this system, regional conflicts are more apt to be settled without dragging the superpowers into direct conflict.

Richard Nixon and Henry Kissinger were both partial creators and at points major recipients of the benefits derived from the shift toward a multipolar international system. Sometimes, as with the overtures to China, there was considerable initiative involved. The Nixon Presidency seemed able to absorb at this time criticisms of American policies as they had emerged in the 1960s. They were also able to profit from changing relationships between the Soviet Union and the Chinese, and the pressures within the Soviet Union for a less costly foreign policy.

It remained to be seen, by the 1970s, just how effective the new international system would be in dealing with a variety of complex problems. The sudden introduction of a genuine crisis into the international monetary system by the increases in oil prices placed a strain on that system. Furthermore, the division of the less developed nations into those with oil resources and those without added an additional dimension of uncertainty.

The changing international system also produced alterations in the nature of internal political support for a changing set of policies and issues. Problems of internal support for the foreign policy operations of Nixon and Kissinger were raising concern by the end of Nixon's first term. Some worried about the tendency for then National Security Adviser Henry Kissinger to operate a large number of the inevitable bargaining relationships himself. More general problems of internal support were also evident. The shift in the international system increased questions of support in two respects. First, one could less readily count on the rhetoric of the Cold War to rally the nation in support during a foreign policy crisis. At the same time, a shifting set of alliances, coupled with mounting international trade issues, made it essential for presidents to seek congressional support for a variety of foreign policy dealings. That process, as we shall see shortly, could be both complex and difficult.

The Foreign Policy Apparatus

The president faces a national security bureaucracy of considerable magnitude.[2] A considerable amount of his time in recent years has been devoted to interactions with that structure. In part due to their sense of frustration in dealing with the maze of units and pressures which are involved, there has been a tendency for presidents, beginning especially with John Kennedy, to centralize that process increasingly in the White House. The national security advisers, including McGeorge Bundy, Walt Rostow, and Henry Kissinger have in turn become key figures in the development of presidential positions. Thus, such practices as the use of the "ex-com" group by Kennedy during the Cuban missile crisis, the extensive discussions of Vietnam strategy by Johnson with his "Tuesday Cabinet," and the extensive discussions and decision making between Nixon and Kissinger alone have become common.

It is not surprising that a president finds the foreign policy bureaucracy difficult to manage. The uniformed military, even with recent cuts, numbers well over two million individuals, and generates management questions ranging from personnel issues to the tremendously complex problems of weapons system development in an age of increasingly complex technological capacity. Weapons issues, such as the prospect of developing the anti-ballistic missile system (ABM), represent decisions involving tens of billions of dollars. President Kennedy's efforts at controlling the Pentagon with an increased use of systems analysis, including the PPB system, was just one manifestation of the difficulties involved.

The Department of Defense also confronts the president with a major set of policy-making activities and interests. Presidents must deal with both civilian heads of the respective armed services and the Joint Chiefs of Staff (JCS). The JCS, comprised of the chiefs of the respective services together with the chairman of the JCS, comprises a body which jealously views threats to its involvement in policy development. In addition, the services have been involved with their own intelligence activities, and have had significant involvement in the operation of United States missions abroad. The Department of Defense has grown in relationship to the Department of State in these activities in recent years, despite the fact that the Department of State stands as a major bureaucratic unit in its own right.

The State Department, and its organization, is a frequent focus for dissatisfaction. At the top are the secretary of state and the undersecretary, who acts as his deputy. Other top-level under and deputy secretaries specialize in such areas as economic affairs or political affairs. In addition, there are both functional bureaus and regional bureaus. The functional units have involved such concerns as congressional relations, economic affairs, international organization, educational and cultural affairs, and intelligence and research. Regional units have included European affairs, East Asian and Pacific affairs, African affairs, Latin American affairs, and Near Eastern and South Asian affairs.[3]

A third major set of activities involves the Central Intelligence Agency (CIA). Organized because of frustrations with the limited intelligence capacities of the American government during World War II, the CIA emerged in 1947. The CIA has had major activities in both intelligence and foreign operations. It is the foreign operations activities, such as the CIA involvement with the internal struggles in Chile during the Allende regime, which have produced intense criticism. In addition, Americans learned to their dismay in late 1974 that the intelligence-gathering activities had not stopped at water's edge, or with the actions of foreign governments. A frightening record was beginning to emerge of CIA surveillance of domestic political activities. The Foreign Intelligence Policy Board, which supposedly had functioned to aid the president in the supervision of CIA activities, came under intense attack amidst both presidential and congressional efforts at reevaluation.[4]

Possible reorganization of the foreign policy apparatus has been a perennial and difficult topic. From the presidential perspective, several basic points deserve emphasis. Even with the devotion of substantial amounts of time, a president cannot easily manage and utilize that apparatus effectively. In their efforts to engage in foreign policy operations, presidents have tended at points to take issues "from the top," without adequate consultation. When they do this, there is the possibility that they will make an unprepared television statement or take a position at a summit meeting which only one or two of the people closest to the president have influenced. Key results then follow. First, there is the possibility that a decision will be made on the basis of individual instinct, as at points happened with President Johnson on Vietnam policy. Second, there is the possibility of "groupthink" within presidential staffs. Finally, there is the problem of various foreign policy agencies, and particularly the CIA, receiving limited supervision.

Specific organizational and reorganizational questions have been considered by a variety of writers.[5] There are obviously no easy answers, given the range of federal government operations today. Without seeking to review the specifics of reform alternatives, a general posture can nonetheless be taken. The presumption that a president will be acting with adequate information and with a well-organized decision process must be viewed with reservations. The automatic aspects of "expertise and coordination" simply may not exist. Implications for reform can be drawn from this general perspective, in looking at Congress and at the possible changes in presidential roles.

A variety of problems with the foreign policy bureaucracy and with the nature of the American foreign policy process are clear as one looks at the decision process surrounding America's most lengthy foreign war. The Vietnam War emerged out of the emphasis on a Cold War orientation in the international system, and occupied both the president and the nation for a tumultuous decade. The collapse of the South Vietnam government in late spring, 1975, served to intensify the question of how the United States could follow a set of policies with such high costs and so painfully few benefits.

The Vietnam Case

The tragic history of American involvement in Southeast Asia shows extremely well the wide range of influences which can come to bear in the development of foreign policy. Major American involvement with Southeast Asia was most emphatically not confined to the period of troop involvement in Vietnam. A major thrust of the Pentagon papers, made public through the efforts of Daniel Ellsberg, was that the work of Pentagon historians underscored a continuing American concern and involvement in the creation and evolution of South Vietnam.[6] Furthermore, the conflict was not confined to Vietnam itself. Enemy troop movements in neighboring Laos and Cambodia produced repeated American involvement, often secretively, in the forms of both troops and bombing missions. Bombing missions increased as troops were being removed during the first Nixon term, and internal conflicts continued in an increasingly beleaguered Vietnam. The de-Americanization of the conflict did nonetheless substantially remove the issue from American political concerns during the period between the Paris Agreements in late 1972 and the fall of the South Vietnam government.

Many lessons and points of emphasis can be drawn in looking at the decision processes during the years in which Vietnam played such a dominant role in both presidential politics and American politics generally. An increasing number of sources have explored aspects of Vietnam policy making in considerable detail.[7] It is useful to review central problems by first considering process characteristics and then looking at the impact of key political forces. Process characteristics should be considered in terms of the level of debate, the completeness of analysis, and then the role of key participants.

Absence of debate.   Lack of meaningful debate, both within the government and involving the electorate, was apparent in several instances in Vietnam decision making. This was not true in all instances, but did occur at key points. Within the Kennedy Presidency the expansion of American commitments in 1961 was not a key issue. Yet it was in 1961, as the nation and the President worried about other foreign policy issues, that the troop commitments began to increase, from 685 men to a total of 16,732 by October 1963. After a fairly substantial debate within the Presidency in 1963 over the American relationship to the Diem regime, the nation experienced in the first months of the Johnson Presidency another period of reduced debate. Critical absence of debate occurred in August 1964, when the Gulf of Tonkin Resolution was hurried through the Senate, since Johnson and the nation seemed more interested in talking about other issues. There was again debate within the Johnson Presidency in early 1965, with George Ball one of the leading critics of further American commitment. Yet by April 1965, the nation was committed to both an air war and an offensive ground operation, without a declaration of war and without having had a major sorting out of opinions and options through a national debate on the importance of Vietnam.

Incomplete analysis.   Care must be taken not to overstate the problem of inadequate analysis, which was also apparent at times. From very early in the Johnson Administration there were questioning analyses, particularly from the intelligence division of the CIA. Daniel Ellsberg has stressed that Presidents did not suffer from incomplete analyses that led them optimistically to take steps which would lead them further into a quagmire of involvement. Rather, according to Ellsberg, the decisions increasing American involvement were a consequence of the fact that Presidents as far back as Truman and Eisenhower were reluctant to appear in the eyes of the voters to have lost Vietnam.[8] Presidential perceptions, colored by the emotional responses to the communist takeover in China, were seen by Ellsberg as dominated more by electoral concerns rather than inadequate analysis. It is also nonetheless true that the nation lacked, particularly in the Kennedy years, any extensive expertise regarding the sociopolitical aspects of the Vietnam situation. Government experts who could even read the language were extremely rare. By 1966, the absence of complete analysis in the hands of the President became more a function of his staff system rather than of the absence of questioning interpretations in the national government. Problems with both adequacy of debate and thoroughness of analysis are at several points apparent as one reviews the roles of key components of the Vietnam decision process.

The elite role.   Members of the elite went through a period of generally quiescent acceptance of the war, until a key break with the Johnson Presidency. Key figures involved as governmental participants in the early decisions of 1964–1965 revealed a substantial elite background. There was also little indication of a serious questioning of the growing war effort on the part of either upper-class Americans or spokesmen for major industries. In March 1968, the situation was dramatically different. One of the important contributions toward Johnson's refusal to accept the request for additional troops in March of that year was the meeting held with an informal, highly skeptical group sometimes labeled the "wize men."[9] These individuals spoke most clearly from the vantagepoint of what writers about the elite have characterized as the American Establishment. Included in that advisory process were such individuals as Dean Acheson, Douglas Dillon, Arthur Dean, and John McCloy. The thrust of their message was that the war no longer was supported by significant segments of the American elite. It is important to recognize, in terms of interpretations of American politics as elitist, that this shift in views was not followed by as rapid a change in policy as some would have liked—there was a lengthy continuation of the air war in Nixon's first term. The elite role was nonetheless important both in allowing the early growth of American commitment without a major debate and also in promoting and legitimizing dissent by 1968.

Bureaucratic influences. Several important roles were also played by bureaucratic influences within the federal government. Graham Allison has correctly emphasized the necessity of considering organizational pressures as one seeks to explain policy outcomes.[10] Vietnam is no exception; the bureaucratic impact took different directions at various points.

One of the several themes in David Halberstam's *The Best and the Brightest* is that the bureaucratic influences in 1964 moved with comparatively little resistance toward an assumption of greater American involvement in Vietnam.[11] The Pentagon papers document the extensive planning which went on throughout that year. The shift at key points, particularly in the Pentagon, was toward considering how to meet future contingencies, what weapons would work best, and how to handle logistical operations. Less is known about State Department activity. From what is known, there seems to have been a tendency for the assumption of a forthcoming greater conflict to harden, with comparatively little debate at key organizational points.

The decisions in the spring of 1968, although accompanied by major impacts from both the electorate and from spokesmen for the American elite, also found organizational politics within the Defense Department (DOD) taking on great importance. The internal push found civilian dissidents in DOD rallying around Clark Clifford in the effort to persuade Johnson against accepting decisions for further troop increases. There was also an impact from some on the staff, such as Harry McPherson, but it was not primarily White House Staff pressure which Johnson had to deal with. Johnson faced a conflict between his generals and their desire for more troops on the one hand, and Pentagon dissidents and skeptics on the other. In this context, one could certainly not view the foreign policy Presidency as one free from substantial organizational pressures and tensions.

Personality and staff. Particularly in terms of reducing debate at some points, personality and staff factors were also involved. The Johnson personality has been emphasized in the writings of James Barber as a key factor in the rigidity of Johnson's position.[12] For Barber, Johnson's insecurities as an individual (characteristic of the active-negative) contributed to a tendency on Johnson's part to personalize the question of war policy in a tragic way. As he became committed, in Barber's view, Johnson took a highly hostile view of dissent, which meant that the staff operations could not readily produce a clear review of policy alternatives. It could also be noted, from a personality standpoint, that Johnson's tendency toward secretiveness in many dealings with the press contributed to his tendency in 1964–1965 to take policy steps in ways which reduced the likelihood of discussion and debate within the electorate.

The flexibility which has been given presidents in recent years to organize their staffs as they see fit produced its logical result with the Johnson staff approach. Johnson could easily choose to meet with an ad hoc group of advisers and thus avoid some of the dissent which reliance upon a more formal structure might conceivably have produced. Despite his openness on aspects of domestic policy, in regard to Vietnam Johnson was able to substantially wall himself off at several points prior to spring 1968 from a variety of skeptics.[13]

The congressional role. This was also tragically muffed at key points. Congress could have taken a different role than its easy acceptance of the Gulf of Tonkin Resolution in August 1964. The Vietnam War produced the spectacle of the nation fighting the longest war in its history on the basis not of a congressional declaration but rather the Gulf of Tonkin Resolution. One can debate the words of that resolution, including support for the president to "take all necessary steps, including the use of armed forces, to assist any member or protocol state of the Southeast Asia Conference Defense Treaty requesting assistance in defense of its freedom."[14] It is far less debatable that when a total of two legislators in both houses (Senators Morse and Gruening) opposed the resolution after limited debate, there was limited legislative awareness of what was ultimately to be involved.

Senator Fulbright played a major role in supporting the resolution, assuring skeptical senators that the President would continue to consult, and that no extensive hearings were needed. Senator Fulbright subsequently showed, beginning in spring 1966, that congressional hearings could be a powerful magnet attracting dissent on the war issue. By that time, however, the various arguments about saving face, coupled with the rigidities of the position held by President Johnson, made the exercise more capable of promoting division in the country than a rapid change in policy.

The public opinion impact. The public reaction to the Vietnam War revealed clearly the limitations in public impacts which can be involved in policy development—particularly when there is a conscious presidential effort to keep the public at arm's length. Some public impacts were ultimately felt. Ultimately, Johnson realized that he could run again only at the risk of most divisive consequences, and that he would not necessarily be successful in seeking reelection. He would point in his memoirs to his early decision not to run again in 1968 as an indication that he did not simply yield to political pressure. Yet there was no denying the difficult situation public opposition presented by spring 1968.

Public opinion was at the same time difficult to arouse, and public resentment could be fairly substantially reduced by reducing American casualties, even while actually increasing the bombing attack.[15] President Nixon, in his first three years in office, dropped more bombs on North Vietnam than Johnson had in his approximately four years of bombing while in office. President Nixon was also successful in seemingly getting his pledge of peace with honor substantially accepted by the electorate even though his major accomplishment was to de-Americanize a continuing conflict. Casualties and televised pictures of combat had an impact on public opinion; continued bombing had a far less substantial impact.

Summary

There is a blending of influences involved in the long series of decisions involving Southeast Asia which makes it difficult to explain outcomes in terms of a single factor, such as elite dominance, quagmires, bureaucratic pressures, electoral perceptions by presidents looking to the next election, or inadequate presidential personality. The closed politics of the Vietnam decisions in the early 1960s did involve some competition, as has been emphasized so often by those looking directly at the foreign policy bureaucracy. Yet in allowing closed politics to persist, with a tendency for fait accompli decisions, other segments of the political system were depending upon a president and a decision process to an extent which easily allowed a perpetuation of a cold-war view of international politics. From this perspective, changing presidential relationships with Congress also deserve specific attention.

Congress: An End to Deference?

The traumas of the Vietnam conflict have drawn renewed attention toward the question of legislative roles involving foreign policy. To approach this question at the outset, it is necessary to review the ways in which the president has, and has not, been uniquely able to get his way with Congress on foreign policy matters.

In his classic study, Aaron Wildavsky found significant differences in congressional willingness to support foreign policy and domestic legislative proposals. Drawing from the *Congressional Quarterly* ratings for presidential success with issues on which they took a position, Wildavsky found in the 1948–1964 period a willingness by Congress to pass presidential legislation only 40 percent of the time on domestic policy (natural resources, labor, agriculture, taxes, etc.), with substantially more willingness to go along on various aspects of foreign policy. Defense policy (disarmament, manpower, etc.) produced over 70 percent passage, and two other groups of foreign policy issues produced, respectively, 70.8 percent and 58.5 percent passage.[16] There are problems with these data, since the intensity of concern and the scope of the measure cannot be determined from the basic support scores. The support scores do nonetheless indicate a fairly basic difference in foreign and domestic policy support during the 1948–1964 period and also point to a commonly held view of presidential roles.

An important study of legislative role call behavior also emphasized presidential ability to lead more easily on foreign policy matters. Aage Clausen studied the behavior of members of the House since World War II, and found a distinct difference between presidential influence on foreign policy matters and in four different policy areas.[17] (The other four were civil liberties, agricultural assistance, social welfare, and governmental management.) Members of the president's own party were significantly more responsive to his foreign policy appeals than they were to his appeals in other areas. Clausen felt that the uniqueness of the foreign policy area was a most significant finding in his study, and stressed factors other writers have mentioned, such as the absence of great concern in many congressmen's districts for foreign policy questions, in comparison to the interest found on domestic matters such as civil rights.

Writers in the early 1960s also often stressed the willingness of Congress to go along with or make only minor changes in decisions on basic weapons systems. The Armed Service Committees were characterized by Louis Dexter as "real estate" committees. That is, the major concern was with the location of projects and not the nature of the overall weapons systems themselves.[18] Samuel Huntington found a pattern in the 1950s in which weapons questions and troop level questions seemed to produce more interest than questions of overall strategy. Huntington found little indication of a willingness for Congress to become substantially involved with basic directions of foreign policy and wondered in that context whether their tendency to show some interest in weapons systems might not produce an unfortunate bifurcation, in which weapons systems were not in keeping with the foreign strategies being pursued.[19]

Evidence emerging by the 1970s began to raise questions regarding the ease with which the president could operate even on foreign policy matters. In part, the support score data was itself shifting. Taking the period from 1965 to 1973, there was virtually no difference in the support scores on domestic and foreign policy matters. The foreign policy area had a 53.1 percent favorable-action score, while domestic proposals drew a 50.8 percent level of support.[20]

There were also indications that a president could encounter considerable difficulty with some of the foreign policy questions which the multipolar international system was generating in increasing number. Presidents had long had difficulty with the question of foreign aid. Despite periodic pleas, the president found his budgets cut by as much as a third on foreign aid proposals. Problems President Ford began to confront in Congress early in his term gave an indication, furthermore, that this type of issue was growing. Aid to Turkey, for example, became a hotly contested issue in October 1974, and the President finally yielded to congressional desires not to offend the Greek government over the issue.

Congressional willingness to take on the Presidency and the foreign policy bureaucracy also produced important results in the weapons field. President Johnson first proposed an ABM system in the fall of 1967. In an excellent review, Morton Halperin traced the gestation of the proposal as a result of confused bureaucratic politics. Johnson ultimately endorsed a proposal which had a doubtful rationale, and which he apparently did not fully understand himself.[21] Congress formed a stiff resistance to the ABM.[22] Critical in that response was the ability of Congress to generate outside expertise and to call into question the seeming expertise of the Department of Defense. The outside expertise included such people as Jerome Wiesner, a former science adviser in the Kennedy Administration. Wiesner and other scientists were able to provide some alternative advice which was useful to the committee, and to focus opinion on an alternative view. Administration spokesmen also revealed the shabbiness of their own presentation, as they were even forced to reveal that a piece of supposedly expert testimony had been obtained in a brief, accidental airport meeting. There was also legislative staff analysis of the cost figures, which increased skepticism about the plan.

Ultimately, in a virtually even vote, Congress did approve a limited start for the ABM system. Sufficient question had been raised in the original debate, however, to cause the start on the proposed plan to be only minor. Congress had taken a rare step in seeking to question the expertise of the Pentagon, and ultimately caused a major alteration in original Pentagon intentions. Congress was clearly in quest of a larger role.

The issue which remains is that of the presidential power to proceed without legislative interference and make decisions in a closed manner. In such instances, Congress has been sufficiently without information so that the President has been involved solely with the foreign policy bureaucracy. These instances, in empirical terms, have been comparatively few. In this sense, Congress has not been a "paper tiger" for the foreign policy president. At the same time, decisions made as a result of closed interactions of the president, his national security advisers, and segments of the foreign policy bureaucracy can be of extreme importance. The early Vietnam decisions were in this category, as were actions of the Nixon Presidency in not only making decisions on Cambodia, but seeking to keep the implementation of those decisions secret.

The foreign policy bureaucracy, as we have seen, has very often presented the president with considerable controversy and difference of opinion. It is easier to perceive the closed process as monolithic when viewing it from a general, outsider's perspective than when viewing it in terms of its integral parts. At the same time, that process is highly dependent upon presidential personality, and upon the adequacy and forcefulness of the different views being developed. Reform implications for aspects of the closed policy process will be apparent as we look further at alternative presidential roles. A preliminary review is now appropriate regarding the foreign-domestic role distinction.

The Foreign-Domestic Distinction

It is easy to overstate the distinctions between respective areas of presidential responsibility. Presidential roles and policy influence are related to underlying conditions rather than simply specific types of substantive concern, such as foreign policy strategy or major domestic policy concerns. Several of the contributors in Emmet John Hughes' useful collection of former staffers' views of the two-presidency concept appropriately stressed that the distinction was not always as clear as some discussions seemed to suggest.[23] President Ford's inability to gain passage in Congress of his proposed military aid as South Vietnam fell in April 1975 was a dramatic indication of the conditional aspects of presidential roles and policy influence. Ford at points must also have felt very frustrated in his domestic dealings in the same period, but it was nonetheless clear that the presumed advantages attributed to the foreign policy presidency were not present.

There has been important emphasis on the latitude of foreign policy actions as one reflects on presidential behavior during the Cold War period. Structural relations with Congress facilitated easier presidential action in foreign policy situations, at least where force was involved. Electoral support for the Cold War anticommunist emphasis produced a consensus which a president could easily build upon for support of specific policy steps. Power relationships found interest more often in domestic than in foreign policy questions, thus leaving the president greater freedom to pursue his own policy objectives. Nonetheless, even at the seeming peak of the president's influence on foreign policy, he could readily lose on issues such as foreign aid or the development of a specific weapons system.

At a time of rapid change in American politics, it is especially important to emphasize that underlying factors can alter likely presidential roles as well as opportunities for policy influence. Presidents may be able to profit from a growing consensus on some domestic and economic management steps, and they may also profit from a desperate sense that "something needs to be done, and done quickly." A sense of urgency can, at least on occasion, influence domestic and economic management issues. Roles are influenced by general policy contexts and electoral expectations as well as by personality, power, and structure. Thus perceptions of both likely and possible presidential roles in respective policy areas must not be overly dominated by the practices of the Cold War period. Opportunities and constraints become additionally apparent in looking at recent mobilizing efforts regarding the electorate and regarding relationships with Congress.

NOTES

[1] Charles Osgood, ed., *Retreat from Empire*, Baltimore, Johns Hopkins Press, 1973; see especially chaps. 1–3.

[2] For a readable discussion of major components, see Roger Hilsman, *The Politics of Policy in Defense and Foreign Affairs*, New York, Harper & Row, 1971.

[3] Hilsman, op. cit., pp. 42–48.

[4] The problem of CIA operations has recently been discussed by Victor

Marchetti and John D. Marks, *The CIA and the Cult of Intelligence*, New York, Knopf, 1974.

[5] See in particular, John Franklin Campbell, *Foreign Affairs Fudge Factory*, New York, Basic Books, 1971.

[6] *The Pentagon Papers As Published by the New York Times*, New York, Bantam, 1971.

[7] See in particular Townsend Hoopes, *The Limits of Intervention*, New York, McKay, 1969; and David Halberstam, *The Best and the Brightest*, New York, Random House, 1972.

[8] Daniel Ellsberg, *Papers on the War*, New York, Simon & Schuster, pp. 42–135.

[9] Halberstam, op. cit., chap. 22.

[10] See the impact of bureaucratic pressures developed in Graham T. Allison, *The Essence of Decision: Explaining The Cuban Missile Crisis*, Boston, Little, Brown, 1971.

[11] Halberstam, op. cit., p. 653.

[12] James David Barber, *The Presidential Character: Predicting Behavior in the White House*, Englewood Cliffs, N.J., Prentice-Hall, 1972.

[13] The tendency for Johnson to retreat with a few key advisers is discussed in Henry Graff, *The Tuesday Cabinet*, Englewood Cliffs, N.J., Prentice-Hall, 1970.

[14] Language is taken from Lyndon Baines Johnson, *The Vantagepoint: Perspectives of the Presidency 1963–69*, New York, Holt, Rinehart & Winston, 1970, p. 117.

[15] The tendency for public opposition to be related to casualties is discussed in John Mueller, *War, Presidents, and Public Opinion*, New York, Wiley, 1973, chap. 8.

[16] Aaron Wildavsky, "The Two Presidencies," in *The Presidency*, ed. by Aaron Wildavsky, Boston, Little, Brown, 1969, pp. 230–243.

[17] Aage R. Clausen, *How Congressmen Decide: A Policy Focus*, New York, St. Martin, 1973, pp. 222–230.

[18] See Louis Dexter, "The Armed Service Committees," in *New Perspectives on the House of Representatives*, ed. by Nelson Polsby and Robert Peabody, Chicago, Rand McNally, 1969, chap. 1.

[19] Samuel P. Huntington, *The Common Defense: Strategic Programs in National Politics*, New York, Columbia University Press, 1961, chap. 1.

[20] I am indebted to Jeff Simon, University of Southern California, for his seminar research on this data.

[21] Morton H. Halperin, *Bureaucratic Politics and Foreign Policy*, Washington, Brookings, 1974. Halperin uses the ABM case to very usefully show the conflicting forces which bear on a president in dealing with the foreign policy bureaucracy.

[22] The legislative response is discussed in Louis Fisher, *President and Congress*, New York, Free Press, 1972, pp. 212–224.

[23] A variety of interpretations of the two-Presidency concept are presented in the responses of former advisers to a series of questions by Emmet John Hughes. See his *The Living Presidency*, New York, Coward-McCann & Geoghegan, 1972, pp. 311–368.

Presidents
and the Electorate

Presidents are continually trying to build and maintain support for themselves and for their programs. The resulting pattern of relationships between presidents and the electorate raises basic questions both about the capacities for leadership which now reside within the office and the problem of legitimacy in American politics. The level of public confidence in the information coming from the White House has fallen drastically in recent years, making institutional legitimacy a major issue. The manner in which a president is able to attract support is significantly related to the nature of political competition.

Strong-presidency advocates have emphasized the opportunities for an effective presidential personality to mobilize policy support within the electorate and in turn gain legislative victories in Congress. Critics today see presidents as largely unable to build policy support directly and apt to be stymied in Congress when they confront various specialized constellations of interests. Presidential rhetoric in this view consequently involves symbols without substance and considerable deception. Actions vis-à-vis Congress in turn involve circumvention rather than leadership. The next two chapters examine key issues involving leadership with the electorate and with Congress. To begin, one must consider the mechanisms through which presidential attempts at electoral leadership and communication emerge.

Channels of Communication

There has been growing restiveness, on the part of both presidents and the electorate, with the major communication channels. Previous discussions of isolation and agendas have pointed to difficulties with the nature of the communication which is received by the president. In terms of what information gets out, the president is not always as successful as he would like, and the electorate has been increasingly indignant at the patterns of secrecy and distortion. The issue moved from some public concern over news management under Kennedy to proclamations of a credibility gap under Johnson and a widespread dismay with the extent of Nixon's dishonesty. Inevitably, the issue reverts fundamentally to the press and to television operations.

Those who engage in covering the Presidency undertake a coveted, demanding, and often frustrating responsibility.[1] Only the large dailies, wire services, and leading news magazines can afford the luxury of a full-time person to follow the daily comings and goings and constant rumor mills of the White House. These individuals tend to possess a substantial amount of political knowledge and have at numerous points contributed insightful interpretations. Reporters' educational backgrounds have improved in recent years. Their daily contact is primarily through the press secretary, and includes innumerable releases, as well as statements in the frequent sessions between reporters and press secretaries, and some staff interviews.

An inherent tension is involved. Members of the press often seem to be unduly hungry for news and, in particular, to be insensitive to timing on issues which an official may consider important. Competition among members of the press, aside from any natural inclinations, prompts this behavior. Attention and promotion goes with access. From the press perspective, a press secretary and, too often, his boss seem to view the press as essentially an instrument for orchestrating waves of public support for the incumbent. Frustration has often surrounded the interaction of White House and press.

The most institutionalized method of interaction between the president and the press has been the press conference.[2] Begun in the early days of this century, the press conference seemed fairly institutionalized in the days between Franklin Roosevelt and John Kennedy, as even the less visible Presidents, such as Eisenhower, had fairly regular conferences. Given the recent decline in press conferences, it is striking to find Clinton Rossiter concluding as of 1956,

The press conference is not a restraining but an enabling device, as our last three Presidents have demonstrated repeatedly; and that, I would guess, is why it will never again be abandoned outright nor even reduced to the cold, gray event it was under Herbert Hoover.[3]

A disintegration of the press conference began with Johnson, as the tensions over Vietnam increased, and reached new lows in both frequency and usefulness under Richard Nixon. President Ford in turn reverted to essentially a pre-1964 degree of frequency. Johnson began to experiment with differing formats and ultimately simply reduced the frequency. President Nixon gradually came to use the press conference so infrequently that there was not even surprise at their steadily decreasing use.[4] Although this disuse was more pronounced as he struggled with the rising sentiment favoring impeachment, the beginnings came midway in his first Administration. It was concluded that televised addresses were more useful for him than the sometimes rather acrimonious meetings with the press.

Presidents have often, nonetheless, not only had the upper hand at press conferences, but actually tended to enjoy them. Friendly questioners can usually be found if a president does not like the direction in which a conference is moving. Answers can be brief if he desires, and he can leave with little opportunity for follow-up questions, because other press members have their favorite questions in mind and are waiting for a chance to inquire. With easily several hundred at a conference, and perhaps 25 questions asked, reporters simply do not tend to follow up on one another's questions. Planting of questions and the use of opening statements can also insure that specific points are gotten across. Presidents can also call conferences quickly, so that they do not face a press which is particularly well prepared to ask the most pointed questions.

Yet recent Presidents have been apprehensive of press conferences. Kennedy was the last President to show much enjoyment of the activities involved. There is, of course, always the chance of the classic faux pas, as when Truman failed to correct the use of the term *red herring* in reference to his views on the degree of importance attached to the issue of communists in government, or when his answer regarding possible use of atomic bombs during the Korean War left the impression that the level of consideration was very active. Johnson and Nixon, however, seem simply to have been apprehensive about questions which were rather obvious, such as questions about the course of the war in Vietnam or the interpretation of aspects of the Watergate scandals.

Press conferences at best reveal only a smattering of the activities in a Presidency at a particular point in time. Even their extensive use would be no substitute for other lines of communication. One may also be somewhat hard pressed to point to substantial amounts of really useful information which has come out during press conferences in recent years which was not also coming out in other contexts. The tendency to concentrate on foreign affairs (with an average of 85 percent of press conference questions involving foreign policy in Nixon's first two years) reduces opportunities for relevant domestic and internal administrative questions.[5] Yet for all their faults, the press conferences did provide one link through which the electorate could receive something other than canned public relations scripts from the White House.

Presidential television has grown as press conferences have declined. Nixon, in addition, sought different audiences, on occasion, with radio addresses. Speeches obviously have, from the nation's standpoint, the disadvantage of including only that which the president wants to discuss. From the vantagepoint of the president, there is a real temptation to go after the viewing audience of easily 70 million or better that watches the major addresses. President Nixon thus tried additional experiments, such as making sure that his speeches would be broadcast during prime viewing time whenever possible. Given the network tendency to drop everything to serve the president when he requests time, there is an easy potential for presidents to exploit the use of television.

Background briefings constitute another very substantial source of information from the Presidency. Starting basically during World War II, the briefings allow administration officials (including presidents on occasion) to develop ideas, plant trial balloons, or seek to undermine an opponent without being directly quoted. The recurring phrase, "according to high administration sources," is the inevitable result. The briefings do provide a basis for more news being released than would be the case if everything was done on the basis of direct quotation. At the same time, they contribute a murkiness to the process in that there is less responsibility for what is said and less public awareness of who is leading what policy moves.

Surrounding the communication flow at many points is the tendency to label activities secret because of their national security implications. The Freedom of Information Act passed in 1966 represented an attempt at reducing the range of information which could be withheld. Yet the legislation also fell back upon the "national security needs" rationale for withholding information. In addition, one had to be able to request information in specific terms. Therefore, if one did not know of specific secret documents on a given matter, information still could not be requested. Reform steps by 1974, as discussed in Chapter 14, did point to important new changes.[6]

It is not easy to be very enthusiastic about the recent ability of the press to provide accurate information on presidential activities. One should recall that the press reporting which led to the pressure for increased investigation of the Watergate scandals came initially not from the White House press corps but from two young reporters on the local desk of the Washington Post.[7] It is in any event through these channels that the nation seeks to stay informed and the president seeks to lead. The consequences now deserve direct attention.

Promoting Electoral Response

Presidents have a seemingly marvelous opportunity for building support for both their policies and for themselves. A television audience during prime viewing time can easily be obtained at no cost. White House conferences and the granting of recognition to individuals and groups in the electorate can promote particular policy interests. Cabinet officials are ready spokesmen for administration policies. It is easy, too, to keep oneself in the public eye. Travel of any kind places the president on the evening news, and the press is always eager for even small bits of information. Yet one nonetheless finds both presidential frustration with support-building activities and also important evidence that they often do have difficulties in creating effective policy support.

Altering Attitudes and Behavior

Presidents can at points alter individual attitudes and behavior. Several of the more successful presidential appeals have come in situations in which the president was not asking individuals to work for specific pieces of legislation, but to engage in some specific act. John Kennedy's interest in physical fitness produced some increased individual activity. Perhaps even more dramatic was the response when Kennedy pushed the individual approach to bomb shelters in 1961.[8] Rather than asking individuals to write their congressman, or accept a basic new federal commitment, Kennedy suggested that individuals seek their own means of providing shelters. That suggestion produced, during the following decade, a variety of converted fruit cellars and backyard white elephants in places like southern California! In terms of presidential impacts, the result was striking. Kennedy found himself confronted with a sudden rise of entrepreneurship which he and his advisers eventually began to question. In such instances, the presidential power of suggestion may even be greater than was originally intended. Attempts at changing behavior can nonetheless result in failure. Thus President Ford found that his "WIN" buttons—produced as part of a campaign to push his philosophy designed to "whip inflation now"—produced considerable cynicism and no significant alteration in consumer behavior.

A president also has the power to activate some specific supporters in the electorate. The White House conference approach has been used fairly extensively for this purpose. President Eisenhower staged a major conference on foreign aid in 1958, with an eye toward activating the business community into greater support of his foreign aid program.[9] Invitations to attend a White House function were generally regarded as an honor, and there was ready acceptance. The granting of recognition to individuals and to interest-group leaders in various ways can provide a measure of new activity in given policy areas. The final result of Eisenhower's conference was some increased communication on the issue by conference participants, but no major impact on Congress. Both Presidents Kennedy and Johnson were highly sensitive to the opportunities involved in activating specific groups of supportors. The difficult task nonetheless comes in trying to convert the momentum achieved into meaningful policy support, particularly where there is opposition at a key veto point in Congress.

Elections themselves also constitute a vehicle for involving new individuals with particular policy issues. The Stevenson campaigns, even though unsuccessful, were nonetheless a good indication of the manner in which the momentum of election activity can bring a new group into political involvement. The Stevenson campaigns produced increases in liberal reform participation in a number of cities throughout the country. The Goldwater campaign also served to further activate supporters of some of his positions. Mass media campaigns, with professional organizers to arrange for crowds, may unfortunately reduce some of this mobilizing dimension of campaign activities.

Presidents can also at points produce substantial indications of public acceptance for specific policies. Rather frequently, these efforts have been in the area of foreign policy, and they have often involved statements as to why a particular step was taken. In explaining these fait accompli steps the president is not asking for a response which will influence Congress, but for public acceptance of what he has recently done. Vietnam has produced the most striking examples. Poll support for Johnson's policies rose a mighty 30 percent after one of his addresses, and support for Nixon's policies rose at one point by 18 percent after a similar television appeal. Domestic policy support scores have generally been more modest, like the 4 percent increase Kennedy received after his televised proposal for a tax change.[10] Once again, the distinctiveness of the foreign policy area, compared with others, is striking.

There are nonetheless serious pitfalls in presidential efforts at policy leadership. Indications of policy support may not be very firm or lasting. At points, the voter may even be affirming contradictory positions. How does one translate, for example, voter approval of simultaneous steps to promote new programs, reduce taxes, and reduce the annual debt? These are the difficult ultimate questions which policymakers must face, and indications of policy support may well not touch the hard alternatives.

There is also the difficult question of translating poll support into action which moves Congress. It has not been uncommon for policies which receive national poll support of 60 percent and better to languish in Congress. This happened with such issues as federal aid to education in the early 1960s. The key sources of opposition in Congress may well be unmoved, as was often the case facing President Kennedy.

The Expectation-Gap Problem

Presidential interest in creating policy support can also produce serious problems of overexpectation. Lyndon Johnson and his War on Poverty have been discussed in this context.[11] There is no question but that Johnson, with his characteristic exuberance, seemed to promise the nation and its poor a great deal in the 1964–1965 period. The State of the Union address in 1965 in particular seemed to make war simultaneously on a variety of existing national problems. The response in the urban ghettoes by 1966–1968 has been seen by some as being significantly influenced by the frustrations which resulted when expectations outran Johnson's ability to deliver on his promises. Insofar as such situations are endemic to presidential leadership, one envisions the president having to overpromise in order to gain any supportive action, yet finding that a combination of limited budgetary resources and veto points in the political process make it impossible for him to deliver on his promises.

Several reservations should be made regarding the degree to which the Johnson problem is inherent in presidential appeals to the electorate. There is no question but that rising expectations can be a problem in advanced industrial societies, just as they are in the nation struggling with early stages of industrialization. One's sense of well-being is always relative to others around him, and television communication in particular can make it most apparent to those in an industrial society who are comparatively bad off that there are others who are doing very nicely.

The Johnson case is nonetheless somewhat unique. In terms of what did cause the urban riots, there were obviously a wide variety of factors which came into play in the mid-1960s. At the same time, some of Johnson's exuberant rhetoric was unnecessary to legislative passage. Rather, it reflected his tendency to picture everything he did in bold, extravagant terms. It does nonetheless remain true that when one is trying to bring groups into more active political involvement which have not previously been effectively involved, a president may confront the problem that the promises needed to bring people out of political noninvolvement are too large to later fulfill.

The Question of Presidential Support

It is also necessary to question presidential abilities to maintain even their own popularity if they choose domestic policy reform. For the strong-presidency advocate, an active mobilizing role is necessary to effective presidential leadership. Some evidence supports a very different view. President Eisenhower was uniquely able to maintain his popularity while taking a very passive domestic role. Johnson's downfall, on the other hand, was seen by some as resulting from his aggressive domestic stance. Nixon could in the same context be seen prior to Watergate as an example of a President who avoided serious slumps in his popularity while concentrating substantially on foreign policy matters.

The extensive studies by John Mueller dealing with presidential popularity as measured in the Gallup Polls constitute an important source of information.[12] Mueller studied presidential popularity from Truman through Johnson and found that changes in Gallup Poll ratings could best be explained by four variables. First, the "rally around the flag" variable finds popularity increasing with a tense international event. The uniform tendency for the president's popularity to go up with an international crisis is dramatic. Presidential blunders, just as well as courageous acts, are greeted with an increase in their popularity. Truman's popularity rose 9 points as the nation entered the Korean War. Eisenhower's rating went up 6 points in the wake of the United States' admission that a spy plane (U-2) had been making secret flights over the Soviet Union—just before a scheduled summit conference. As John Kennedy was admitting guilt in the ill-conceived Bay of Pigs invasion, his popularity rating was jumping a full 10 points—to 82 percent. It is small wonder that concern was expressed in the wake of Nixon's collapse in 1973 that an international incident would be provoked in an effort at rallying support. The October 1973 alerting of the armed forces in the middle east crisis was questioned by some as a move stemming from his desire to shift attention and muster support for his tottering Presidency.

Engaging in a lengthy war is nonetheless apt to produce a decline in presidential popularity. Truman's popularity gradually declined after the Korean War began, a fact which is explained in part by voter dissatisfaction with the war. The drop of Johnson's popularity in the polls was even more dramatic, as both the Vietnam War and electoral opposition to that war increased during the last years of his Administration. One suspects, in fact, that these two experiences will constitute a powerful restraint on other presidents as they contemplate the prospect of lengthy military involvement.

Economic conditions produce a most intriguing impact on presidential popularity. The often rather pained observation of incumbents that they are blamed for the bad things while not praised for their accomplishments is at least partially borne out in the economic and popularity data. Recessions do produce an impact tending to decrease presidential popularity. Conversely, there is no indication that improvement in economic conditions will assist a president in maintaining or developing high popularity ratings.

The domestic variable is especially significant as it relates to leadership potential. Mueller categorizes the domestic impact as one which bears the "coalition of minorities" phenomenon. That is, policy steps frequently tend to produce a decrease in popularity among those who wanted more done or wanted something else done. As a result, he finds that time in office is related to a gradual decline in popularity, because of the growing number of those who have suffered disappointment at one time or another. Eisenhower is the exception in the Mueller data, and of course also the least domestically active of the Presidents from Truman through Johnson. Through 1972, the flatness of the Nixon popularity ratings, with few peaks or valleys, could be seen as a partial exception to the tendency for time in office to be associated with declines in popularity, although one would need to specifically repeat Mueller's analysis to speak with certainty of the absence of other factors. A not unreasonable conclusion, and one which Mueller partly suggests for Eisenhower, is that the president who initiates comparatively little domestic policy is apt to maintain higher levels of support.

If Mueller's interpretation of the reasons behind a general fall in support is correct, then it is a seemingly devastating blow to the idea of a president being able to lead by mobilizing public support for new domestic policy solutions. One would expect a politically astute and longevity-seeking president simply to emphasize foreign policy matters and seek to avoid recessions and lengthy foreign wars. Several qualifications must be made, however, before one reaches this conclusion.

There are curious exceptions to the tendency for domestic action and advocacy to be associated with a decline in popularity. Most striking is the maintenance of Johnson's popularity without serious fall as he was enacting basic aspects of the Great Society throughout 1964 and early 1965. The measures themselves were also initially highly popular with the voters.[13] Johnson's decline really began with the Vietnam War, and not with the domestic thrusts he was undertaking in Congress. Economic steps, such as Nixon's new economic policy in 1971, may also produce a jump of several points in poll ratings.

Even more striking is the tendency for incumbents to do well in their efforts at reelection despite the frequent decline in their popularity by the latter stages of the first term. Gallup has not included his question on presidential popularity in his polls during campaigns, so it is impossible to speak with assurance regarding the popularity trend during reelection years. Mueller sees the election process as involving a rekindling of interests and support. The tendency for domestic support to trail off and yet for incumbents to be reelected is a striking phenomenon, particularly in view of the tendency seen in Chapter III for the incumbent to capture more votes in his second effort.

One possible interpretation is that the reelection efforts are apt to involve a substantial foreign policy impact. Nixon clearly profited from a voter tendency to see his foreign policy moves in favorable terms in 1972. Foreign policy steps were apt to receive two to three times as many favorable comments as were any of his domestic moves.[14] Eisenhower also profited more from personality and foreign policy assessments than favorable views of his domestic policies in 1956. Unfortunately, information is more limited on earlier reelection efforts. One must also recognize in looking at Nixon and Eisenhower that Republicans have often tended to get comparatively higher assessments on foreign policy matters.[15]

Reelection success despite modest domestic support is a phenomenon with important implications. The frequent victories of incumbents are impressive in light of their major problems in sustaining domestic policy support. Furthermore, one has an intriguing insight into the problem of presidential miscalculation. Incumbents have tended to view their reelection as a mandate on their policies. This was most evident with Richard Nixon and his more aggressive stance after the 1972 election. Insofar as the elections do reflect a general advantage for incumbents because of emphasis on the symbols of office rather than enthusiasm for policies, there is an obvious basis for the frequent tendencies of second-term officeholders to overestimate their political support for subsequent policy moves.

As several writers have emphasized, we need better analyses of the nature of public support. The value of the Gallup Poll Index is in part that it has been repeated identically for about three decades. Gallup asks, "Do you approve or disapprove of the way (the incumbent) is handling his job as President?" The tendency for political activists and Washington leaders to follow the Gallup ratings gives them additional importance. Richard Neustadt has argued rather strongly that the maintenance of prestige with the electorate is an essential resource for the president who seeks to maintain his influence. Yet it remains unclear just what the Gallup question measures. Some of the components were explored by the CBS television network, and their insights were reported in the volume *Public Opinion*.[16] A highly partisan orientation is readily seen in the respondents' evaluations, with some regional variations. It nonetheless remains unclear just how the popularity ratings relate to subsequent voting decisions and to willingness to support specific policies.

There is a need for a clearer picture of how indications of falling presidential support in the polls relate to voter choices at subsequent elections. Elections must ultimately test voters not in their degree of enthusiasm for particular candidates, but in their preference between two alternatives. The tendency toward a more issue-oriented voting, as opposed to party-identification voting, portends opportunities for both incumbents and challengers to develop a greater amount of issue-oriented support than in the past. Depending upon the degree to which domestic issues emerge in future campaigns, there would seem to be greater opportunities for both gaining and losing support on key policy issues.[17] If policy-oriented voters dislike the challenger even more than the incumbent, then lack of support as reflected in the Gallup Poll may have little to do with reelection opportunities. On the other hand, the inability to satisfy various domestic policy desires can also make the situation of the incumbent more difficult, and reinforce the tendency to emphasize such nonpolicy-oriented cues as leadership ability and the general managing of foreign relations.

The difficulties confronting the president in developing and sustaining policy support nonetheless seem, overall, rather substantial. It is often difficult to translate personal popularity into action which moves Congress. In turn, the president faces the danger of unwisely raising expectations in efforts directed toward mobilizing new segments of the electorate. In the face of these difficulties, a president nonetheless possesses other resources for sustaining his popularity. Symbols, deception, and secrecy comprise other devices for relating to the electorate.

Policy Leadership, Symbolism, or Deception?

All presidents engage in some degree of symbolic politics. Murray Edelman has emphasized in his writings that a substantial amount of the activities of recent administrations can be categorized as efforts at symbolic reassurance.[18] Edelman sees presidents engaging in symbolic activities if they sense that real, material changes in programs will not be successful, or that they will cost too much, either in terms of the political resources of the president or in terms of financial resources.

Symbolic appeals are a less scarce resource than tangible policy rewards in that they can be employed simultaneously with a variety of groups. They also require no real knowledge of how a given problem might be solved—the president simply acts and speaks in ways which comfort various segments of the population.

A wide variety of presidential activities can be seen as stemming at least primarily from the desire to generate symbols which will increase acceptance and support of the occupant of the Oval Office. The use of the symbols of the office itself constitutes an effort at merging the identification between a particular individual and the sense of nation among the American people. President Nixon, in particular, worked very hard with this type of appeal. The American system gives ample opportunity for such undertakings. Presidents also at points appoint commissions or propose legislation simply to give the electorate a sense of comfort that something is being done. These steps may lead to meaningful proposals, but they can also simply serve to reassure.

In other situations, a president seeks to show particular segments of American society that he cares about them, that he shares common values. President Nixon liked to congratulate athletes and coaches. Football fan though he indeed was, this could also be seen as an effort at establishing common value identification with the millions of other Americans who enjoyed their favorite teams on television. Visits to the states of so-called middle America constituted another step toward showing a given geographic segment of the nation that he cared about them. The location of the Western White House at San Clemente, California, was seen by some as another symbolic gesture toward a portion of the country.

At points, it becomes difficult to distinguish symbolic appeals from more tangible types of action. The appointment process on occasion takes on largely symbolic dimensions. Even though the position is largely routine, it was considered, for example, good politics for Nixon to appoint a chicano as the U.S. treasurer (not to be confused with the secretary of the treasury). White House Staff appointments may also be substantially symbolic; a president wants some people on his staff to at least symbolically represent various groups which have conscious political identities. The appointment process in other contexts becomes more tangible. Southerners or blacks on the Supreme Court may, for instance, make decisions directly involving major policies.

Symbols are important to presidential leadership. All coalition building involves at least some symbolic activity. FDR at points promoted specific, tangible rewards for several key groups he sought to gain support from in the electorate. These have been reviewed in Chapter 3. Yet Roosevelt was also a master at both reassuring rhetoric and rhetoric which made several segments of American society during the 1930s feel that he really cared about them.

Confusion or absence of symbolic cues can in fact make it difficult for legislation with real substance to be achieved. Perhaps the most interesting recent case was with Nixon and his Family Assistance Plan.[19] The origin of the phrase "Look at what we do and not what we say" (which surely looked grotesque in the wake of Watergate!) was in the fight over family assistance. As Daniel Moynihan has perceptively observed, one of the problems with the bill was the great difficulty for Nixon in generating the symbolic cues to potential recipients of the additional aid. Several potential benefactors became, in fact, leading opponents.

Symbolic politics nonetheless create serious difficulties. Presidents may resort to the use of symbolic politics to cover up changing circumstances which ought to be revealed to the electorate. With Nixon, this reached the point of absurdity at points. Nixon continually reassured the nation in 1970 and 1971 that the economy would soon be performing better than ever. In the process, his staff even eliminated the independent announcement of unemployment figures, hoping thereby to eliminate the attention they were receiving. Nixon apparently felt that if only the electorate would believe in prosperity and stable prices, then that belief would help them occur. There are some very specific economic situations in which such a phenomenon can be observed, generally when there is inadequate consumer demand. Certainly the establishment of electoral confidence that things would get better was a key ingredient in Roosevelt's success with early economic steps in his Administration. Yet the danger is that a president and his advisers will look increasingly foolish to at least major segments of the electorate. Given the problems in managing a modern economy, the parallel growth of both governmental economic involvement *and* a crisis of credibility seems more than coincidental.

Symbolic appeals may also cover up the fact that in reality nothing is being done about a problem which does indeed deserve serious attention. In reassuring the electorate, a president may be preventing a hard look at the concrete realities which must ultimately be confronted. One suspects also on occasion that members of the Presidency may end up primarily deceiving themselves. One view of the rise of the Cold War has stressed the impact which presidential rhetoric ultimately had on the focus of thinking on the part of Truman and his advisers.[20] The adherence of Johnson and his aides to a hard line in Vietnam may also have been influenced by this phenomenon. It is easy for members of the president's staff, ever desirous of being loyal, to respond to their own symbolic rhetoric.

The tendency to relate to the electorate with an emphasis on symbols can also lead to direct distortion of facts.[21] The list of instances involving presidential deceit is getting painfully lengthy. Presidents may be buying time, as with Kennedy's announced "head cold" in October 1962, as the response to the Soviet missiles in Cuba was considered. Presidents may also be trying to cover policy failures, as when the Eisenhower Administration initially lied about its staging of a U-2 flight over the Soviet Union shortly before a scheduled summit meeting in May 1960. In that instance, the subsequent admission that the Administration had both taken a foolish move and then lied in an effort to cover it up seriously undermined the forthcoming summit conference. In some instances, presidents have also seemed to enjoy telling "tall tales," as when Johnson's ancestor was discovered—to the shock of historians who knew better—to have been among those who died at the Alamo.

Presidential lies may also distort policy situations, or else create a false sense of needed support. President Johnson clearly saw advantages in using specific events in Vietnam as rationales for expanding American commitments. The Gulf of Tonkin incident and the raid at Pleiku were the most dramatic.[22] The Tonkin development was used as a basis for rushing the Tonkin resolution through Congress in August 1974. The raid at Pleiku was seen by one of Johnson's key advisers as a handy rationale. Pleikus were, in the words of McGeorge Bundy, like streetcars—if a person waited long enough, one was sure to come along.[23]

The Nixon Administration also practiced deception to a major degree, and on issues other than the cover-up of Watergate and the cover-up of the cover-up. Henry Kissinger was publicly stating a pro-Indian version of President Nixon's position on the American position in the Pakistan-Indian War, for example, while in private indicating that the President wanted very much to have American policy tilt toward the Pakistanis. The distortion became public in early 1972, much to the embarrassment of the Nixon Administration.[24]

The Cambodian bombings during Nixon's Administration constituted the most widely publicized recent instance of official presidential lying. Bombing raids were specifically denied; American neutrality in Cambodia was supposedly being maintained. Yet the Administration subsequently admitted that over 3,000 raids had taken place; an elaborate form of double bookkeeping had been required to deceive Congress and the American people.[25] The desire to cover this up was, in fact, a major reason for wanting to cover up national security leaks—by wire taps, if necesary.

The Watergate revelations substantially broke open the pattern of presidential distortion. They also produced the dramatic result of outright disbelief in the ·President's word for a large majority of Americans. The Nixon Presidency thus culminated—given the disclosures—a growing electoral disbelief in presidential rhetoric.

One should be uneasy with efforts at drawing a trend line on presidential distortion. Some measure of distortion in revealing information is probably about as old as politics itself. Neither the press, scholars, nor Congress has been particularly successful in getting a truly accurate reading of recent presidential records. One can speak with greater confidence in stating that the issue of presidents directly lying to the American electorate has now become a substantial one in general perceptions of the Presidency. The Watergate cover-up, as we shall see, also raises a special case.

Recent concern over presidential use of symbols also seems warrated. The Nixon Administration was more heavily populated with public relations roles than any other in history. As many as 100 individuals were in some manner involved, and extreme emphasis was placed on terminology and symbols.[26] At one point in the debate over the possible release of the tapes, there was even an effort by Nixon at redefining the issue as one of separation of power rather than executive privilege. Presumably it was reasoned that the former was the better-sounding term. The transcripts Nixon released in April 1974, contained frequent references to how decisions could be interpreted to look good before the electorate.

An observer must be careful not to denounce a given Presidency for its use of symbols simply because he happens to dislike, for example, football fans, the values of some so-called middle Americans, or other groups a president may be seeking to attract. It is all too easy to forget that in some measure a wide range of symbols have been used by various Presidents. Nonetheless, a high concern for appearance and use of words does seem to have characterized in particular the Nixon Presidency.

Summary

Current relationships between presidents and the electorate show immense tension. Presidents Johnson and Nixon produced electoral distrust which substantially outdistanced the reaction to news management in the Kennedy Administration. Tension in these relationships is to some extent understandable. Presidents want to use the media to gain support for their policy thrusts and for themselves.

They have become increasingly the dominant political figures in media coverage and are understandably interested in making favorable impressions. Individuals within the media are motivated both by a desire to get as much information as possible, and to gain an enhanced personal position by the information they are able to reveal. Yet despite the frequent presidential and staff feeling that the press is too zealous in the pursuit of information, there are all-too-frequent situations in which major policy developments—and failures—are hidden from the public.

It is comforting to blame individuals for what has been observed in the past decade. With Johnson and Nixon in particular, this was certainly partly deserved. Nixon had always placed high emphasis on rhetoric and had a low regard for telling the truth on political matters. Johnson also tended to embellish various actions—it seemed a part of his character.

Two other factors nonetheless must be considered. Symbols and deception are one means of dealing with cross-pressures for any political figure. Given the nature of various cross-pressures in recent years, there has clearly been a temptation for presidents to resolve their problems in this way. From this perspective, it is not easy to be terribly optimistic about changes in presidential approaches to the electorate. Yet one other key factor is involved. Part of the temptation for deception clearly came from the belief in the White House that it was possible to get away with acts of deception. Surely Richard Nixon could never in his wildest dreams have imagined that his Presidency would crumble in the face of public disclosure of the deceptions of his Administration. From this perspective, there is a potential for modifying future behavior by modifying the opportunities for secrecy.

NOTES

[1] White House correspondents have produced both useful accounts of their own roles and important interpretations of aspects of the Presidency. Stewart Alsop, *The Center*, New York, Harper & Row, 1969; and Douglas Cater, *The Fourth Branch of Government*, Boston, Houghton Mifflin, 1959, are extremely useful.

[2] Histories of press conference use are provided in Elmer Cornwell, *Presidential Leadership of Public Opinion*, Bloomington, Ind., University of Indiana Press, 1965.

[3] Clinton Rossiter, *The American Presidency*, New York, Mentor, 1971, p. 87.

[4] Roosevelt averaged 1.5 press conferences per week, holding a total of 998. Truman met with the press almost once a week. Eisenhower held

conferences twice a month. Nixon, in turn, went 13 months without a conference, even prior to Watergate. David Wise, *The Politics of Lying*, New York, Vintage, 1971, pp. 463–464.

[5] This figure is based upon a Nixon staff study quoted in Newton Minow et al., *Presidential Television*, New York, Basic Books, 1973, p. 58.

[6] Journalist David Wise provides an interesting account of his considerable frustrations in seeking to use the provisions of the Freedom of Information Act in the State Department. See Wise, op. cit., pp. 149–150.

[7] The difficulties encountered are revealed in Bob Woodward and Carl Bernstein, *All the President's Men*, New York, Warner Paperback Library, 1975.

[8] The civil defense responses are discussed in Eugene Wigner, *Who Speaks for Civil Defense?*, New York, Scribner, 1968.

[9] This effort was extensively examined by James Rosenau in *National Leadership and Foreign Policy*, Princeton, N.J., Princeton University Press, 1963.

[10] Minow, op. cit., p. 19.

[11] Aaron Wildavsky, "The Empty-Headed Blues: Black Rebellion and White Reaction," in *The Revolt from the Masses*, ed. by Aaron Wildavsky, New York, Basic Books, 1971, pp. 52–65.

[12] John Mueller, *Presidents, War, and Public Opinion*, New York, Wiley, 1973, chap. 9.

[13] Johnson's popularity and the popularity of the programs as he gained their enactment is discussed in James Sundquist, *Politics and Policy: The Eisenhower, Kennedy, and Johnson Years*, Washington, D.C., Brookings, 1968. See in particular pp. 496–497 for levels of policy support as of 1965.

[14] The substantially greater popularity for Nixon's foreign rather than his domestic policy moves is documented in the Louis Harris poll data as of August, 1972. See *Newsweek*, August 28, 1972, p. 18.

[15] The Republican tendency to do better on foreign policy assessments is traced through 1964 by Donald Stokes in "Some Dynamic Elements of Contests for the Presidency," in *The Presidency*, ed. by Aaron Wildavsky, Boston, Little, Brown, 1969, pp. 346–364.

[16] The poll data is reported in Robert Chandler, *Public Opinion*, New York, Bowker, 1972, chap. 6.

[17] The impacts of greater issue oriented voting are effectively discussed by Richard W. Boyd in James David Barber, ed., *Choosing the President*, Englewood Cliffs, N.J., Prentice-Hall, 1974, pp. 175–201.

[18] Murray Edelman, *Politics as Symbolic Action*, Chicago, Markham, 1971. See also his *Symbolic Uses of Politics*, Urbana, Ill., University of Illinois Press, 1964.

[19] On Nixon's difficulty in generating supporting symbols with the logical groups, see Daniel P. Moynihan, *The Politics of a Guaranteed Income*, New York, Vintage, 1973, chaps. 4, 5.

[20] Bertram Cochran, *Crisis and the Truman Presidency*, New York, Funk & Wagnalls, 1973, p. 187.

[21] The most extensive recent discussion of presidential lying is Wise,

op. cit. See also Bruce Ladd, *The Crisis of Credibility,* New York, New American Library, 1968.

[22] On the Tonkin incident, see David Halberstam, *The Best and the Brightest,* New York, Random House, 1969; and Joseph Goulden, *Truth is the First Casualty,* Chicago, Rand McNally, 1969.

[23] The view that Pleiku constituted a convenient rationalization has been attributed to Johnson's National Security Adviser, McGeorge Bundy. See Halberstam, op. cit., p. 533.

[24] The duplicity in the Nixon Presidency was publicized through the efforts of columnist Jack Anderson. See his *The Anderson Papers,* New York, Random House, 1973, pp. 205–269.

[25] The congressional outrage at this direct deception of Congress was serious enough to promote introduction of an impeachment article in the House Judiciary Committee proceedings. The deception was specifically admitted by the secretary of the air force in testimony before Congress.

[26] The contemporary reliance on public relations is vividly discussed by Thomas Cronin in "The Presidency Public Relations Script," in Rexford Tugwell and Thomas Cronin, eds., *The Presidency Reappraised,* New York, Praeger, 1974, pp. 168–183.

Presidents and Congress

Presidential relationships with Congress present a curious paradox. It is common to observe that Congress has declined in policy-making importance vis-à-vis the president in recent decades, yet presidents often complain that it is extremely difficult to move Congress on specific issues. John Kennedy voiced a frequent concern as he claimed that Congress looked a lot stronger from the White House than it did from the vantagepoint of an individual Senator's office. Each president since 1960 has had a very different relationship with Congress, a fact which further complicates efforts at generalization. Congress, in the brief period of slightly more than a decade, has been both a chief villain and a major source of hope for many observers.

Several topics deserve attention in unraveling aspects of presidential relationships with Congress. Patterns of interaction must be considered, along with the major resources of presidential influence. Differences in levels of success can then be considered, along with tendencies for circumvention. Analysis of presidents and Congress will then conclude with an examination of recent changes taking place in Congress as it seeks a more active policy-making role.

Patterns of Interaction

Patterns of presidential involvement with Congress have become substantially institutionalized. Back in the days of Teddy Roosevelt, concern for the implications of separation of power motivated Roosevelt and House Speaker Joe Cannon to meet in a secret manner, with Cannon carefully entering the White House so as to be unnoticed. Yet by Kennedy's day there was a substantial liaison staff, with an office in the Capitol. About the only remaining homage paid to separation of power was Lawrence O'Brien's reluctance (as top liaison man for Kennedy) to sit in the galleries when Congress was voting.[1] The federal government simply could not handle its present range of activities if legislative-executive relations remained ones of passing occasional smoke signals to one another.

Presidents now use several mechanisms in relating to Congress. Meetings with party leaders are held when Congress is in session, to review forthcoming legislation. Presidents want to know how their programs are doing, and what the flow of business is going to be. They are also interested in expressing their sense of urgency on various issues to the party leaders. It has not been uncommon for these meetings to occur as frequently as once a week, often at breakfast gatherings.

The legislative liaison office is responsible for the routine interactions. Legislator's voting positions need to be continually assessed, and in turn the president can communicate his sense of the importance of various policy matters. Liaison officials work closely with party leaders; the House of Representatives in particular presents major problems of coordinating likely voting information because of the number of individuals involved. Liaison officials also work at points with their counterparts in the respective departments in an effort at coordinating the mustering of support for specific measures.

Presidents also meet with, and contact by phones, individual legislators. President Johnson in particular liked to engage in extensive direct contact with legislators. Often, these efforts involve efforts at gentle—and on occasion not so gentle—acts of presidential persuasion on specific bills. In other instances, there will be a direct exchange of information on a variety of matters. One of the more interesting friendships in recent years was between Johnson as President and Senator Dirksen, the Republican minority leader in the Senate. Numerous meetings were held on Vietnam matters, with Dirksen generally reassuring Johnson in his positions.[2] This is one of the instances in which the importance of friendships coming from long mutual involvement in Washington politics produces activity which is too often not emphasized in textbook discussions.

Of the recent Presidents, Johnson was the most actively involved with Congress, Kennedy did the most in terms of developing an institutionalized structure, and Nixon was the most strongly criticized for his own and his staff's inabilities to maintain either an informed or an active set of relationships with Congress. The removal of Bryce Harlow from his position as head of legislative liaison was widely seen as one early indication of frustrations in Nixon's relationships with Congress. Nixon's shift to his "Operation Candor" in the fall of 1973, with its inclusion of White House meetings with large numbers of legislators, was in part an outgrowth of limited and fragile earlier relationships.[3] Regardless of how disdainful presidents and their staffs may feel toward Congress on occasion, there is no escaping some measure of continuing interaction.

Presidential Power and Congressional Resistance

Despite the extensive set of interactions which normally takes place, presidents face major restraints in their efforts to deal with Congress, and with individual Congressmen. Independence of committee chairman has been a continuing key factor. Presidents have had no real say, given seniority, in the selection—or firing—of committee chairmen. The 1975 actions in overturning 3 House chairmen was in turn an important development, but did not necessarily mean that presidents themselves would have a voice in future removals. As a result, chairmen even of the president's own party will on occasion act with tenacious independence. John Kennedy found Southern chairmen difficult to deal with on numerous occasions.[4] Concern for tax measures found Kennedy, for example, wooing Senator Byrd with steps including a presidential appearance at Byrd's birthday party at his Virginia farm. Congressman Rooney, whose subcommittee had a lot to say about embassy budgets (at a time when Kennedy was hoping to get more individuals appointed as ambasssadors on the basis of merit rather than personal fortune), was invited to Florida for a personal visit. Neither action had a decisive impact; the fact that the President used such techniques reflects the lack, basically, of more decisive power resources.

Lyndon Johnson had fewer problems with committee chairmen, for several reasons. Friendship ties were helpful on occasion, given Johnson's background in the Senate and his Southern origins. Critically, Johnson also had, after the 1964 elections, a surplus majority which was extremely helpful in breaking conservative coalition resistance on key matters. Additionally, both the veto capacities of the Southern delegation and their numbers in chairmanships were declining after 1964. Richard Nixon's problems became somewhat more those of dealing with Congress in general, although he still faced difficulties in dealing with such independent and powerful chairmen as Wilbur Mills, as Mills headed the House Ways and Means Committee in its review of tax policies.

Lack of influence on the electoral success of legislators is at the root of the presidential problem, with both chairmen and congressmen in general. Safe seats and the tendency for incumbents to be fairly easily reelected limit the amount of interest congressmen have in presidential assistance. Presidents *have* on occasion entered primaries to aid their friends and to attack foes. The most famous case was Roosevelt's effort (largely unsuccessful) to purge senators in 1938 who were opposing his New Deal measures.[5] Public awareness of presidential efforts may well cause a negative response in the local electorate and can even backfire. Furthermore, a young legislator from a marginal district is more readily toppled than the senior figure who is specializing in a committee role and is giving presidential programs a rough time.

The less visible resource that a president may use, either for purges in his own party or to help in general elections, is campaign contributions. Money can be made available and is a most useful resource for the president. The indirect route is to steer donors to candidates whose favor the president wants to gain. Money can also flow more directly. Thus, a key issue in the controversy over Herbert Kalmbach's handling of Republican money left over from the 1968 campaign was the use of that money in legislative races. The quiet provision of funds for legislative races was seen in the Nixon camp as an important step in gaining a more friendly Congress after 1970.

Presidential support in general legislative elections can also have some impact. The active support of a president, with perhaps an appearance in a legislator's district or at least pictures and kind words, is often sought. It is unusual to have the candidates shun the president, as occurred with Nixon in the wake of his political collapse. A popular president, during his own run for office, generally helps bring out some voters who would otherwise be staying home. He can also pull some congressmen into office. Midterm elections repeatedly find the president's party doing worse, sometimes rather substantially. Especially bad showings often come in the midterm elections for a president in his second term.[6] Part of the loss is built in, if a president has created an artificially large majority by helping to carry a number of marginal districts the year his name was at the top of the ticket. The best a president can generally hope to do in a midterm election is to minimize losses to the opposing party. President Nixon made a major endorsing effort in 1970 in Senate races and encouraged the entrance of what seemed to be the most attractive candidates. That effort was nonetheless substantially unsuccessful.

Presidential actions, in short, are more apt to change the overall size of their party's delegation, rather than to eliminate key opponents of presidential programs. If purges are not often successful, there nonetheless remains the possibility of altering a legislator's position on a specific piece of legislation.

Aid and favors to help solidify support for a legislator in his district or to help him accomplish his own objectives is at points helpful in terms of specific votes, regardless of the overall composition of Congress. Even recognition is sometimes deemed important. Appointment to a commission or honorary position may seem attractive to a legislator who labors under the typical lack of public attention given to congressmen. Appointments for his friends can also be important to the legislator as he seeks both to build a political base and to show his influence in Washington. Aid for his district is an additional key incentive. Presidents at points clearly utilize this resource for legislative influence. President Kennedy was reported to have responded after meeting with Wilbur Mills on tax matters in 1963 that he recognized the value of the Arkansas River Project (aiding Mills' home state) for the first time. River and harbor improvements have been traditionally emphasized as a bargaining resource for presidents, although a glance at the budget figures today indicates the limited scope when compared to other programs. Army Corps of Engineer funds (cut substantially by Nixon) were by 1973 only in the $2 billion range. Science and research and development projects, running better than $15 billion, have provided a growing source of potential bargaining. Interest on the part of Midwest legislators in gaining a larger share of science funds produced at one point direct discussion of the issue with President Johnson.[7] In developing support for specific programs, it can be most helpful to have NASA funds going significantly to the South, or Sea Grant funding aiding states with key legislators. The more difficult trade is to generate support for a bill by spinning off a benefit for a particular legislator which is unrelated to that particular bill. It can be difficult for even an enterprising president to find oceans to study in Kansas, or a rationale for supporting major science research at struggling, marginally successful state universities.

Defense contracts provide the largest single category of potentially bargainable assistance for districts.[8] Even with increasing personnel costs, there may be in the neighborhood of $40 billion to deal with. The location of payrolls is also important, in terms of legislative interest. Yet presidents face limitations with this legislative sanction. On the largest contracts, the political factors seem often to relate to the president's own opportunities for reelection. Widespread unemployment in California, for example, is something which Richard Nixon had a clear personal interest in avoiding in 1972, irrespective of votes by the state's Democratic senators against several weapons system proposals introduced by the Nixon Administration. Thus there were limits on his ability to sanction the California legislators even if he could manipulate contracts to accomplish that objective. The president also faces the necessity of either breaking the contracting process down into fairly small units, with resulting costs in time and possible efficiency, or else having a rather limited number of plums which can be distributed to entice key votes. If he chose the latter course, he might influence the most critical vote or two in a given session, but many other votes would have to go unaided by this type of influence. It should be noted, however, that the threat of a sanction and the implicit promise of aid if a congressman is on good behavior, expands somewhat the scope of the contract bargaining.

The appeal of party loyalty must also be recognized.[9] This is obviously of no help with the opposition, but the argument that the defeat of the president is also a defeat for his legislative party can—particularly if the president is generally in good standing—have an impact on potentially wayward party members. Despite the importance of coalitions and the impact of districts, party cues and a sense of identification with party do remain a strong influence in congressional politics.

The other route the president can take is to seek a ground swell of support for specific legislation. Richard Neustadt's *Presidential Power* emphasized the importance of electoral appeals. The problems with this strategy in terms of public responses have been considered in Chapter 10. Had John Kennedy lived for a second term, the evidence would be somewhat clearer on uses of electoral support, since he had considerable popularity with the electorate. In his actual record, he seemed somewhat reluctant to try to convert his popularity to specific issue support, especially on domestic matters, and he also had considerable difficulty with Congress. A review of the recent record gives further indication of the strengths and weaknesses of respective presidential resources for influencing Congress.

The Recent Record

Presidents Kennedy, Johnson, and Nixon had very different experiences and degrees of success in dealing with Congress. In simple terms, Kennedy was often stymied; Johnson (especially through 1966) was very uniquely successful; and Nixon suffered substantial defeats, yet managed to produce a wide variety of policy impacts. Often, Nixon's success was not in persuading a majority in Congress, but rather in achieving some means of accomplishing his objectives without the direct consent of Congress. Each pattern deserves consideration.

There is a long-standing dispute over the evaluation which should be made of Kennedy's level of success with Congress.[10] He suffered serious liabilities which were inherent in his situation. The size of the Democratic majority in Congress actually declined in 1960. Southern points of resistance were intense, particularly in key committee chairmanships and the influential Rules Committee in the House. Kennedy was also dealing with several issues which had been stalemated 10, 20, or even 25 years. Kennedy had also been a victor by a narrow margin, and was often reported to be highly conscious of his seemingly narrow base of support. Finally, Kennedy devoted, particularly in 1961, a very high segment of his time to foreign policy matters and the several crisis issues being confronted.

The defense of Kennedy has generally been twofold. First, he did gain passage of some significant domestic measures. Aid for depressed areas, manpower retraining programs, and emergency public works measures are often mentioned. The year 1962 also produced the important foreign policy step of Congress ratifying the Test Ban Treaty restricting the testing of nuclear weapons. Second, Kennedy's record tends to be defended in terms of his promoting greater public interest in measures which were subsequently passed by Johnson. Randall Ripley partially accepts the importance of Kennedy's preliminary work in his review of that legislative record.[11] It is nonetheless apparent that Kennedy was often stymied by the operation of a variety of congressional veto points. A President with popularity in the polls often found the going in Congress difficult.

Johnson's record is conversely one of unique accomplishment, particularly on domestic policy issues.[12] He was the inheritor of several favorable developments. There was some sentiment toward the passage of Kennedy's programs as a tribute to the dead President. After the 1964 elections, Johnson had a substantially greater legislative majority to mobilize. In the House, the impact of Goldwater's poor showing at the top of the ticket gave the Democrats a net gain of 37 seats and an important ability to override the impact of the conservative coalition. Public support for such measures as aid to education and Medicare was also high as Johnson began to mobilize for the passage of these programs. Finally, Johnson was a President who clearly felt at home in the legislative arena and with domestic politics. His years as majority leader in the Senate had given him a shrewd sense of timing and of coalitions.

The result was a President who was phenomenally successful. The remaining elements of the New Deal agenda, plus a basic civil rights bill, was basically passed by 1966. A war on poverty, a tax cut, Medicare, federal aid to education, and a tough civil rights act all came rolling through the Johnson-charged Congress. That period compares favorably with the Wilson efforts in 1913–1914 and the first years of the New Deal as a period in which presidential leadership coupled with fortuitous circumstances in Congress produced a basic legislative modification of policies and commitments. Such key veto points as committee structures, filibusters, and the position of the House Rules Committee began to fade in strength. Johnson was sensitive to the importance of making his legislative mark early if he was going to have major achievements, and he was remarkably successful in his efforts.[13]

Nixon's record with Congress reflected a return to squabbling and frequent presidential defeat, even prior to the Watergate issues. Nixon began with major limitations.[14] His was the minority party, and he, like Kennedy, lacked strong support in the electorate (unless one coupled the Wallace vote with Nixon's 43 percent). The electorate also seemed more uncertain of the new President than is usual, with a decidedly large number of responses in the "not sure" category when Gallup asked voters to indicate how they felt the new President was doing. Nixon also sought to relate to Congress after having been away from Washington for eight years, and with a staff which was remarkably inexperienced in legislative matters.

Nixon's record produced serious defeats and also low overall ratings.[15] In an unprecedented response, Congress turned down his first two attempts at appointing members to the Supreme Court. Not since the days of Herbert Hoover had a president lost a Supreme Court nomination. The Family Assistance Plan passed in the House, but became hopelessly mired down in the Senate Finance Committee. The supersonic transport (SST) funding was ended, despite a strong White House plea, and the President ran into unexpectedly strong resistance on such weapons measures as the development of the ABM missile system. Nixon did manage to promote successfully the shift to a volunteer army and the first phase of his revenue-sharing program. Nonetheless, in terms of passage of bills with presidential backing, he slumped quickly to levels lower than both Kennedy and Johnson. Measures were less apt than in the Kennedy period to be killed in committee, but both committee measures and presidential programs were more apt to be altered or killed in floor votes. Stalemate and an inability on Nixon's part to produce legislative majorities became the dominant pattern.

A president, as Johnson made clear, could move Congress under a set of favorable conditions. Yet stalemate and frustration were typical for both Kennedy and Nixon. Rather than making Congress happy with a newfound influence in blocking the Presidency, the Nixon years produced an intense unhappiness with the role Congress was able to fulfill. To understand that unhappiness, one must consider the all-important situation in which presidents find that they can accomplish their objectives without direct legislative support.

Presidential Discretion

Crucial to an understanding of legislative-executive relationships is an assessment of the changing scope of presidential discretion.[16] In various ways the congressional tendency to delegate roles to the Presidency and to executive agencies with broad statements of authority has been characteristic of Congress since at least the 1930s. Preisdents have also often found that the frustrations of dealing with Congress can be resolved by simply devising means of bypassing specific congressional approval.

Presidential ability to bypass Congress has been glaringly obvious in foreign policy matters.[17] Congress has not even been required to declare a war since World War II. Significantly, President Nixon also found means of avoiding the impact of substantial legislative hostility toward his Vietnam policies in his first term. Congress passed the Cooper-Church Amendment in 1969, seeking to prevent the use of troops in Thailand and Laos. In 1970, Nixon and his strategists chose, instead, to enter Cambodia. (Efforts at legislating a specific date for the end of the war proved popular with some in Congress, but until 1973 never a majority. The Hatfield-McGovern Amendment failed in the Senate in 1970 by a 55-to-39 vote.) Furthermore, as subsequently became apparent, a policy of sustaining bombing in Cambodia without revealing those actions to Congress enabled the Nixon Administration to fly over 3,000 bombing missions into Cambodia. Despite legislative skepticism, Nixon was able to pursue his policy of decreased troop commitments and increased bombing throughout his first four years in office.

Specific legislative delegation to the president of responsibility for broad policy making has also often occurred. Tariff policies have been substantially an executive function since the 1930s. Executive authority was continued in this area even in the face of the massive legislative concern with the behavior of the Nixon Presidency. Wage and price controls involved another delegation, with only the vaguest suggestion of policy directions from Congress. It is difficult for Congress to be very specific, yet the result is that the Presidency is in effect asked both to make policy and to supervise the implementation of the resulting decisions.

Several other techniques have been employed to give the president considerable discretion in recent years, with varying degrees of controversy. The use of executive orders by the president has at points been an important policy tool. The custom has simply developed historically for the president to issue a variety of orders pertaining to the administrative operation of the government. At points, with the expansion of the federal bureaucracy and the scope of the government's concerns, executive orders have taken on considerable importance in setting general policy directions. President Truman achieved the desegregation of the armed forces by this route. More recently, President Kennedy sought to promote integration in public housing by the executive order route, as well as seeking to eliminate discrimination in housing sales which were covered by such loan programs as that of the Veterans Administration. Major aspects of these executive moves were given a statutory base by the civil rights acts of 1964 and 1968. Ruth Morgan concluded an extensive survey of executive order use by concluding that on occasion the president not only promotes law making, but also makes laws.[18] The Morgan analysis was fairly enthusiastic, made as it was in the context of advances which had been made with civil rights issues. Regardless of how one might feel as to the policy results being achieved, the president nonetheless had an important tool for avoiding Congress.

Impoundment of funds appropriated by Congress emerged in the Nixon Presidency as a highly explosive presidential technique for achieving policy objectives without direct legislative support. There were long-standing precedents for a president not spending all of the funds appropriated by Congress. On occasion, as with President Jefferson and the Louisiana Purchase, they also exceeded appropriation levels. Presidents immediately prior to Nixon had used the impoundment technique quite extensively. Eisenhower's impoundments averaged over $7 billion per year, Kennedy's over $6 billion, and Johnson's over $7 billion. There is some dispute as to how Nixon's figures should be counted, but a conservative judgment is that he averaged over $11 billion. Yet in relationship to the total size of the federal budget, the percentage of funds being impounded was actually less in many cases than had been impounded by preceding Presidents.[19]

The issue with Nixon and Congress surrounded the scope of impoundment and the permanence of Nixon's decisions.[20] Many of the earlier impoundments had been of funds for military procurement, with a tendency for commitments to be delayed. Nixon impounded only marginally funds for defense matters, but impounded funds for a variety of programs being espoused by Congress extensively. Impoundment affected legislative favorites, such as programs for the cities and for the environment. A group of legislators even went into court to try to get the President to spend appropriated highway funds, and they achieved significant success.

The impoundment technique, it should be emphasized, has been significantly altered by recent action.[21] The Presidency must now supply lists of impounded funds every 30 days. Furthermore, if the impoundment is not approved by Congress within 60 days, then the impounded funds must be spent. It remained to be seen as the new procedures were enacted just how effective they would be; the procedures were nonetheless significantly altered. Not only was Congress seeking a voice, but it was up to the Presidency to get another affirmative vote rather than for Congress to produce an opposing vote. This represented an important shift from the earlier pattern of legislative-executive relations, in which a variety of procedures were assumed to be permissible unless Congress acted to reject them.

The reorganizing authority given to the president in the Reorganization Act of 1939 has at points also been an important tool for presidential influence. Positions on the White House staff can be shuffled at will, allowing changes giving different people major policy impact. Nixon also sought by the reorganizing authority to eliminate the Office of Economic Opportunity (OEO) in 1973. He was fought successfully in the courts, on the basis of a ruling that the agency's statutory existence made it improper for a president to eliminate it entirely. After a series of compromises in Congress, OEO's functions were nonetheless phased into several domestic departments. Nixon also sought, after his cabinet reorganization proposal had been defeated in 1971, to achieve partial reorganization by shuffling cabinet positions himself into a supercabinet structure which would have given three cabinet officials greater influence. That plan was abandoned in the confusions of Watergate.

The veto process produced an unusually extensive opportunity for President Nixon to achieve his objectives without majority support in Congress. The phrase "one-third plus one" did not originate with impeachment discussions in the Nixon staff, but with the sense that they could often achieve their goals through vetoes which Congress could not override with the needed two-thirds vote. Nixon did not veto an unusually large number of measures in his first term. His 28 vetoes compared with 30 for Lyndon Johnson, 21 for John Kennedy, and 181 for Eisenhower.[22] Nixon was more willing than his predecessors to veto major legislation. Thus, he became the first President since Eisenhower to veto an appropriation bill, and he vetoed a number of substantial domestic measures. Disagreements over the substance of policy were clearly reflected in Nixon's veto process. Nixon's opportunity for using the veto effectively was related to his basic desire to reduce a variety of domestic programs. A president seeking to advance new commitments could not use the veto with the same degree of effectiveness. Under specific conditions, the veto nonetheless emerges as an important tool for a president in influencing policy without winning a majority in Congress.

The powers which Richard Nixon was employing were in several respects in keeping with past trends. There were also several instances in which the opportunity for presidential discretion was not grudgingly yielded, but was willingly granted by congressmen who felt a need for speed and expertise, or perhaps a desire to be able to criticize policy without really being responsible. Vetoes and impoundments proved to be the highly controversial measures. The Nixon Presidency, in sum, could often block Congress and proceed without majority support in Congress, even though it often could not gain majority support for new policy thrusts. Presidential discretion, if not new, was dramatically extensive.

A Changing Congress

By 1975, Congress was in a mood to seek a substantially different role. The actions of a Democratic majority interested in asserting its policy desires more emphatically against those of President Nixon had provided an initial reform thrust. As in the past, recent institutional change has often not been the result of an apolitical discussion of institutional niceties. Yet Congress has continued to reveal numerous resistances to changes within the context of its highly institutionalized procedures. These were at some points most apparent in the post-Watergate response. Looking at the patterns of continuity and change in recent years, several developments involving both functions and structure of Congress deserve emphasis.

Issue Raising

There are few firm measures of the sometimes rather complex manner in which various participants contribute to the raising of new issues and policy ideas. Historically, there have been some rather dramatic cases of legislatively spawned issues, as in the spring of 1950, when Senator Joseph McCarthy launched the question of communist infiltration into government as an issue which would occupy immense amounts of time, as well as significantly retarding the development of the State Department and violating many individual's civil rights. Among observers of the contemporary period, there has been both a frequent emphasis on the marginal dimension of the legislative role and also a persistent defense of that role as being larger than expected when one examines issues closely. Ronald Moe has been one of the staunch supporters of the view that Congress has done a substantial amount of initiating.[23] John Johannes takes something of a middle position in a thoughtful discussion of alternative conditions under which various roles can be performed.[24] Johannes stresses instances in which Congress may lead indirectly as issues are preempted by the president. Eisenhower's belated support for a civil rights bill in 1956 and Johnson's takeover of the antipollution and consumer protection issues are cited among the examples. At the same time, the tendency for legislative initiation to occur under specific conditions of an activist majority in Congress and a more passive president constitutes for Johannes a limitation on the ease with which one can generalize about the legislative initiating role.

Regardless of how one reads the trend, the recent past has found a significant role for congressmen in raising issues. Interest groups are finding that it is most helpful in gaining momentum to get some legislators interested. At the same time, ambitious legislators are often looking for issues to champion. Many legislators lack extensive ability to gain media attention, but they can at least promote discussion among some specialized audiences.

Recent cases are numerous. Environmental legislation got a major thrust in the water pollution area in the mid-sixties with the efforts of Senator Muskie. Women's rights have been advanced by legislator attention. Consumerism was aided at early stages by several legislative proponents. The handling of radioactive waste by the army was raised as an issue by a young congressman. Early discussion of revenue sharing, long before it became a major reform thrust of the Nixon Administration, was promoted by Congressman Reuss of Wisconsin. Opposition to weapons systems, as when the critics of the ABM system emerged in 1969–1970, involved an important legislative role. Even if they lack substantial expertise themselves, congressmen have found that they can at points serve an important role in allowing those with questioning voices a chance to be heard. There have indeed been important instances in which Congress has been instrumental in either raising a new issue or providing a focal point for those seeking to criticize an existing or emerging policy coming from the Presidency. Issue raising has in fact meant that new groups and interests have been able to find some access in the political system.

Altering Policy Outcomes

Congress has shown a substantial willingness to alter program recommendations handed to it by the president. Indeed, as the coalition shift became pronounced between the branches, this was increasingly basic in the embroilments between Nixon and Congress. Traditionally, Congress has often tended to influence outcomes by refusing to act; committee vetoes and filibusters were the dominant pattern, with racial matters often the dominant issue.

There have been important changes since 1969. The issue of defense versus domestic spending has become a recurring issue between the president and Congress. Senator McGovern reflected the salience of that issue within his own legislatively oriented world as he sought to take the issue of guns versus butter to the general public in 1972. Significantly, the issue has produced some tendencies for priority matters to reach the floor of both houses. Cuts in such areas as space and defense have tended to come not from the specialized committees, but in the context of floor debates. This is in marked contrast to the days of the 1950s and 1960s in which defense appropriations sailed through floor deliberations as recommended from committee. In those days, an entire defense appropriation might be approved in a couple of hours.

The picture which Richard Fenno carefully detailed of the limited legislative use of the power of the purse had altered at points by the mid-1970s.[25] Congress approved some very large changes from those requested by the president. In 1972, the total congressional appropriation involved such changes as over $10 billion more than requested for Labor and Health, Education and Welfare (this was vetoed), and over $5 billion less for defense. Several other specific programs, such as space and foreign aid, also received substantial cuts, while environmental and consumer protection measures were among those increased.[26] Several of these changes became involved in either presidential vetoes or impoundments, as relations between Nixon and Congress faltered. The issue was not total spending as much as priorities, despite the Nixon tendency to blame Congress for deficits and to justify the need for his vetoes. Nixon himself was proposing large deficits, and Congress was at points actually cutting more than adding to his budget proposals. With Congress controlled by the opposing party and seeking different priorities, Nixon was clearly attempting to alter policy outcomes. This was also the point at which presidential discretion entered into the Nixon Presidency, with the impact of impoundment and vetoes.

Program Evaluation and Administrative Oversight

Congress has increased somewhat its involvement with the assessment of programs.[27] Committee bureaucracies have continued to grow, as has the time spent by congressmen in committee, precisely because of this expanded activity. Several of the issues which have been raised through congressional action have come as a result of the review function. At points, reviews have been both substantial and thorough.

Military programs have occasionally received more substantial review than tended to be the case in the past. Instrumental in this regard has been the activity of the Joint Economic Committee. On occasion, as with the revelations of the cost overruns on the C5-A cargo plane, an important change comes from the review. Those overruns were exposed as being over $2 billion, through the willingness of a Pentagon official, A. Ernest Fitzgerald, to testify.[28] One should not overstate the case regarding review capacities. Some additional capacity was developed in the past decade. At the same time, because of the magnitude of potential topics for examination, many programs are still explored in the traditional, rather cursory manner, with friends of the programs often on the review committees and congenial witnesses being called to testify. The incentives of a congressman may well be away from careful review, given his needs for dealing with constituents and taking some stand on a variety of issues.

Educating the Electorate

Few could deny, in the wake of the impact of the Ervin Committee hearings in the summer of 1973, that legislative action could have a major impact in educating the electorate. The Ervin Committee transformed the Watergate issue into one from which millions of Americans gained a direct sense of the magnitude of the abuses which had taken place in the Nixon Presidency. If Nixon's spokesmen often confused the culprits and the exposers of wrongdoing in their attacks on Congress, they nonetheless correctly sensed that the educational impact of congressional activities was substantial.

Congress has nonetheless been somewhat reticent in the educational role. Television has not often been used as effectively as it might. Party leaders have not found it a particularly useful vehicle. Floor proceedings in the House and Senate are similarly reported only by the printed word.

The educational role is sometimes criticized in that it is often associated with the work of ambitious individuals. A popular hearing is an excellent vehicle for a senator seeking to develop a mass constituency. The sudden rise in interest in a presidential bid by a formerly obscure Republican, Senator Howard Baker, was a good recent reminder of the usefulness of popular hearings in terms of personal publicity for participating legislators. A legislative hearing can easily produce the plays to the media which were so common in the Joseph McCarthy era, when one saw the pursuit of dramatic witnesses and the purposeful creation of exciting incidents to capture maximum press coverage.

The actions of an ambitious congressman can nonetheless have important consequences. One can only wonder what the impact might have been in 1964 had a more critical role been chosen by the head of the Foreign Relations Committee. The Vietnam hearings in the spring of 1966 revealed very forcefully that hearings can perform an important role in allowing dissenting views to be expressed, and in so doing promote a more substantial public interest in an issue. Part of the hope behind the War Powers Act passed in 1973 is essentially that of providing greater opportunity for dissidents to focus their attention, with the legislature acting as a public forum. Given the tendency for presidents to feel so often that they must present seemingly final solutions, the educational role of Congress can be a most important one.

Congressional activities thus relate in basic ways to the nature of presidential policy roles. The general thrust has been, first of all, to increase the chances that a president may act to ratify bargains made in Congress. The stakes of the bargaining process also sometimes shift, as a president must consider congressional interest more seriously. The mobilizing role is in turn being shared to a greater extent, insofar as congressmen are engaged in raising issues and developing support for particular solutions. Insofar as the overseeing function of Congress is expanded, the responsibilities for supervision within the Presidency are reduced somewhat. Finally, the hope behind such recent steps as the War Powers Act has been to reduce somewhat the likelihood of fait accompli steps being taken by a president. Reform considerations regarding Congress must be sensitive to the changing legislative functions and the capacities for further modification.

A Changing Structure?

Through most of the Nixon Presidency, changes in the functioning of Congress were more obvious than changes in structure. The American Congress is a highly institutionalized body, with committee procedures and patterns of leader selection which have existed in several instances since at least the turn of the century. Barbara Hinckley's *Stability and Change in Congress* has clearly elaborated the tendencies toward persistence in congressional structure.[29]

Actions taken in the latter stages of the Nixon Presidency and in the first portion of the Ford Administration collectively began to modify the picture of never-changing legislative structures. Both committee operations and the role of party structures showed significant alterations.

Committee leadership patterns did show some bending in the face of public criticism. Committee chairmen were still chosen on the basis of seniority, but with an opportunity for their removal. By 1975, the magnitude of this change became very forcefully apparent. Besides the resignation from the chairmanship of the Ways and Means Committee by Wilbur Mills in the wake of his much-publicized meetings with a local dancer, there were removals of three other chairmen involving differences over policy directions in the committees— veteran House chairmen W. R. Poage of the Agricultural Committee, F. Edward Hebert of the Armed Services Committee, and Banking and Currency Committee head, Wright Patman. Practices largely predating 1900 had been significantly modified.

Jurisdictional issues for the committees proved more vexing. The basic jurisdictions which existed as of 1974 were created in the reforms of 1946. Those reforms themselves involved a number of compromises, and the evolution of jurisdictions since has often been a function more of the power of particular chairmen than a logical plan for division of labor. As a result, it is widely concluded that present jurisdictions make little sense. Witnesses often must appear before several different committees on the same issue, and seemingly related programs are not compared by the same committee. There is some merit in a measure of competition being instilled in program review; yet in the eyes of many observers the contemporary committees overlap excessively. The Democrats fought in caucuses in early 1974 over possible realignment of committees. Richard Bolling, a long-time reform advocate from Missouri, saw his proposals fail in the face of intriguing alliances between chairmen who did not want to lose power and lobbyists who desired to maintain the influence patterns of the status quo. Some changes were made in October 1974, and again in early 1975, but the most thorough proposals were still defeated.

A potentially major reform was achieved in June 1974, with the agreement to revised budgetary procedures. There had been substantial interest for several years in the development of a procedure which would give Congress a more substantial ability to confront the key choices represented in a given year's budget. The old practice of separating taxing and spending issues, as well as separating the actions of the two houses and thus forcing repeated compromises, was often criticized. The new procedures agreed to were to be phased in slowly.[30] They involve an effort at agreement on total appropriation levels prior to decisions on specifics, new committees for examining budgeting and taxing alternatives, and a projected timetable for deliberations, including an October 1 ending of the fiscal year, in order to expand time for review. The new procedure was to be phased in for 1976. An important indication of the importance some attached to the new procedure was the willingness of Senator Muskie to resign from the Senate Foreign Relations Committee to devote greater energy to his chairmanship of the Senate Budget Committee.

Party organization issues showed by 1975 a mixed congressional response. The most startling development was happening in caucus organizations of the Democratic Party. Those caucuses at points in the 1950s would meet for a single brief session at the beginning of a new term to reelect the party's same leaders. Senator Proxmire found to his amazement in 1958 that the first caucus he attended lasted about two minutes, and simply reelected all of the existing party leadership.

The resurgence of the caucus actions of the Democrats in the late 1960s was a striking phenomenon, particularly in the face of frequent references to the decline of party organizations and party identification in the electorate. With the infusion of 75 new Democratic faces in the House Democratic Party in 1975, there was a further interest in using the caucus as a vehicle for developing general policy positions. This movement, by January 1975, even produced a caucus pronouncement of a new economic policy prior to the unveiling of President Ford's own plans. The prospect of a sharp, permanent increase in the development of policy positions through a majority caucus was considered a possibility by some, particularly if Democratic majorities in Congress continued to face Republicans in the White House.

The selection of party leaders has been somewhat more resistant to change. Some of the vitality of early Congresses came as party leaders emerged very quickly. Henry Clay was even elected speaker of the House as an entering freshman. (The vitality of early legislatures was also aided at points by a large infusion of newcomers; perhaps as many as half or more, in comparison with the frequent 10 to 15 percent of recent years.) Party leaders gradually came to be chosen through a process of slow movement from lesser to more important positions of responsibility. Substantial seniority plus institutional loyalty have been central in that process. As a result, party leaders have often been competent individuals, but not persons apt to capture the imagination of the electorate as political leaders who could help rally support for major policy position.

Summary

Presidential relations with Congress present difficult problems. A sharing of functions is never easy. Presidents have had strong influence with Congress under the impact of several conditions: a genuine crisis, as in 1933; an unusually high majority for the president's party in Congress, as in 1965–1966; or an unusually high electoral consensus as to the appropriateness of particular policy steps. Presidential skills have also been important to the president's role with Congress, as are the opportunities which come in the first year or two of a new president's term. Given the national uncertainty on many policy questions in the Nixon years, it is not terribly surprising that conflict between the president and Congress was common. Yet the limitations of the president's political resources for modifying the positions of stubborn congressmen and altering the often highly specialized centers of policy-making involving congressmen, agencies, and clienteles are often very apparent.

The trend toward presidential action through legislative delegation raises difficult questions. Presidential staff roles have grown, and new commitments have come at points as fait accompli steps, at least for Congress. There may be prior debate and a bargaining relationship among key participants within the Presidency. Nonetheless, in these situations, power has shifted to a group of the policymakers who are selected at points without even legislative concurrence and who are often unavailable for consultation because of the doctrine of executive privilege. In the process, access can easily become quite restricted.

The congressional response by 1975 added up to a substantial effort at modifying relationships between the branches. The War Powers Act stood as an attempt at expanding legislative involvement in foreign policy decisions. Impoundment of funds would now be more difficult because of the procedures enacted in 1974. Use of executive orders under emergency proclamation authority had been repealed, reducing the likely scope of the executive orders. The legislative confirmation of the director of the Office of Management and Budget had been finally agreed to, allowing Congress to potentially exercise a slightly stronger influence on the operations of that critical component of the Presidency.

Yet nagging questions remained as to possible future roles. Congress could more easily declare that it wanted to be consulted than it could organize and proceed in different ways. Not only did various centers of policy-making activity which had been frequently identified by such writers as Lowi and Redford persist, but in some cases the creation of additional subcommittees made the protection of a specific interest even easier. Congress also seemed to have its typical problems in reaching major policy positions, with the process of developing a majority coalition on any measure still difficult.

Congress also remained low in public esteem. Whereas better than 60 percent of the electorate gave Congress good or excellent ratings as of the mid-1960s, the number had fallen to barely over 20 percent by 1974. The electorate seemed to be saying, a plague on both your (or our!) houses. There seemed no easy indication than the checks and balances concepts of Montesquieu and Madison would guarantee that at least one of the branches would be in good working order. Evaluation of reform prospects must await, however, a consideration of the Nixon collapse and the overall state of the theory and practice of presidential politics.

NOTES

[1] The status of the liaison roles as of the early 1960s is extensively reviewed in Abraham Holtzman, *Legislative Liaison: Executive Leadership in Congress,* Chicago, Rand McNally, 1970.

[2] The Dirksen-Johnson friendship is insightfully discussed in Neil Mac-Neil, *Dirksen,* New York, World, 1970, chap. 12.

[3] The strained relations between Nixon and Congress are discussed in Rowland Evans, Jr., and Robert D. Novak, *Nixon in the White House,* New York, Vintage, 1971, chap. 5.

[4] Kennedy's problems with Congress are stressed in Louis Koenig, *The Chief Executive,* New York, Harcourt Brace Jovanovich, 1964, chap. 6.

[5] Presidential attempts at influencing legislative races are reviewed in William Riker and William Bast, "Presidential Action in Congressional Nomination," in *The Presidency,* Aaron Wildavsky, ed., Boston, Little, Brown, 1969, pp. 250–167.

[6] An extensive review of midterm elections has been undertaken by Barbara Hinckley. For a summary, see her work *Stability and Change in Congress,* New York, Harper & Row, 1971, chap. 2.

[7] Johnson's interest has been discussed in several sources. See, for example, Daniel S. Greenberg, *The Politics of Pure Science,* New York, World, 1967, chap. 10.

[8] Limitations with the view that legislators can be counted upon, in general, to support defense appropriations if levels of spending are high in their district or state are discussed in Bruce Russett, *What Price Vigilance?,* New Haven, Conn. Yale University Press, 1970, chap. 3.

[9] The persistent importance of partisan voting cues has been stressed in many studies. Informal aspects of party are discussed in Donald Matthews, *U.S. Senators and Their World,* Chapel Hill, N.C., University of North Carolina Press, 1960. For party voting, see in particular, David Mayhew, *Party Loyalty among Congressmen,* Cambridge, Mass., Harvard University Press, 1966. On presidential abilities to influence members of their party, and the comparative greater impact of presidents in foreign than in domestic policy concerns, see also, Aage Clausen, *How Congressmen Decide: A Policy Focus,* New York, St. Martin, 1973, especially chap. 8.

[10] A strong defense of the Kennedy legislative record is contained in Theodore Sorenson, *Kennedy,* New York, Harper & Row, 1965, chap. 14 and appendix A.

[11] See Randall Ripley, *Kennedy and Congress,* Morristown, N.J., General Learning Press, 1972.

[12] On Johnson's successes, see in particular James Sundquist, *Politics*

and Policy: The Eisenhower, Kennedy, and Johnson Years, Washington, D.C., Brookings, 1968.

[13] According to staff aide Harry McPherson, Johnson commented, "You've got to give it all you can that first year. Afterwards, you tend to find Congress running for its own neck." Harry McPherson, *A Political Education,* Boston, Little, Brown, 1972, p. 268.

[14] An extensive review of legislative-executive relations published in 1969 pointed to the underlying difficulties facing Nixon and the likelihood of difficult relations, with a minority for the President in Congress and an aging majority coalition. See Randall Ripley, *Majority Party Leadership in Congress,* Boston, Little, Brown, 1969.

[15] Nixon's success score by 1973 was the lowest in 20 years, a mere 51 percent on measures on which he took a stand. Both Kennedy and Johnson had significantly better records; Johnson achieved over 90 percent in his best year. It should be noted, however, that it is difficult to get truly accurate measures of success which relate to the importance of various pieces of legislation. For a recent summary of presidential successes, see *Congressional Quarterly,* January 19, 1974, pp. 99–100.

[16] An extremely thorough historical review is provided in Louis Fisher, *President and Congress,* New York, Free Press, 1972.

[17] The growth of presidential discretion in foreign policy matters is the major thrust in Arthur Schlesinger, Jr., *The Imperial Presidency,* Boston, Houghton Mifflin, 1972.

[18] Ruth Morgan, *The President and Civil Rights,* New York, St. Martin, 1970, p. 86.

[19] Democratic Study Group, "Special Report," February 15, 1973, pp. 5–6. See also Fisher, op. cit., chap. 4.

[20] The tendency for Nixon impoundments to involve policy issues is discussed in Louis Fisher, "Impoundment of Funds: Uses and Abuses," *Buffalo Law Review* 23:1 (Fall 1973), 141–200.

[21] For a useful review of the impoundment shift, see the *National Journal,* May 18, 1973, p. 731. The new procedure also sought to emphasize legislative involvement with policy-oriented impoundments, while making the more routine impoundments still possible.

[22] The historical record on vetoes is contained in *Presidential Vetoes,* Washington, D.C., GPO, 1969.

[23] Ronald Moe and Steven C. Teel, "Congress as Policy-Maker: A Necessary Reappraisal," in *Congress and the President,* ed. by Ronald Moe, Pacific Palisades, Calif., Goodyear, 1971, pp. 32–52.

[24] John R. Johannes, *Policy Innovation in Congress,* Morristown, N.J., General Learning Press, 1972.

[25] Richard Fenno carefully documents, as of the early 1960s, the tendency for Congress to deviate only slightly from executive proposals on most budgetary matters. See Richard Fenno, *The Power of the Purse,* Boston, Little, Brown, 1966.

[26] For a useful summary of differing legislative responses on appropriations, see William T. Murphy, Jr., and Edward Schneider, *Vote Power,* New York, Anchor, 1974, chap. 1.

[27] An extensive discussion of the oversight function and the efforts to use computer technology is presented in John Saloma, *Congress and the New Politics*, Boston, Little, Brown, 1969; see especially chap. 6.

[28] Senator Proxmire has reviewed several of the efforts at legislative oversight in his *Uncle Sam: The Last of the Big Spenders*, New York, Simon & Schuster, 1972.

[29] Hinckley, op. cit.

[30] The modified procedures are discussed in the *Congressional Quarterly*, June 15, 1974, pp. 1590–1594.

The Collapse
of the Nixon Presidency

The collapse of the Nixon Presidency forcefully demonstrated many recent problems with presidential politics. Tensions raged involving Nixon's relations with Congress, the Federal bureaucracy, the electorate, the press, and even his own staff. The power of the incumbent to marshall extraordinary resources for his own reelection, and to conceal activities, at least initially, became distressingly apparent. A nation which had generally avoided theoretical pursuits and had prided itself on the unique wisdom involved in the creation of its political institutions, slowly realized the existence of fundamental difficulties.

The abuses of the Nixon Presidency resulted from both recent institutional practices and Richard Nixon's glaring inadequacies. The extent to which Nixon's behavior could be "credited" to one or the other of these factors constitutes both a difficult and an extremely important question. The Nixon record and the more proximate causes of major abuses deserve first attention. The following chapter considers underlying tensions in the contemporary theory and practice of presidential politics. Vital reform issues then emerge: In what ways might recent traumas become the basis for a reconstruction of a more adequate presidential politics?

The Nixon Record

There is an obvious need for continuing study of the Nixon record. Scholars will rightly labor for years over aspects of the Nixon record and his presidential downfall. It does not take much imagination to envision a whole series of counterarguments and revisionist views emerging. Yet much information did quickly become available, and the outlines of key activities did emerge. Never in American history was the public so readily informed about so many presidential activities as occurred in the 1973–1974 period.

The Senate Watergate Committee investigation report includes a useful summary by the chairman, Senator Ervin, of the incredible record. That report states:[1]

> Watergate was a conglomerate of various illegal and unethical activities in which various officers and employees of the Nixon Re-election Committees and various White House aides of President Nixon participated in varying ways and degrees to accomplish these successive objectives:
>
> 1. To destroy insofar as the presidential election of 1972 was concerned the integrity of the process by which the President of the United States is nominated and elected.
> 2. To hide from law enforcement officials, prosecutors, grand jurors, courts, the news media, and the American people the identities and wrongdoing of those officers and employees of the Nixon Re-Election Committees, and those White House aides who had undertaken to destroy the integrity of the process by which the President of the United States is nominated and elected.
>
> To accomplish the first of these objectives, the participating officers and employees of the Re-Election Committees and the participating White House aides of President Nixon engaged in one or more of these things:
>
> 1. They exacted enormous contributions—usually in cash—from corporate executives by impliedly implanting in their minds the impressions that the making of the contributions was necessary to insure that the corporations would receive governmental favors, or avoid governmental disfavors while President Nixon remained in the White House. A substantial portion of the contributions were made out of corporate funds in violation of a law enacted by Congress a generation ago.
> 2. They hid substantial parts of these contributions in cash in safes and secret deposits to conceal their sources and the identities of those who had made them.
> 3. They distributed substantial portions of these hidden contributions in a surreptitious manner to finance the bugging and burglary

of the office of the Democratic National Committee in the Watergate complex in Washington for the purpose of obtaining political
intelligence; and to sabotage by dirty tricks, espionage and scur-
rilous and false libels and slanders the campaigns and the reputa-
tions of honorable men, whose only offenses were that they sought
the nomination of the Democratic Party for President. . . .

4. They deemed the departments and agencies of the Federal Government to be the political playthings of the Nixon Administration
rather than impartial instruments for serving the people, and undertook to induce them to channel federal contracts, grants, and
loans to areas, groups, or individuals so as to promote the re-election of the President rather than to further the welfare of the
people.

5. They branded as enemies of the President individuals and members
of the news media who dissented from the President's policies
and opposed his re-election, and conspired to urge the Department
of Justice, the Federal Bureau of Investigation, the Internal Revenue Service, and the Federal Communications Commission to per-
vert the use of their legal powers to harass them for so doing.

6. They borrowed from the Central Intelligence Agency disguises
which E. Howard Hunt used in political espionage operations,
and photographic equipment which White House employees
known as the "Plumbers" and their hired confederates used in
connection with burglarizing the office of a psychiatrist which
they believed contained information concerning Daniel Ellsberg
which the White House was anxious to secure.

7. They assigned to E. Howard Hunt, who was at the time a White
House consultant occupying an office in the Executive Office Building, the gruesome task of falsifying State Department documents
which they contemplated using in their altered state to discredit
the Democratic Party by defaming the memory of former President
John Fitzgerald Kennedy. . . .

The Ervin Committee report summarized other charges, as well:

They sought to persuade the FBI to refrain from investigating
the sources of campaign funds which were used to finance the bugging
and the burglars.

They made cash payments totaling hundreds of thousands of
dollars out of campaign funds in surreptitious ways to the seven
original Watergate defendants as "hush money" to buy their silence
and keep them from revealing their knowledge of the identities of the
officers and employees of the Nixon Re-Election Committees and the
White House aides who had participated in the Watergate.

Events between the end of the Ervin Committee hearings in
August 1973 and the July 1974 hearings of the House Judiciary Committee (chaired by Peter Rodino) revealed an increased involvement
of the Presidency with the agencies in questionable ways, but most

importantly they ultimately forced the disclosure of the recording of Nixon's June 23rd, 1972, conversation with H. R. Haldeman, which clearly indicated Nixon's awareness of his staff's involvement in the Watergate matter at that time.[2] Rather than gradually learning in the spring of 1973, Nixon had clearly known of a substantial involvement even when he was carefully denying any wrongdoing on the part of his staff. This fact proved, ultimately, to be the source of his downfall. Even the 10 members of the Rodino Committee who had stuck with their defense of the President to the end felt that the taped revelation of knowledge on the part of the President made the obstruction-of-justice charge undeniable.

The shift on the part of Nixon's last defenders in Congress produced a growing sense in both Congress, the electorate, and parts of Nixon's staff that Nixon's resignation was now inevitable. Plans for transition grew rapidly, even as President Nixon made a last defense before his cabinet of his intentions to stay. The events of a better-than-two-year period finally climaxed. Nixon addressed the nation, announcing his resignation in fairly restrained terms, held an emotion-laden session with those around him the morning of his departure, and boarded *Air Force 1*. A somber Gerald Ford was sworn in as President and addressed the nation even as the Nixon party was flying west to what quickly became virtual seclusion at San Clemente.

Departure did not end questions surrounding the Nixon Presidency. By the early action of pardoning former President Nixon of any charges stemming from his actions as President, his successor only closed the door to some of the lines of inquiry. Two central questions lingered. How did the Nixon record compare with others, and what produced that incredible record?

There is perhaps no more vexing question confronting analysts of the contemporary Presidency than the comparison of abuses of power. Given the limitations of past records, the better strategy is perhaps to seek to skirt the issue. One must recognize that previous administrations were not subject to a comparable scrutiny. Democratic presidents had majority party support in Congress, and no investigators had access to the inner processes of previous presidencies which the Nixon tapes made available. Any individual author cannot help but realize, moreover, that the perceptions of all Americans—including most certainly his own—can easily be colored by various aspects of personal political preferences.

The question of comparison is nonetheless of immense importance.[3] The view that Nixon simply got caught doing what everyone else was doing reflects on the legitimacy of the institution, the historical position of his predecessors, and perhaps most crucially, the importance of differing reform orientations. One must seek, however tentatively, to place the abuses of power in a comparative context.

1. *Personal finances.* One is hard pressed to find an instance in which other presidents have been as interested in expanding their personal fortunes while in office. Roosevelt and Kennedy had always been wealthy and could even afford the luxury of donating their salaries as President to charity. President Truman, the poorest of modern presidents, was never particularly interested in expanding his personal estate. He continued to live modestly after leaving the White House. President Eisenhower did accept some gifts for his Gettysburg farm, but never appeared to be a person seeking clever financial transactions.

President Johnson raises a more interesting question. There is no dispute with the proposition that he got rich while in politics. Income from his lucrative television station license and his Texas investments grew handsomely during the 1950s. Johnson was a millionaire several times over by the time he reached the White House. The further expansion of his estate was not, according to the admittedly sympathetic views of those around him in the White House, a significant concern.[4] He was seen, in fact, as being highly sensitive to his wheeler-dealer image and concerned that his actions not jeopardize his Presidency.[5]

Richard Nixon was interested in expanding his estate as he came into money only late in life. He also surrounded himself in his New York days with individuals who were used to making financial transactions in a manipulative, if not illegal, manner. His net worth, prior to his repayment of income taxes judged due, had tripled while in office, from just over $300,000 to almost a million dollars. The use of vice-presidential papers as an income tax deduction had enabled him to pay a token sum in 1971, although the use of that deduction was finally judged to have been improperly handled. Government-funded improvments at the San Clemente estate were also questioned, with considerable embarrassment at the General Services Administration. The House Judiciary Committee ultimately voted against an impeachment charge on the basis of the tax evasion material, but it was difficult not to conclude that presidential finances had been handled in a most opportunistic manner.[6]

2. *Corruption in high office.* The distinguishing characteristic of the acts of "traditional" corruption for individual gain which occurred in the Nixon Presidency is the large sums of money involved and the number of high-ranking officials. This perspective emerges as one compares earlier instances of corruption in government.

The scandals of the Harding Presidency constitute one important comparison.[7] Harry Daugherty, Harding's attorney general, was widely viewed as a classic influence peddler, and had spent a lot of money getting Harding elected. He seemed determined to make his position a personally profitable one, and received questionable sources of income while in office. Although he resigned, he was never convicted of a criminal charge—to the surprise of many. (The final jury verdict was 11 to 1 for conviction.) The head of the Veterans Bureau did, however, go to jail for conviction of conspiracy to defraud the government in the handling of veterans hospitals.

The handling of oil leases in government reserves became the most controversial issue in the Harding Administration, and ultimately produced the one instance prior to the Nixon Administration in which a cabinet official was sentenced to prison. The Secretary of the Interior, Albert Fall, made several highly lucrative leases to oil developers including Harry Sinclair and Edward L. Doheney. Fall had also received over $400,000 from the two oil developers, as he was struggling with the development of his large land holdings in New Mexico. The evidence was enough to bring a conviction, and Albert Fall became the first cabinet official to enter prison. Significantly, the lengthy investigations of the various wrongdoing in the Harding Administration never produced any indication that Harding was personally involved.

More recently, interest in corruption in government has focused on issues beginning with the Truman Administration. The Roosevelt Administration did produce, during the haste of military preparations and contracting, instances of influence peddling and corruption in the handling of war contracts.[8] Truman was nonetheless substantially more often criticized, and Eisenhower made "the mess in Washington" a telling campaign issue in 1952. Favors to staff members included gifts of a freezer and a mink coat to peripheral figures in Truman's staff.[9] The Reconstruction Finance Corporation, a federal lending agency established during the depression, was more substantially involved; most notably, the Democratic Party chairman resigned over his influence-peddling role. Significantly, the Internal Revenue Service was also involved. The two top officials resigned, and there was a general housecleaning, including 200 lesser employees. The issues were, again, those of influence peddling for personal gain.

Despite Ike's reference to cleaning up the mess in Washington, his Administration was in fact confronted with more serious scandals than was Truman's.[10] Most widely heralded was the departure of his chief aid, Sherman Adams (the staff director, a role comparable in many respects to H. R. Haldeman's role for Nixon) after he was accused of intervention with the Federal Trade Commission on behalf of his friend, Bernard Goldfine, a New England businessman, from whom he had accepted gifts. Adams proclaimed his innocence throughout, claiming that the gifts (hotel rooms, a vicuna coat for his wife, and an oriental rug) had nothing to do with his routine checking of regulatory commission matters for Goldfine. Other Eisenhower officials who departed under clouds of suspicion included two General Services Administration officials, three members of regulatory commissions, and an assistant secretary of the Air Force. How different history might have been if one other suspected individual—his young vice-presidential nominee Richard Nixon—had been removed from the ticket when the propriety of his receipt of a fund from businessmen in his district for use in facilitating his Senate activities was questioned during the campaign! Generally, in the Eisenhower period individuals left quietly; they did not go to jail.

The Kennedy Presidency was comparatively free of major scandal. The case which generated the greatest public attention was that of Billie Sol Estes, a Texas business promoter who illegally received credit from banks by misrepresenting his federal grain allotment holdings. Federal funds were not lost, but there was a substantial defrauding of businesses involved. Orville Freeman, the secretary of agriculture, dismissed three employees without waiting for investigation, and an investigation by Congress did not produce additional indications of wrongdoing on the part of governmental actors. The TFX military aircraft controversy also produced cries of conflict of interest and an extensive investigation. Secretary of the Navy Fred Korth was under particular suspicion because of his involvement with a Fort Worth bank which was doing business with General Dynamics, the firm which ultimately received the TFX contract award.[11] In Robert Art's review of this case, he concludes that the trail of suspicion was substantially the result of the underlying uncertainty in the respective military services about the merits of the plane, plus the sheer size of the contract.

The Johnson Presidency raised the question of possible corrupt practices quite forceably, since Johnson was clearly in a position of having gotten rich while in public life. Johnson was, in turn, clearly embarrassed by the Bobby Baker scandal which emerged in 1963–1964.[12] Baker ultimately went to jail as a result of business transactions which had allowed him to parlay a nominal governmental salary into a net worth of over $2 million in less than 10 years. Johnson quickly sought to sever ties with Baker as the news of the scandal developed, pointing out that he was not his personal secretary in the Senate but rather the secretary to the majority caucus. No direct tie to Johnson's involvement was ever established.

President Johnson was also viewed by some as having a rather intense local pride in the airline routes and the decisions he made in the context of legally required presidential concurrence with changes in airline routes. No direct financial transaction was ever traced, however. It was also in the Johnson period that Robert Winter-Berger traced several questionable transactions involving aides to Democratic leaders in the House. There was substantial opportunity for the Democratic influentials in Congress to engage in questionable practices. What one did not find, however, was an indication that those patterns trailed into the White House, or into the Oval Office directly.

The Nixon Presidency, in comparison, produced a *substantial* number of corrupt transactions, and transactions which *repeatedly reached high levels* in the Nixon Adminstration, including *serious suspicion of the President himself.* First is the case of the Vice-President.[13] Spiro Agnew was allegedly receiving payments for hoped-for favors while he sat in the Vice-President's office. The plea bargaining which Agnew engaged in prevented a full disclosure of the corruption in which Agnew had been involved.

Then there is the series of cases involving influence peddling. The three most widely discussed cases involved the relationship of the International Telephone and Telegraph Corporation (ITT) to the Nixon Administration, the impact of the dairy lobby contributions on milk prices, and the efforts of Robert Vessco. The ITT case was the most serious of the three and involved a wide range of individuals.[14] The case initially involved a scheduled contribution of $400,000 by ITT for the Republican convention to be held in San Diego in 1972. A famous memo from ITT lobbyist Dita Beard included such references as "I am convinced, because of several conversations with Louie re Mitchell, that our noble commitment has gone a long way toward negotiations on the mergers eventually coming out as Hal wants them" and "if it gets too much publicity, you can believe our negotiations with Justice will wind up shot down."

The central issue behind the ITT case was ITT's desire to acquire the Hartford Insurance Company, the sixth largest insurance company in the United States, as a major source of stable revenue for the diverse operations which ITT was then conducting on a global basis. That merger was approved by the Justice Department. A lengthy series of congressional investigations and then court inquiries followed, which resulted in the convictions of the lieutenant governor of California, Ed Reineke, and the U.S. attorney general, Richard Kleindienst, for perjury in testimony before the investigating authorities. President Nixon's own involvement was a subject of intense dispute in the impeachment inquiry. His defenders claimed that his involvement was only in terms of a general antitrust philosophy, while his critics argued that he was aware of the funds being contributed and had acted on that basis. The case was still in the courts as of the fall of 1974.

The dairy industry case also produced questions of corruption which reached the President himself. Basic facts are known.[15] The dairy industry had been a substantial source of Republican campaign funds in 1968, and there were promises of substantial sums for 1972. In March 1971, the industry leaders expressed extreme disappointment at the pegging of price supports for "manufacturing milk," which is used for butter and cheese. On March 22, 1971, a dairy industry political fund contributed $10,000 to Republican committees, and as meetings were held on the milk price issue the contributions continued. An estimated $422,500 was ultimately contributed to the Nixon campaign effort. After dairy leaders had met with Nixon and the Agricultural Secretary, Charles Hardin, Hardin then changed his mind and announced that the price would be raised—from the original $4.66 to $4.93 per 100 pounds. Once again, the Nixon contributor won.

A third major case involved the activities of one Robert Vesco. Vesco operated a sickly mutual fund enterprise (International Overseas Services) which he had acquired from its exotic founder, Bernie Cornfeld. Vesco was in trouble with the Securities Exchange Commission (SEC), and hoped for favorable treatment. While his case was pending, he promised $250,000 to the Republican campaign through Maurice Stans. Both Stans and former Attorney General John Mitchell were indicted for their roles in acting as intermediaries for Vesco with the SEC. In a case which was confused by Vesco's departure from the country, both Stans and Mitchell were acquitted in late 1974.

The corruption issues related, in the final analysis, to the manner in which approximately $60 million was raised for the 1972 campaign. That issue must now be considered directly.

3. *Fund-raising activities.*[16]   It is essential to consider, in comparing fund-raising efforts of different candidates, that the entire process in the past decade has been characterized by a sharp increase in total sums involved. Even so, Nixon's efforts at raising almost $60 million represented an unusually massive effort. It is also significant that Nixon's effort was out of keeping with the actions of past incumbents. There is, of course, nothing necessarily illegal in raising substantial sums of money. There is, however, an indication of zealousness on the part of an incumbent in asking people for specific sums of money.

It must be emphasized that specific violations of the 1971 Federal Election Campaign Act as it went into effect in 1972 were not confined to Richard Nixon, or to the Republicans. There had been for some time a definite conflict between the legal requirements for campaign fund raising and the accepted norms. Some of the restrictions were actually rather unrealistic and were commonly violated by both parties. It is not terribly surprising, in short, that one finds indications that in 1972 there were violations by both parties of the new legislation. Insofar as 1972 was unique, it was in terms of the Nixon Presidency tending to be more specific as to how much money would be accepted and what favors would be forthcoming in the future. There is a difference, in other words, between appointing large contributors ambassadors (as was, for example, John Kennedy's father as a Democratic financial supporter in the 1930s) and making it very explicit what office is being sold and what the cost will be. It is also worth noting that the question of financial manipulations did not have as much of an impact on the public as did some of the other Nixon abuses.

4. *Political espionage and corrupt election practices.* Infiltrating an opponent's campaign to obtain good information and sometimes seeking to disrupt his campaign are rather time-honored practices in American politics. Infiltration has been practiced at all levels, including the presidential races themselves. The fragmented nature of the party organizations and the tendency to put together new organizations makes this comparatively easy. There have also been such tactics as those of the legendary Dick Tuck, who has done such things as giving a signal for the Nixon bus in 1960 to pull out without Pat Nixon aboard, thus causing some delay, as the bus had to return for the candidate's wife.[17]

It has also been long recognized that local voting practices have not always been completely honest. "Vote for the candidate of your choice—and vote often!" has not in some instances been a joke. Pencil ballots, for example, lent themselves to such tactics as having ballot counters place graphite under their fingernail, making a second mark on some ballots, and then later contesting them as being incorrectly marked. The nation experienced a situation in 1960 in which the ballot counting in Illinois and Texas was most assuredly conducted to the advantage of the young Democrat, John Kennedy. It is worth recalling, furthermore, that at least one national election was won by a highly questionable handling in 1876 of the electoral college votes of two southern states.

In view of this history of espionage and dishonesty in elections, the aspects of Nixon's operations which are nonetheless impressive involve their *extent*, the *highly organized manner* in which they were carried out, and their *direct ties to the White House*. In terms of the burglaries at the Watergate headquarters of the Democratic National Committee, it was the *second* attempt which failed, and wire tapping had been going on for weeks. This was also in the spring, and not in the final weeks of a campaign. Furthermore, there were plans for other areas as well, including the Miami convention.

The involvement in high places became of course the subject of a massive investigation. From the volumes of material, it slowly became evident that several of the President's closest advisers were either directly involved or knew of illegal plans. What was involved was not a willingness to go along with local political mores which would help a candidate in a given part of the country, but rather a plan from the top to make sure that the President's phrase, "We gotta win," (June 23, 1972) would be carried out.

One must emphasize also, regarding political espionage, that the Nixon Administration invented some of these techniques before spring 1972. The break-in at the office of Daniel Ellsberg's psychiatrist in February 1971 was one indication that activities which had been practiced on those perceived as political radicals were being turned, by 1972, onto the affairs of more conventional party politics. This takes one to the critical area of efforts to subvert agencies of government for political purposes.

5. *The subverting of governmental agencies for political objectives.*[18] This fifth issue, perhaps the most devastating, was at the heart of Nixon's downfall. The recording of his conversation with Robert Haldeman on June 23, 1973, just six days after the break-in at the Democratic National Headquarters, was critical in his downfall. Nixon's own transcript reveals him asking if the FBI could not be called off the investigation by telling them that there was CIA involvement. This possibility was reviewed several times during the incredible discussions involving various attempts at concealing both the illegal activities and the cover-up of those activities.

Use of the FBI and the Internal Revenue Service for political purposes also became clear with the unfolding of additional evidence before the Rodino Committee. An FBI investigation of newspaper reporter Daniel Schorr was ordered, even though he was not being considered for a government job as the cover story given by Nixon spokesmen indicated. FBI information was also produced through wire taps, and information which was not just of a national security nature was reported back through White House channels. In addition, there was the attempted use of the Internal Revenue Service to audit the returns of those who were regarded as enemies of the Nixon Presidency.

The question of comparison is difficult. Little is known about the relationships of past Presidents to the CIA or the FBI and the

IRS. What did emerge was a picture of a White House Staff which was both extremely anxious to gain additional information and also willing at points to pull either the information- or the intelligence-gathering activity itself into the White House.

Other issues of impeachment. Other issues were also raised in the impeachment inquiry. The question of the unauthorized bombing of Cambodia was the most intriguing. The House Judiciary Committee confronted a most unusual situation. The secret bombing of Cambodia seemed blatantly unconstitutional. Yet the fact that Nixon had let a few members of Congress know of his actions seemed similar to the pattern of other Presidents in dealing with Congress. Foreign policy secrets had in other instances also been handled in a confidential manner. Furthermore, in a comparative context, the role of the operations division of the CIA had been periodically one of involvement with clandestine military operations. One can debate the seriousness of various actions. Yet what is most apparent is that the Nixon actions on this issue did indeed have some precedents in foreign policy roles which had evolved since World War II. In this respect, Nixon's actions were not as unique as some would have liked to believe—either out of a dislike for Nixon, or a concern for the manner in which institutional practices had evolved. In this situation, the Judiciary Committee decided against an impeachment charge based upon the illegal bombings in Cambodia.

It is also difficult to develop a precise reading on the question of the presidential cover-up of transgressions. Nixon's own record became tragically clear. There was systematic lying to the American people in a constant effort to downgrade the seriousness of the affair and the degree of involvement on the part of the President and his immediate staff. The President was in a two-year process of seeking to find some means of concealing the magnitude of the activities of his staff. Yet presidential lying has been depressingly familiar in the contemporary President. A key difference between Nixon and former Presidents is that the known instances of presidential lying have come primarily in foreign policy operations and not in covering partisan political activities.

Ultimately, it was the extensive cover-up activities which produced both Nixon's downfall and the convictions of the lengthy list of Nixon staff aides in 1973 and 1974. As a result of their efforts at concealment, perjury and obstruction of justice became the common bases for conviction. Such specific events as the Watergate burglary, the handling of campaign funds, and the effort at obtaining psychiatric files on Daniel Ellsberg produced some convictions. The ultimate indictment and conviction of over 15 fairly influential (and some *very* influential) members of the Nixon Administration, along with numerous other convictions of lesser individuals, nonetheless resulted frequently from the cover-up activities and, in turn, the attempt to cover up the cover-up activities.

In a comparative context, the Nixon record produces a mixed picture. The number of specific influence-peddling cases, other than that of the Vice-President, was not drastically out of keeping with some other administrations. As to campaign fund raising in 1972, a variety of candidates did not meet the letter of the new laws. The specificity with which potential donors were approached by Nixon's staff did, however, strike a number of observers (including some who were approached) as unusually aggressive. Here, as in so many other contexts, one had an issue of the tone and style of the Nixon operations as they seemed to embellish past precedents and tendencies.

There is also little indication of precedents for the *systematic* manner in which enemies were confronted by the Nixon Presidency. Wire tapping, audits by the IRS, and the break-in at the Democratic National Headquarters were part of an unusually systematic effort to ruthlessly attack political opponents. One simply does not have a comparable record of another administration and Presidency covering mistakes in the political arena by operating a plan which involved not only deception but "paying off" individuals to keep them quiet and working to thwart FBI investigations by hinting of CIA concern.[19]

Nixon was *not* simply a President who "happened to get caught doing what all the others did." Precedents were expanded, and several new roles were developed. Yet there is also some truth in the view that some public indignation was based upon a short, inaccurate, and at points partisan perception of what had happened in earlier Presidencies. Given this perspective, it is important to begin exploring factors contributing to the consistent abuses of power in the Nixon Presidency.

The Search for Causes

The record of abuses in the Nixon Presidency has produced a most understandable search for explanations. The Ervin Committee investigations, which began as a probe into campaign finance activities in the spring of 1973, often found questioners searching for more general explanations. Questions about motivations of individuals who were being questioned and staff organization questions often surfaced in that endeavor. A precise articulation of causes will remain illusive and will certainly involve many continuing probes. Key relationships can nonetheless be reviewed, granting the difficulties involved in placing precise weights on some factors. One must necessarily consider the impact of Nixon's personality, the men around Nixon, the growth of secrecy, changing business-government relationships, and the withering of party structures.

Nixon's Contribution

Responsibility for the abuses of the Nixon Presidency must begin with the President himself. Central characteristics in the Nixon personality have been discussed, including a basic shyness, a ruthlessness and cynicism in political dealings, and a tendency to resolve personal insecurities by an emphasis on his handling of crisis situations. Nixon did have a capacity for thinking through problems in international relations without undue rigidity. Yet ultimately he was simply disastrously misplaced in the office he had spent a lifetime seeking to acquire.

The full impact of Nixon's ruthlessness emerged with the tape disclosures of the extensive conversations on various cover-up plans. Little indignation was expressed by Nixon as a host of illegal maneuvers were discussed to keep the original burglary quiet. Knowledge of other illegal plans, such as the Huston Plan for operating a surveillance function within the White House Staff on the activities of radicals, also did not produce an immediate presidential veto. Winning in 1972 similarly emerged as an objective which the President regarded as taking priority over some of the seemingly established norms for political operations.

Nixon also contributed personally to the development of a staff operation which was uniquely hierarchical. This reflected his basic shyness and dislike for extensive oral communication. The development of his staff system with H. R. Haldeman as, in effect, chief of staff, was substantially a reflection of Nixon's own personality. That staff system, in turn, was the classic example of a hierarchy in which important bits of political information could be withheld from the President. Obviously, as the tapes revealed, Nixon knew much more than he was telling regarding the cover-up. Yet various staff activities also could be undertaken in the Nixon White House with the realization that presidential awareness was unlikely.

Presidents invariably have a major impact on their staff and its operations. This has been seen repeatedly with various Presidents. They help establish a tone for those operations, and they substantially influence the nature of their own communication flow. This impact does not necessarily alter the overall policy outcomes of their Presidency on many issues, or the overall policy response of the national government. Yet on the Watergate issues the impact was substantial, and for a basic reason. The procedures of the staff, and their partisan political operations, became the central issue in question. Various presidents in the Nixon years would have had difficulty ending the American involvement in Vietnam and dealing with the constricting resources available for domestic policy activity. The Nixon personal impact was strongest in precisely the area which caused his Presidency to end in a shambles: misuse of power for the purpose of seeking to stay in power.

The President's Men

President Nixon recruited the men on his staff, and he helped set the tone for their operations. Yet these individuals themselves must be given some "credit" for the collapse of his Adminstration. The growth in staff power, and the tendency to recruit ambitious individuals without previous elective office experience has been seen as part of the general evolution of the Presidency. Because Nixon did not come to the Presidency from the legislature and had been away from Washington for eight years, he had a staff which was uniquely lacking in familiarity with Washington operations in general and the legislative arena in particular.

The Nixon staff was characterized, in turn, by a tremendous sense of loyalty to the advancement of his Presidency.[20] The comments of Charles Colson, one of the more infamous proponents of political abuses, are illustrative. In the wake of his sentencing, Colson observed that he did not once think of the constitutional issues involved in his actions, even though he had been trained as a lawyer. What counted—and apparently the only thing which counted—was getting things done which the President desired. The Nixon staff did indeed seem to resemble a sect. Loyalty and unthinking obedience were the central tenets as aides sought both to advance the Nixon Presidency and, in so doing, to perpetuate their own positions as part of the "Nixon team."

The staff also reflected the long-standing tendency in Richard Nixon and his associates to adopt a cynical, "anything which works is okay" view of the political process. A substantial number of staff members had been involved in political campaigns in California—a state in which a combination of weak parties, early use of public relations techniques, and a rapidly mobile and politically disorganized electorate had long produced rather questionable tendencies in political campaigns. Specifically, H. R. Haldeman had been involved with Nixon's 1962 campaign for governor, in which a mailing under a false label produced a Democratic court suit. (That suit was ultimately dropped, as Richard Nixon was already obviously the loser.)[21] Several of the lesser figures in the Watergate scandals, such as Donald Segretti, had emerged in that California political milieu. Ronald

Zeigler, the press secretary who aided in the cover-up, came from the same political environment.

The staff both reflected Richard Nixon and also revealed the manner in which recent staffs had been recruited. In that sense, the issue was more basic than simply the lack of adequate personalities on the Nixon staff. Structurally, they were able to develop positions of influence—and opportunities for political intrigue—as a result of the evolution of the institution itself in recent decades.

Secrecy

The abuses of the Nixon Presidency were clearly undertaken with an anticipation of continued secrecy. Nixon and his aides obviously never in their wildest dreams could have imagined the unraveling of their Administration's record which occurred in the second term. Executive privilege and the rationale of national security were to be the "security blanket" under which the various actions, legal and otherwise, would be covered. The "imperial presidency" as Arthur Schlesinger, Jr., has called the contemporary institution, has been one in which a host of questionable and illegal activities could be undertaken, seemingly without fear of reprisal. The absence of a sense of restraint due to fear of disclosure was thus fundamental.

The importance of secrecy also underlay tensions between the Nixon White House and the two key agencies of surveillance in American society—the CIA and the FBI. Nixon and key aides were clearly disappointed with aspects of the operations of both of these agencies. The CIA, on its intelligence division side, had long had major reservations about the Vietnam War, which endeared them to neither Johnson nor Nixon. The FBI was, in turn, seen as providing insufficient information on the political left and on campus dissidents. Because of secrecy and the lack of external controls over these agencies the White House was able to absorb aspects of the political intelligence role itself. Both the Ellsberg break-in and the plan for direct intelligence activities, the so-called Huston Plan, represented White House efforts at establishing their own secret intelligence operations. The too infrequently studied relationship between the White House and the intelligence community, with the strains which a zealous President and his staff placed upon it, was an important factor in the Nixon abuses.

Business, Money, and Politics

Richard Nixon occupied the Presidency at a time when the importance of governmental decisions in regulating the economy was increasing. This trend has been seen in operations since the days of John Kennedy. The step of introducing wage and price controls in August 1971 still constituted a vast addition to the regulatory role. In an age of increased governmental involvement with the economic success of various firms and sectors of the economy, it is not surprising to find a substantial zeal in the business community for the establishment of at least comfortable access to the Presidency, if not in fact specific political influence.

One should not overstate the newness of this phenomenon. Of the three most widely discussed instances of questionable campaign fund use (ITT, the dairy industry, and the affairs of Robert Vesco), only the dairy industry price increases involved new policy considerations. It may also be argued that Richard Nixon and his associates helped to create the milieu of expectations of substantial governmental assistance to business, with their aid to such firms as Lockheed and Penn Central Railroad. It nonetheless seems fair to emphasize the growing dependency of business on governmental decisions. Coupled with the frequent peripheral position of Congress, this creates a situation in which an increased number of individuals and firms find it to their distinct interest to establish good patterns of access to the White House.

The Withering Political Parties

The close ties of the 1972 campaign to the White House reflected the marginal position of party structures in contemporary politics. Nixon was not the first incumbent President to release individuals from his staff for campaign purposes, or to deal with extensive strategy considerations in the context of on-going presidential operations. Presidents Johnson, Eisenhower, Truman, and Roosevelt had done this in varying degrees as incumbents. The Nixon operations simply built upon this tendency, with the typical Republican penchant for comparatively more formal political organizations.

The result of the Nixon campaign organization was to provide the basis for a trail of corruption leading directly to the White House. Campaign abuses of various kinds which in the past had been a part of local political cultures thus tended to be absorbed by the White House itself. The zealousness of Nixon's staff aides and their instincts for strict hierarchical organization could easily mold the campaign organization, since the party organizations themselves had continued to atrophy. The result was tragic: The tangle of campaign abuses was unraveled to reveal the White House intimately involved.

Individual or Systemic Problems?

It would be comforting to place the blame for the abuses of the Nixon Presidency in the hands of an inadequate presidential personality surrounded by highly loyal political operatives who would do anything for the sake of pleasing their boss and gaining reelection. One could then add the regulation of campaign finance and measures for keeping campaigns out of the White House as both logical and sufficient reform thrusts. Coupling these reforms with the selection of a more adequate presidential personality in future elections could then be expected to produce something like a return to "normalcy" in presidential politics.

It can indeed be argued that the worst of the Nixon abuses were not inevitable. A different presidential personality and a different staff would certainly have had troubles with Congress, assuming the then-existing partisan divisions and the nation's constricting resources, plus the lack of consensus as to what was to be done. The termination of American military involvement in Southeast Asia was also not an easy task for many to confront. Yet Nixon's troubles were not primarily those of handling policy questions, but ones stemming from a ruthless commitment to reelection at any cost. Nixon and his aides most unquestionably exacerbated problems with the contemporary office.

The comforting view is nonetheless incomplete. Even a look at some of the proximate factors involved in the Nixon abuses has taken us back to several underlying relationships. Presidents have had a relatively free hand in developing staffs, and these have been used for a variety of purposes. The problem of relationships with secret agencies is certainly not new, nor is the temptation involved with government having a major influence on the economic fortunes of innumerable business firms. Party decline and the tendency for presidential activity to dominate reelection campaigns were certainly not new to the Nixon Presidency. Finally, pushing back into more basic relationships, it has to be recognized that the selection process produced a Richard Nixon and that the voters were persuaded of his virtues not only twice, but almost three times—he lost in 1960 by only slightly over 100,000 total votes. To fully comprehend the plight of the Nixon Presidency, it is necessary to consider basic tensions in the contemporary Presidency itself.

NOTES

[1] *The Senate Watergate Report,* vol. 1, New York, Dell, 1974, pp. 8–10.

[2] The hearing evidence is summarized in *The Impeachment Report,* New York, New American Library, 1974.

[3] One useful historical survey is contained in the special report for the Judiciary Committee under the direction of C. Vann Woodward. See C. Vann Woodward et al., *White House under Fire: Responses of the Presidents to Charges of Misconduct,* New York, Dell, 1974.

[4] On Johnson's record, see ibid., pp. 319–339.

[5] A highly critical account of Johnson's finances is contained in J. Evetts Haley, *A Texan Looks at Lyndon,* Canyon, Tex., Palo Duro Press, 1964.

[6] An informative discussion of Nixon's finances is contained in the *New York Times Magazine,* January 13, 1974.

[7] An extensive review of the Teapot Dome scandals is found in Burl Noggle, *Teapot Dome,* New York, Norton, 1962.

[8] Problems of wartime profiteering are reviewed in the context of attempted investigations in Donald H. Riddle, *The Truman Committee,* New Brunswick, N.J., Rutgers University Press, 1964.

[9] Truman's problems are reviewed in David A. Frier, *Conflict of Interest in the Eisenhower Administration,* Baltimore, Penguin, 1969, chap. 1.

[10] Ibid.

[11] On the TFX case, see Robert J. Art, *The TFX Decision,* Boston, Little, Brown, 1968.

[12] The Bobby Baker case is discussed in Rowland Evans, Jr., and Robert D. Novak, *Lyndon Johnson: the Exercise of Power,* New York, New American Library, 1966, pp. 436–437.

[13] Agnew's transgressions are reviewed in Richard M. Cohen and Jules Witcover, *One Heartbeat Away,* New York, Viking, 1974.

[14] General background on the development of this case is provided in Anthony Sampson, *The Sovereign State of ITT,* New York, Fawcett, 1973. More specific details are reviewed by a London *Sunday Times* team, in Lewis Chester et al., *Watergate,* New York, Ballantine, 1973, chap. 8.

[15] See Chester et al., ibid., pp. 93–94; and *The Impeachment Report,* op. cit.

[16] The fund-raising abuses are extensively reviewed in *The Senate Watergate Report,* op. cit.

[17] For a Democratic view of the campaign which stresses the lesser magnitude of earlier abuses, see Frank Mankiewicz, *Perfectly Clear,* New York, Quadrangle, 1974, chap. 3.

[18] Issues involving the use of governmental agencies for political purposes became central to the House Judiciary Committee debates, creating a different central focus than the Ervin Committee investigations, with their emphasis more substantially on campaign finance questions. Aspects of that evidence had a major impact on the three impeachment articles which were ultimately voted by the House Judiciary Committee. For one review, see *The Impeachment Report,* op. cit.

[19] There is obviously not agreement on this point. For an emphasis on the tendency for earlier Presidents to hide political mistakes, see the comments of Congressman Wiggins, a Nixon defender, in *The Congressional Quarterly* 32, no. 52 (December 28, 1974), 3446.

[20] For a retrospective discussion of that strong sense of loyalty, see Jeb Stuart Magruder, *An American Life: One Man's Road to Watergate,* New York, Atheneum, 1974. A more critical account, emphasizing the absence of men with independent ideas and stature, is found in Richard J. Whalen, *Catch the Falling Flag,* Boston, Houghton Mifflin, 1972.

[21] The 1962 campaign is discussed in Mankiewicz, op. cit.

Theory and Practice

The state of the Presidency as revealed in the collapse of the Nixon Presidency was a rude jolt to two commonly held ideas in American political thought. Both advocates of strong presidential leadership and believers in a pluralistic view of the American political process faced major difficulties. It was understandable that many longed for a return to practices which fit those theories more fully. In so doing, the easiest route was to consider the Nixon and at least aspects of the Johnson period to be an unfortunate episode evolving primarily from their individual limitations.

Many Americans did subscribe to the "individual blame" view. Although alienated and frustrated with existing operations, they tended to retain the belief that the American system could work. An impressive 89 percent responded to pollster Louis Harris in late 1973 that they felt the American system was basically sound. Difficult questions nonetheless had to be confronted. Were not underlying tensions and contradictions in the theory and practice of presidential politics at least significantly and perhaps even substantially responsible for the problems which developed? One also had to wonder about future presidential roles. Without significant reform, was there not a likelihood of future difficulties of considerable magnitude? The tensions and dilemmas involved in both presidential theory and power relationships demand careful review.

Perspectives on the Presidency Reconsidered

Several key topics and relationships have been interpreted very differently by respective theories of presidential politics. To consider respective views, it is necessary to consider presidential personality, staff roles, policy mobilizing capabilities, the claims for the superiority of the respective branches, and contemporary checks and balances. Recent experiences with these areas demand a careful review.

The Search for Ideal Personalities

It is far more obvious now than a decade ago that there are major difficulties in getting adequate individuals into the Oval Office. The recruitment net which is cast is fairly narrow and tends to elevate those individuals who can mobilize large amounts of money and successful media attention in getting a campaign started. The declining ability of the parties to direct the nominating process, and the likelihood of fractional victories, mean that there may be comparatively few good choices available to the electorate in final elections. The situation is particularly difficult where incumbents do not face effective challenge.

Presidential candidates have tended to come from the ranks of the politically experienced. Yet political experience can easily become a detriment. Such strong-presidency enthusiasts as Richard Neustadt did of course recognize that the truly effective president should be a skilled politician with a particularly suitable temperament. It nonetheless becomes apparent that the skilled politician may run into serious problems if he becomes perceived by the electorate as being too clever and too manipulative in his operations. The American tendency to venerate the Presidency and to be skeptical of politicians can come back to haunt the White House occupant who is seen as overly political and lacking in a larger sense of purpose. President Johnson's dismal fall from public favor is a forceful example. The president surely needs political skills in sensing coalitions, pacing issues, and avoiding political pitfalls in taking various actions. Yet if the American public concludes that the exercise of political skills is his overriding interest, his ability to sustain support either for himself or for his policies begins to fall into jeopardy. Highly politicized presidents can create serious problems for themselves—thus making the question of obtaining effective presidential personalities extremely difficult.

Recent presidential behavior has also thrown into serious question the extent to which the public can count on socialization into proper norms of conduct to act as a restraint on the abuse of power. Nixon was certainly not the only President in recent times who seriously distorted the public acounts of what his Administration was doing. A serious probing of recent White House occupants' perceptions might well reveal a shift in their interpretations of what can be considered justifiable and acceptable conduct. Their behavior has nonetheless been in conflict with widely prevailing public norms as to the limits on acceptable uses of power.

Richard Neustadt is still correct in his argument that presidents need a fair degree of political skill. Writers such as Lasswell and Rogow are also still correct in arguing that the old maxim, Power corrupts and absolute power corrupts absolutely, is too simple. Yet it is also increasingly evident that the individual who can operate successfully because of his political skills and will also act with voluntary restraint out of a sense of what constitutes proper presidential behavior is a rare individual—and a difficult individual to get elevated into the Presidency. Furthermore, this type of behavior becomes all the more difficult to achieve given the restricted and unique conditions under which a president can meet various expectations for his performance. Unfortunately, the shift to scarcity promised by the mid-1970s to make the difficulties of the president increasingly intense.

Impacts of the Institutionalized Presidency

The evolution of the Executive Office of the President has long been supported in the quest for efficiency and coordination in the development of public policy. That evolution has in turn made the Presidency a vastly different institution than the one which existed prior to the 1930s. It is a fundamentally different institution, also, from the one which existed when many of the Constitutional precedents regarding the Presidency were developed. The consequences of vast expansion in the institutionalized Presidency have been enormous.

The expanded size and scope of present operations often serves to increase the power of the staff rather than that of the president. The restraints seen in the president's agenda are immense, and they are not easily solved by having him work longer hours or emphasize competitiveness within his staff. There are simply too many questions evolving within the staff, and they are often highly complex. The expanded expertise may at points make the president, just like members of Congress, unable to effectively influence the evolution of policy choices. Presidents have shown substantial interest and ability to learn on occasion, particularly where economic issues are involved. Yet this cannot be done across the range of issues at any particular point in time. The result is most obvious: Where the number of issues going into the White House increases, *and* decisions are simply ratified by a president, then it is the staff which has increased its power within the political system.

Coordination and expertise are elusive concepts in looking at operations of the contemporary Presidency. Some policy steps on fairly specific problems have shown the impact of expert analysis in seeking concerted actions. The more serious problems arise in considering the decisions which emerge across wider ranges of alternatives. Additional data on health care costs or the killing capacity of a new bomber may help in choosing between alternative health delivery systems or between two bomber prototypes. Such data is of far less help, however, as the Presidency lurches toward the cardinal decisions involving overall expenditure and policy thrusts. As these decisions are made, political calculations tend to become overriding. Unless one can tend to avoid hard decisions by using something-for-everyone decision rules, competition within the Presidency can become intense. DeGrazia is correct, in these instances, in arguing that the Presidency is like Congress—but with a tent over it.

The growth of the institutionalized Presidency also raises in new ways the question of governmental secrecy. The concept of executive privilege is used to cover a wide range of policy-making activities. As some now want the doctrine applied, one is talking about a vastly different set of considerations than when the nation worried as to whether one of Washington or Polk or Lincoln's aides should testify before Congress. Reform has to confront this issue.

One further difficulty with the contemporary Presidency and its institutionalized staff must be emphasized. Those mechanisms which were established to aid the president can also serve to isolate him. We have seen the issue of isolation to be a complex one, and one which is influenced by differing personalities in the Oval office. It is also a phenomenon which is easily emphasized by those in the electorate who feel that their policy choices are not being considered. Yet the tendency for the president to operate in a world which is molded and shaped by his staff and advisers has also been apparent. The proposition that one strengthens the president and adds coordination and expertise to governmental decisions simply through staff additions contains all too many contradictions and negative consequences.

Reevaluating the President's Policy Mobilization Role

The strong-presidency advocates have often emphasized the importance of presidential efforts to mobilize support in the electorate and in Congress as key ingredients in achieving effective policy change. Proponents of this view envision leadership and also a fairly open and competitive political process. Problems also emerge with this emphasis.

Presidents do have substantial resources for capturing the attention of the American public. Large television audiences are available to them on virtually a moment's notice. Presidents can at points focus issues. Kennedy could even seize the initiative on the space program and gain support for his commitment to landing a man on the moon before 1970 without serious congressional objection. Presidents can also, by serious emphasis, sometimes increase the opinion poll indications of support for given policies. Yet difficulties are also apparent.

Presidents have often had major difficulties in converting popular support into the political resources which will produce a policy change in Congress. The answer to the question of what would happen if the number of voters polled who indicated approval of a proposed bill increased by 10 percent was often "Very little." Polls take a national sample, and key congressmen may well be responding to a more specific constituency. Various interests and elites may be able to defend themselves in Congress even if there is generalized congressional support for change. Furthermore, a president may lack either the skill, the time, or the interest in working directly or with his aides to prevent various delaying tactics in Congress.

The one situation since 1960 in which a President was able to mobilize support and alter bargains on a range of domestic issues very successfully was in the 1964–1965 period. Several conditions, however, made that situation unique. There was a generalized public sentiment already built up for several of those steps, Johnson was an avid legislatively oriented President, and after the 1964 elections he had an unusually large partisan majority to work with. Presidents Kennedy and Nixon had substantially less success in mobilizing support for policies which required specific legislative approval.

A president may find his efforts at mobilizing public support producing unrealistic expectations. This is particularly difficult if he is seeking to deal with segments of the population which have received limited previous attention, and which have had limited integration into the political process. Some of Johnson's difficulties with rapid rises in expectation were undoubtedly a consequence of his tendency to want to describe so many programs and activities in unnecessarily gigantic proportions. A different president might well have had considerable policy-mobilizing success with a lower level of rhetoric. Johnson also faced the problems of changing internal dynamics within the black populations of the center cities, which contributed to the rising upheavals during his Administration. The problem of presidents overselling programs in an effort to mobilize support will nonetheless remain, particularly as a future president may again seek to activate political support from the have-not segments of American society. We have also seen recent incumbents, in their efforts at mobilizing public support, tending to emphasize symbols and employ deception. Where presidents are blocked in achieving more tangible policy results, this is one likely avenue to pursue. The emphasis on the presumed capacity of the president to solve problems which has been so characteristic of the strong-presidency orientation is conducive to presidential action which at least gives the appearance that all is well, or that something is being done about a whole variety of policy questions. In the face of difficulty in mobilizing support and moving Congress, there is also an obvious pressure for the president to seek substantive policy shifts unilaterally. Willing legislative delegation and presidential uses of secrecy and such devices as impoundment to circumvent Congress, which we saw in discussing presidential-legislative relations, have an underlying logic, given the difficulties presidents have in mobilizing direct approval. Thus, the mobilizing role, like the emphasis on staff, can lead to consequences vastly different than those intended by the strong-presidency advocate.

Validity of the President as Majority Spokesman

It is now increasingly obvious that the nature of the policy choices emerging from Congress and the Presidency, respectively, do not automatically produce a clearly defined majority interest within the operations of presidential politics. Some of the debate on the merits of presidential versus legislative majorities during the 1950s and 1960s was very clearly the result of coalition politics. By the late 1960s, Congress gained different supporters as it emerged as the center of opposition to the Vietnam War and a rallying point for those who felt that the balance of defense and domestic spending could be tipped more substantially toward domestic needs.

Arguments for the superiority of either legislative or executive decisions as being representative of majority sentiment confront difficulties. Congressional elections are often uncompetitive, and internal procedures can easily thwart majority preferences within that institution. Nonetheless, claims of superiority for presidential decisions should be viewed skeptically, rather than with automatic acceptance. A president is, to be sure, the only public official who must think about the entire nation as his electoral constituency. Nonetheless, the Presidency may be significantly skewed on particular issues. A president may be reflecting his own personality needs in sticking to a position, or he may be reflecting a staff system which does not allow him to process information effectively. Furthermore, there may well be specific lobby impacts on the president which influence specific decisions. Since there is no opportunity for public hearings, these may actually be more hidden than is the case with Congress.

The implications of this analysis for future practices are important. Automatic virtue should not be imputed to the position of either branch. Differences need to be worked out on their merits on specific issues, and with an eye toward good faith bargaining between leaders of the respective branches. Procedures should allow for a resolution of conflicts, without the presumption that one of the branches is inherently superior to the other on all major policy questions.

Checks and Balances

Traditional debates over the nature of presidential politics have produced sharply divided views as to the manner in which checks can and should operate. Issues involve not only all three branches, but the position of the political parties, the press, and interest groups and elites. Recent experiences can be reviewed for each source of potential checks.

Congress. The legislative check on the Presidency has often not been very effective in recent years. This has been most obvious in terms of foreign policy, and especially those questions involving the use of force. More generally, the legislative check has been weak in the frequent situations where major policies do not require specific legislative concurrence. Presidents often find that they cannot move Congress, but that it is possible to move without Congress. This was particularly true of the Nixon Presidency, in part because of his disdain for Congress and in part because the steps being initiated by Nixon were attempting to restrict governmental programs. It is easier for most actors in the American system, including presidents, to get their way when their desire is to prevent something from being done. The use of secrecy in executive operations also proved a major detriment to an effective legislative check on the executive at several points. It is more than a little difficult to prevent abuses of power if one does not even know that those actions are taking place.

The courts. The Supreme Court does not often take on questions of presidential operations and possible abuse of power. As of the mid-1950s, Glendon Schubert concluded his extensive review by emphasizing the tendency toward judicial restraint on questions of presidential power.[1] The refusal of the courts to confront the questionable constitutionality of the Vietnam War was a good example of a common pattern. The willingness of the Supreme Court to examine the executive privilege question, even on narrow grounds, in ruling against Nixon in July 1974, thus constituted an interesting exception to the general tendency of avoiding explosive issues between president and Congress.

Both the courts and the judicial process have nonetheless proven very important in some developments which potentially stand to alter aspects of national policy-making activity. The thrust of such legislation as the Environmental Protection Act of 1969 is to allow the courts to be used more substantially to determine the outcome of specific issues. The adequacy of environmental impact reports in particular often become a legal issue. Rather than another bureaucratic unit to be supervised, presumably by the president, one thus had a shift in the focus of decision. The use of the courts has been important in facilitating the development of an alternative focus for some interest-group activity. If not a direct check, the judicial process nonetheless promises some potential for different lines of conflict resolution. (The rise of such phenomena as class action suits and the thrust of Ralph Nader's operations in the quest for a public-interest law orientation was similarly facilitated by developments involving a different use of the judicial process.)

Political parties. The inabilities of the political parties to provide a check on presidential politics have been apparent for both the majority and the minority parties. The president's own party has been glaringly weak as a source either of strength in policy development *or* as a check on his actions. Richard Nixon's operations would never have been approved in 1971–1972 by at least many within the hierarchy of his own party, yet party officials were so uninvolved as to be unaware of those events.

The position of the party opposing the president in Congress has also been weak. The role of the titular leader of the opposing party has always been an ambiguous one in the American system. The difficulties of that role were compounded in the wake of the Watergate revelations because of an extraordinary juxtaposing of events. Had Senator Edward Kennedy himself been less suspect in the eyes of many because of the death of his young female companion under mysterious circumstances during a weekend at Chappaquiddick, he might have been in a position to play a more active role in focusing criticism on the Nixon Administration. The disarray of the parties nevertheless makes it difficult for forceful opposition to incumbents to be expressed through partisan mechanisms.

The media. In reviewing the formal lines of competition around the contemporary Presidency, it is most understandable to find, even prior to Watergate, the Nixon Presidency's harshest words regarding an opposing force most often directed toward the press and the television networks. Presidential spokesmen from Spiro Agnew to Patrick Buchanan persisted in portraying the media as far too hostile to the Nixon Presidency. In these views, the press was far too critical of Nixon and his policy accomplishments.

The power of the media in focusing criticism is substantial. The recent presidential pattern of announcing decisions with little prior notice served, at the same time, to intensify the importance of press and television coverage. President Johnson increased the tendencies for his Administration to be frustrated with the press by his tendency to seek secrecy prior to announcing decisions to an extreme degree, often on fairly routine matters. President Nixon repeatedly took major steps which had received little prior public attention, in the fait accompli role. The Cambodian invasion, the establishment of wage and price controls, and several Watergate actions come readily to mind.

Television is a major force in both speeding and intensifying electoral responses as the president engages in dramatic moves. Television provides instant commentary from a variety of sources, and perhaps even poll responses and rapid readings of public opinion. The result can indeed be, as in the wake of Nixon's firing of his key investigator, Archibald Cox, a "firestorm" of activity. It is not surprising that presidents and their spokesmen feel checked, or at points threatened, by these responses.

It is, however, difficult to conclude that the media have been either highly critical, or particularly effective, in serving as a check on presidential operations.[2] Although the press ultimately helped in uncovering the corruption in the Nixon Presidency, this came many months after the major events had occurred. Furthermore, it was not the network commentators or the White House regulars who were instrumental, but rather two lowly reporters on the local desk of the *Washington Post*. One compliments, rather than demeans, the work of Bob Woodward and Carl Bernstein by pointing out the number of people who were unable to penetrate the corrupt inner sanctum of the Nixon White House.[3]

Presidents get angry with the media in part because it can direct prompt responses, but also because presidents become so used to the impact of television being highly favorable. As the authors of *Presidential Television* have very forcefully documented, the media are a very important resource for presidents.[4] They can help the astute incumbent orchestrate the majesty of his office and dramatize his range of activities—particularly in the foreign policy field. If television can hurt a president on occasion, it can also be of frequent service to his interests.

It is understandable, given the withering of other sources of competition and the speed of today's politics, that the role of the media is a point of frequent debate. It obviously is of great importance. The question of how information is to be disseminated and the related problem of secrecy must be continuing issues in the evolution of presidential politics.

A Basic Paradox

Traditional checks on the Presidency produce a fundamental paradox. It has generally been difficult for a president to lead in the manner prescribed by the strong-presidency enthusiast. Yet the checks on the Presidency have often been rather weak. It has therefore been possible for both the president and the Presidency to operate in ways circumventing those checks, at points in a fairly secretive and manipulative manner. The mobilizing and bargaining roles may be weak, but too often the traditional checks have also been limited.

The Power Question

For the strong-presidency enthusiast, a competitive political process constituted the most important check on presidential politics. The recent pattern of presidential politics, and especially the revelations of scandals and abuses of power in the Nixon Presidency, have raised serious questions regarding that check which emphasize problems seen by both elitists and those stressing autonomous and uncompetitive tendencies in national policy-making. Each of these views must now be reviewed in the wake of recent experiences.

The Elite View

Some aspects of contemporary presidential politics do follow patterns emphasized by major elite writers. The recruitment process has placed a large number of individuals from elite backgrounds in cabinet positions, often including the most important cabinet posts. Particularly at the White House Staff level, many presidential appointees were from upper-middle-class backgrounds. Presidents themselves, while not born into elite status in most instances, have generally had substantial economic means by the time they entered the White House. A president, while in office, lives a life of luxury. The total range of experiences has not often altered that basic life-style. The national newsworthiness of a president taking the time to eat breakfast with rank-and-file Americans, as occurred with Nixon in the spring of 1974, is a manifestation of the uniqueness of such activities. Significantly, the men around the president have often demonstrated a greater measure of upward mobility than the often elite-raised members of the cabinet. Individuals who were successful in their advising activities could often count on substantial economic good fortune once they left the White House. It is important to note that neither social backgrounds nor achieved status necessarily determined political attitudes.[5] Yet the backgrounds of many and the generally swank setting of virtually all presidential activities could easily contribute to an ethos reflecting the lack of direct reminders of the everyday problems confronting millions of Americans.

The Nixon Presidency brought to a dramatic climax the growth of campaign contributions. Leading families were contributing large sums, reaching the six-figure level in some instances. Major economic operations also produced tremendous sums. The oil industry contributed over $5 million to Nixon, and defense contractors contributed better than $2.5 million to various Republicans.[6] The milk producers contributed about $2 million overall that year, in the transaction which ultimately became devastating not just for the Nixon Presidency, but for a variety of congressmen and a Texas governor (and former secretary of the treasury for Nixon), John Connally.

Substantial amounts of money were given by those affected by government regulation. The airline executives began to reveal by 1974 that they had virtually all been contributing, in part, it seemed, out of a desire not to be isolated as the sole uncooperative firm in a situation in which every other firm had been contributing. The tendency for money to be involved in a competitive process in this manner suggests that there was not necessarily a specific buying of presidential favors by single corporations. The flow of money did, nonetheless, show a tendency for both various functional areas of the economy and specific firms to contribute in a major way to an incumbent president.

Policy outcomes themselves, in some views, have given considerable support to aspects of the elite interpretation. Statistics on incomes before taxes display a pattern in which the rich do indeed enjoy a substantial proportion of the income being distributed to all Americans. Census Bureau figures reveal the basic pattern. Dividing all families in the nation into five equal population categories, the percentage of the total income of all Americans being received as of 1971 was as follows: lowest fifth, 5.5 percent; second fifth, 11.9 percent; third fifth, 17.4 percent; fourth fifth, 23.7 percent; and highest fifth, 41.6 percent. In terms of individual incomes rather than families, the disparities were even more striking. While the bottom fifth received 3.4 percent, the top 5 percent received 20.6 percent, and the top fifth received 50.4 percent.[7]

The effect of federal taxes, despite the seeming progressiveness displayed in the individual tax booklets each year, has also been strikingly minor. After federal income and payroll taxes, and also after cash payments to individuals, percentages of total income were as follows: lowest fifth, 6.3 percent; second fifth, 9.1 percent; third fifth, 14.6 percent; fourth fifth, 22.8 percent; and highest fifth, 47.1 percent.

It is important to recognize the substantial degree of stability in income distribution over several decades, particularly in family income before taxes between World War II and 1970. Yet also running through the recent data is the impact of a greater degree of regressiveness in tax policies. Robert Lekachman, a major student of incomes policy, stated in late 1973 that the impact of five years of Nixon had been a decline in the more progressive taxes on business and income of some $25 billion, while at the same time the more regressive payroll levies (such as social security) increased by $20 billion.[8]

There had been some progress through the 1960s in bringing additional individuals above the government-declared poverty levels. In 1959 almost a quarter of the American population, 39,490,000 persons, was below the poverty level. By 1969, the proportion had declined to 12.2 percent, and the number of individuals to 24,289,000.[9] Yet with the ravages of inflation in the 1970s, people asking the question of how to live at or somewhat above the poverty level were becoming increasingly desperate. Indeed, those in middle-income categories began to ask the same question, as they found their real income (figures corrected for inflation) undergoing an actual decline.

Focusing on policy outcomes in terms of income distribution must be done with care. The process through which income distribution takes place is a complex one. At points, policy efforts may be made for altering income distribution which are substantially unsuccessful and thus not apparent in the data. The process through which governmental action contributes to the pattern of income distribution will also be reviewed shortly in the context of the functional area dominance view.

Foreign policy operations have also produced a mixed picture on the elite dominance issue. From the vantagepoint of the president and the constellation of competing forces he has faced, the process has clearly been a competitive one. The picture of the foreign policy apparatus presented by both Graham Allison and Morton Halperin is clearly one in which a range of options are often being debated.

There has also been considerable indication of competition taking place for the same resources and policy advantages. Defense contractors want weapons produced not just in general, but by their firms. The different branches of the armed services desire an expanded share of the overall defense budget, as well as hoping for an expanded pie to divide.

Foreign policy operations have also showed international pressures which are not emphasized in the analyses exposing the substantial ties various corporate entities have had to the defense weapons operations. Changing international systems cannot easily be molded by just a single nation, regardless of how strongly a major component in one of those nations might desire a foreign policy which is also advantageous for their economic position.[10]

Elite ties and involvement have nonetheless been substantial at some points in the foreign policy process. The Vietnam decisions revealed in several instances an important impact by those often identified as part of the American elite. Particularly where decisions were made in a fairly closed manner, elite involvement was apt to be substantial. The ease with which those from elite backgrounds gained the president's ear did not necessarily mean that there was one elite interest versus that of everyone else, but they did raise questions about both access and the range of values being considered.

Presidential politics have also revealed lines of conflict not emphasized in the Domhoff-Mills line of analysis. There were major issues, particularly racial matters, which divided the lower and middle classes, and which found segments of the elite divided. The concept of the limousine liberal, along with the concern for backlash among white Americans, emerged in the 1960s as indications of the manner in which social-class and racial issues could divide adversaries on a basis other than of the elite versus everyone else. Cleavages involving religion and alternative life-styles were also present. Finally, income distribution below the elite level was also influenced by various policy-making activities involving unions and professional groups, which did have an impact on incomes being received. Aspects of the manner in which governmental expenditures related to income distribution results can also be seen in the context of those analyses emphasizing functional area dominance.

Functional-Area Dominance

Several aspects of federal government operations also fit the concepts of those seeing presidential politics operating in the context of dominance by uncompetitive and autonomous interests. In this view, there are multiple centers of policy-making activity which are often highly biased toward the best-organized interest or interests in a particular area of concern. The central problem in this view is a political system which has parceled out those policy-making interactions in a way which makes it impossible for central guidance to occur. Rather than being a problem of control by a single coordinating elite, the problem is seen to be one of a politics which lacks direction and guidance.

From the vantagepoint of the president and those working around him, there are repeated indications of conflict over various policies. Economic policies, in particular, have produced a variety of economic functional areas, such as banking, housing, defense contracting, agricultural operations, and construction and public works, in which those suffering from current economic operations are anxious to have new policies and expanded assistance. It is not surprising that those who have worked in the White House tend to view the policy-making process, because of their perspective, as a highly competitive one.[11]

Process characteristics also fit the concept of functional area dominance in some respects. The amount of attention which can be given at "the center" of presidential operations in the White House has often been very limited. Certainly the president himself has been limited in the coordinating role he could perform. Furthermore, presidential frustration with the fragmentation faced in various governmental operations has often been substantial. The regulatory commissions, trust fund operations, and veto points in Congress have been periodic points of frustration. The phenomenon Emmette Redford identified as "policy subsystems" could make life difficult for a president who wanted to alter the operation of a particular policy.

Total expansion in the federal government's spending has been an important indication of the difficulties either a president or Congress can have in operating the budgetary process in a manner which restrains pressures from various segments of the population wanting those policies which affect them expanded. The federal government *did* expand its total outlays significantly in the period between Kennedy and Ford. The budget increases from less than $100 billion to over $300 billion indicate in part an expanding gross national product, an expanding population, and changes in nomenclature used in budgeting operations. A more accurate indicator of comparative spending is the figures on outlays as they relate to the total gross national product (GNP). Between 1955 and 1970, the federal portion of the GNP increased from 19.5 percent to 21.4 percent. In that same period, the increase for all governments was sharper: from 29.9 percent to 34.0 percent. The shift in defense allocations is also significant. There was a net increase of 5.7 percent in nondefense spending, with a decrease of 2.4 percent in defense spending, as those figures related to the gross national product.[12]

The various shifts toward nondefense spending thus occurred at the same time federal government operations were showing very little impact on the total distribution of income in American society. This link fits the concerns of those who see the various policy-making interactions around governmental expenditures often dominated by the interest or interests with privileged access and a better chance to take advantage of governmental programs once they are enacted.

Agricultural payments are a classic example. Because of ties with important legislative committee members, subsidy programs were continued as they increasingly gave benefits not to the struggling farmer but to the large farms and agribusinesses. Subsidies are based upon the productivity of each farm unit, and as a result the large and more efficient operators get the lion's share of the payments. Specifically, in a recent Department of Agriculture study it was concluded that the largest farms, with incomes averaging $20,900.00 per year, also received 62.8 percent (4.64 billion dollars) of all price support assistance. At the other end of the scale are the 1.5 million small farmers averaging less than $8,000.00 in annual income (including non-farm sources) and yet receiving only 9.1 percent ($670 million) of the total benefits.[13]

Ties to both the White House and to Congress in agricultural policy development has become increasingly clear. The dairy producers were contributing over $2 million to political campaigns in 1972, and even a lowly first-term member of the House (who happened to be on the dairy and poultry subcommittee) would receive $32,000 for his campaign. It was most evident that agricultural policies were involved with a set of interactions not destined to rapidly alter policy away from those with the best access—and those who provided a valuable source of support for the politician.[14]

Regulatory operations have produced examples, also, of interactions which have tended to substantially influence a particular policy outcome by the mobilizing of those with the most immediate, and specific, interest. There was an effort at tightening the regulation of the tobacco industry in the face of additional information linking smoking and lung cancer back in 1965.[15] To fight that effort, members of the Tobacco Institute (a lobby organization for the major tobacco companies) got together, using ex-Senator Clements, and engaged in a major lobbying campaign in Congress. The specific interest won; President Johnson did nothing through the whole process, and ultimately signed (despite the protests of consumer groups demanding a veto) a bill which in effect prevented the tougher stand recommended by the Food and Drug Administration from being considered.

Other interests have often mobilized to protect their positions. One of the more intense operations in recent years has been that of the Seafarers International Union and the shipping companies. They seek to protect the position of the Merchant Marine, and in the process the volume of traffic and the salaries and working conditions of its members. They have been suspicious of reorganizing efforts and desirous of maintaining what in the eyes of some is a highly privileged employment position. A target of their favors was Congressman Edward A. Garmatz of Maryland. He received $17,000 in publicly reported union funds in 1966. In 1968, 90 percent of his funding came from the shippng interests. In 1970, the industry raised a reported $37,000 for him, even though he was unopposed for reelection. As the reader can easily guess, Garmatz was in a strategic position: He served as chairman of the Merchant Marine and Fisheries Committee.[16]

There are nonetheless some indications that functional-area dominance by a tight-knit set of supporters can be modified, if not in fact broken. At points, seemingly established governmental programs have been substantially modified, and in other instances there have been indications that seemingly closed policy-making interactions can be forced to accommodate a wider range of values and interests.

Atomic energy policy making constituted in the 1950s and 1960s a good example of closely knit operations in which few outsiders made a major impact. The complex subject matter facilitated a situation in which the Atomic Energy Commission, responsible both for promoting peacetime uses and for regulation, received too little effective scrutiny from Congress. Concern for safety operations by the late 1960s altered the picture. The Atomic Energy Commission found itself on the defensive, and a debate involving safety regulations finally led to a fundamental reorganization of the regulatory practices themselves.[17]

Environmental considerations produced other important results. The operations of the Army Corps of Engineers were long regarded as one of the better examples of a tight-knit set of mutually supporting relationships between congressmen desiring projects for their districts and the Corps itself, with its desire for expansion. Committee operations (headed for years in the House of Representatives by Michael Kirwin) involved trading of support among committee members for various projects and often an easy time for river and harbor development interests. Congress itself took an important step in altering river and harbor politics by requiring environmental impact reports. The surprising results included the defeat of the plan for the development of the Florida Barge Canal.[18]

A large number of policies have remained largely unexamined by other than the most interested participants. Specialization in Congress and the president's lack of time or interest clearly contributed. There have nonetheless been some indications that the practice of policy-making through functional-area dominance by the most interested party or parties could be "cracked." The cracks in functional-area dominance will provide an important clue for the reform agenda.

Pluralism

Those who saw presidential politics operating in the context of an open competitiveness, with easy access for a wide variety of groups, received serious challenges from the developments since the early 1960s. The nature of policy outcomes, with its high level of elite benefits, has been discussed. The operation of presidential politics in a context of frequent elite recruitment for cabinet positions and the selection of highly upwardly moble presidents has also been shown. Several points deserve additional emphasis.

Pluralists can point to instances in which electoral politics has had an important influence on policy development. President Nixon was clearly looking toward the 1972 election with such decisions as the establishment of wage and price controls in 1971 and in his efforts at stretching out decisions on desegregation which were offending white (and particularly 'Southern) constituents.[19] The Vietnam War can also be viewed in the context of electoral impacts. Johnson ultimately found himself in a position in which running again would have been an extremely distasteful (and not necessarily successful) effort, Furthermore, insofar as Daniel Ellsberg's emphasis on presidential unwillingness to assume responsibility for "losing Vietnam" is correct, one has an additional indicaton of the importance of potential electoral sanctions on presidential policy making. Given the specific directions in which these influences by the electorate tended to take public policy, it is perhaps worth emphasizing the obvious point: Presidential politics will at points operate in response to majority wishes as correctly perceived by leaders and yet produce policy results which are repugnant to some with intense policy concerns.

Pluralistic views suffer in terms of the difficulties confronting those who seek to organize and participate in a bargaining process. From the vantagepoint of presidential politics, a fundamental problem is apparent. With whom does one bargain? Presidents are often too preoccupied with other matters to give a significant amount of attention to domestic issues. In turn, the concentration of authority in the Presidency has meant that the question of access is often most difficult for those without established patterns and well-established lobbyists. A major political region and its (white) representatives may find their way into the White House bargaining activity. The points of access are not so open for those with a variety of new issues, interests, and demands. When David Truman developed his emphasis on bargaining in executive politics, his emphasis was almost exclusively on the federal bureaucracy and the agency-clientele relationships. This picture of a bargaining process was at points more accurate in the years prior to the expansion of staff operations. The ease of access was clearly more questionable as one saw the growth of a Domestic Council, an Office of Management and Budget, and even wage and price control mechanisms. Interests having ties to a lower-level agency might well have no real access to the White House.

Some of the frustrations expressed by those seeking access to the Nixon Presidency resulted from the coalition he sought to build, and not simply from governmental structures. The picture which emerges is nonetheless clear: High dependence on governance by the Presidency makes it difficult to envision the American political system as one in which access for a wide variety of groups (particularly if they do not already have strong ties somewhere in the political system) easily occurs.

Ultimately, the pluralist lost most fundamentally with the electorate itself. Pluralism was closely wedded to the American belief, as of the early 1960s, that the government was responsive if one sought relief. As the authors of *The Civic Culture* made clear, this was a uniquely American belief. By the early 1970s, the public opinion polls were telling a very different story. The polls confirmed what many had sensed by themselves and in conversations with others. The analysts could develop lines of analysis showing that the elite dominance models did not always hold. Yet for the average American, the points of political access seemed frighteningly remote.

Ultimately, questions involving power relationships in presidential politics are not easily answered. From the vantagepoint of the president and his staff, the process is clearly a competitive one. They are kept more than busy with conflicting pressures. Yet access to that process can also be quite limited and unevenly distributed throughout the population. Furthermore, some potential issues are less apt to be raised than others simply because of the resources which are possessed by the upper class and the major corporate interests in American society.

The question of power relationships is difficult to answer because there exist simultaneously several different patterns of political activity and power relationships. Some conflicts resemble the elite model, while others at the same time show characteristics emphasized by those stressing autonomous and uncompetitive policy-making activity. Some issues also reveal substantial access and competition, as emphasized by the pluralist writers.[20]

A president, in short, generally faces not only issues on which there may be a substantial amount of elite consensus, but also situations in which power is fragmented and in which he may feel genuinely impotent. In addition, there are some situations in which the more open and bargaining-oriented process does come into operation. Reform in presidential politics must therefore contend with more than one type of power configuration. It is time now to return to the question of presidential roles.

An End to Superman?

Thomas Cronin aptly used the phrase "Superman, the Textbook President" to describe the thinking of many Americans and a large percentage of the textbook writers as of the late 1960s.[21] That overly dependent expectation, as should now be apparent, produces serious problems. Presidents are unable to operate in the prescribed fashion of a strong President if they are unable to fill the mobilizing role and if they become overloaded with issues. Given the tendency for the number of issues facing the American political system to expand, there may well be less chance for future presidents to fill the expectations of the strong Presidency model than was the case in earlier decades. The tendency is then for power to grow within the Executive Office of the President, and for the president to be involved with a ratification of staff action. Since selection processes produce inadequate personalities, and since cross pressures in electoral expectations make mobilizing difficult, there is also a tendency for hidden politics and the use of fait accompli roles to increase. In that context, those with access to the presidential decision process may be extremely limited in number.

The direction of much reform discussion in the post-Watergate period has been motivated by an intense desire to reduce some of these tendencies. Yet in the extreme, this "antipresident" posture also confronts difficulties. For a president to be encouraged to engage in ratifying roles and to resist bargaining and mobilizing roles seems to constitute an open invitation for little significant policy change to emerge. In short, the American presidential dilemma emerges all over again.

Possible directions for reducing this dilemma can nonetheless be drawn from our analysis of alternative roles. First, it is essential that decisions which are ratified by a president be worked out with a greater degree of participation and an opportunity for alternative values to be considered. These presidentially ratified decisions need not be either solely staff decisions or those developed in a set of interlocking alliances with privileged interests dominating. Fortunately, the cracks seen in the tendencies for uncompetitive and autonomous interest-group activity to dominate decision-making provides an important clue to opportunities for this reform thrust. Second, the situations where the president and the Presidency must be involved with at least a partially fait accompli process need to be reduced, and when they are necessary, the degree of secrecy after the initial decisions must be reduced. There *are* ways in which the dilemmas of presidential politics can be confronted.

NOTES

[1] Glendon Schubert, *The Presidency in the Courts,* Minneapolis, Minn., University of Minnesota Press, 1957.

[2] There are numerous volumes discussing this problem. One useful bibliography and set of basic materials is in Newton N. Minow et al., *Presidential Television,* New York, Basic Books, 1973.

[3] Their intriguing account is Carl Bernstein and Bob Woodward, *All the President's Men,* New York, Warner Paperback Library, 1974.

[4] Minow, op. cit., pp. 171–191.

[5] This issue is discussed in Donald R. Matthews, *U.S. Senators and Their World,* Chapel Hill, N.C., University of North Carolina Press, 1960, chap. 6.

[6] *The Congressional Quarterly* 32, no. 40 (October 5, 1974), 2679.

[7] Charles L. Schultze et al., *Setting National Priorities, 1974,* Washington, D.C., Brookings, 1973, p. 41.

[8] Robert Lekachman, "The Economics of Inequality," in *What Nixon Is Doing to Us,* ed. by Alan Gartner et al., New York, Harper & Row, 1973, p. 6.

[9] Daniel P. Moynihan, *The Politics of a Guaranteed Income,* New York, Vintage, 1973, p. 36. The definition of poverty did also increase, rising to $4,137 by 1971 for a nonfarm family of four.

[10] See John W. Spanier and Eric M. Uslander, *How American Foreign Policy Is Made,* New York, Praeger, 1974.

[11] One interesting discussion of fragmentation and competition seen through the eyes of a long-time budget official is in Harold Seidman, *Politics, Position, and Power: The Dynamics of Federal Organization,* New York, Oxford University Press, 1970. On page 97, he specifically states,

> Whether he wants to or not, President Nixon cannot ignore the trend toward fractionalization and compartmentalization of Federal programs which has made the subgovernments powerful and arrogant and permitted public power to slip into private hands. More is at stake than economy and efficiency. Unless checked, these developments could bring into question the viability of our democratic system.

[12] Schultze, op. cit., p. 9.

[13] See William Proxmire, *Uncle Sam: The Last of the Bigtime Spenders,* New York, Simon & Schuster, 1972, pp. 148–155.

[14] *The Congressional Quarterly,* op. cit.

[15] The actions of the Tobacco Institute are well documented in A. Lee Fritschler, *Smoking and Politics: Policymaking and the Federal Bureaucracy,* New York, Meredith, 1969.

[16] Mark J. Green et al., *Who Runs Congress?,* New York, Bantam, 1972, p. 23.

[17] The modifications in the AEC are discussed in *The Congressional Quarterly* 32: 34 (August 24, 1974), 2323.

[18] The importance of the congressional role in opening environmental politics to broader participation was stressed in remarks by Congressman Les Aspin, a Wisconsin Democrat, in a public address at the University of Southern California, May 3, 1974.

[19] On the Nixon civil rights maneuvers, see Rowland Evans, Jr., and Robert D. Novak, *Nixon in the White House*, New York, Vintage, 1971, chap. 6.

[20] This is the position developed by Theodore Lowi in his famous review of Raymond Bauer et al., *American Business and Public Policy*. For a useful summary of that position, see Randall B. Ripley, *Public Policies and their Politics*, Boston, Little, Brown, 1966, pp. 27–40. The original essay appears as "American Business, Public Policy, Case-Studies and Political Theory," *World Politics* No. 4, July 1964.

[21] Thomas E. Cronin, "The Textbook Presidency," in *Inside the System*, ed. by Charles Peters and John Rothschild, New York, Praeger, 1973, pp. 6–19.

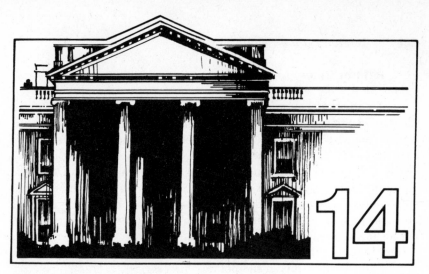

Confronting
the Reform Agenda

The American Presidency does show significant capacity for change. Both the enactment of many post-Watergate reforms and the impact of President Ford as a distinct contrast to his predecessor dramatized the capacities for change by the mid 1970s. The occupant of the White House can make significant differences in the organizational pattern within the institution, and in the characteristics surrounding at least aspects of the relationships with the press, the federal bureaucracy, Congress, and major interests. Election returns and an indignant electorate revealed, by 1975, a capacity for altering presidential relationships with Congress rather substantially for at least a short-run period.

The rush of reform activity in the wake of the Watergate scandals often seemed to be primarily directed at a reduction in the chances that another President would behave as arrogantly as did Richard Nixon. This was obviously not a modest objective! At the same time, there is a good deal more to effective presidential politics than achieving situations in which the president no longer finds it necessary to proclaim, as did Nixon, that he is not a crook.

Reform Goals

To adequately confront the question of possible reform in presidential politics, it is essential to consider basic goals. Obviously, there cannot be easy agreement on either the goals themselves or the strategies and techniques most suited to the achievement of major goals. Some adjustments in institutions can be made in an effort at avoiding difficult situations in the future but with little sense of partisan advantage and policy preference as they are being enacted. Reform in such areas as the selection of vice presidents might come in an uncontroversial context. Many other changes, however, are inexorably tied to the nature of the policy outcomes which are preferred by various participants in the political process.

The question of goals in presidential politics reintroduces the issue of American political values. Issues involving democratic politics, policy effectiveness, and political legitimacy are all involved. Concern for democracy requires a concern for the distribution of access to decision-makers and for the distribution of resources for influencing decisions. Clearly, a concern for democratic politics must also involve an opposition to secretive, manipulative use of executive power. Within the category of democratic concerns, there are good reasons for individuals to differ on the extent to which such values as expanded participation ought to be sought.

The goal of democratic politics may well be challenged more seriously in the next years than in the past by those looking for a more rapid movement toward particular policy goals. Periods of economic difficulty and of declining faith in national achievements can indeed foster greater interest in the abandonment of democratic commitments. It is well worth emphasizing, in the context of these issues in America, that the more autocratic regimes can also have major difficulties in developing effective policies. The demands which changing resource levels place on a system may be impossible to resolve, and the tendencies toward groupthink, executive isolation, and inadequacies in leader's personalities can produce major problems.[1] At the same time, emerging policy issues can rightly be interpreted as placing a very real strain on the American democratic commitment.

Concern for effective public policy must be basic in efforts at reforming presidential politics. Public confidence in presidential politics is not going to be restored solely by more earnest personalities, or different staff patterns. Process concerns and political styles can be important, but electoral orientations are often strongly influenced by the nature of the policies emerging from the operation of presidential politics.

Seeking to define effective policy is obviously a task of potentially limitless proportions. Broadly, it is useful to recognize three views of possible modifications in the effectiveness of public policy. (1) For some, Americans are encouraged to lower expectations and simply declare yesterday's seemingly unsatisfactory results to be the best attainable state of affairs in the future. (2) A second view emphasizes economies of scale and more efficient use of resources. Mass transit systems, school systems with greater effectiveness as well as lower per-pupil costs, and regional health centers are among the policy thrusts which fit this orientation. (3) In another view, the answer to effective policy must now come with redistributive approaches to income and wealth distribution and in alterations in the relationships between business and government. Proposals for major taxes on wealth, various income policy steps, and nationalization of such industries as health services and defense procurement receive attention from this perspective.

More satisfactory policy results from presidential politics are not apt to develop easily from an overwhelming emphasis on just one of the three approaches. Lowered expectations may be forced on Americans at some points, given the greater scarcity of resources which the coming years portend. Yet it seems unnecessary to abandon in total the quest for policies which improve life for Americans through effective use of presidential politics. Economies of scale and more effective use of resources are, in principle, attainable in a variety of policy situations. Furthermore, even with a possible redistributive thrust in public policy there will still be a need for improving the way in which various services are made available for the average American. It also seems apparent that the redistributive issues cannot be ignored. In part, resources held and influence weilded by corporations and the wealthy make it difficult at points for more efficient policies to emerge. Transportation policies with a dependence on highways, resource policies with a dependence on oil, and housing policies influenced by the impact of tax advantages through manipulating tax loss provisions all show aspects of this problem. In addition, the question of the distribution of wealth contains some possible answers for confronting aspects of the scarcity issue.

Effectiveness in policy relates, in turn, to the question of public confidence in presidential operations. The legitimacy of American political institutions has dropped sharply in recent years, including the Presidency. Reform in presidential politics must be concerned with actions which facilitate both greater electoral confidence and also a greater sense of fairness in basic operations. Efforts at tax reform, for example, involve the question of how *fairly* the public judges the government to be operating, and not simply the question of what additional revenue can be generated.

Expanding the democratic dimensions of presidential politics, improving its policy-developing capacities, and increasing public support involve fairly difficult choices. It can be difficult to foster several political values at the same time within a given political system.[2] For example, greater participation in the name of expanded access to the Presidency may conflict with the objective of policy-formulation which reacts fast enough to economic conditions to keep employment high. Similarly, the pursuit of greater openness in government can produce situations in which public confidence is further undercut by the information which is revealed. Reform would indeed be a much easier task if goals were never in conflict.

Efforts at moving presidential politics toward various goals are also restricted in that reform tends generally to focus on structural aspects of the Presidency. Formal institutional arrangements and requirements *are* important. Requiring a president to release information, or allowing for changes in legislative committee chairmen, for example, may alter not only the prevailing political practices but important policy outcomes as well.

The totality of presidential behavior is also shaped by several other factors, including presidential personality, power relationships, general policy contexts, and electoral expectations. Several of these factors can also be altered, as political resources for influencing presidential selection are altered by restrictions on campaign finance, or as the presidents correctly sense that the electorate is tired of false promises. In several contexts, the future Presidency has clearly been altered in likely behavior by the traumas which Richard Nixon encountered. Regardless of the specific thrusts of campaign reform legislation, for example, a president's fund-raiser in the future will be more cautious—perhaps to the point of even avoiding the job. Major aspects of the reform agenda must nonetheless be structural, and they deserve careful attention along with a consideration of ways in which other factors may change or be changed in the evolution of presidential politics.

The Reform Agenda

Responses to the Watergate scandals did produce significant reform activity. Several reform issues emerged on the nation's agenda at the same time. In considering that reform agenda, it is useful to look at presidential selection, presidential information systems, the secrecy questions, policy analysis, modifications in access to policy making activity, the role of Congress, and electoral expectations. In looking at reforms in these areas, it is important to keep in mind the general directions which are being prescribed for modifying presidential politics. First, there must be increased opportunities for policy change without direct presidential leadership, and second, it is essential to reduce opportunities for the manipulative and miscalculating uses of the fait accompli role. Concerns involving not only a more democratic politics, but policy effectiveness and electoral support are related to this thrust in several ways.

Improving Presidential Selection

Effective presidential selection is both crucial and difficult.[3] The abuses and inadequacies of the Nixon Presidency have dramatized the possible impact of an individual presidential personality. The failures of Nixon and the problems of recent Presidents will be important lessons surely recognized by future occupants of the Oval Office. Yet in several possible areas of reform there is no easy way to compel a president to act as reformers desire. It is extremely difficult to legislate staff patterns and approaches to the media and the electorate. Wise presidential selection is vital.

James Barber has intriguingly argued that the selection process should pay considerably more attention to the personality, rather than the policy statements, of prospective presidents. Given the problems which presidential personalities have created, this is in some respects an enticing suggestion. Furthermore, the lack of continuity between platform positions and subsequent actions suggests limitations with an extensive focus on a candidate's platform in evaluating him. One wonders how many voters for Richard Nixon in 1968 expected wage and price controls, advocacy of a guaranteed income plan (Family Assistance), detente with the Russians, and recognition of Communist China! The observable decline in party attachments can be seen as a further basis for arguing that voters should simply seek out the best presidential personality.

Barber's suggestion nonetheless confronts a basic problem. Despite the evolution of a more fluid party system, a president does not start from scratch in developing policy positions once elected. There are coalition patterns which remain, and party mechanisms in dealing with Congress. One suspects, in the wake of Nixon's collapse, that voters will pay more attention to the personalities of the persons being considered for the Presidency. To ask voters to discount coalition relationships, however, is to ask that that still significant avenue for voter influence on policy be reduced.

The obvious hope should be that the nominating process can produce opportunities for voters to choose between two well-suited candidates. Two steps can be taken to help broaden the recruitment net. A greater sharing of policy-making activities can mean that there will be a greater opportunity for a variety of governors and congressmen to gain public recognition. Better opportunity for exposure to the media is also essential. Easier access to media exposure could in part be accomplished by voluntary action on the part of the television networks. Specific policies granting free time to emerging candidates should also be considered.

Several influential dimensions of the selection process are difficult to alter. The building of an organization for the primaries and the financing of that effort is difficult to remove from the individual efforts of candidates. As a result, a substantial number of potential candidates are eliminated. Altering primary practices themselves requires the coordination of action by respective state legislatures. States could agree, regionally, to a limited number of primaries as one means of reducing the burden of those races on candidates. The suggestion of a single national primary has received periodic interest. Despite some reduction in the burdens on prospective candidates, this step could also reduce aspects of bargaining which remain in the present process. National primaries could increase the chances for factional victories, which are already a problem. A broader recruitment net and expansion of candidates' opportunities for access to public attention are the most feasible proposals.

The process for selection of the vice-president also cries out for improvement. It would seem difficult in many respects to structure a more accident-prone process. History has in a sense caught up with the inadequacies of traditional procedures. The nation experienced in a period of one year both the removal of a vice-presidential nominee (Senator Eagleton) because of the questions raised as to the significance of his earlier hospitalization for reasons of mental depression and the resignation of Vice-President Agnew as he pleaded no contest to charges of income tax evasion. The likelihood of vice-presidents becoming president makes improvement in their selection imperative. Besides the ever-present possibility of an incumbent vice-president assuming the Presidency, there is always a possibility that the recognition he receives will lead to future election. Of the seven Presidents from Truman through Ford, four had previously been Vice-Presidents (Truman, Johnson, Nixon, and Ford); and the nation was greeted in 1968 with a choice between two former Vice-Presidents (Nixon and Hubert Humphrey).

At a minimum, the procedure used by the Democrats after Senator Eagleton's removal from the ticket in 1972 could be employed. Since the candidate is virtually always chosen by the presidential nominee anyway, having the decision made after the convention and then ratified by the national committee would not change the basic power relationships. Presidents would gain potentially valuable time to choose their running mates. This is obviously no guarantee of a wise choice. Richard Nixon, after all, had four years to review the credentials of Spiro Agnew. Some of the pressures of immediate and possibly deeply regretted choice could be eliminated, however, by giving more time to the nominees.

Widespread attention to the impact of the Twenty-fifth Amendment has also developed in the wake of the unique results during Nixon's second term. The phenomenon of both a president and a vice-president holding office without having been elected by the voters produced considerable concern. In part, the selection of more adequate men in the first place could hopefully reduce this problem. It also seems unlikely that both publicly elected officials will depart office in a single term very often. Some alterations can be made in the machinery and techniques for replacement, but the potential problem is basic so long as elections are held only every four years.

Providing for Presidential Removal from Office

The far more basic reform would be to abandon the practice of fixed elections every four years. Various proposals for this more basic modification began to emerge in the wake of frustrations not just with the Vice-Presidency, but with the mechanisms available for removing individuals from office. Good arguments can be made for and against both legislative votes of no-confidence and a possible recall procedure.[4]

A basic motivation behind the arguments for abandonment of present practices, which allow the electorate to decide whether to remove an incumbent only every four years, stems from the sense that impeachment is an unlikely tool for removal. Many wondered whether the Nixon resignation would have evolved without the evidence from his own tapes, and it seems most obvious that future presidents will not again make such tapes.

Motivation for suggested no-confidence or recall procedures also stems from the sense that a given president may simply be unfit for the nature of the issues facing the country. With a more rapid change in issue agendas facing the nation, the chances of a president facing quite different problems than the ones on voters' minds when he was selected becomes greater. Thus, for the proponent of change, there is the hope that the nation can change leadership without waiting in a stalemated situation for many months or even several years, as is possible in the present system.

Proponents of legislative no-confidence procedures also envision a change in the bargaining relationships between the president and Congress. The threat of a no-confidence vote and the calling of a new election could be an important factor in helping Congress to force alterations in presidential behavior. Congress acquires, in this view, a means of holding the president accountable, even if Congress cannot be directly involved with some of the more specific policy developments.

There are problems with the proposed reforms. Given the nature of present party structures and nominating processes, it is difficult for new candidates to emerge quickly. In supporting the rapid calling of new elections, it is also necessary to envision the nominating process becoming more centralized and better organized than is now the case. This might be possible and could have advantages in reducing some of the laboriousness of the present nominating process. Some change would nonetheless be necessary.

Recall, in particular, also raises the possibility of a president being enticed to engage in short-run policies to placate the electorate. A president facing the circulation of a recall petition might well take some of the short-run economic steps and use the symbolic reassurances which have already been widely condemned in looking at presidential behavior.

A legislative no-confidence vote also raises the question of whether congressmen also ought to immediately stand for reelection if they force a president to do so. As a practical matter, a proposal to that effect is not apt to gain favor in Congress; it was not considered in the original proposal introduced in the House by Congressman Reuss (Dem. Wisconsin) in 1973. Members of the House can argue that they are already asked to face the electorate every two years. For members of the Senate, the luxury of being able to hold office for six years would not be easily abandoned.

Electoral confusion and uncertainty must also be considered. The four-year election cycle has added a measure of stability to the electoral process. Given the low levels of confidence and participation with the present system, this advantage is perhaps easily overrated. Yet undue complexity in alternative methods could also increase uncertainties with the selection process.

Methods for removing a president other than impeachment or voting him out after a four-year period deserve serious consideration. The price paid for deadlocked or leaderless government, as witnessed in 1973–1974, and such earlier periods as 1919–1920 and 1931–1932, is high. Furthermore, the nature of the issues now confronting the national government is such that even higher costs could occur in the future. Even if used only once or twice in a generation, the benefits of a new method could be considerable. At the same time, the past record of reforms producing unintended consequences suggests the importance of extended research and debate. Hopefully, better recruitment and a modified set of roles and procedures will in any event make frequent removal of tainted presidents unnecessary. It

is important to look at those changing relationships and possible reforms directly.

Strengthening Presidential Information and Decision Systems

Some strengthening of presidential information and decision systems is possible. In part, this will remain a function of individual
personalities. If a president does not want critical analysis of alternatives, or adverse information, it is difficult to mandate those procedures. This basic fact constitutes a key reason for the tremendous
importance of the recruitment process itself. Several possibilities
nonetheless emerge.

A president should give attention to the issues of both competition and overspecialization of his information channels. The importance of staff competition will remain as a factor in reducing presidential isolation. In part, competition is enhanced if the president selects
staff with an eye toward gaining a variety of viewpoints and if he
is willing to facilitate interaction which does not produce undue deference. Presidents themselves must be sensitive to the possibility of
the "groupthink" phenomenon as it has been described by Irving
Janis.

Some writers have advocated the development of a formal advocacy system, described by such terms as "multiple advocacy."[5] This
involves designated roles for individuals who will seek to provide
the president with a range of alternatives. With multiple advocacy,
attention is given to the degree of access and the bargaining resources
which go to the proponents of various views within the orbit of presidential decision making. The problem with multiple advocacy, of
course, is that a president must himself want that process in order
for it to evolve. The position taken by Richard Johnson is, overall,
very sensible.[6] Whatever the limitations of the information system
which the president gravitates toward, there must be a periodic sensitivity toward corrective action. A president who is tending toward
the formalistic staff orientation needs periodically to introduce other
individuals and proponents of alternative views into the process. Conversely, the individual who tends toward a high emphasis on politically feasible alternatives needs to be encouraged periodically to take
a longer-run look at alternatives.

A subtle but important dimension of the staff information process
has to do with the nature of the interactions and activities which
the staff engages in. The tendency has grown in the period since about
1960 for staff aides to put in long hours, spend little time away from
the White House, and for their activities to involve a constant emphasis on the importance and prestige of the White House. Proposals
emerged in the Ford Presidency for means of altering the nature

of the environment staffers tend to operate in. Forced time out of Washington and away from the office, plus a reduction in the luxuries surrounding the possession of those positions, received consideration.[7] General environments are obviously only one of many factors influencing decisions and actions; attention to modifications in those environments is nonetheless in order.

Questions involving presidential information and decision systems also involve the question of shared functions. As is most evident in considering the presidential agenda, it is simply impossible for a president to possess as much information on various issues and organizational procedures as one might like to imagine. No information system, regardless of how cagey the president is in using a competitive approach, will prevent the possibility of various activities of some importance escaping his attention. It is for this reason that an improved oversight and review of administration activities both by Congress and by various outsiders is essential. Furthermore, where the question is one of malfeasance in a governmental operation, the very threat of greater exposure can be a deterrant to questionable action.

Presidential information and decision systems raise, finally, the critical question of secrecy. Presidents have often proceeded in the recent past with the sense that important transactions could be undertaken without the prospect of scrutiny by others. This has involved opportunities for using executive privilege and the classification system as vehicles for protecting, at times, not only the decision process but the nature of those decisions themselves. The secrecy issue ultimately involves not only the immediate presidential operations, but the federal bureaucracy as well.

Limiting Secrecy

The possession of secret knowledge is a resource of major importance in any political system. In the wake of the Watergate scandals, it was scant cause for rejoicing for Americans to be informed that in comparative terms they possessed one of the least secretive of modern governments. The question of governmental secrecy is critically misunderstood if it is regarded as essentially an issue of State Department and foreign policy secrets as they involve presidential operations. The question of secrecy is ultimately one critically involving all areas of governmental operations, and presidential staffs and regular departments as well as presidential operations themselves. Knowledge, for example, of likely oil company profits gained through leasing arrangements proposed with the Department of Interior can be important to legislators and to the public.

The scandals of the Nixon Administration finally brought home to millions of Americans the tremendous power of secrecy. Major military operations were hidden from the public, not just delicate negotiations. Surveillance capacities in the White House were obviously sought without serious consideration of the possibility of either being caught or held responsible. Ultimately, as Justice Brandeis once suggested in a famous analogy, the sunshine of the truth can turn out to be a "great disinfectant." Yet critical issues remained surrounding the restraints Americans were willing to tolerate on an open flow of information. Interpretations of executive privilege and the development of practices involving the Freedom of Information Act constitute the focus for continuing issues.

The concept of executive privilege was not in the least enhanced by the now-obvious efforts of Richard Nixon to hide grave abuses of power behind the curtain of a widely defined doctrine of executive privilege. In an extreme interpretation, Nixon tried to assert that the concept covered all federal employees, former employees as well as those currently involved with the government. Rather quickly, a review of legal studies made it clear that the Nixon claims were not based on the supposedly solid precedents he was asserting. Indeed, with the extensive writings of Raoul Berger, many were persuaded to a rather strikingly different conclusion: Executive privilege was a very modern doctrine, which had evolved extensively from the assertions of President Eisenhower in his efforts to abate the anti-Communist investigating activities of such congressional zealots as Senator Joseph McCarthy.[8]

Extensive use of executive privilege is in any event clearly modern. The various reviews of the early precedents found Presidents generally finding some means of getting at least portions of the desired information to Congress. A lengthy memorandum prepared in 1954 by the then-attorney general, William Rogers, to support Eisenhower's position emphasizing the number of early precedents for executive privilege, did not stand up at all well under scholarly scrutiny. Yet Rogers' memorandum was often referred to as a basic document for the "time-honored precedent of executive privilege." Recent Presidents have made the extensive use, as the Library of Congress found in noting some 49 instances in which the doctrine had been employed between 1952 and March 1973. Significantly, 19 of those instances had occurred as of that date with the Nixon Administration.[9] There was also a tendency for usage to cover a wide range of issues and agencies. In 1974, a *National Journal* study found less than half of the instances of recent use involving questions of foreign affairs.[10]

The Supreme Court action against President Nixon's claims of executive privilege in July 1974 was instrumental in the ultimate collapse of the Nixon Presidency and yet of little import in ultimately settling the question of executive privilege. The surprisingly unanimous (8–0) decision came with emphasis on the specific conditions of the case: A president could not asset "an absolute, unqualified presidential privilege of immunity from judicial process under all circumstances."[11] The court hinted at the possibility of the concept being used under other conditions, but avoided (perhaps wisely, in an emotion-packed summer) the task of spelling out those conditions.

A strong case can be made for a more restricted view of legitimate presidential secrecy. Given the events of the Johnson and Nixon years, it is apparent that less secrecy is needed, to reduce the chances that a president will seek to hide not only the deliberations on a policy but the actual policy itself.

It is also questionable just how adverse a reduction in secrecy would be for the presidential advising process. One of the most persistent claims during Nixon's embroilment over executive privilege was that there had to be complete confidentiality if the advising process for both Nixon and his successors was to produce candid advice. The Supreme Court decision also implied partial acceptance of this view, as they stated, "The President's need for complete candor and objectivity from advisers calls for great deference from the courts." Yet it was necessary to wonder: Just who is being protected by secrecy? If an adviser gave good advice which was not followed, it would clearly be the president, and not the adviser, who would prefer that the information be withheld. George Ball, an early dissenter on Vietnam policy, must certainly not have minded having his role known. Given some of the tendencies toward groupthink and a yes-man ethos in the White House, and the mistakes which have ensued, it is also necessary to question just how effective the advising process is which proponents of executive privilege seek to protect.

There is an admitted problem of timing in the release of information. A president may make some justifiable claims for needing some time to deliberate his response to new information. It is sobering to ponder how a restricted doctrine of executive privilege might apply to situations such as the first sighting of Soviet missiles in Cuba in October 1962, which produced President Kennedy's announced head cold as he retreated for deliberation. Yet the problem with extensive use of executive privilege is that it can easily facilitate a closed decision process which then presents the electorate with fait accompli actions.

Ultimately, part of the question of presidential secrecy must be worked out in the ongoing relations between president and Congress. Staff aides who are involved in major policy developments should not be able, either legally or as an accepted practice, to avoid Congress entirely simply by asserting their privileged relationship to the president. Conditions can be worked out in which information about individuals which is not germane to policy questions is left out of staff accounts to Congress, and in which the answers to specific questions may be briefly postponed to another date. Where there is disagreement, it is appropriate for the courts to play an arbitrating role.

A variety of specific procedures also deserve careful review. Part of the issue of secrecy appropriately involves the issue of ultimate public knowledge of actions taken. If presidents cannot always be judged instantly, they should at least recognize that they will be judged by an accurate history of their actions. The classification system, which places perhaps 100 million papers into a classified category, deserves more careful pruning. The time limit involved in the release of papers can also be shortened, although one faces the problem that information may not be put down in written form if there is a rapid dissemination process. Professor Schlesinger has perceptively discussed this issue, as he draws the conclusion that perhaps a 10-year period prior to disclosure is the best compromise.

The Freedom of Information Act stands as an additional key procedure for a wide variety of transactions.[12] That act was originally passed in 1966, and Congress sought successfully (over a Ford veto) to strengthen the act in 1974. The original act presented problems for those seeking information, as they had to claim an interest in a very specific document (rather than information on a general topic), and they fairly easily confronted the classification system with its restrictions on the basis of national security. In addition, agencies found a variety of methods for stalling in providing requested documents. The new act promised greater potential for those seeking information from governmental agencies. Documents did not have to be requested as specifically, and classified portions were to be divided in a more flexible manner to allow a greater release of information from the unclassified portions. In addition, agencies which contested and lost had to pay the court costs of those seeking the information.

A working out of effective procedures for the release of information from the federal bureaucracy emerges as an important strategy in seeking to conduct a politics which is less dependent upon cliques of government bureaucrats and their key allies. Environmental politics, for example, has often produced situations in which limited information has increased the chances that participants in policy struggles would simply exchange symbolic rhetoric rather than systematically explore policy alternatives on an informed basis.

The quest for a more open politics thus does not involve only the president, nor exclusively foreign policy issues. The drawing of precise lines and specific procedures can never be easy. There is also the possibility that the release of some information could further reduce public confidence in the government, as policy uncertainties became more clear to the nation. Yet the recent past has shown all too clearly opportunities for hiding both policies and deliberations, and a tendency for officials of the White House to imagine that they can hide a wide variety of actions from public scrutiny. Granting the difficulties involved in drawing ultimate lines on conditions allowing for secrecy, it is nonetheless clear that efforts at reducing opportunities for abuse as seen in the recent past are essential in post-Watergate reforms.

Expanding Policy Analysis Capacities

Knowledge can be influential in the development of public policy, and in turn for those who possess considerable expertise. It is, to be sure, quite true that resources can be easily wasted on policy research. One might well sympathize with the comment of one congressman by the mid 1960s who complained that additional poverty researchers had primarily one useful impact in his district—they put a little money into the economy when they bought their lunches. Yet overall it remains true that we know too little about both the consequences of past policies and the feasibility of new alternatives. As Charles Schultze aptly observed after heading budgeting operations for President Johnson, we have often opted in favor of slow change to allow policymakers to learn with each new step, and yet we still have used the time thus allotted poorly and have invested little in the systematic analysis of what those policies have produced.

Policy analysis must confront issues which have too often not been extensively discussed. Consequences of tax laws in such situations as ghetto housing and the enrichment of agribusinesses at the expense of small farmers need to be confronted more directly. The income distribution implications of various policies must also be given greater attention. This type of information may well at points intensify conflicts over given policies as it becomes clearer who *in reality* benefits from major aspects of such programs as urban renewal, agricultural price supports, and federal aid for higher education. Yet both concerns for policy effectiveness and for income distribution issues necessitate that a broader concept of policy analysis be developed.

The expansion of policy analysis capacities need involve additions neither directly to the White House Staff nor the Executive Office of the President. It is important that presidents have good translators of policy analysis and various social and economic projections on their staffs, but large analytic units do not necessarily aid a president. Organizational rigidity, and a tendency to isolate the president can be the all too frequent result. Rather, the capacities for looking at public policy should be strengthened at several points throughout the political system. Private research operations, university research facilities, and flexible organizations loosely attached to both Congress and the Executive Office of the President can all help. Policy analysis capacities can also be developed within various interest groups more effectively. This is important as an additional basis for improving bargaining processes, and in avoiding a sterility which can set in if policy analysis is overwhelmingly undertaken in aloof Washington offices rather than in the context of interaction with individuals suffering directly from the problems and existing policies being examined.

Broadening Access in Policymaking

The importance of interest-group and elite activity has emerged repeatedly in looking at contemporary presidential politics. Altering power relationships in some of these interactions is vital to the achievement of more effective public policies. In an age of constricting national resources, this is of critical importance. The quality of public services being offered, including such areas as transportation, education, medical care, and recreational facilities, are all involved. Where the regulatory process confronts government-business relationships, such issues as the safety, the nature, and the price of the products available to consumers are also very much involved. Often, these interactions also have important impacts on overall income distribution patterns. Several key strategies for reform can be pursued.

Campaign finance. Modifications in campaign finance procedures will not, by themselves, produce a cure-all which allows for the development of more effective public policy. It is all too easy to envision producing a sudden flowering of more effective policy in the wake of the Watergate scandals by simply reducing the dependence of politicians upon campaign contributions. Alterations in this process are nonetheless absolutely essential. They could increase the likelihood that the president will be ratifying decisions or working to mobilize and alter bargains in a context in which financial contributions no longer promote some values rather than others as much as in the past.

Regulation of campaign finance is no easy task. Even by 1972, the American system had more regulatory provisions than other Western democracies. The provisions of the 1971 legislation, and the April 7, 1972, deadline for accepting funds without using the new disclosure procedures, constituted one of the points of confusion leading to some of the Watergate-related abuses.

The response to Watergate throughout 1974 was substantial.

Campaign finance laws were passed in no less than 40 different states. California voters went the farthest, with the passage of an initiative in June 1974, which was substantially more comprehensive than the federal legislation. Contributions were limited, particularly for lobbyists, and overall ceilings were established which would substantially lower the total amount spent in campaigns. Disclosure provisions were made which included a requirement that an individual contributor's place of employment be provided as a means of checking for multiple individual gifts by corporations. A regulatory commission to police the future operations was also provided by that initiative.

The final response by Congress was also substantial. With the passage of the 1974 legislation, the Campaign Reform Act, opportunities for presidential aspirants to gain public funding in the primaries were established by the provision requiring that those who had raised at least $5,000 in 20 different states were entitled to matching federal funds. An important step toward reducing dependency upon private financing in large sums for presidential nominating politics had clearly been taken. More stringent measures against donations in large amounts by both individuals and organizations were also included in the act. Provisions against circumvention by use of multiple committees were not as stringent, however, as many would have liked. Perhaps most importantly, the 1974 act also provided for both disclosure and a review of disclosure records by a specially appointed commission. Given the failures of campaign finance reform in the past, the process of continual monitoring was of critical importance.[13]

Governmental agencies. Important steps can also be taken in the nature of governmental agencies which develop in the future. The organizations of the future, as students of management have argued, need not be as hierarchical as in the past. Managers need to be able to manage conflicts more effectively, a goal which could be achieved in part simply in terms of the ways in which they are trained.

Some agencies have shown a capacity for a more open adjustment to shifting values. Thus, for example, the U.S. Forest Service engaged in a process of adjusting to new values in the 1950s, with the advent of greater recreational concern, and in the 1960s, with the impact of environmental concerns. Budget changes occurred, and there were changes in regulatory operations which came from the internal dynamics of Forest Service operations. Relations of agencies to their clienteles can involve the accommodation of a wider range of values.

Regulatory agency operations also require change. The practice of having individuals serve a short time and then return to the private-sector organizations from which they came has not lent itself to the development of effective regulatory practices. Techniques for avoiding dominance by special interests must be vigorously sought. A president himself can not often give. extensive attention to these issues, but there can be experimentation with such steps as tighter conflict-of-interest laws and greater publicity of abuses. Ultimately, organizational issues also must involve the question of interest-group activity.

Interest groups. Interest-group activity constitutes a critical lever in bringing a greater consideration of values into various policy-making activities. In reviewing the recent interest-group process, it is absolutely essential to recognize that this process need not necessarily be dependent upon a presidential leadership role. The civil rights movement was not invented by Lyndon Johnson or John Kennedy. The movement began with key events such as the Montgomery bus boycott, and the momentum gained in the wake of the 1960 student sit-in in Greensboro, North Carolina. By 1964, President Johnson was important in providing an impetus for civil rights legislation, but this was well after the civil rights movement had gained substantial impetus.[14]

Environmental and consumer movements also grew very substantially without presidential initiatives. The focus was often on Congress and particular committees, with such individuals as Senator Edmund Muskie (on water pollution) playing a major role. Ralph Nader, beginning with the publication of his *Unsafe at Any Speed,* also revealed several ways in which consumer organizations could organize throughout the states, again without major encouragement from the Oval Office.[15]

The rise of Common Cause has also been a striking recent phenomenon. Under the leadership of John Gardner, that organization quickly developed a mass-based organization which was highly active as a citizens' lobby on such issues as campaign reform and the modification of the seniority system in Congress. With fairly specific targets, it became apparent that participation could be expanded rapidly through interest-group activity.

The development of more effective policy-making interactions is not destined to proceed with any single strategy. Tensions must also be confronted, especially since some of the steps may increase chances that any new policy steps will be vetoed, rather than creating more effective new decisions. The environmental field in particular has shown aspects of this difficulty. More effective policy analysis nonetheless can increase the likelihood that effective policies will emerge from the bargaining processes, however, and both analysis and bargaining are absolutely essential as the nation confronts the necessity of using resources more wisely and more efficiently.

Broadening access in policy development does not require that future policy-making avoid a concern for general goals. Writers such as Theodore Lowi and a variety of supporters of general planning processes have argued that the American system suffers from an inability to commit itself to basic plans and goals.[16] Discussion of general directions for public policy can be useful, and there are points at which agreement on a basic standard may be the most effective means of developing more effective public policy. Too often, however, discussions of goals in presidential politics have been largely exercises in symbolic politics and have been of limited value. Expanding participation in policy-making activities should be sought both to bring values to policy development which are sometimes ignored and also to give those values a position of political influence.

Modifying Congressional Functions

Congress can perform more essential functions in the political process. At the same time, Congress does not seem destined to suddenly follow any specific model for reorganization of its overall operation. Possible changes for Congress flow from our general picture of the problems in presidential politics today. Tendencies for fait accompli decisions by the president need to be reduced, and opportunities for an enlarged bargaining process need to be expanded. There are important clues in the record of the recent past as to this possible role.

Congress has been impotent, and the Presidency has been prone to the problems of inadequate personality and inadequate staff relationships, in situations where there has been little legislative knowledge as to what was actually being decided. This is the issue we have considered in terms of executive privilege and the lack of interaction between the Presidency and Congress. Various steps being taken, such as requiring congressional confirmation of a larger number of officials in the Presidency, can provide a larger basis of information. Reducing the secrecy surrounding the handling of funds through impoundment is also a useful step which fortunately has now been taken. Congress needs to expand its ability to receive existing information rather than simply seeking to generate more of its own information.

Another extremely important role for Congress is that of influencing the nature of access to the political process. This relates to the broadening of values involved in policy-making activities, and the nature of those groups involved in various bargaining processes. Congress has often been successful when it has facilitated greater access and involvement by diverse groups. The environmental politics movement, including achievement of the legislation requiring preparation of environmental impact reports on many proposed construction projects, had the effect of allowing new voices to be heard in the evolution of a wide variety of decisions.

Congress has also at points been able to increase the number of alternative views being heard on foreign policy issues. The ability of the Congress to thwart the deployment of the ABM was due in part to the access which they gave to informed voices from the science community. This case may have been somewhat unique, in terms of the presence of such highly informed experts as Jerome Wiesner and a group of scientists at Harvard-MIT. It nonetheless did allow for a wider range of debate.

The War Powers Act passed in late 1973 over President Nixon's veto can also be viewed in terms of the range of policy debate which is likely to occur. Under the provisions of that Act, a president must notify Congress in writing within 48 hours after any emergency military action in the absence of a declaration of war. Within 60 days, the combat action must either end or be approved by Congress, and Congress can also within the 60 to 90-day period order an immediate removal of American forces by a majority vote. If an ordered removal should occur, that majority vote in Congress cannot be vetoed by a president.

The hope behind the Act is in part that presidents will exercise restraint before taking any action because of the debate and congressional action which will follow. Proponents such as Senator Javits were obviously strongly motivated by the absence of debate as Congress approved the Gulf of Tonkin resolution in 1964. The hope behind the War Powers Act is thus that Congress can serve as a center for debate perhaps resembling the manner in which debate was promoted on the Vietnam War beginning in the spring of 1966. More opportunity is provided, in short, for the process of debate and dissent.

The War Powers Act has nonetheless been reviewed skeptically by several observers.[17] For some, there is a suspicion that it might actually be easier for a president to get the nation involved in a foreign commitment than before simply because it could be difficult to remove troops after sixty days. For others, the prospect of a constitutional crisis over the nature of the constitutionality of the War Powers Act also raised concern for possible uncertainty in future military commitments. There are significant grounds for questioning how the new procedure might work, depending upon the motivations and behavior of key participants in a future use. Hopefully, a shift in presidential behavior toward greater consultation and a shift in policy-making toward greater involvement of both congressmen and interested segments of the electorate will flow from this legislative effort at asserting a stronger role on foreign policy questions.

Economic questions pose vexing issues. Some have argued that the Presidency should be given a larger role, perhaps being allowed to modify taxes for a limited period without legislative consent in an effort at speedier fiscal policy response. This proposal was advanced in the face of the experiences of Kennedy and Johnson, where legislative slowness seemed to be a drag in fiscal policy response. The delays in enacting a tax cut as a fiscal policy in the 1961–1964 period have often been cited by proponents.

Limitations with this view are nonetheless impressive. Economic policy choices are not neutral steps, but ones in which difficult choices among alternative values are at stake. There is no logical reason why the preferences of the Presidency are necessarily better, or preferable to those of the legislative branch. An expanded bargaining relationship is, in short, reasonable. In this regard, the opening up of the Ways and Means Committee in 1974 with an expanded membership and a less dominant chairman portended some opportunities for improved policy development.

The question of decentralization also raises issues of proper legislative activity.[18] Congressmen have tended to persist in a desire for the specialized approach to grants-in-aid, in part because this seems to please constituents, and in part because this was one way in which they could feel some degree of effectiveness, because they achieved tangible results. If Congress is destined to do more in bargaining with the Presidency, then it can also stand to do less in terms of trying to oversee literally hundreds of specific programs.

The question of decentralization also presents, however, the issue of access. Some congressmen (often Democrats) have objected to revenue sharing out of a feeling that the federal government is the most responsive to the needs of those with less involvement in the political process—and generally, those receiving fewer rewards in American society. For those whose political concerns emphasize the problem of limited access for many less privileged Americans, the hope has to be that, with decentralization, new federal funds will provide a sufficient "bait" to attract additional participation and involvement in state and local politics. Again, attention to access in the political process is important.

Congress will undoubtedly continue to experiment with structural arrangements as it seeks alternative roles. It was difficult, in the wake of the Watergate scandals and responses, to envision how these specifics would evolve. Opportunities for basic commitments to emerge were present with a less veto-oriented committee process due to the reduced use of seniority, the use of party caucus on occasion, and the use of floor votes for basic positions. Thus, there were some grounds for hope that Congress could hold the Presidency more accountable by reducing secrecy, contribute to a more dynamic political process by watching opportunities for access to that process, and engage in a more general bargaining process with the Presidency on major policy questions.

Altering Electoral Orientations

Electoral views of the Presidency reveal understandable differences depending upon partisan and ideological preferences and levels of political knowledge. Those views are not easily changed by books producing recommended orientations and structural ideas. Ideas do nonetheless have some influence on attitudes, and attitudes can be a force for change in political behavior. Electoral views of the Presidency are of particular importance as they involve both what should and should not be expected.

The public should expect the president to play an important role in promoting greater amounts of discussion of major goals and possible policy alternatives. Presidents have too often tended to speak *after* riots, environmental crises, and energy problems have occurred. This is in part an inevitable result of their own crowded agendas. President Eisenhower, for example, was planning a series of educational efforts when problems of international affairs (and his own declining health) intervened.

Educational efforts are extremely important as the nation faces the necessity of adjusting to a politics of scarcity and redefining national identity. Scarce resources are going to necessitate a reassessment of the traditional American emphasis on growth and expansion as the proper, and perhaps even self-evident, pattern of events. In a period of changing values and uncertainty in national identity, the president's educational role can have an important impact. Election debates can be of some use, as well as rhetoric from the incumbent in the White House.

The educational task neither can nor should be undertaken by the president alone. Too often, when operating alone on a policy question, presidents tend to wait and assume a fait accompli stance with the electorate. Many voices are needed. It is at this point that a sharing of functions is again of importance.

Public orientations must eschew the view that presidents should be larger-than-life solvers of national problems. There has been a reciprocal relationship in recent years in which the public has seemed to expect a great deal from the president, and recent incumbents have in turn taken a rather flamboyant approach to their rhetoric. As we have seen, an expectations gap is the obvious result. Particularly in a time of frustration over such national issues as economic policy, it is all too easy for the electorate to fall into the wishful thinking that somehow getting the right man in the Oval Office can resolve difficult national issues. In this regard, it was striking to have President Ford criticized by some early observers of his Administration as being too "un-Presidential," only weeks after President Nixon had been forced to resign, in part because many felt that he had given a far-too-lofty definition to permissible presidential behavior.

One would hope that an electorate less dependent on the president can also depend upon itself to a greater extent. The opening of various policy-making activities to greater participation and a greater sharing of functions among different institutions comes down finally to a question of greater citizen involvement. This step will not always make life easier for presidents themselves. It is easier to manage people who are quiet, and a president may even proclaim the virtues of a "silent majority." Yet in a modified process, citizens may help leaders decide more wisely *and* at points come themselves to a more full appreciation of why there are no magic wands which can be waved in various policy controversies to make all concerned participants happy. Precisely because the Presidency has been so central in American electoral orientations, a modification in the perception of that office should also alter other attitudes and forms of political behavior.

The Presidential Dilemma

Presidential politics does ultimately confront Americans with a series of dilemmas. Expansion of the Presidency in a quest for coordination and the use of expertise in policy development can easily lead to an isolated president and an expansion in staff power. Access to the Presidency can too easily become quite limited. Electoral expectations, at the same time, can lead to an overdependence upon a president who can supposedly orchestrate wise solutions to difficult problems. Inadequate presidential personalities then simply aggravate possibilities for deceitful and manipulative operations.

Yet hoping that a president will return to a uniformly passive role is also inadequate. There are situations in which a president appropriately fills his role by working to close bargaining relationships and by mobilizing support for new policy steps. Simply cutting the president "down to size" and turning the Presidency into a museum for visitors would not insure wise policy development during difficult times for the nation.

A perspective for reducing tensions over presidential roles nonetheless does emerge. There *are* important indications that policy alteration can take place without presidential involvement, and these need to be strengthened. In turn, presidents must be restricted from engaging in the more manipulative and secretive policy-making activities.

From this perspective, our view of the reform agenda deserves final emphasis.

Changes in the selection process to decrease the likelihood of inadequate presidential personalities in the future can be pursued, through the provision of a better screening process and a more substantial opening of the recruitment process. Presidential information systems can also be strengthened. This is particularly important in the situations where the president must inevitably make some decisions in a fairly closed manner. Reduction in secrecy is in turn essential, so that at least the decisions themselves are not hidden.

Expanded assessment of overall trends and policy impacts in American society is also essential to more adequate policy development. This does *not* mean that more units need be added to the presidential staff. Rather, expanded information must be generated to provide a more adequate general public debate.

Various policy-making activities need to be opened up to the consideration of a wider range of interests and values. Statutory provisions reducing the likelihood of budgetary examination should be reduced, and analytic tools for examining policy consequences expanded. At points, this can happen at "the center," either with a president promoting interest, or a debate focusing on the floor of Congress. Where issues are in central focus, there is no ready ground for arguing that the plans from either president or Congress are superior; a good faith bargaining process is needed between the two institutions, with Congress possessing enough of the information leading to executive plans so that it can respond intelligently.

Much policy making must nonetheless take place away from the center of concern either for the president or for Congress in general. Actions in the federal bureaucracy and in state and local governments will often have significant consequences. An important federal government role should be to increase the chance that these activities will not be dominated by a veto process created by a few congressmen, a few campaign contributors, an inflexible agency, or a few individuals with highly privileged access. Controlling access to policy making activities is a critical role in all federal government operations.

A reduced dependency upon either the president or the Presidency for directing policy change does not *necessarily* mean that the political process will become stagnant and resistant to continual evolution of various policies. Groups can develop on their own initiative, agencies can evolve different policies and relationships with their clienteles, and legislative action can modify both programs and levels of funding. Some presidential closing of bargaining processes and some mobilizing can occur and will sometimes be absolutely necessary. Attention must be given to the range of access various segments of the population have to these processes and the nature of the political resources which count. Fortunately, the turn away from the campaign funding practices of the recent past offers some hope that money may be a less important resource in the future.

It was difficult to be overly sanguine or overly certain in viewing presidential politics as the nation undertook the celebration of the two hundredth anniversary of the signing of the Declaration of Independence. The American system, historically, enjoyed very definite advantages in not having to confront very many issues at the same time. Then in the brief period since the early 1960s conflicts and tensions involving race issues, environmental and energy concerns, a lengthy and divisive war, and an economy running into serious difficulty all buffeted presidential politics. American desires for democratic politics, effective policy, and a government warranting and receiving citizen confidence and trust were obviously under considerable stress.

America nonetheless remained dynamic in many respects. A politics of dynamic adjustment, involving less assumed dependence upon the president, more informed bargaining, wider policy-making access, less secrecy, and better policy information seemed to offer reasonable hope. One conclusion was in any event clear: Americans have for too long lived too comfortably under the illusion that all major questions of institutional development have been effectively settled.

NOTES

[1] For a strong statement emphasizing the problems with autocratic regimes in the context of comparative research, see Alexander T. Groth, *Comparative Politics: A Distributive Approach,* New York, Macmillan, 1971, especially Chap. 11.

[2] The relationships between legitimacy and policy effectiveness are usefully discussed in Seymour M. Lipset, *Political Man,* Garden City, N.Y., Doubleday, 1960, chap. 3.

[3] Recent selection issues are effectively discussed in James David Barber, ed., *Choosing the President,* Englewood Cliffs, N.J., Prentice-Hall, 1974.

[4] The major proposal for legislative no-confidence votes as a basis for calling new elections was introduced in 1974 by Congressman Henry Reuss, a Wisconsin Democrat. The interest in a presidential recall was in part manifested by the efforts of The People's Lobby, a California organization which was instrumental in achieving successful passage of a campaign finance reform initiative in that state in June 1974.

[5] The major statement is that of Alexander L. George, "The Case for

Multiple Advocacy in Making Foreign Policy," *American Political Science Review* 66 (September 1972), 751–785.

[6] Richard T. Johnson, *Managing the White House*, New York, Harper & Row, 1974, chap. 8.

[7] On the early development of Ford's staff ideas, see "How Ford Runs the White House," *U.S. News and World Report*, September 23, 1974, pp. 28–33.

[8] For a major review of precedents, see Raoul Berger, *Executive Privilege: A Constitutional Myth*, Cambridge, Mass., Harvard University Press, 1974, especially chap. 6.

[9] Norman Dorsen and Stephen Gillers, eds., *Government Secrecy in America: None of Your Business*, New York, Viking, 1974, p. 29.

[10] *The National Journal* 6, no. 36 (October 17, 1974), 344–345.

[11] Language from the Supreme Court decision in *U.S.* v. *Richard Nixon* is taken from the decision as reported in *The Congressional Quarterly* 32, no. 30 (July 27, 1974), 1432–1435.

[12] For an extensive review of problems with the original act, see Dorsen and Gillers, op. cit.

[13] The provisions of the 1974 Campaign Reform Act are reviewed in *The Congressional Quarterly* 32, no. 52 (December 28, 1974), 3431.

[14] The degree of presidential involvement in the development of the civil rights movement is traced in James L. Sundquist, *Politics and Policy: The Eisenhower, Kennedy, and Johnson Years*, Washington, D.C., Brookings, 1969, chap. 6.

[15] The tendency for groups to find access in Congress is emphasized in Hugh G. Gallagher, "Presidents, Congress, and the Legislative Functions," in *The Presidency Reappraised*, ed. by Rexford G. Tugwell and Thomas E. Croin, New York, Praeger, 1974, chap. 13.

[16] The importance of goal-setting activity to reduce the tendency for major policy areas to be dominated by key interests is stressed by Theodore J. Lowi, Jr., in *The End of Liberalism*, New York, Norton, 1969. See especially chap. 10. For an emphasis on the opportunities for bargaining processes to produce change in policy without agreement on goals, see Charles E. Lindblom, *The Intelligence of Democracy: Decision Making Through Mutual Adjustment*, New York, The Free Press, 1965.

[17] For an extensive review of problems and issues, see Arthur M. Schlesinger, Jr., *The Imperial Presidency*, New York, Popular Library, especially chap. 9.

[18] The question of decentralization as it relates to issues of access and participation is effectively discussed in Michael Reagan, *The New Federalism*, New York, Oxford University Press, 1972.

Appendix I
Presidential Success Scores with Congress

Since 1953, the *Congressional Quarterly* has rated presidential success with Congress on the basis of the percentage of bills which were passed where the President took a clear position. No effort is made in these evaluations to consider the degree of importance of different pieces of legislation, but the scores do show, in particular, the tendency for presidential success to decline over time for a given president. The percentages for each year since 1953 are as follows.

President	Year	Percentage of Bills Passed with Clear Presidential Support	President	Year	Percentage of Bills Passed with Clear Presidential Support
Eisenhower	1953	89%	Johnson	1964	88%
	1954	83%		1965	93%
	1955	75%		1966	79%
	1956	70%		1967	79%
	1957	68%		1968	75%
	1958	76%	Nixon	1969	74%
	1959	52%		1970	77%
	1960	65%		1971	75%
Kennedy	1961	81%		1972	66%
	1962	85%		1973	50.6%
Kennedy–Johnson	1963	87%	Ford	1973	59.6%
				1974	58.2%

293

Appendix II
Presidential Ratings

The rating of Presidents according to degree of historical "greatness" is a frequent point of discussion. The preference for activists is clearly borne out in surveys of the academic community. One major study was conducted by Arthur M. Schlesinger, Sr., who polled 75 distinguished historians regarding their personal rankings of presidential greatness. The results of that 1962 survey are as follows.

Ranking	President	Period in Office	Ranking	President	Period in Office
1	Lincoln	1861–1865	17	Van Buren	1837–1841
2	Washington	1789–1797	18	Monroe	1817–1825
3	Franklin Roosevelt	1933–1945	19	Hoover	1929–1933
4	Wilson	1913–1921	20	Benjamin Harrison	1889–1893
5	Jefferson	1801–1809	21	Arthur	1881–1885
6	Jackson	1829–1837	22	Eisenhower	1953–1961
7	Theodore Roosevelt	1901–1909	23	Andrew Johnson	1865–1869
8	Polk	1845–1849	24	Taylor	1849–1850
9	Truman	1945–1953	25	Tyler	1841–1845
10	John Adams	1797–1801	26	Fillmore	1850–1853
11	Cleveland	1885–1889	27	Coolidge	1923–1929
		1893–1897	28	Pierce	1853–1857
12	Madison	1809–1817	29	Buchanan	1857–1861
13	John Quincy Adams	1825–1829	30	Grant	1869–1877
14	Hayes	1877–1881	31	Harding	1921–1923
15	McKinley	1897–1901			
16	Taft	1909–1913			

Appendix III
The President
in the Constitution

Periodically, as in 1974, questions of presidential politics take the nation back to the constitutional document. Major provisions relating directly or indirectly to the position of the president are as follows.

Preamble

We The People of the United States, in order to form a more perfect union, establish justice, insure domestic tranquility, provide for the common defense, promote the general welfare, and secure the blessings of liberty to ourselves and our posterity, do ordain and establish this Constitution for the United States of America.

Article I/Section 3/Clause 6

The Senate shall have the sole power to try all impeachments. When sitting for that purpose, they shall be on oath or affirmation. When the President of the United States is tried, the Chief Justice shall preside: and no person shall be convicted without the concurrence of two-thirds of the members present.

Article I/Section 3/Clause 6

Judgement in cases of impeachment shall not extend further than to removal from office, and disqualification to hold and enjoy any office of honor, trust or profit under the United States: but the party convicted shall nevertheless be liable and subject to indictment, trial, judgment and punishment, according to law.

Article I/Section 7/Clause 1
All bills for raising revenue shall originate in the House of Representatives; but the Senate may propose or concur with amendments as on other bills.

Article I/Section 7/Clause 2
Every bill which shall have passed the House of Representatives and the Senate, shall, before it becomes a law, be presented to the President of the United States; if he approves he shall sign it, but if not he shall return it, with his objections, to that house in which it shall have originated, who shall enter the objections at large on their journal and proceed to reconsider it. If after such reconsideration two-thirds of that house shall agree to pass the bill, it shall be sent, together with the objections, to the other house, by which it shall likewise be reconsidered, and if approved by two-thirds of that house it shall become a law. But in all such cases the votes of both houses shall be determined by yeas and nays, and the names of the persons voting for and against the bill shall be entered on the journal of each House respectively. If any bill shall not be returned by the President within ten days (Sundays excepted) after it shall have been presented to him, the same shall be a law, in like manner as if he had signed it, unless the Congress by their adjournment prevent its return, in which case it shall not be a law.

Article I/Section 7/Clause 3
Every order, resolution, or vote to which the concurrence of the Senate and House of Representatives may be necessary (except on a question of adjournment) shall be presented to the President of the United States; and before the same shall take effect, shall be approved by him, or being disapproved by him, shall be repassed by two thirds of the Senate and House of Representatives, according to the rules and limitations prescribed in the case of a bill.

Article II/Section 1/Clause 1
The executive power shall be vested in a President of the United States of America. He shall hold his office during the term of four years, and, together with the Vice President, chosen for the same term, be elected as follows.

Article II/Section 1/Clause 2
Each state shall appoint, in such manner as the legislature thereof may direct, a number of electors, equal to the whole number of Senators and Representatives to which the State may be entitled in the Congress: but no Senator or Representative, or person holding an office of trust or profit, shall be appointed an elector. [The second paragraph of this clause was eliminated by the 12th Amendment. For those details, refer to that amendment.]

Article II/Section 1/Clause 3
The Congress may determine the time of choosing the electors, and the day on which they shall give their votes; which day shall be the same throughout the United States.

Article II/Section 1/Clause 4
No person except a natural born citizen, or a citizen of the United States, at the time of the adoption of this Constitution, shall be eligible to the office of President; neither shall any person be eligible to that office who shall not have attained to the age of thirty five years, and been fourteen years a resident within the United States.

Article II/Section 1/Clause 5
In the case of the removal of the President from office, or of his death, resignation, or inability to discharge the powers and duties of the said office, the same shall devolve on the Vice President, and the Congress may by law provide for the case of removal, death, resignation, or inability, both of the President and the Vice President, declaring what officer shall then act as President, and such officer shall act accordingly, until the disability be removed, or a President shall be elected. [See also the stipulations of the 25th Amendment.]

Article II/Section 1/Clause 6
The President shall, at stated times, receive for his services, a compensation, which shall neither be increased nor diminished during the period for which he shall have been elected, and he shall not receive within that period any other emolument from the United States, or any of them.

Article II/Section 1/Clause 7
Before he enter on the execution of his office, he shall take the following oath or affirmation — "I do solemnly swear (or affirm) that I will faithfully execute the office of President of the United States,

and will to the best of my ability, preserve, protect and defend the Constitution of the United States."

Article II/Section 2/Clause 1

The President shall be the commander in chief of the army and navy of the United States, and the militia of the several States, when called into the actual service of the United States; he may require the opinion, in writing, of the principal officer in each of the executive departments, upon any subject relating to the duties of their respective offices, and he shall have power to grant reprieves and pardons for offenses against the United States, except in cases of impeachment.

Article II/Section 2/Clause 2

He shall have power, by and with the advice and consent of the Senate, to make treaties, provided two thirds of the Senators present concur; and he shall nominate, and by and with the advice and consent of the Senate, shall appoint ambassadors, other public ministers and consuls, judges of the Supreme Court, and all other officers of the United States, whose appointments are not herein otherwise provided for, and which shall be established by law: but the Congress may by law vest the appointment of such inferior officers, as they think proper, in the President alone, in the courts of law, or in the heads of departments.

Article II/Section 2/Clause 3

The President shall have power to fill up all vacancies that may happen during the recess of the Senate, by granting commissions which shall expire at the end of their next session.

Article II/Section 3

He shall from time to time give to the Congress information of the state of the Union, and recommend to their consideration such measures as he shall judge necessary and expedient; he may, on extraordinary occasions, convene both Houses, or either of them, and in case of disagreement between them, with respect to the time of adjournment, he may adjourn them to such time as he shall think proper; he shall receive ambassadors and other public ministers; he shall take care that the laws be faithfully executed, and shall commission all the officers of the United States.

Article II/Section 4
The President, Vice President, and all civil officers of the United States, shall be removed from office on impeachment for, and conviction of, treason, bribery, or other high crimes and misdemeanors.

Article XII [adopted in 1804]
The electors shall meet in their respective States and vote by ballot for President and Vice President, one of whom, at least, shall not be an inhabitant of the same State with themselves; they shall name in their ballots the person voted for as President, and in distinct ballots the person voted for as Vice President, and they shall make distinct lists of all persons voted for as President, and of all persons voted for as Vice President, and of the number of votes for each, which lists they shall sign and certify, and transmit sealed to the seat of the government of the United States, directed to the President of the Senate. The President of the Senate shall, in the presence of the Senate and House of Representatives, open all the certificates and the votes shall then be counted. The person having the greatest number of votes for President shall be the President, if such number be a majority of the whole number of electors appointed; and if no person have such majority, then from the persons having the highest numbers not exceeding three on the list of those voted for as President, the House of Representatives shall choose immediately, by ballot, the President. But in choosing the President the votes shall be taken by States, the representatives from each State having one vote; a quorum for this purpose shall consist of a member or members from two-thirds of the States, and a majority of all States shall be necessary to a choice. And if the House of Representatives shall not choose a President whenever the right of choice shall devolve upon them, before the fourth day of March next following, then the Vice President shall act as President, as in the case of the death or other constitutional disability of the President.

The person having the greatest number of votes as Vice President shall be the Vice President, if such number be a majority of the whole number of electors appointed, and if no person have a majority, then from the two highest numbers on the list the Senate shall choose the Vice President; a quorum for the purpose shall consist of two-thirds of the whole number of Senators, and a majority of the whole number shall be necessary to a choice. But no person constitutionally ineligible to the office of President shall be eligible to that of Vice President of the United States.

Article XX [adopted in 1933]/Section 1
The terms of the President and the Vice President shall end at noon on the 20th day of January, and the terms of Senators and Representatives at noon on the 3rd of January, of the years in which such terms would have ended if this article had not been ratified; and the terms of their successors shall then begin.

Article XX/Section 2
The Congress shall assemble at least once in every year, and such meeting shall begin at noon on the 3rd day of January, unless they shall by law appoint a different day.

Article XX/Section 3
If, at the time fixed for the beginning of the term of the President, the President elect shall have died, the Vice President elect shall become President. If a President shall not have been chosen before the time fixed for the beginning of his term, or if the President elect shall have failed to qualify, then the Vice President elect shall act as President until a President shall have qualified; and the Congress may by law provide for the case wherein neither a President elect nor a Vice President elect shall have qualified, declaring who shall then act as President, or the manner in which one who is to act shall be selected, and such person shall act accordingly until a President or Vice President shall have qualified.

Article XX/Section 4
The Congress may by law provide for the case of the death of any of the persons from whom the House of Representatives may choose a President whenever the right of choice shall have devolved upon them, and for the case of the death of any of the persons from whom the Senate may choose a Vice President whenever the right of choice shall have devolved upon them. [See also the 25th Amendment.]

Article XXII [adopted in 1951]/Section 1
No person shall be elected to the office of the President more than twice, and no person who has held the office of President, or acted as President, for more than two years of a term to which some other person was elected President shall be elected to the office of the President more than once. But this article shall not apply to any person holding the office of President when this Article was proposed by the Congress, and shall not prevent any person who may be holding the office of President, or acting as President, during the term within which this Article becomes operative from holding the office of President or acting as President during the remainder of such term.

Article XXV [adopted in 1967] Section 1
In case of the removal of the President from office or of his death or resignation, the Vice President shall become President.

Article XXV/Section 2
Whenever there is a vacancy in the office of the Vice President, the President shall nominate a Vice President who shall take office upon confirmation by a majority vote of both Houses of Congress.

Article XXV/Section 3
Whenever the President transmits to the President pro tempore of the Senate and the Speaker of the House of Representatives his written declaration that he is unable to discharge the powers and duties of his office, and until he transmits to them a written declaration to the contrary, such powers and duties shall be discharged by the Vice President as Acting President.

Article XXV/Section 4
Whenever the Vice President and a majority of either the principal officers of the executive department or of such other body as Congress may by law provide, transmit to the President pro tempore of the Senate and the Speaker of the House of Representatives their written declaration that the President is unable to discharge the powers and duties of his office, the Vice President shall immediately assume the powers and duties of the office as Acting President.

Thereafter, when the President transmits to the President pro tempore of the Senate and the Speaker of the House of Representatives his written declaration that no inability exists, he shall resume the powers and duties of his office unless the Vice President and a majority of either the principal officers of the executive department or of such other body as Congress may by law provide, transmit within four days to the President pro tempore of the Senate and the Speaker of the House of Representatives their written declaration that the President is unable to discharge the powers and duties of his office. Thereupon Congress shall decide the issue, assembling within forty-eight hours for that purpose if not in session. If the Congress, within twenty-one days after receipt of the latter written declaration, or, if Congress is not in session, within twenty-one days after Congress is required to assemble, determines by two-thirds vote of both Houses that the President is unable to discharge the powers and duties of his office, the Vice President shall continue to discharge the same as Acting President; otherwise, the President shall resume the powers and duties of his office.

Appendix IV
Sources of
Presidential Study

The range of sources available for presidential study has fortunately been expanding substantially. Text references have been prepared, and indexed, with an eye toward aiding the quest for additional information. The following general points may also be helpful in the search for additional materials.

1. The *National Journal Reports,* published weekly, constitute an excellent source on both staff activities and substantive issues in presidential politics. Periodically, helpful materials are also published by the Center for the Study of the Presidency.

2. The *Congressional Quarterly* publishes both weekly reviews of legislative activities and also an Almanac and a variety of specialized reports. Year-end summaries in January of each year are often particularly useful.

3. Presidential documents are themselves increasingly available. Some information on staff changes can be found in the *Weekly Compilation of Presidential Documents* (Washington, GPO, 1965 to present). The *Public Papers of the President* now includes several volumes for each year, including press conferences, major speeches, and some general documents.

4. The data on presidential popularity and on electoral issue orientations on a variety of issues is now conveniently available in a three-volume series, *The Gallup Poll: Public Opinion, 1935–1971,* New York, Random House, 1972.

5. Changes in policies, and the issues involved, are helpfully discussed in annual publications by the Brookings Institution, generally bearing the title *Changing National Priorities,* usually with Charles L. Schultze as the senior author.

6. The major Watergate documents are now available in paperback. The most comprehensive single source is by the Congressional Quarterly, entitled *Watergate: The Chronology of a Crisis* (Washington, 1975). Judiciary Committee materials are available in libraries carrying major government documents.

7. Recent foreign policy developments are often thoughtfully analyzed in two quarterly documents, *Foreign Affairs* and *Foreign Policy.*

8. Developments during 1975 regarding CIA domestic political activities are reviewed, including the Rockefeller Commission Report, in the *Congressional Quarterly,* vol. 33, no. 22, June 14, 1975, pp. 1207–1210. For the original charges regarding the CIA, see the *New York Times,* December 22, 1974.

9. Several new empirical studies have recently shown opportunities for expanded insight into aspects of presidential politics. John H. Kessel, *The Domestic Presidency: Decision-Making in the White House,* Belmont, Calif., Duxbury, 1975, explores the position of the Domestic Council as of 1972. Robert Presthus, *Elites in the Policy Process,* New York, Cambridge University Press, 1974, contains important interview data relating to the question of elite dominance. James N. Rosenau, *Citizenship Between Elections: An Inquiry Into The Mobilizable American,* New York, Free Press, 1974, contains both a valuable review of recent evidence on electoral responses to decision-makers, and also new data on differing responses to specific appeals and events.

10. Some materials are beginning to suggest comparative dimensions of executive behavior. Two readers with many useful materials are Lewis J. Edinger, *Political Leadership in Industrialized Societies,* New York, Wiley, 1967, and Dunkware A. Rostow, *Philosophers and Kings: Studies in Leadership,* New York, Braziller, 1970. Regarding individual countries, interestingly comparative developments in the executive bureaucracy in Canadian politics are traced in C. Bruce Doern and

Peter Aucoin, ed., *The Structures of Policy-Making in Canada,* Toronto, Macmillan of Canada, 1971. On Great Britain, see in particular Richard Rose, *Policy Making in Britain,* New York, Free Press, 1969. On French politics in recent years, the works of Stanley Hoffmann are also suggestive of ways in which trends in American presidential politics in recent years have some parallels in other industrial societies. See in particular his *Decline or Renewal?: France Since the 1930s,* New York, Viking, 1974.

Index